301.363   L334u

Larsen, Lawrence Harold
AUTHOR

The urban west at the end of the
TITLE   frontier

115559

DATE DUE	BORROWER'S NAME

301.363   L334u
Larsen, Lawrence Harold
The urban West at the end of the frontier
115559

THE URBAN WEST
AT THE END
OF THE FRONTIER

THE URBAN WEST AT THE END OF THE FRONTIER

by Lawrence H. Larsen

THE REGENTS PRESS OF KANSAS
Lawrence

Library of Congress Cataloging in Publication Data

Larsen, Lawrence Harold, 1931–
    The urban West at the end of the frontier.

    Bibliography: p.
    Includes index.
    1. Cities and towns—The West—History. 2. The
West—History—1848–1950. I. Title.
HT123.5.A17L37   301.36′3′0978   77–12019
ISBN 0–7006–0168–6

TO

Elmer and Arleen

Contents

Contents

List of Tables

Preface

During the frontier period Americans built cities west of the ninety-fifth meridian that were carbon copies of those constructed earlier in the older parts of the country. By 1880—the last federal census prior to the official closing of the frontier—there were twenty-four towns of eight thousand or more people in the West. Ranging in size from Lawrence, Kansas, to San Francisco, California, they constituted a vibrant urban society that mirrored the emerging social, economic, and political values of the Gilded Age. Western cities, made possible by tremendous advances in transportation and the railroad in particular, were in the traditions of American urbanization. San Francisco and Denver were "instant cities," but so were Chicago and Minneapolis–St. Paul. Los Angeles was an "oasis," just as Cincinnati was at an earlier date. "Privatism"—a made-up word relating to the dominant role of private enterprise in city building—functioned in Kansas City, along the same lines as in Philadelphia. There was as much "social mobility" in Omaha as in Boston. Little was unique or new about the young cities of the West.

The twenty-four cities grew for a variety of reasons. Omaha benefited from its role as the eastern terminus of the Union Pacific Railroad. St. Joseph was the railhead on the frontier for eastern lines for several years. Through entrepreneurial decisions, Kansas City obtained the first railroad bridge over the Missouri River, and, hence, regional supremacy. Atchison and Leavenworth were competing commercial centers that sought trunk railroads with limited success. Lawrence, started as an antislavery center, achieved stability as an agricultural marketing point. State government accounted for the growth of Lincoln and Topeka. Gold and a superior harbor explained the rise of San Francisco. Oakland, a mere adjunct of the Golden Gate metropolis, rose from a squatters' field. San Jose, Sacramento, and Stockton survived the fate of many gold-rush cities by adroitly changing their economic bases from services connected with mining to agricultural activities. Gold made and broke Virginia City, high in the mountains of Nevada. Portland's strategic location in Oregon enabled its conservative leadership to hew out a prosperous hinterland in the Willamette Valley. At the end of the frontier, Los Angeles was essentially a real-estate promotion awaiting a boom. Galveston relied on ships and Houston on railroads, as the two cities fought to control the Texas economy. San Antonio was an old Spanish town that gained population rapidly after the arrival of the railroad, as did two newer communities, Austin and Dallas. Mineral wealth helped Denver in a limited way, but railroads made the Queen City the heart of the Rocky Mountain Empire. Leadville demonstrated that valuable ores alone were not enough to raise up a viable city. Religious convictions led to the establishment of Salt Lake City. The end result was an urban network that brought civilization to over two million square miles of the United States.

I hope that this analytical study will shed new light on the western urban experience and help other researchers in the field. The project evolved over a period of several years. It grew out of a conversation with the late George L. Anderson, a distinguished historian of the West who taught for many years at the University of Kansas. He felt that urbanization was one of the few remaining themes of the western experience that needed exploring by professional historians. As much as possible, I have tried to rely on hard facts and statistics to reach conclusions and to portray the sweep of the western urban experience. I have adopted a method that differs somewhat from the case-study approach, which has proved useful in studying urban history. In that method, a researcher deals with a single city or with one or two basic themes. Given the mass of data, this is the only practical way some subjects can be done. If enough studies are completed a synthesis is possible. What I have done is to deal with a cross section of urban life in twenty-four cities, and to use comparative data from the other sections of the country. Given the fact that until recently historians have ignored the western city, this book would have been impracticable to undertake except for the availability of three things: the vast amount of urban materials in the 1880 United States census, the data in unstructured local and county histories, and a few works of high quality on western urbanization by professional historians.

So many people gave me encouragement and assistance that it would be impossible to acknowledge all of them. Robert L. Branyan, the graduate dean at Central Michigan University and a former colleague and collaborator, helped develop the concept of dealing simultaneously with many cities. The two of us co-authored an article on urban services in frontier communities. R. Reed Whitaker of the Kansas City Federal Archives and Records Center provided insights on federal archival materials and read the manuscript. Richard Elrod, a historian of Central European diplomatic affairs, patiently listened to material far afield from his interests and offered judicious suggestions. Other colleagues in the University of Missouri–Kansas City history department, Jesse V. Clardy, Herman Hattaway, Richard McKinzie, Louis Potts, and Stanley Parsons, gave help and encouragement. Charles N. Glaab, Patrick McLear, Lyle Dorsett, James C. Olson, William Petrowski, and A. Theodore Brown all contributed in many ways. William E. Lass read the transportation sections, Philip A. Hernandez provided the formula on how to determine urban dwellers of Spanish and Mexican descent, James Walker explained census enumeration districts, Joseph Boudreau helped with information on San Jose, and Dwayne Martin delineated the Kansas City black quarter. At UMKC, Neal Willis, George Gale, and Van Rothrock, professors of psychology, philosophy, and international business and law, respectively, all offered advice. Helen L. Bennett and Bernice Miller of the UMKC General Library unlocked the gates of knowledge. James and Marian Cottrell furnished an island in Canada. Vernon Carstensen taught concepts of western history that bore fruit. Elizabeth Bailey typed the final draft. My wife, Barbara, contributed in many ways and typed earlier drafts of the manuscript.

Of course (though both custom and prudence demand it be said), I am responsible for errors of fact or interpretation.

LAWRENCE H. LARSEN

CHAPTER 1

The Urban West

    The concept that the West was a unit distinct from the rest of the nation played a major role in shaping the dynamics of American society. A certain vagueness associated with defining the precise boundaries of the vast territory added to the image; as pioneers moved across the continent, what was West in one decade became East in the next. Scholars found the moving frontier an apt subject for investigation and speculation. Frederick Jackson Turner argued in 1893 that the frontier was the cutting edge of democracy. Turner's thesis greatly affected formal scientific research and writing in western history.

    For decades professional historians produced studies that supported or repudiated Turner and raised many questions. Were the Populists of Nebraska democratic? Did they practice anti-Semitism? Was the West a place of escape for dissatisfied eastern factory workers? If they moved there, what were their chances of acquiring land? Did federal legislation help individuals or corporations? What impact did foreign capital investments have on the cattle and mining industries? Was Indian policy a vicious negation of republican principles? Did quantitative analysis prove or disprove Turner? While intensive research on these and other subjects contributed in many ways to an understanding of the West, the studies did not tell us much about the people themselves. How many farmers living in sod houses in Nebraska thought in serious dialectic terms about the relationship of agricultural overproduction to the problem of industrial wage levels? How many frontier

1

human society, emerging from the ocean basins, is at present climbing; the two halves front face to face; they march to meet—to unite and harmonize over this summit. . . . Hither the continental slopes mounting upwards from all the oceans converge and culminate: from hence all the descending waters radiate."[2]

Inherent disadvantages of a site—the inconvenient location of natural resources, the enormous technological problems of water supply, the lack of transportation—did not mean that different methods were used to build a town. It was a normal practice in America to construct cities in advance of the development of agricultural hinterlands. Entrepreneurs founded Holyoke as a manufacturing town, Atlanta as a railroad junction, and St. Louis as a fur-trading post. Kansas City and Omaha antedated farming in Kansas or Nebraska. Denver helped to generate the mining boom in Colorado that made the Mile High City a distributing and transportation point. San Antonio's establishment came long before the opening of the cattle frontier; Houston and Galveston aspired "to wear a city's crown" prior to the peopling of most of Texas. Portland, Sacramento, and San Francisco predated solid regional commercial growth. Los Angeles and Dallas were founded before railroads provided outlets to markets.

The urban frontier was much less colorful than other aspects of the western experience. The platting of a town hardly had the drama of a massive cattle-drive north from Texas. The erection of a few wooden and tar-paper shacks scarcely compared with a gold strike in Nevada. The arrival of a small group of immigrants hardly had the impact of an Indian battle in Montana. The coming of the iron horse to a remote desert hamlet seemed mundane when considered against the building of railroads through the mountains of Colorado. Still, the undramatic process of organizing towns significantly shaped frontier society.

In the older sections of the country, a few cities had gained predominance over others: New York defeated Boston and Philadelphia to dominate the Northeast; Chicago emerged victorious against St. Louis in the Midwest; Baltimore, Louisville, and New Orleans shared control in the South. In the West, where the struggle for economic supremacy continued unabated, all except a few of the eventual victors had firm foundations by 1880. Of course, there were a few exceptions. Seattle was a small village until the arrival of the railroad in the mid-eighties; in 1900 it ex-

ceeded 100,000 in population. San Diego and Phoenix had never appeared to have bright prospects. They languished until the twentieth century. Aircraft manufacturing and naval activities accounted for dramatic progress in San Diego during the Second World War; Phoenix benefited from the postwar resort and land businesses. Oklahoma City and Tulsa remained unimportant until the 1900s. Started as cattle and marketing towns, they obtained metropolitan status as oil centers. Some other cities that progressed rapidly at an early age lost momentum. Stockton fell to San Francisco, Virginia City stagnated after the mines stopped producing, and Leavenworth gave up without much of a fight to Kansas City. It was axiomatic that a community, even one that experienced sudden expansion from a gold strike or cattle boom, could ill-afford to rest on its laurels. The stakes in town building were too high to allow complacency.[3]

Every place with aspirations needed promoters. With gusto these persons—sometimes owners of real estate, but frequently journalists with little personal wealth and at best a tenuous financial interest in the community they championed—portrayed even the smallest of way stations as the next Babylon and Tyre or, depending on the chief forms of business and recreation, Sodom and Gomorrah. A pamphleteer bragged in typical style: "No one can doubt that the sum total of Tacoma's resources, domestic and foreign, together with the entire aspect of her own and the world's present environments, are vastly superior to those of Chicago in 1852, and that it is only a question of TIME when a greater city than Chicago or New York will flourish on the more salubrious shores of Puget Sound." A harder-sell booster in Austin wrote in 1877: "Hundreds of costly residences greet the eye on every side; a dozen church spires point aloft to the clouds; institutions of learning to prepare the youthful mind for the duties of maturer years are numerous. The daily papers carry the news from all quarters of the globe to their thousands of readers, while the hum of the mill-wheel, the ring of the anvil, and the scream of the steam-whistle attest the already developing manufacturing interests of the city."[4]

Some promoters viewed the future of their chosen city in a broad context. They exhibited maps of "paper towns" in Kansas and Nebraska with lots set aside for the federal capitol, a national cathedral, a national university, and a national observatory. Fre-

5

quently, the plans pinpointed a massive union station, from which trunk lines radiated to all parts of the land. It made little difference that the place actually consisted of a gambling den, a brothel, and a few decrepit hovels.[5] Every place hoped to become a Chicago or even a Milwaukee or Indianapolis. No one denied that a few towns would survive out of the thousands platted in the early days of a new territory. The question was which ones, and that was a choice the promoters attempted to determine.

William Gilpin believed throughout the 1850s that a "Centropolis" of fifty million people would develop within a hundred years in the vicinity of Kansas City. "There must be a great city here," Gilpin declared, "such as antiquity built at the head of the Mediterranean and named Jerusalem, Tyre, Alexandria, and Constantinople; such as our own people name New York, New Orleans, San Francisco, St. Louis."[6] He said that Kansas City was in the center of the North American continent, a "symmetrical and sublime" concave bowl that focused all forces to the center, ensuring a harmonious pattern of social development. Of particular importance were the Missouri River and the plains of Kansas. He described the great river as a "glorious mirror" and "throne of the Invincible" that would ensure commercial greatness for Kansas City. He called rural Kansas the "Garden of the World," stating that the region's pastoral agriculture was destined to become "a separate grand department of national industry." He dismissed assertions that the area was actually a desert, contending that the "supreme engineering of God" would more than solve any irrigation problems. Even more fortuitous, Kansas City was within the isothermal zodiac, lay astride the axis of intensity, and had an ideal "gravitational" location. He pirated a theory of urban gravitation from S. A. Goodin, an obscure and unsuccessful Cincinnati promoter, to prove mathematically, using "leagues" as the common denominator, that Kansas City lay in the exact center of the "Great Basin" of the North American continent. Other major cities would grow by "natural law" around Kansas City in circle fashion every five hundred to seven hundred "leagues." After Gilpin moved to Colorado he blandly admitted an error in his calculations; the correct location of the great city of the world was at Denver.[7] Such shifts were common among promoters. Jesup Scott variously placed the great city of the world at

6

Cincinnati, Alton, and Chicago, before settling upon Toledo, where he had large property holdings.

In the 1880 census—the last before the official end of the frontier—the West contained twenty-four cities with populations of eight thousand or more (see Table 1-1). This was the breaking point used to differentiate between important and unimportant places; throughout the nineteenth century experts considered population statistics a measurement of progress. As in other sections of the country, most of the cities were on the borders of the region. Eight towns formed a jagged line near the ninety-fifth meridian: Omaha, Lincoln, Atchison, St. Joseph, Leavenworth, Lawrence, Topeka, and Kansas City. Eight cities were on or near the Pacific Ocean. Five were close together in northern California: San Francisco, which ranked ninth nationally, Oakland, Sacramento, San Jose, and Stockton. The remaining far western communities were Portland, Virginia City, and Los Angeles. On the Gulf Coast were Galveston and Houston. Three other Texas localities were of significant size: San Antonio, Austin, and Dallas. On Gilpin's vaunted eastern slope, in Colorado the solitary places of consequence were Denver and Leadville. Salt Lake City was in Utah Territory. Although the various cities constituted only a small percentage of the 286 in the United States of more than eight thousand, they formed a virile and propitious urban frontier.[8]

Vast distances separated the cities. It was over 1,800 miles from Kansas City to San Francisco and 2,200 miles from Houston to Seattle. Even within the subdivisions—the edge of the central plains, the Pacific Coast, the Texas plains, and the mountains—the towns seemed far apart in an age in which fast passenger trains averaged under 30 miles an hour. Dallas and San Antonio were 270 miles from each other, Lawrence and Omaha about 200 miles, Denver and Salt Lake City 500 miles, and Los Angeles and Portland almost 1,000 miles. Yet the distances were relatively unimportant except in terms of travel time. The cities were all small or nonexistent at mid-century, and many exploded into life as a result of minerals and rails. They all experienced boom and bust and, in the case of most, natural disasters. By the closing days of the frontier the road to stability and continued success was clearly marked. Urban leaders needed to consolidate the gains of the early years and to develop solid hinterlands rich with agricultural and mineral wealth. While they shared a common experience,

7

TABLE 1-1
Frontier Cities and Their 1880 Populations

Cities	Populations
California	
Los Angeles	11,183
Oakland	34,555
Sacramento	21,420
San Francisco	233,959
San Jose	12,567
Stockton	10,282
Colorado	
Denver	35,629
Leadville	14,820
Kansas	
Atchison	15,105
Lawrence	8,510
Leavenworth	16,546
Topeka	15,452
Missouri	
Kansas City	55,785
St. Joseph	32,431
Nebraska	
Lincoln	13,003
Omaha	30,518
Nevada	
Virginia City	10,917
Oregon	
Portland	17,577
Texas	
Austin	11,013
Dallas	10,358
Galveston	22,248
Houston	16,513
San Antonio	20,550
Utah Territory	
Salt Lake City	20,768

they also competed against each other. Their histories prior to 1880 afforded some indication of future prospects.

Kansas City had the best chance of exercising economic, political, and social mastery over the central plains. In 1821 St. Louis interests started a fur-trading post near the Kawsmouth. By mid-century the town of Kansas had few people and a flimsy economy supported by the Indian trade and the outfitting of immigrants. The fifties saw a flurry of railroad booms, which were ended abruptly by the Civil War. The first eastern rail connection, the Pacific Railroad, reached Kansas City from St. Louis in 1865. During the immediate postwar period, Kansas City and other Missouri River towns fought for dominance. Victory came when the Hannibal and St. Joseph Railroad decided to construct an extension of its main line through Kansas City into the Southwest. In 1869 the first railroad bridge over the Missouri River opened at Kansas City. Massive outlays of capital from Chicago started banks, packing houses, and stockyards; New York and Boston firms established regional headquarters for insurance companies and mercantile concerns. Kansas City became a major receiving and distributing point. The depression following the Panic of 1873 had no prolonged effect on the city. By 1880 Kansas City was the most important transportation hub in the nation west of Chicago.[9]

Omaha challenged Kansas City for supremacy in the central plains. The Council Bluffs and Nebraska Ferry Co. founded Omaha in Nebraska Territory in 1854, laying out 322 blocks, each 264 feet square. Overcoming opposition from other towns in the territory such as Bellevue and Nebraska City, Omaha became the territorial capital and by 1857 had an estimated fifteen hundred people. "The spirit of speculation abroad over the whole country was speedily developed in that city," an old settler recalled. "Money was easily made; corner lots commanded absurdly inflated prices; 'wild cat' banks, established without authority of law, and having no substantial basis of capital, were numerous; city scrip assisted in increasing an already abundant currency, and the future of the place looked very bright to the owners of real estate within its limits."[10] Overnight, the situation changed. The Panic of 1857 severely affected Omaha—banks closed, real estate slumped, business and population dropped. Prosperity returned in 1859, when merchants equipped prospectors going to the Colo-

rado gold fields. A major turning point came a few years later. On 8 December 1863 construction started out of Omaha on the Union Pacific, the eastern half of the first transcontinental railroad. The road stimulated the economy and brought in more people. Promoter George Train called the city the place "where the Almighty placed a signal station at the entrance of a garden seven hundred miles in length." Things went so well that in 1867 local merchants dropped their opposition to moving the capital to another location. They felt that Omaha no longer needed government activities to sustain a flourishing economy. But, after the Union Pacific's completion in 1869, the slow settlement of the hinterlands and the national depression brought several bad years. In the late seventies an influx of newcomers into Nebraska led to a sharp upturn that caused Omaha leaders to entertain fond hopes of surpassing Kansas City as an urban center. Both places owed their success to adroit promotion and the fact that they were key rail links to other parts of the land. By 1880 they had thwarted many rivals, some of which had seemed blessed with more advantages a few short years earlier.

St. Joseph on the Missouri River had at one time entertained large aspirations. Organized in 1843 at the site of Joseph Robidoux's old trading post, it quickly vanquished nearby Sparta to dominate Missouri's Platte Purchase and become the county seat of Buchanan County. St. Joseph, according to boomers, was "the principal frontier town west of the Mississippi."[11] By 1859 the Hannibal and St. Joseph Railroad had reached St. Joseph, and the Pony Express ran through the city. The town of 8,932 inhabitants was an important national transportation center. Fifteen uninterrupted years of progress followed the Civil War, and by 1873 a magnificent $1,500,000 railroad bridge spanned the Missouri River at St. Joseph. In 1880 the city had 2,000 more inhabitants than Omaha. However, while St. Joseph added 13,000 persons in the seventies, Omaha gained 14,000 and Kansas City 23,000.

On the western bank of the Missouri River, Leavenworth had delusions of grandeur. A company of thirty-two Missourians "claimed" and platted it in 1854 at the opening of Kansas Territory. They spent $4,500 cutting timber and brush, and netted $12,000 in a quick sale of lots. After this beginning, Leavenworth moved forward quickly. By 1860 it had 7,429 inhabitants, graded streets, churches, schoolhouses, and imposing homes. Impressive

mercantile buildings lined the main thoroughfares; river steamers crowded the levee. Unlike other border towns, it prospered during the Civil War, because of increased military activities at Fort Leavenworth. After the end of hostilities and the withdrawal of thousands of soldiers, the city entered a period of severe depression. The failure of Kansas to grow as expected hurt Leavenworth—at one time one-fifth of all the people in the state resided there—as did the defeat at the polls of several local bond issues intended to promote railroad construction. It gained a reputation as a dead town. During the 1870s Leavenworth, the erstwhile Queen City of the West, lost over a thousand residents and its metropolitan hopes.[12]

Twenty miles up river, the Atchison Town Company, controlled by seventeen Missourians, platted Atchison in 1854 at a "great curve" on the Missouri. "The peculiar configuration of the earth was not favorable for the easy building of a metropolis on the site of Atchison," commented an observer. "Abrupt bluffs stood up from the banks of the river, rift only to allow an unromantic stream, with unstable banks, to empty its feeble current into the uncontrollable Missouri." Two competitors, Doniphan and Sumner, were better situated. Nevertheless, Atchison survived and prospered. The village served as the headquarters for several overland freighters. It remained relatively free of the troubles in "Bleeding Kansas" and by 1860 had evolved into a fairly stable community of 2,616. Following the Civil War, Atchison thrived briefly and then experienced a prolonged downturn. Still, the population doubled in the seventies, primarily because of railroad construction. "Atchison is the natural gate-way of the West," said the board of trade, "and as a distributing point has advantages superior to those of any other city in the Missouri Valley."[13] By 1880 the community had a bridge over the Missouri, a $120,000 union station, and several railroads. The Atchison, Topeka and Santa Fe Railroad was partially owned by Atchison interests. Despite optimism and aggressive leadership, Atchison could not alter fixed commercial patterns that limited its growth.

Political considerations were important in the settlement of three other cities. When Nebraskans selected Lincoln as a compromise choice for a capital in 1867, there was only one house at the site. Three commissioners surveyed lots, and construction proceeded on a capitol, penitentiary, university, and lunatic

11

asylum. These projects stimulated expansion; Lincoln added 11,000 residents in thirteen years.[14] Topeka progressed in much the same fashion. After winning a statewide election to choose a capital for Kansas, Topeka undertook a massive building program which led to an increase of over 10,000 inhabitants between 1870 and 1880. The Atchison, Topeka and Santa Fe established its offices and machine shops in Topeka, and the future looked very bright. "The location of this city enables it to hold the key to the far new west," said the editor of a city directory. "It is nearer the base of frontier operations than any other town of pretensions."[15] The population of Lawrence, which lost the statehouse when Leavenworth voters, embittered over a railroad controversy, cast their ballots for Topeka, increased by only 190 persons in the same period. All things considered, the seemingly ill-starred municipality had done rather well. Founded with the assistance of Massachusetts and Connecticut emigrant aid societies, it became an antislavery center. Lawrence was first called Wakarusa, then Yankeetown, and after that New Boston. The early settlers adopted the name Lawrence out of respect for New England industrialist Amos Lawrence, who gave them a reported $10,000 for "education purposes." Proslavery elements besieged and burned Lawrence twice in the 1850s. During the Civil War, Confederate raiders led by William C. Quantrill killed 180 people and wrought damage amounting to $2,000,000. Rebuilding the town stimulated business, allowing Lawrence to flourish as an important local marketing town.[16]

Meanwhile, halfway across the continent, San Francisco was attaining hegemony over northern California. In the spring of 1848 almost everyone in the old Spanish town of one thousand people had gone to the gold fields, leaving behind 135 houses, 10 unfinished structures, 12 stores and warehouses, and 35 shanties. But new settlers appeared within months, and fortune seekers transformed San Francisco into a roaring camp. Prosperity followed, despite disastrous fires that swept away inflammable tents and wood structures, hard times from fluctuations in mining, vicious criminals, and violent riots against Orientals by white workingmen. Vigilance committees were formed to maintain order. Mineral strikes in California and Nevada, along with expanding agricultural production in California, furnished a firm economic base. "The condition of affairs in San Francisco at the

12

present time is gratifying," the mayor asserted in 1880. "Much encouragement has been given to manufactures, and a determined effort is being made to procure the immigration to California of good settlers to assist in developing the resources of the state."[17]

The great commercial metropolis had a number of satellites, the most important of which was Oakland, directly to the east across San Francisco Bay. Squatters settled in the place in 1850; for the next decade and a half land-title cases clogged the courts and discouraged migrants. Plans to make the city the western terminus of the transcontinental railroad revived interest; after the arrival of the first overland train on 8 November 1869, Oakland enjoyed many years of economic well-being and rapid physical growth. It won the Alameda County seat and annexed neighboring Brooklyn. Harbor improvements and the construction of railroads throughout California encouraged commerce. Ferry lines ran from Oakland to San Francisco.[18] Of all these things, the ferries on the bay were the most significant, because they made Oakland an adjunct of San Francisco.

Sacramento, Stockton, and San Jose were the other jewels in San Francisco's crown. Sacramento, platted in December of 1848 near Sutter's Fort at the juncture of the American and Sacramento rivers, was a trading post and gambling den during the gold rush. Merchants averaged profits of 200 percent. A horseshoe cost sixteen dollars, a shot of whiskey fifty cents. According to an eyewitness, "every saloon was crowded and every table blockaded by an eager crowd of gamesters." The city survived severe floods, epidemics, squatters' riots, and fires. "After 1850 the place sank into a dignified tranquility," a local historian noted, "disturbed only by floods and fires, and such unromantic incidents as the entrance of the first railroad or the establishment of the state capital."[19] Serious problems impeded the founding of Stockton at the head of a navigable slough three miles from the San Joaquin River. Fear of Indian attacks led to the abandonment of settlement efforts in 1843 and 1844; an attempt in 1846 failed when the Mexican War began. After permanent settlement in 1847 the town survived epidemics, floods, and conflagrations that happened with clocklike regularity. Just before the Civil War, Stockton experienced what officials called the "transition from the gold period to the wheat period."[20] The community moved ahead, firmly connected to San Francisco by daily passenger steamers. San Jose,

13

organized in 1777 seven miles below the southern tip of San Francisco Bay in the lush Santa Clara Valley, had the twin distinction of being the oldest municipality in California and the meeting place of the first state legislature. Once a supply base for gold prospectors, it evolved into an emporium for surrounding agricultural lands.[21] San Jose and the other two cities had all successfully managed the difficult procedure of shifting economic bases at propitious times.

Virginia City failed to find an economic alternative to mining, with dire results. Started as a Nevada mining camp on Mount Davidson, Virginia City became a flourishing place with cultural pretensions, following the discovery in 1859 of the Comstock Lode. After overcoming nearby Gold Hill, it surged to an estimated population of twenty-five thousand in 1876. Then the mines were exhausted, and close to fifteen thousand persons left in the next four years. The future held little hope for Virginia City because it was impossible to develop an agricultural base in the surrounding mountains. Most of the $300,000,000 in profits from the Comstock Lode went to San Francisco speculators. Indeed, even the houses on "Millionaires' Row" in Virginia City were dismantled and taken to San Francisco for reassembling.[22]

Portland, on the west bank of the Willamette River twelve miles from its juncture with the Columbia, was the largest of the other two West Coast cities. Chartered in 1851, it had a number of competitors. A contemporary noted, "Nearly every man in Oregon has a city of his own and it is impossible to tell what point on the Columbia will take the preference." William Gilpin, active in the region at the time, later took credit for laying out Portland, although he never presented proof. Even though the town had what promoters considered an excellent location, title controversies slowed progress until the mid-1850s. From then on, it enjoyed what spokesmen called a "remarkable" expansion based on the steady agricultural settlement of western Oregon, the opening of railroads and water navigation in the Willamette Valley, and the exploitation of mineral deposits. By 1880 Portland impressed visitors as having many New England attributes. A regional magazine claimed, "Invoke the spirit of the lamp and transport a resident of some Eastern city and put him down in the streets of Portland, and he would observe little difference be-

tween his new surroundings and those he beheld but a moment before in his native city."[23]

Los Angeles lay in what boosters called "semitropical" California. Situated twelve miles from the Pacific Ocean at a rather undesirable spot for commercial activities on the banks of the sluggish Los Angeles River, the town owed its origin in 1781 to a group of discharged Spanish soldiers from the neighboring mission of San Gabriel. When California entered the Union, Los Angeles had only 1,610 inhabitants, almost all of whom were Mexicans. In the 1860s and 1870s, during the first southern California land boom, speculators started the neighboring villages of Santa Monica, Anaheim, Long Beach, and Pasadena, allowing Los Angeles to gain a suburban dimension in advance of metropolitan status. Experts believed that the Los Angeles basin could sustain a population of one million. The main concern was transportation; the only locally owned railroad was the eighteen-mile long Los Angeles and Independence. The San Francisco–owned Southern Pacific Railroad, which ran through Los Angeles, charged high shipping rates.[24]

On the Gulf Coast, Galveston and Houston were fighting for urban supremacy in Texas. Galveston occupied the northeast portion of Galveston Island. Before the city obtained a charter in 1838 several communities, including the pirate town of Campeachy, had occupied the site. Galveston thrived as the port for the Republic of Texas, suffered in the first decade of American rule when other seaports cut deeply into foreign trade, staged a major recovery in the late 1850s with the reestablishment of some old connections, lost half its population during the Union blockade in the Civil War, and moved forward after hostilities. "We cannot help observing how rapidly business is increasing in Galveston," a newspaper editor wrote in May of 1865. "The wharves are already crowded by steamers and other craft laden with merchandise. Old stores are being fitted up; dwellings converted into shops. All our merchants seem busy. Galveston is rapidly regaining her former commercial position." In the seventies, Galveston was the nation's third largest cotton and fourth biggest coffee market.[25] A general increase in exports, coupled with the arrival of railroads and manufacturing industries, generated optimism.

Similar confidence existed fifty miles away on the shores of

Buffalo Bayou. The promoters who planned Houston in 1836, within months after the nearby Battle of San Jacinto assured Texas independence, wanted to construct a railroad terminal; they named the first roadway Railroad Street. Nothing came from this and other schemes until after the Mexican War, when New England capitalists invested in projected lines and the Texas legislature made liberal grants to the railroads. By the Civil War there were 357 miles of track in Texas, almost all of which radiated out of Houston. During Reconstruction a further influx of capital from northeastern investors prompted further construction. In 1879 the city's lines shipped 459,697 cotton bales, 2,000,000 pounds of hides, 250,000 pounds of wool, 8,000 hogsheads of sugar, 18,600 barrels of molasses, and 24,000 barrels of sirup.[26] Much of this traffic helped Galveston, just as that town's ocean trade aided Houston. The two rivals were dependent upon each other.

The Texas interior towns predated the railroads. San Antonio, founded as the capital of Spanish Texas in 1718, remained relatively small until the advent of American rule, when it flourished as the center of the Texas cattle industry and various military activities. After the arrival in 1877 of the Galveston, Harrisburg and San Antonio Railroad, almost every train brought new settlers. Manufacturing thrived at good water-power sites on the San Pedro and San Antonio rivers; the wool, hide, and cotton trades progressed. A Texan found many anomalies. "Old houses, whose fort-like appearance speaks of a time when Indian wars were a constant source of apprehension, stand side by side with the wooden warehouses," he said. "The old mission buildings of the pious Catholic priest look out upon the railroad station, and gas-pipes run through streets still intersected by the irrigation ditches of the early Spanish settlers." He called the city "almost a shrine" to "sons of Texas," for in the streets had "flowed again and again the blood of heroes, fighting for home, for liberty, and for independence."[27]

In 1837 a board of commissioners selected Austin, located on an unnavigable stretch of the Colorado River, as the capital of the Republic of Texas. Its final report, which dwelled on the "fertile and gracefully undulating woodlands and luxuriant prairies," predicted a "truly national city" worthy of serving as "the home of the brave and the free." Austin never realized those great ex-

pectations, although it finally became something more than a meeting place after the coming in 1871 of the Houston and Texas Central Railway.[28]

The Houston and Texas Central's main line reached Dallas in 1872, changing the thirty-one year old Peter's Colony village from a quiet county seat into an incipient commercial and manufacturing point. In 1880 a proud official commented, "Eight years ago the present prosperous city of Dallas was a little village of perhaps 1,500 inhabitants, contented and well-to-do, who little expected that their city, which had been thirty years in reaching the point at which they saw it, would in less than ten years increase over six times in population, while in importance it would pass from a quiet village to a thriving city."[29] The same statement applied to other Texas towns; railroads opened a whole new era.

Denver, founded by New England speculators as a "paper city" in 1858 at the base of the Colorado Rockies at the juncture of South Platte Creek and Cherry Creek, subdued several competitors in its immediate proximity and prospered temporarily as a trading and mining-supply hub. Enumerated at 4,749 in 1860, Denver added only ten people in the ensuing decade, surviving a disastrous fire in 1863 and a serious flood the following year. Railroad promotion was the key to community hopes. In the 1870s the city successfully contested with other places on the eastern slope for trunk connections. The Union Pacific–Eastern Division connected with eastern roads at Kansas City and the transcontinental at Cheyenne; the Denver and Rio Grande Railroad promised a link to the Southwest; and the Denver, South Park and Pacific Railroad served central Colorado. The population of Denver increased seven times over in the seventies. It profited from mineral strikes and obtained a great deal of capital from northeastern investors at the expense of once-promising Cheyenne. Denver hewed out the Rocky Mountain Empire so quickly that its sole remaining challenger in Colorado was left far behind. "Who can guess the future of this great city?" a booster trumpeted in 1880. "Before the ordinary course of events is likely to check our growth, Denver will at least double her present population and increase her wealth by at least one-half."[30]

In the heart of the Rockies, at an altitude of ten thousand feet, Leadville had managed to augment roads that were open part of the year with railroad connections to other parts of the region

via the Denver and Rio Grande and the Denver, South Park and Pacific.[31] But Leadville was unable to overcome serious handicaps. The precipitous mountains precluded agriculture; almost all investments went into mining. So, when the mines stopped producing or silver glutted the market, the city declined and became a decaying curiosity that catered to a small tourist trade.

Latter Day Saints led by Brigham Young platted Salt Lake City in 1847, at the base of the Wasatch Mountains and near the southeast shore of the Great Salt Lake. The arrival of a thousand to six thousand Mormons annually in Utah, most of whom first came or stayed in Salt Lake City, assured a hinterland for the city. "Taking up the connecting social links, it may be repeated that not only Salt Lake City, but all the cities of Utah grew up under the most perfect system of colonization that the world has seen in latter times," said an old settler. "Indeed the early travelers to California invariably spoke of it as a system of religious communism, which Brigham Young and his apostolic compeers were attempting to establish upon the Old and New Testament plans, in the virgin valleys of the Rocky Mountains, where a new social experiment seemed eminently proper, viewed from a strict sociological standpoint." Status as the territorial capital and the church headquarters counterbalanced floods, prolonged droughts, and insect plagues. The first major commercial activity occurred when merchants sold forty-niners provisions at high prices, including flour after harvest time at twenty-five dollars per hundred pounds. Usually, winter brought depression conditions. "Merchandise was supplied almost entirely by ox-teams from the Missouri river, 1,000 miles east, which could travel only in the summer," an official declared. "Most of the staple goods thus brought were generally sold out by Christmas or soon after, so that the market was thenceforth bare of them until fresh supplies were obtained." More hard times came in 1856 and 1858 when most people fled United States troops sent to subordinate Utah Territory to the federal government. More economic trouble followed the Panic of 1873.[32] Only the support of the church hierarchy kept the city ahead of other important Mormon settlements, Fillmore City, Logan, Ogden, and Provo. Without the religious motivation of the people, Salt Lake City might have remained small and unimportant.

The urban frontier represented a unique aspect of the west-

ern experience. City building was neither a proving ground for democracy nor a battlefield for cowboys and Indians. It was not a response to geographic or climatic conditions. Rather, it was the extension of a process perfected earlier, the promotion and building of sites no matter how undesirable into successful localities. Uncontrolled capitalism led to disorderly development that reflected the abilities of individual entrepreneurs rather than most other factors. The result was the establishment of a society that mirrored and made the same mistakes as those made earlier in the rest of the country.[33]

CHAPTER 2

Demography, Society, and Economics

For years cowboy dramas delineated the western frontier population as white, Anglo-Saxon, and Protestant. Until the 1970s few blacks appeared in these stories except in the most minor of supporting roles, although viewers of these dramatic productions tacitly understood that downtrodden Indians represented black victims of segregation. Almost all presentations depicted westerners as native Americans, born and bred in the region. With little apparent schooling, they spoke perfect English with just a trace of a western accent. Eastern tenderfoots, despite living in the nineteenth century, knew little about horses; "school marms" from Ohio or Vermont talked as if they had degrees from Vassar, Smith, or Mount Holyoke. Hardly anyone used a foreign vernacular; Indians spoke in a childlike tongue, and Mexicans—almost always coarse and sadistic bandits—conversed in a sing-song fashion that passed for a Spanish-American dialect. Immigrants were few and far between. The few Jewish peddlers, English adventurers, Scandinavian families, and Chinese cooks disappeared early, eliminated by bullets, disease, or dropped plot lines. The West of the back lots of the movie studios had few blacks, foreigners, or easterners. Actually, while the region as a whole was not as cosmopolitan as the rest of the nation, it was not significantly different. The ethnic and religious compositions of the western frontier cities were as diverse as their eastern counterparts.

A majority of the native Americans in the western cities in 1880 were from other sections. People's origins reflected geography

21

and transportation. Large numbers of New Englanders had gone to Portland; it was easier for them to reach Oregon by sea than to go by land to Colorado or Texas. The San Francisco Bay region received a massive influx of prospectors from all over the nation, as gold fever overcame problems of accessibility. Northeastern abolitionists encouraged migration to Lawrence; religious beliefs brought persons from across the land to Salt Lake City. In most other places, the pioneers had traveled from neighboring states, following the traditional pattern. Omaha's nucleus came from Iowa, especially from Council Bluffs, where prospective home-steaders had waited patiently for the extinguishing of Indian titles and the creation of a new territory. The same happened in Kansas, where the first settlers in Atchison, Leavenworth, and Topeka crossed over from western Missouri. Called "Border Ruffians" by the northern press, which described them as depraved slavehold-ers, complete with whips, chains, and human chattels, the settlers almost invariably placed land speculation ahead of the slavery issue.

Population sources seldom remained fixed for very long. Civil War veterans from both sides went to Omaha to work on the Union Pacific. Unreconstructed Confederates moved to St. Joseph, believing the city proslavery in sentiment. Kansas City, which drew its early inhabitants from Missouri and Kentucky, gained large numbers of men from the Midwest and Northeast, who sought employment on the railroads and in the packing houses. The Americans in most western towns stayed on the move. People left in droves after staying a couple of years or less in one place. Few municipalities, large or small, could make the claim that Leavenworth did in the census: "No radical changes have occurred in the character of the population."[1]

In 1880 native Americans predominated in the three largest cities. San Francisco had 129,715 residents born in the United States, representing 55 percent of a total of 233,959. Native Californians numbered 78,144, or 33 percent of San Francisco's total population. All other states that contributed in excess of 1 percent were in the Northeast—16,001 came from New York (7 percent), 8,244 from Massachusetts (4 percent), 3,709 from Pennsylvania (2 percent), and 3,233 from Maine (1 percent). Fewer had moved from neighboring jurisdictions: 490 from Oregon and 484 from Nevada (each 0.2 percent), and 33 (0.01 percent) from

Arizona Territory. More people than that had journeyed halfway across the continent. An enumerated 1,334 (0.6 percent) migrated from Missouri, 2,152 (0.9 percent) from Ohio, 1,935 (0.8 percent) from Illinois, and 81 (0.03 percent) from Nebraska. In Kansas City 83 percent of 55,785 inhabitants were native-born. Missourians numbered 18,023, accounting for 32 percent of all Kansas Citians. Two northeastern states furnished sizable contingents: New York, 3,858 (7 percent), and Pennsylvania, 2,540 (5 percent). Kansas Citians from midwestern states included 3,347 from Illinois (6 percent), 3,340 from Indiana (6 percent), and 1,061 from Iowa (2 percent). There were few southerners. Kentucky sent 2,574 (5 percent), Tennessee, 1,113 (2 percent), and Arkansas, 126 (0.2 percent). Other aggregates numbered 1,317 (2 percent) from Virginia and 86 (0.2 percent) from South Carolina. Fewer residents than might have been expected were from Kansas: 1,629 (3 percent).

Denver's natives were primarily from the Northeast and the Midwest. While Americans totaled 26,924 out of 35,629 (76 percent), just 3,804 (11 percent) of all Denverites were from Colorado. This percentage was only slightly more than that for New York, which contributed 3,712 (10 percent). Additionally, 8 percent were from Illinois (2,795); 6 percent from Missouri (2,249), Ohio (2,211), and Pennsylvania (2,165); 3 percent from Iowa (1,233); and 2 percent from Kansas (615). Among individuals from other places were 119 (0.3 percent) from Minnesota and 47 (0.1 percent) from Utah Territory.[2] Taken together, the figures for the three municipalities showed the diverse nature of internal migration.

Western cities had significant minorities of blacks or foreign-born, and sometimes both. Generally, the mix reflected sectionalism. Places in or near the former slave states had more blacks; those settled from the free states contained larger numbers of foreigners. San Francisco, Kansas City, and Denver had black quarters—28 percent of Census Enumeration District 6 in Kansas City was black. (Table 2-1 indicates the number and percentage of blacks and foreign-born in the 1880 frontier cities.)[3] Kansas City had 9,301 immigrants and 8,143 blacks, the largest number in the West. San Francisco, with the biggest foreign-born population, 104,244, had 1,628 blacks. Houston and Topeka had more blacks and fewer foreign-born. Conversely, Omaha, Virginia City,

TABLE 2-1
FOREIGN-BORN AND BLACKS IN 1880

City	Total Population	Number of Foreign-Born	Percentage of Foreign-Born	Number of Blacks	Percentage of Blacks
California					
Los Angeles	11,183	3,204	29	102	1
Oakland	34,555	11,021	32	593	2
Sacramento	21,420	7,048	33	455	2
San Francisco	233,959	104,244	45	1,628	1
San Jose	12,567	3,834	31	101	1
Stockton	10,282	3,430	33	199	2
Colorado					
Denver	35,629	8,705	24	1,046	3
Leadville	14,820	3,918	26	279	2
Kansas					
Atchison	15,105	1,842	12	2,787	18
Lawrence	8,510	1,021	12	1,995	23
Leavenworth	16,546	3,382	20	3,293	20
Topeka	15,452	1,862	12	3,648	24
Missouri					
Kansas City	55,785	9,301	17	8,143	15
St. Joseph	32,431	5,656	17	3,227	10
Nebraska					
Lincoln	13,003	2,407	18	576	4
Omaha	30,518	9,930	33	789	3
Nevada					
Virginia City	10,917	4,791	44	96	0.1
Oregon					
Portland	17,577	6,312	36	192	1
Texas					
Austin	11,013	1,385	13	3,606	33
Dallas	10,358	1,323	13	1,921	19
Galveston	22,248	5,046	23	5,348	24
Houston	16,513	2,273	14	6,479	39
San Antonio	20,550	5,598	27	3,036	15
Utah Territory					
Salt Lake City	20,768	7,673	37	86	0.4

Denver, and San Jose had more foreign-born and fewer blacks. Two exceptions to the general rule relating to slave states and free states were in Texas and Kansas: Galveston and Leavenworth. Otherwise, the statistical relationships differed little from elsewhere in the country: South Bend was 26 percent immigrant and 2 percent black, Montgomery 4 percent immigrant and 59 percent black, and Lawrence, Massachusetts, 44 percent immigrant and 0.4 percent black.[4]

The large percentages of foreign-born in many western localities—45 percent in San Francisco, 44 percent in Virginia City, and between 30 and 37 percent in Omaha, Oakland, Sacramento, San Jose, Stockton, Portland, and Salt Lake City—made them as much "immigrant cities" as New York (40 percent), St. Paul (36 percent), Scranton (35 percent), and Cleveland (37 percent). Six other western towns had immigrant proportions of between 20 and 30 percent, and nine of from 12 to 20 percent. Writing about San Antonio at the end of the eighties, a resident concluded, "San Antonio is now probably the most cosmopolitan spot on the face of the globe. Representatives of every race of the earth have been counted here, except perhaps the aboriginal Oceanicans. The larger elements of the existing population are American, Mexican, German, Colored, with smaller groups of French, Italian, Polanders, Irish and many other nationalities."[5] The same thing could have been said about most other places. Yet even though no community was under 12 percent immigrant, the tendency was to think of ethnic ghettos in terms of crowded tenement blocks in the Northeast rather than congested districts in Denver, Leadville, or Galveston. Actually, only 2 out of 176 cities of ten thousand or more in the North were more than 40 percent immigrant, against 2 out of 23 in the West. Cities in the Midwest, Northeast, and West had about 30 percent foreign-born.

Most immigrants who arrived in the United States prior to 1880 were from northern and western Europe. The statistics for the frontier cities reflected this movement. Dallas, Austin, and Galveston, in keeping with early colonization trends in Texas, had disproportionate numbers of Germans when compared with the national totals, but so did St. Louis, Cincinnati, and Milwaukee. Portland received many foreign-born from Germany and Great Britain; those in Leavenworth were primarily from Ireland and Germany. Three nationalities accounted for at least 1 percent

of the people in Kansas City and Denver. The former had 3,526 Irish (6 percent), 2,209 Germans (4 percent), and 1,004 English (2 percent). The latter had 2,095 Germans (6 percent), 1,922 Irish (5 percent), and 1,436 English (4 percent). While Omaha contained Germans, Scandinavians, and Irish, sizable numbers of Czechs, most of whom worked in the packing houses, imparted a degree of Bohemian culture absent elsewhere. San Francisco was more cosmopolitan. The population included 19,928 Germans (9 percent), 15,077 Irish (6 percent), 4,160 French and 3,860 Canadians (each 2 percent), and 3,086 English and 2,491 Italians (each 1 percent).[6]

Cities on the West Coast in 1880 had large populations of Orientals. There were 21,745 Chinese enumerated in San Francisco, representing 9 percent of all inhabitants. Chinese in other places totaled 1,668 (9 percent) in Portland, 1,781 (8 percent) in Sacramento, 687 (7 percent) in Stockton, 1,974 (6 percent) in Oakland, and 634 in San Jose and 605 in Los Angeles (5 percent each). Away from the Pacific Coast, there were 519 Chinese (5 percent) in Virginia City and 238 (1 percent) in Denver. No other city had many Chinese. Omaha reported 14, St. Joseph 2, and San Antonio 7.[7] The only Japanese counted were 45 in San Francisco and 5 in Oakland. Throughout the West, whites disliked Orientals; in Portland officials called them "Mongolians." A California writer accused the Chinese of transacting "dark and devious affairs" involving "the smuggling of opium, the traffic in slave girls and the settlement of their difficulties." He claimed that in San Francisco's Chinatown, "The Chinese lived their own lives in their own way and settled their own quarrels with the revolvers of their highbinders." Only the "very lowest outcasts" among whites lived in the quarter.[8]

American Indians and Mexicans rounded out the ethnic components of western towns. Indians were few, with the most the 97 in Los Angeles, 76 in Virginia City, 45 in San Francisco, 37 in Omaha, and 11 in Salt Lake City. There were none in three places, Lincoln, Topeka, and Austin. San Antonio had the most persons with Hispanic last names, 4,876 (24 percent). Another southwestern city, Los Angeles, had the second largest percentage. There were 920, representing 8 percent of the population. In two other selected communities, there were 697 individuals (6 percent) with Spanish names in San Jose, and none at all in Topeka.[9] In San

Antonio there were Mexicans in all walks of life. Most of those in Los Angeles were laborers or farmers. The Indians were outside the mainstream of society.

Eighteen of the twenty-four cities had more males than females (see Table 2-2).[10] Women had a 52 percent to 48 percent statistical advantage in Salt Lake City, a special case for religious reasons. Other western towns in which females had an edge were Lawrence, Leavenworth, and Houston, all with 51 percent, plus Austin and Galveston, just over 50 percent. Females made up less than 45 percent of the inhabitants in several places: 44 percent in Omaha; 43 percent in Kansas City, Sacramento, San Francisco, and Stockton; 42 percent in Virginia City; 40 percent in Portland and Denver; and 27 percent in Leadville. In other sections of the country, northeastern localities of over ten thousand population tended to have more women than men, as did almost all such towns in the South and about half in the Midwest. The cities in the West required many manual laborers. Yet the totals reflected migration patterns to a greater extent than the needs of employers. A majority of early arrivals were young adult males lured by mining strikes and other speculative opportunities. Leadville (27 percent female) illustrated the short-term impact, while Leavenworth indicated how ratios evened out in the long-term.

Media productions, while concentrating on the depraved side of the western experience, carefully noted that religion played an important part in the lives of the "good people." Some stories concerned pastors trying to construct churches to bring the first vestiges of civilization to cow towns or mining towns. This was fairly close to reality and, if anything, underemphasized. In 1890 the census made its first successful comprehensive attempt to gather statistics on religion. The compilations for the sixteen former frontier cities surveyed that then had populations in excess of twenty-five thousand are shown in Table 2-3.[11]

Usually the cities had fewer church members than those of comparable size in other sections. Cincinnati with 296,908 people had 115,777 communicants (39 percent) as opposed to 92,872 (31 percent) in San Francisco (298,997 population); Bridgeport with 48,866 people had 19,983 communicants (41 percent) contrasted with 18,490 (38 percent) in Oakland (48,682 population); and Wilkes-Barre with 37,718 people had 15,738 communicants (42

TABLE 2-2

Male and Female Populations in 1880

City	Males	Females	Percentage of Females
California			
Los Angeles	5,910	5,273	47
Oakland	18,117	16,438	48
Sacramento	12,271	9,149	43
San Francisco	132,608	101,351	43
San Jose	6,553	6,014	48
Stockton	5,870	4,412	43
Colorado			
Denver	21,539	14,090	40
Leadville	10,781	4,039	27
Kansas			
Atchison	8,616	6,489	43
Lawrence	4,181	4,329	51
Leavenworth	8,171	8,375	51
Topeka	8,140	7,312	47
Missouri			
Kansas City	31,999	23,786	43
St. Joseph	17,832	14,599	45
Nebraska			
Lincoln	7,140	5,863	45
Omaha	17,104	13,414	44
Nevada			
Virginia City	6,280	4,637	42
Oregon			
Portland	10,514	7,063	40
Texas			
Austin	5,473	5,540	50
Dallas	5,462	4,896	47
Galveston	11,066	11,182	50
Houston	8,029	8,484	51
San Antonio	10,673	9,877	48
Utah Territory			
Salt Lake City	9,953	10,815	52

TABLE 2-3

VITAL RELIGIOUS STATISTICS, 1890

City	Population	Organizations	Church Edifices	Value of Church Property	Members	Percentage of Communicants
San Francisco	298,997	150	125	$4,241,100	92,872	31
Omaha	140,452	95	81	1,990,825	18,658	13
Kansas City	132,716	123	101	2,672,355	31,600	24
Denver	106,713	98	81	2,884,142	33,613	31
Lincoln	55,154	49	37	490,932	8,653	16
St. Joseph	52,324	59	55	803,175	14,588	28
Los Angeles	50,395	78	62	951,507	18,229	36
Oakland	48,682	66	52	1,052,491	18,490	38
Portland	46,385	60	46	1,479,550	16,815	36
Salt Lake City	44,843	49	32	602,094	17,502	39
Dallas	38,067	55	45	619,425	11,711	31
San Antonio	37,673	40	39	460,850	11,102	29
Topeka	31,007	72	50	519,725	11,554	37
Galveston	29,084	33	38	606,950	13,748	47
Houston	27,557	52	49	379,650	8,712	32
Sacramento	26,386	30	22	337,100	9,059	34

percent) compared to 11,102 (29 percent) in San Antonio (37,673 population). Some exceptions were Chattanooga with 29,110 people and 9,830 communicants (34 percent) against 13,748 (47 percent) in Galveston (29,084 population), and Des Moines with 50,093 people and 16,142 communicants (32 percent) compared to 18,229 (36 percent) in Los Angeles (50,395 population). Normally, cities with large numbers of Roman Catholics reported a higher number of communicants. Both the Northeast and the Midwest had more Catholics than the West and the South.

Membership totals for religious faiths are shown in Table 2-4.[12] Every city had many different denominations. Nevertheless, in six places Roman Catholics accounted for more than half of all members: San Francisco (70,670 out of 92,872), Denver (18,039 out of 33,613), Portland (9,140 out of 16,815), San Antonio (6,283 out of 11,102), Galveston (8,200 out of 13,748), and Sacramento

TABLE 24

Communicants by Denomination, 1890

City	Regular Baptist	Catholic	Jewish	Lutheran	Methodist Episcopal	Presby- terian	Protestant Episcopal
San Francisco	1,110	70,670	4,075	2,096	3,115	2,812	2,446
Omaha	1,107	7,675	1,035	1,277	1,859	1,708	1,228
Kansas City	4,490	11,900	825	838	3,195	1,333	1,143
Denver	2,498	18,039	895	540	2,858	1,896	1,820
Lincoln	681	2,570	27	531	1,625	696	301
St. Joseph	1,044	5,896	490	318	948	321	653
Los Angeles	1,282	6,154	460	375	3,002	1,873	979
Oakland	1,109	8,000	750	287	1,469	1,665	830
Portland	722	9,140	1,165	347	781	1,110	676
Salt Lake City	171	1,350	100	24	347	223	465
Dallas	2,250	3,275	200	90	445	164	518
San Antonio	1,075	6,283	200	500	590	130	525
Topeka	1,345	2,145	58	526	2,144	1,118	612
Galveston	734	8,200	850	787	841	95	670
Houston	1,265	3,350	75	....	935	....	591
Sacramento	370	6,000	250	148	458	256	330

(6,000 out of 9,059). Roman Catholics claimed the most communicants in all the other towns except Salt Lake City, where 14,276 of 17,502 church members were Mormons. Generally, religious ties reflected pluralism. Kansas City had 123 different organizations, Dallas 55, Galveston 33, and St. Joseph 59. There was great diversity among Protestant groups, with no special pattern throughout the section. Jews constituted the second largest denomination in San Francisco. Six synagogues had 4,075 members. In comparison there were 3,115 Methodists, 2,812 Presbyterians, and 2,466 Episcopalians. A number of other places had impressive Hebrew assemblies: Portland (1,165), Omaha (1,035), Denver (895), Galveston (850), and Kansas City (825). The western cities were no less or more religious than those in other parts of the country. As in the older sections, there were strong religious ties.

By 1880 all the frontier cities had public school systems. Well-organized administrative structures, long annual reports, comprehensive budgets, and detailed courses of study concealed serious deficiencies. Most teachers had neither professional training nor secondary diplomas. The curriculums stressed the basic skills of reading, writing, and arithmetic; students bothering to attend normally appeared completely disinterested. Pedagogical methods were authoritarian—"scholars" marched to and from classes to the beat of drums, submitted to corporal punishment, and recited by rote. Instructional material was minimal, there was little equipment and less innovation; classes averaged sixty to one hundred students. Still, many places remained proud of their schools; Leavenworth authorities claimed that pupils completing the four-year high school had "little difficulty entering Harvard with no other preparation." An 1879 graduate of Central High School in Lawrence probably better caught the climate of education in Kansas. Decades later, she said, "I don't recall anything that was spectacular about those four years, and practically all of my vivid memories center around the extracurricular activities, the preparation for commencement and the commencement proper."[13]

Cities spent as little as possible on schools. Appropriations in 1879–80 ranged from $15,346 in Houston to $875,448 in San Francisco. Buildings were customarily converted houses or modest structures. A conspicuous exception was the Omaha High School,

31

erected in 1872 at a cost of $200,000. The four-story building, which occupied a ten-acre campus at the city's highest point, had 17 classrooms, 4 large recitation halls, handsome offices, commodious library facilities, and several "apparatus rooms." More typical were the 19 wooden schools in St. Joseph, or the 10 with a total of 72 rooms in Kansas City. Teachers' salaries were low. Houston instructors made an average of $41.50 monthly; Virginia City cut the pay of teachers to make up a budget deficit. No place had an adequate staff: 34 educators taught 3,060 students in Leavenworth, and 22 instructed 1,584 in San Antonio. St. Joseph's student-teacher ratio in two black schools was a hundred to one. High absentee rates abounded. In Topeka daily attendance averaged 1,288 out of 1,926 pupils; in Denver 1,953 attended of 3,210. Throughout the West a little less than half of those eligible matriculated in public schools. Even so, the few denominational institutions remained modest endeavors. Omaha's Episcopal St. Barnabas School had 60 pupils; Atchison's Roman Catholic academy had 200 students.[14] About the only consolation was that the places of learning in San Jose, Salt Lake City, and Leadville compared favorably with those in Norristown, Cedar Rapids, and Mobile.

What passed for higher education was modest in character. The University of Nebraska at Lincoln had 2 buildings, 10 faculty members, 90 students in college courses, and 2,700 library books. Over 250 persons attended Omaha's Creighton College, a Roman Catholic Jesuit institution housed in a new $63,000 hall. The nondenominational St. Joseph College in St. Joseph claimed an enrollment of 177. In Lawrence the University of Kansas had 114 students and 16 professors. The library claimed to house 3,800 books, although a student thought the number closer to 200. There were two other small schools, all in Kansas: Congregationalist Washburn in Topeka, and Roman Catholic St. Benedict's in Atchison. Farther west, plans called for starting the University of Southern California in Los Angeles and reopening the moribund University of Denver. Aside from the University of California at Berkeley and the College of Santa Clara at Santa Clara, there were no other important learning centers in the entire region. Conditions were not much different from the older sections, where few schools approached Harvard College's 886 students and 187,300 books. Rutgers College had 101 students and 9,600 books, the University of Wisconsin 340 students and 4,000

books, and the University of Mississippi 184 students and 500 books.[15] Whether public or private, lower or higher, poorer or richer, the level of western urban education was as undistinguished as elsewhere. A Portland spokesman summed the matter up when he said, "Education is guided by Americans from New England and the northern states."[16]

The frontier cities boasted of many literary, musical, and artistic activities. Portland and San Francisco both had literary societies at an early date, and the latter saw the establishment in 1872 of the Bohemian Club for aspiring artists. Salt Lake City supported a variety of journals concerned with the Mormon community, Los Angeles promoters produced tracts designed to promote the "land of sunshine," and Portland interests began the magazine *West Shore* to glorify communities and individuals in the Northwest. Unfortunately, no real climate of cultural enrichment existed. There was not a single art gallery or library worthy of the name; serious musical fare failed to attract audiences. Hardly any successful author, artist, or musician remained long in the West. Most literary magazines died young. The *Territorial Enterprise* in Virginia City and the *Golden Era* in San Francisco enjoyed their greatest days during the Civil War, when some aspiring literary figures went West to avoid the fighting. After the *Overland Monthly*, designed to draw entirely on West Coast talent, appeared in 1868 in San Francisco, distinguished personality Henry George predicted that writers in the city would soon make a living by practicing their calling rather than "digging sand, peddling vegetables, or washing dishes in restaurants." But the *Overland Monthly* changed its format after eight years of publication, and George, Bret Harte, Samuel Clemens, and others left, some returning to the East.[17]

Western newspapers were shrill, intense, promotional, and numerous. The *Leavenworth Times* and *Omaha Bee* devoted many pages to "puff" articles extolling the virtues of their respective communities. There were thirty-four papers in San Francisco during the mid-1870s, all of which a reader claimed were "not calculated to elevate, but rather to lower the tone of public feeling." He contended "the press does not strive to lead or educate the latter, but rather to follow it, and follow it down to a low depth." A Denver politician admitted that the city's four dailies challenged "the admiration of every one who appreciated pluck

33

and perseverance." Kansas City's journals, perpetuating a tradition started by editor Robert T. Van Horn of the *Journal of Commerce,* were little more than extensions of the business community. While the *Deseret News* in Salt Lake City spoke for the Mormon hierarchy, a succession of "gentile" sheets, including the *Salt Lake Tribune,* denounced theocracy and polygamy. One reader called the *Tribune* "a decided anti-Mormon journal." The *Portland Oregonian* dominated the news by successfully controlling the Associated Press wire.[18] Many people resented newspapermen. Irate subscribers had already shot three San Francisco editors before William Randolph Hearst took over the *Examiner* in 1887. He recruited reporters skilled in the art of sensationalism to help perfect the techniques of "yellow journalism." When he applied the same methods in eastern dailies, critics associated the style with the West, ignoring the fact that since colonial days the press in America had frequently been accused of irresponsible reporting.

Various forms of urban recreation were much the same in the West as in the East. Voluntary associations were active everywhere. The Austin resident who noted that the community had "Masonic lodges, Odd Fellows' lodges, Hebrew Associations, and other secret and benevolent societies" could have been discussing just about any place in the United States.[19] Such fads as roller skating and bicycle riding quickly spread across the nation; westerners avidly followed boxing, horse racing, and baseball. Just as in the East, the newspapers carried the results of major sporting events. Several western towns built race courses. While some romanticists attributed racing to a county fair tradition, the sport owed its rise to the great eastern tracks: Belmont, Pimlico, Saratoga, and Churchill Downs. Prize fighting spread to the West after many eastern cities outlawed boxing as barbaric. San Francisco and Virginia City were important boxing centers. Baseball flourished; Houston had a team that competed with neighboring towns as early as 1861. In 1886 Kansas City gained a National League franchise. This first attempt by a western team to challenge the East in competitive athletics ended ignominiously. The club, characterized by poor hitting, pitching, and fielding, won 30 and lost 91 games. After one season it moved east to Indianapolis.[20]

Another significant aspect of urban diversions in the West evolved around private places of amusement. The combination

dance hall, gambling casino, restaurant, theater, hotel, and sporting house, which flourished in New Orleans, thrived in the West.
Men coming out of the mines or off the range wanted to do as
much as possible in a few hours. A tired pleasure-seeker could
drink, eat, gamble, ogle the "girls," and watch theatricals without
ever leaving his seat. Rough in the beginning, these saloons and
casinos changed over the years into more respectable theaters and
opera houses.

By 1880 all the twenty-four frontier cities had multipurpose
entertainment centers. There was an indistinct line between them
and so-called beer gardens, lecture halls, and opera houses. In
Kansas City the Coates Opera House sat two thousand people, and
the Gillis Opera House over twenty-two hundred. There were
three open-air beer gardens and the gigantic outdoor Theater
Comique, which claimed a capacity of six thousand. Denver had
four theaters and halls, plus four large gardens that were "toler-
ably well patronized in summer." However, a booster admitted,
"Denver, it must be confessed, is sadly deficient in places of legitimate amusement, though concert halls are unhappily only too
plenty in the lower part of the city." He claimed the Denver
Opera House was small, uncomfortable, and poorly ventilated.
Two dance halls in Los Angeles had indifferent luck in securing
a steady clientele. Austin had several large beer halls and two
opera houses. Not to be outdone, Houston had an auditorium
seating seven hundred and one seating eight hundred; San Antonio had three large halls, the smallest of which sat six hundred.
Salt Lake City's pride was the fifteen-hundred seat Salt Lake
Theater, built by Brigham Young from boards and nails abandoned by the United States Army. Another large structure, the
Mormon Tabernacle, held several thousand. Twelve theaters
operated in San Francicso. One was the Grand Opera House, the
social and cultural heart of the city. On special occasions two
thousand people, dressed in formal evening clothes, gathered
amidst ornate splendor. The Chinese Royal and the Chinese
Grand theaters served Chinatown. Citizens of all classes attended
events at the four-thousand seat Woodworth Pavilion, operated
in connection with a popular amusement park. Leadville had
several large dance halls, with names as diverse as the Carbonate
Beer Hall, the Gaieties, and the Academy of Music. They competed for male patrons with numerous houses of prostitution.

While many uplifting activities spiced everyday life, a Portland official admitted what was true throughout the section; the dance halls were "exceedingly well patronized, much more so than the theaters and lecture-rooms." Even so, western towns consistently provided better theatrical facilities than their eastern counterparts: Boston, with 362,839 people, had eleven theaters; a single decrepit hall dating from 1825 seating an estimated eight hundred served 90,758 Albany inhabitants.[21]

The western cities were old enough to have workers engaged in the wide variety of different occupations associated with urban areas. Because the towns functioned as marketing and distributing points, most employees were in commerce and related personal or professional services. There were, of course, exceptions. Men in Leadville and Virginia City labored in outlying mines; commuters in Los Angeles and Salt Lake City went daily to suburban farms, vineyards, and orange groves; several towns required many industrial workers.

San Francisco, Kansas City, and Denver had the largest working forces. Table 2-5 shows their main occupational components.[22] In San Francisco there were 7,867 laborers, 4,656 sailors and longshoremen, and 2,070 draymen. Domestic servants totaled 9,666, traders 7,150, clerks 6,778, launderers 3,077, and hotel and restaurant workers 2,705. There were 2,155 commercial travelers, hucksters, and peddlers. Manufacturing operatives included 5,858 in textiles, 3,358 in boots and shoes, 2,938 in cigar making, and 2,613 in carpentering. Professional classifications showed 583 physicians, 765 musicians, and 249 journalists. In Kansas City there were 4,550 laborers, mostly in the packing houses. The number of clerks was 2,101, of domestic laborers 1,830, of railroaders 1,311,

TABLE 2-5
MAIN OCCUPATIONAL GROUPS IN 1880

City	Total Work Force	Professional and Personal Services	Trade and Transportation	Manufacturing and Mechanical
San Francisco	104,650	35,060	30,150	37,475
Kansas City	25,081	9,811	7,625	7,393
Denver	15,737	5,127	3,764	6,422

and of carpenters 1,301. Laboring (1,680) and carpentering (1,035) were the only occupations in Denver that employed over a thousand. More than half of San Francisco's workers were foreign-born: 67,181, of which 17,012 were from Ireland, 12,394 from Germany, and 6,076 from Great Britain. The Irish aggregated 2,461 of the domestic servants and 3,467 of the laborers. Most of Kansas City's 5,620 foreign workers were Irish (2,208) or German (1,375). Irish accounted for 1,226 and Germans for 1,242 of 5,247 foreign-born employees in Denver. Kansas City had the most black workers, many of whom were listed as laborers, launderers, or domestic servants. Females in occupations aggregated 14,142 in San Francisco, 3,645 in Kansas City, and 1,681 in Denver.[23] The three cities, while having a low percentage of working women, had some of the largest proportions of persons gainfully employed compared with total population in the nation. Only eight other localities matched or surpassed the 44 percent for Denver and the 45 percent for San Francisco and Kansas City. The census explained, "This is due to the fact that great numbers of inhabitants of any one of these cities have recently gone thither to seek their fortunes, leaving the women, the children, and the aged behind in the older communities from which they came."[24]

Every western town claimed vast factories. A Dallas spokesman called attention to "6 large flour-mills, an extensive cottonseed-oil factory, 2 iron foundries, 3 planing-mills, several broom factories, and other flourishing establishments." Representatives of the Leavenworth Board of Trade proudly proclaimed in 1880, "From the feeble beginning made only a little more than a decade ago, the manufacturing industries of Leavenworth have increased and developed, grown and multiplied till the city is now everywhere recognized as the manufacturing center of the Great West, and occupies the same relation to the states west of the Mississippi that Pittsburg [sic] occupies to the Middle States."[25] In actuality, the "extensive" firms discussed in promotional statements were almost always two- or three-man operations with limited capital. Still, by 1880 ten of the twenty-four frontier communities had considerable manufacturing. Although the value of products of all except San Francisco ranked in the bottom fifty among the nation's hundred principal cities, the rise of industry added an important dimension to urban life in the West. The industrial statistics for the ten centers are shown in Table 2-6.[26]

TABLE 2-6
INDUSTRIAL STATISTICS IN 1880

City	Rank According to Population	Rank According to Value of Product	Number of Establishments	Capital	Average Number of Employees	Value of Materials	Value of Products
Denver	50	53	259	$2,301,850	2,944	$5,715,215	$9,367,749
Galveston	82	94	170	871,350	684	1,283,246	2,375,065
Kansas City	30	69	224	2,147,305	2,548	3,723,916	6,382,681
Oakland	51	91	72	1,371,457	1,387	2,012,695	3,181,066
Sacramento	90	87	160	1,672,400	924	2,911,889	4,093,934
St. Joseph	57	77	238	1,423,650	2,238	3,210,080	5,143,585
Salt Lake City	93	95	166	860,415	928	812,736	1,610,133
San Antonio	96	100	71	310,050	361	328,476	642,412
San Francisco	9	9	2,971	35,368,139	28,442	47,978,072	77,824,299

The most extensive works were in San Francisco. The Bay metropolis had 2,971 establishments capitalized at $35,368,139 that employed an average of 28,442 operatives producing products valued at $77,824,299 annually. It ranked ninth nationally and had more establishments, capitalization, employees, value of materials, and value of products than all the other western cities combined. The largest single industrial category in San Francisco was foundries and machine shops. There were 58 capitalized at $2,391,739, employing 1,921 laborers, and producing products valued at $3,889,503. In addition there were 310 boot and shoe factories capitalized at $1,090,772, 47 tanneries worth $1,161,800, and 110 men's clothing businesses evaluated at $1,126,164. These firms, plus a number with smaller overall capitalizations in women's clothing, corsets, dressed furs, millinery apparel, men's furnishings, gloves, and hats, gave San Francisco a virtual clothing monopoly on the Pacific Coast. Several other industries had a capitalization of more than $1,000,000. These were 38 breweries ($1,666,520); 152 printing plants ($1,744,755); 56 shipyards ($1,681,523); 147 tobacco, cigar, and cigarette makers ($1,687,603); and 24 slaughterhouses ($1,586,200). San Francisco produced just about every conceivable product: safes and explosives; guns and caskets; axle grease and carriages. It was a volatile industrial complex; severe rioting swept the city in 1877 and 1879. White operatives banded into workingmen's parties, advocating what their employers called "quasi-socialist" ideas, and assaulted Oriental laborers who supposedly worked for less money.[27]

The factories in other cities appeared capable of rapid expansion. Denver's plants supplied goods for a large area of virtually untapped potential. There were six $100,000 lines: brick and tile, flour and grist, malt liquor, printing, foundries and machine shops, and carriages and wagons. Galveston, with 170 establishments capitalized at $871,350, producing goods valued at $2,375,965, had one large industry, printing and publishing. Five concerns had 134 employees and a capitalization of $87,000. Three flour and grist mills worth $40,000 producing products worth $205,000 led manufacturing in San Antonio. The only two $100,000 industries in Salt Lake City were malt liquor and printing; Oakland and Sacramento, in the shadow of San Francisco, had a wide variety of small concerns. The most important St. Joseph lines, all capitalized at over $100,000, were malt liquor, printing

and publishing, flour and grist, and slaughtering and meat packing. Omaha and Kansas City had more extensive manufacturers. While the $285,000 malt liquor industry was the largest in Omaha, the most important was slaughtering and meat packing. Five firms, evaluated at $249,200, employed 148 and produced goods worth $991,790. The value of products on the capital investment in packing houses was not on the surface as large in Kansas City, $965,000 against a capital investment of $437,500, but important holdings were outside the city limits. Capitalists had already consolidated meat packing into three companies. And, unlike Kansas City's other $100,000 industries—foundries and machine shops, paints, and printing and publishing—meat packing had tremendous national potential in light of developments in refrigeration and availability of railroad connections.[28] As the frontier neared an end, many cities were going through a process experienced earlier in Racine and Selma, and before that in Lowell and Lawrence, Massachusetts.

The average capitalization of individual western factories in 1880 was small, and the annual wages varied markedly, as Table 2-7 indicates, helping to explain why neither western manufacturers nor workers held community power.[29] The proliferation of small plants impeded union activities and, at the same time, made it difficult for one or two men to speak for the industrial community. Manufacturers had not yet gained a dominant voice

TABLE 2-7

AVERAGE CAPITALIZATION AND WAGES OF INDUSTRY IN 1880

City	Average Capitalization Per Establishment	Average Annual Wage Per Establishment
Denver	$8,887.45	$534.79
Galveston	5,125.59	730.68
Kansas City	9,586.18	557.58
Oakland	9,048.01	547.00
Omaha	11,920.77	430.63
Sacramento	10,452.50	592.74
St. Joseph	5,981.72	397.14
Salt Lake City	5,183.22	458.55
San Antonio	4,366.90	381.66
San Francisco	11,904.45	524.87

in most places. Nevertheless, they could take heart from past examples.[30]

By 1880 economic and political power throughout the West had passed into the hands of a privileged few. A succession of western frontiers fell to large operators. After the initial strikes in the gold fields of California, the silver lodes of Nevada, and the lead veins of Colorado, big corporations appeared, bought or crushed independents, and achieved monopolistic positions. The same thing occurred on the fishing frontier along the Columbia River, the lumber frontier in the Northwest, and the cattle frontier of Texas, Colorado, Wyoming, and Montana. Agriculture had corporate characteristics from an early date in California, and when farmers moved onto the Great Plains they found themselves subservient to transportation interests that had benefited from the largesse of government in establishing empires of rail. People going west to find opportunity, instead discovered a closed society reigned over by "cattle barons," "bonanza kings," "lumber magnates," "silver millionaries," and "railroad tycoons." Because wealth translated into power, the rich held political control over state and territorial legislatures from Nebraska to Oregon, and Texas to Montana. Here, again, the West followed in the footsteps of the East.[31]

The extension of corporate tentacles into the western cities was incomplete in 1880, with the notable exception of San Francisco, dominated by a few families on Nob Hill—the Crockers, the Stanfords, the Huntingtons, and the Hopkinses. "The men we find at the head of the great enterprises of the Pacific Coast have a great business power—a wide practical reach, a boldness, a sagacity, a vim, that can hardly be matched anywhere in the world," an observer noted. "London and New York and Boston can furnish men of more philosophies and theories—men who have studied business as a science as well as practiced it as a trade—but here in San Francisco are the men of acuter intuitions and more daring natures; who cannot tell you why they do so and so, but who will do it with a force that commands success. Illustrations of such men and their bold and comprehensive operations may be seen in the Bank of California—the financial king of the Pacific States, with five millions of capital—the California and Oregon steam navigation companies, controlling the inland navigation of the two states, the great woolen mills and machine shops of San Fran-

cisco, the Wells-Fargo Express and Stage Company, in the mining companies, especially the Comstock lode, in the Central Pacific Railroad Company, even in the large farms of the interior valleys, and in the wheat dealing 'rings' of the city." Robert Louis Stevenson called the Stock Exchange "the heart of San Francisco; a great pump . . . continually pumping up the savings of the lower quarters into the pockets of the millionaires upon the hill."

Those who played important roles in the affairs of San Francisco came after the first wave of speculators. They made their fortunes elsewhere, in Sacramento and Stockton. The great transportation system that they thrust eastward had a western terminus in Oakland. They moved to San Francisco, not out of a desire to dominate the city, but because it was the place to go. When they made the decision to centralize their operations on Market Street, the Monarch of the West was already on a course toward urban greatness. They marshaled their wealth to wed the town to their own ends just as they had earlier planned and executed a Pacific railway strategy. Bitterly resented by some, condemned by many for vicious labor practices, and envied by all, their presence was a mark of San Francisco's preeminence. In the eyes of many, San Francisco was the Rome of the Pacific Coast; all roads led to it.[32]

Community leadership in western towns had first rested with those who had an early stake. Many times persons became casually involved in an Austin, San Jose, or Topeka. Kansas City was an excellent example. During the 1840s physicians, clergymen, and merchants received land payments in lieu of cash for services. Individuals with no speculative intentions found themselves with impressive holdings. In 1856 they founded the Kansas City Chamber of Commerce. Over the next fifteen years, through abortive railroad booms, wartime adversity, and postwar success, they remained together in a period when the leadership in nearby Independence and other competitors overturned. Thus, Kansas City had a crucial edge in working for the railroad connections that brought regional ascendancy.[33]

The very success of Kansas City lessened the role of the original business leaders. They had functioned on the proposition that politics was divisive, and so, whether Republican or Democrat, they had assiduously avoided controversy in formulating an economic policy. Conditions changed following the obtaining of

42

trunk railroads, when Chicago, Boston, and New York transportation, mercantile, and financial interests moved to the city. Armour and Swift engaged in banking as well as meat packing. At the close of the frontier, Kansas City experienced what San Francisco went through earlier. In exchange for a life of ease, the older leadership allowed outsiders a major share of community power.

Houston and Omaha experienced upheavals in their business communities. In the Texas city the arrival of New England railroad speculators had important consequences. Using eastern money, they diversified their investments into a number of enterprises. They blended in with the local leaders, replacing them in some instances, and helped to establish an oligarchy that ran the city through two commercial organizations, the Houston Board of Trade and the Cotton Exchange. In Omaha an ambitious speculator intruded upon local interests. George Francis Train, a Union Pacific investor and organizer of the scandal-ridden Crédit Mobilier, formed Crédit Foncier to build towns along the UP's route. He used hard-sell techniques to promote Omaha, where he owned six hundred acres, and the town's hinterland. Train realized only modest gains; he moved to Denver, where he failed and died poor. After Train left, Omaha's power structure returned to a combination of real estate and mercantile interests, with a measure of influence granted the Union Pacific. Meat packing brought in Chicago capital. The growth of industry, plus the growing corporate impersonality of the Union Pacific, left a major share of economic decision-making in impersonal hands.

By 1880 the dominant power arrangements in a majority of places had fallen into deceptively settled patterns. Cautious merchants from New England managed Portland. Fiscal conservatism and a reluctance to take risks contributed to a failure to successfully check the rise of Seattle. The Mormon leadership in Salt Lake City, after looking unfavorably on "gentile" businesses and mining, became more liberal after severe economic reversals. In 1880 an observer claimed that Salt Lake City was the main street for one large mining camp. Increased cooperation between the church-sponsored Board of Trade and the "gentile" Chamber of Commerce helped achieve economic stability. At Denver, William Larimer, quoted as saying in 1859, "I am Denver," led an aggressive group of entrepreneurs, who demonstrated skill and zeal in taking advantage of mining strikes, in outmaneuvering

43

competitors for railroads, and in thwarting eastern investors. A small group of men in Galveston controlled the Galveston Wharf and Cotton Press Company, which monopolized activities in the port.

Other cities in the West of 1880 had little to fear from outside interests, because they had limited aspirations or, supposedly, little potential. Speculators with political connections in Nebraska directed Lincoln's fortunes; they encouraged the state to finance the exploration of nearby salt deposits, which ultimately netted $100 annually, far short of expectations. Aggressive railroad promoters in Atchison had impressive local mansions and wide commitments in other places. A different set of mining interests predominated after every strike in Virginia City and Leadville. When they left, a few storekeepers remained behind. Merchants formed the main groups in Leavenworth, Topeka, and Lawrence. No threats appeared on the horizon; Kansas City's rise discouraged investment in lesser places. A tightly organized oligarchy in St. Joseph exhibited more interest in Kansas land and New York bonds than in St. Joseph's future. Stockton, Sacramento, San Jose, and Oakland retailers had no plans to challenge San Francisco. Businessmen in Dallas, Austin, and San Antonio believed that railroads offered opportunities for economic advances. They searched for ways to procure capital, unaware of oil deposits awaiting exploitation. For a time, however, the power arrangements appeared stable.

In Los Angeles a small group of merchants and speculators patiently awaited prosperity. Even though the arrival of the Southern Pacific Railroad had proved of limited value, the promoters of Los Angeles remained undeterred. They did not intend to give up easily. After all, they had paid the Southern Pacific a cash subsidy of $600,000, plus numerous other concessions, to build through their town rather than behind the mountains to the east. Continuing to view a viable railroad as an absolute necessity to community progress, they placed their hopes in a rival line, the Atchison, Topeka and Santa Fe. When it arrived in 1887 spectacular results rewarded their efforts. On a single day, real-estate sales in the Los Angeles area were three times the amount of the subsidy paid the Southern Pacific, and for the year 1887 the city ranked third nationally in land sales. The bottom dropped out of the boom in 1888, destroying many paper cities and

resulting in an estimated $40,000,000 in book losses. By then, Los Angeles was a well-established city. The business community, led by *Los Angeles Times* publisher Harrison Grey Otis, who organized the Chamber of Commerce and distributed promotional literature, emerged stronger than ever. The leading members made tremendous profits in real-estate transactions throughout the Los Angeles basin, and the survival of some of the boom towns added to the importance of the surrounding hinterland. A combination of rails, real estate, and patient businessmen made Los Angeles a success. Although there was no program for building a great city, the Los Angeles story came as close as any to providing a model account of how a band of entrepreneurs developed and followed a community policy that enabled them to stay in power during an unsettled period. When wealthy Henry E. Huntington moved from San Francisco to Los Angeles in 1898 to construct interurban lines and real estate developments, he found a durable and prosperous business community.[34]

The dominant groups exercised enough control in the twenty-four cities so that city politics and city government were unimportant. No matter who won an election, the views of a privileged few prevailed. "Boss" or "reform" administrations had no alternatives; business leaders either ignored hostile officials or threatened to leave town. The structure of government flowed along traditional lines. Cities owed their existence to legislative action. While the granted charters of incorporation contained restrictive provisions on such matters as the selection of appointed officials and vote percentages needed to pass bonds, the question of "home rule" was not a burning issue; state constitutions allowed a considerable degree of self-government. The chief official was a mayor who presided over a council of varying size. The scope of activities was relatively small—Austin spent about $70,000 annually. There were few employees, and elected officials served on a part-time basis.[35] Frontier city governments had no apparent means of developing innovative techniques. The legacy of the alliance between business and politics was a series of machines—Abraham Ruef's in San Francisco, James Pendergast's in Kansas City, and Robert Speer's in Denver. The innovative Commission Plan that evolved in Galveston after the tidal wave was the result of an accident of nature and had nothing to do with the frontier experience.

45

By 1880 the urban West clearly showed a debt to the East. The statistics for the native and foreign-born populations displayed no dramatically different characteristics. Religious affiliations were as diverse. Primary, secondary, and upper education copied national trends, as did literature and journalism. Sports moved directly west; places of amusement, while innovative, offered little new. No special occupational groupings evolved from the western urban experience. Manufacturers in California and Colorado sought to emulate counterparts in Michigan and Massachusetts. Large interests assumed dominant roles; smaller units hoped to maintain their status. The Turner thesis did not work in the city.

Improving the Environment

The West offered an opportunity for urban environmental experimentation. A blending of the latest eastern architectural styles with Spanish and Indian designs held great hope. The missions of the Southwest, the haciendas of Santa Fe, the cliff dwellings of Mesa Verde, and the pueblos of Taos combined beauty with forms that followed functions suited to the climate and the topography. Technological progress in Victorian America freed builders from the height and engineering restraints of antebellum days. During a period in which flux and innovation marked architecture, dramatic developments seemed within reach. Just as exciting was the possibility of major breakthroughs in urban planning. A golden opportunity existed to escape from the monotonous grid so prevalent in eastern cities. The hilly surface of the San Francisco Peninsula, the stark plains of Texas, and the foothills of the Colorado Rockies challenged the talents of planners. Few older communities had undertaken concerted efforts to design parks. The showcase projects that existed—Central Park in New York, Prospect Park in Brooklyn, and Fairmont Park in Philadelphia—had recent roots. The wide-open spaces in the West provided cheap land for meaningful and pleasing vistas aimed at enhancing the quality of life. Unfortunately, the same kind of commercial considerations that superseded esthetic factors in the Northeast, Midwest, and South prevailed west of the ninety-fifth meridian. And, no one seemed to care about another problem of everyday life: the condition of the streets. With few ex-

ceptions the parks were undistinguished, the planning poor, the architecture mundane, and the thoroughfares muddy.

Westerners sought to build cities that looked as much as possible like those in the older sections. They wanted to make Galveston another Mobile, Denver another Indianapolis, and San Francisco another New York. To achieve these goals cities used a progression of different architectural configurations that had no relationship to indigenous patterns. No place paid attention to the Indian experience; "Anglos" erected few structures in Texas or Southern California that even casually resembled Spanish architecture. San Antonio, despite its venerable missions, wore what one local writer called an "Anglo-Saxon skirt." He claimed that the city had "more of the appearance of an old world town than any in the Union—Boston not excepted." A dramatic negation of native cultural patterns occurred in Los Angeles, which had impressed a visitor in 1879 as "still a mere village,—mostly Mexican." By the start of the real-estate boom of the mid-eighties, downtown Spring Street looked much the same as College Avenue in Appleton, State Street in Madison, and Wisconsin Avenue in Milwaukee.[1]

During their early days, what passed for architecture in western towns was very primitive. Fur traders in Kansas City and St. Joseph lived in log cabins. Some of the first buildings in Leavenworth and Atchison were prefabricated structures transported from the East. Tar-paper shacks and clapboard stores with false fronts were familiar sights on the Great Plains. Tents sufficed in the mining towns; because there was a sudden influx of settlers building materials were scarce, and entrepreneurs were reluctant to invest in permanent construction until economic foundations were stable. A Sacramento leader, recalling gold-rush days, said, "While merchants, bankers, and corporations would hazard nothing in architectural ornament, gamesters were erecting magnificent saloons at enormous cost. A few poles stuck in the ground and covered with a wind-sail constituted the first gaming rendezvous. In the summer the famous 'Round Tent' was put up, where every species of gambling was carried on in its most seductive aspect."[2] A tent city was of short duration. Sometimes the tents literally folded, swept away by winds; a fire in a tent city was disastrous.

Successful communities gradually acquired more substantial

buildings patterned after those in the East. While single-family dwellings of one and two stories predominated throughout the section, a combination of high land values and topography in San Francisco led to the construction of low wooden row-houses reminiscent of brick ones in Baltimore and Washington. Local versions of Greek Revival and Romantic architecture predominated in Galveston. Two- or three-story buildings made up "business blocks" in western cities that were similar to main thoroughfares in the rest of the country. Some of the more ornate business districts contained arcades. Kansas City, San Francisco, and Portland had several impressive mercantile houses with cast-iron façades fabricated in James Borgardus' New York factory. The large packing houses in Omaha had counterparts in Chicago. Every western town had stone warehouses, pretentious brick hotels, elaborately decorated opera houses, magnificent churches with spires thrust toward the heavens, fine stores, and the beginnings of special sections for the wealthy containing rows of large mansions designed in the latest styles.[3]

Several localities had metropolitan trappings. The five-story Tabor Block in Denver was as impressive as any structure of its kind in the country. Built with money made in the Colorado mineral fields, it reflected the varied sources of commercial architecture in America. So did the three-story Pico House hotel and the neighboring Merced Theater in Los Angeles. Many stately Victorian Gothic mansions graced the bluffs above the Missouri River at Atchison. The business district in Leavenworth reminded visitors of those in northeastern centers. Of particular interest was the "mammoth" three-story Robert Keith & Co. building, which housed a furniture company. In Kansas City three- and four-story buildings of yellow and red brick housed commercial establishments on busy Delaware Street. The block-long Board of Trade symbolized community progress; the Pacific House Hotel hosted a generation of cattlemen, speculators, and gamblers. The city's leading hotel, the Coates House, stood a short distance away on Broadway in the heart of the theatrical district. Along prestigious Ninth Street, northeastern concerns had either built or planned to build gigantic offices; New York Life hired the nationally known firm of McKim, Mead, and White to design a regional headquarters. Because of their newness, many cities were in the forefront of the more eclectic aspects of the Romanesque Revival

movement, pioneered by Boston's Henry Hobson Richardson. Portland was so much like a New England city that a critic concluded that the town seemed old even in youth. A spokesman disagreed, stating it had "a metropolitan appearance unlooked for in a place of its size."[4] While other places made similar claims, there was really only one great western metropolis: San Francisco.

By the last stages of the frontier, San Francisco had numerous ornaments of urban aggrandizement. The imposing Bank of California dominated Market Street; the Lick House enjoyed a reputation throughout the West as a first-rate hotel. The Palace Hotel, constructed in 1876, sprawled over two and a half acres. The luxurious facility had 750 rooms, most of which opened on a large court. An English visitor called it a combination of the Louvre and the Grand Hotel of Paris. Most tourists saw the mansions on Nob Hill, the Seal Rocks from the multi-story Cliff House, and the clogged lanes of Chinatown. A resident said, "The Chinatown dwellings were old business blocks of the early days; but the Chinese had added to them, had rebuilt them, had run out their own balconies and entrances, and had given the quarter that feeling of huddled irregularity which makes all Chinese dwellings fall naturally into pictures." San Francisco already had a reputation as an interesting place to visit. Unlike its later cosmopolitan image as a "Paris on the Bay," the view in the eighties was that of an aggressive and flamboyant city; a western Chicago where the rich and poor toiled to create an urban center that evoked brute strength as its finest virtue. A foreigner caught some of the flavor in 1881, when he described the new city hall, considered by residents to rank with the guildhalls of Brussels and Amsterdam, as "an awkward pile of red bricks, with a huge tower somewhere, the whole caravansary having somewhat the appearance of those gigantic breweries to be found in the great cities of the Northeast."[5]

Western cities had an opportunity to advance the art of urban planning. Attempts at designing communities had started in the colonial period. William Penn produced comprehensive plans for Philadelphia; Williamsburg's design blended together landscape gardening and Georgian architecture. Later attempts ranged from Thomas Jefferson's proposals for "checkerboard" towns with squares laid aside for recreational purposes to the systematic plats prepared by paternalistic Boston capitalists for industrial "cities

in nature" throughout New England. Almost always economics dictated the course of events; buildings covered Penn's projected parks, and Jefferson's plans never gained popularity. Inadequate zoning thwarted the desires of manufacturers in the Massachusetts mill towns of Lawrence, Lowell, and Holyoke. Williamsburg remained beautiful, because it stayed a small governmental and educational center. More emblematic were the identical grids used by the Illinois Central Railroad for communities along its route. The printed maps contained a blank for the name of the town.[6] Urban planning in America was often done by drunken fur traders over a bottle of whiskey, who might draw a map for St. Louis based on their recollections of their native New Orleans, or by promoters, who crowded as many lots as possible into a small tract in the middle of a vast, uninhabited valley.

Commercial and exploitative reasons had determined the locations of the western frontier cities. Despite promotional claims of "natural advantages," geographical considerations were secondary. Leadville and Portland were cases in point. The "natural advantage" of Leadville over its rival, Independence, Colorado, was the proximity of mineral deposits. The flow of commerce favored Portland over Vancouver, Washington. Leadville's mining district had a radius of from fifteen to twenty miles, embracing the west slope of the Park Range and the east slope of the continental ranges. Leadville smelters treated and reduced ore from throughout the area. In addition, the town acted as a distribution point for food, tools, and other necessities. Portland was at the head of a valley 150 miles long in which over half the people in Oregon resided. While the founders of Leadville and Portland had attempted to find the best spots possible, taking under advisement the flatness of the site, the compactness of the underlying soil, the natural drainage, and the accessibility of drinking water, economics had predominated from the first. So, Leadville rested on the sloping and bleak treeless side of an alluvial plain at the foot of the Park Range, almost two miles above sea level, while Portland, high above the Willamette River, perched on basalt rocks covered with soil and trees. Both places had spectacular mountain views. The Colorado Rockies surrounded Leadville; persons in Portland could see the snow-capped summits of the Cascades.

The sites lent themselves to such design concepts as winding

roads, spacious open areas left in a natural state, and buildings set back on large lots to capture the best features of the surroundings. On the stark slopes high in the Rockies and in the hills of the Columbian basin, no planner designed western versions of Williamsburg, fitted the city into the environment, related the architecture to the beauty of the region, or fashioned new concepts of urban living. Both places lost the promise of pioneering new modes of planning. Leadville emerged as an almost rectangular town of small square blocks and undersized lots, split down the middle by a single main thoroughfare. The street plan was much like that of any number of older cities; Leadville appeared misshaped and jammed together.[7] While lost opportunity in Portland did not lead to ugliness, it resulted in an attempt to apply eastern concepts to a western location. With a great deal of determination, the men who platted Portland laid the streets out in a gridiron pattern, running them as straight as possible up the hills, creating a compact community in the wilderness. A map of Portland in 1880 resembled that of Des Moines. The difference was that the Iowa city occupied a relatively flat prairie. Portland retained a high degree of natural beauty, a circumstance that had absolutely no relationship to the planning process. A lack of vision prevented a different course.

Several western cities were on level land far removed from hills, mountains, and lush vegetation.[8] All owed their existence to entrepreneurs who had overcome many disadvantages. The hard give-and-take and high risks of town promotion had made major design expenditures impractical; survival took precedence over esthetic considerations. As might have been expected, none of the places emerged with imaginative, well-formulated, or interesting plats. Austin was on the Colorado River in country without marshes, ponds, or lakes. The town consisted entirely of rectangular blocks, with the principal streets running south toward the river. Houston's features were just as pedestrian. Dallas, by the Trinity River, on flat and sloping prairie, had an irregular layout because of new subdivisions built in the 1870s after the coming of the railroad. Prior to that the grid was a conventional one adjacent to the river. The opposite happened in San Antonio. "Although the modern business blocks and fine residences, with all their adjuncts in the way of the conveniences of civilization so largely predominate," stated an observer, "yet the

ancient looking houses here and there, the crooked streets and alleys, the plazas, the relics of an older and altogether different dynasty—lend the city a venerable air that is particularly pleasing to the visitor's eye so used to straight, wide streets and compact blocks laid out in the mathematical precision of a chess board."⁹ The inconsistent features of the old Spanish districts contrasted with the American sections laid out in gridiron fashion.

Lincoln had an uninviting location, which the founders failed to improve. Only the grounds of various state agencies interfered with the gridiron street arrangement. Topeka had an even squarer lineament, cut by the Kansas River. Although a booster declared that the city stood "upon high ground, commanding a fine view of some of the most charming prairie-landscape scenery of the West," the site, near the edge of the tree line, was bleak and generally flat. Denver, with an elevation varying 125 feet from the lowest to highest points, which belied promotional claims that it occupied a "series of plateaus," had a commonplace outline.¹⁰ Sacramento and Oakland had unexceptional plans, but they seemed almost like masterpieces of planning when compared to Stockton. The town was absolutely square, eleven blocks by eleven blocks, for a total of 122 blocks. Only the sloughs cut through the design. Seldom had the art of city planning fallen to as low a level. While Stockton was not altogether characteristic, the lackluster design further indicated the failure of westerners to do much more than the obvious in placing towns on level ground.

A number of frontier communities presented interesting planning possibilities. Galveston's island was low and almost level, being three to nine feet above sea level. Fine, sandy soil posed few construction problems. The loess prairie at Omaha rose gently away from the Missouri River bottom. Hills surrounded Atchison, transversed from west to east by White Clay Creek. Leavenworth, St. Joseph, and Kansas City were on tree-covered bluffs high above the Missouri River. Lawrence was in a wooded area in the Kansas River valley, at its juncture with the Wakarusa valley. Inside the city, Mount Oread rose 175 feet. The Wasatch Mountains towered above Salt Lake City. Mountainous Virginia City had an undulating surface. Luxuriant valleys set San Jose and Los Angeles apart from neighbors with fewer blessings.

Unfortunately, the quality of the planning had little relationship to location. Galveston, despite the curve of Galveston Island,

had an almost square grid. Straight streets and rectangular blocks stretched away from the river at Omaha. Railroad tracks and factories occupied the bottom lands; then came the downtown, and farther to the west most of the dwellings. In Atchison, which featured a grid, the main effort was to reduce grades and to flatten the White Clay Creek valley. Kansas City faced a more complex problem; the bluff dropped sharply to the bottoms from the hilly central business district. Land clearance projects facilitated the platting of a regular gridiron; earth machines made straight cuts through the bluff. Leavenworth and St. Joseph had streets that were as straight as possible, given the topography. At Lawrence, city fathers used a square plat with rather large rectangular blocks. Streets ran straight up precipitous Mount Oread. Salt Lake City had what an official called "an irregular and broad-faced L" design, with large square blocks and very wide streets.[11] Virginia City sprawled across Mount Davidson in no particular order. San Jose and Los Angeles had comparatively square contours.

San Francisco, which contained hills over four hundred feet in height, personified the failings of urban planning in the West. So intent were the builders on developing a square design that they ran streets up and down Telegraph and Nob hills with no regard to the grades, creating serious access difficulties for heavy vehicles. A New England tourist observed, "The early comers, having begun wrongly on the American straight line and square system of laying out the city, are tugging away at these hills with tireless energy, to reduce the streets to a grade that man and horse can ascend and descend without double collar and breeching help; but there is work in it for many a generation to come. They might have better accepted the situation at the first, made Nature engineer and architect in chief, and circled the hills with their streets and buildings, instead of undertaking to go up and then through them. Such a flank attack would have been more successful and economical, and given them a vastly more picturesque city. Boston had the advantage of cow-paths to establish its streets by; but no estray cow ever visited these virgin sand-hills of San Francisco, as innocent of verdure as a babe of sorrow or vice." A local observer admitted, "The hills are steep beyond conception. Where Vallejo street ran up Russian Hill it progressed for four blocks by regular steps like a flight of stairs. It is unnecessary to say that no teams ever came up this street or any other like it, and grass grew long

among the paving stones until the Italians who live there-abouts took advantage of this herbage to pasture a cow or two. At the end of four blocks, the pavers had given it up and the last stage to the summit was a winding path."[12] In the thirty years prior to 1880 the city spent $30,000,000 to level sand dunes and gullies. The projects involved the filling in of over three hundred acres of San Francisco Bay.

The cities that blossomed in the eighties repeated the earlier design mistakes. At Tacoma a subsidiary land company of the Northern Pacific Railroad, which hired landscape architect Frederick Law Olmsted to formulate plans and then ignored his proposals, attained little success in trying to achieve orderly settlement. Rudyard Kipling, after visiting Tacoma in 1889, wrote, "The town was thrown like a broken set of dominoes over all . . . . hotels with Turkish mosque trinketry on their shameless tops, and the pine stumps at their very doors . . . houses built in imitation of the ones on Nob Hill, San Francisco—after the Dutch fashion."[13] Seattle went a step further and actually used hydraulic mining machines to regrade hills in order to make conventional square blocks. An even more bizarre failure occurred in the Los Angeles area, where developers deliberately followed a policy of real-estate decentralization intended to bring residential and commercial dispersal. The aim was to avoid congestion and to create a metropolis that blended together the best features of urban and rural life. The result was totally uncoordinated growth after idealism vanished and economic values became paramount.

Most of the western frontier cities did an inadequate job of providing parks, places of amusement, and grounds for leisure activities. Private interests often furnished the last two: Dallas had a forty-acre race track, and the Winter Palace amusement center operated in Galveston. Parks, almost always under public control, were a relatively new innovation in the United States. Several colonial cities, in particular Philadelphia and Boston, had parks; the original plans for Washington had called for land-scaped malls. Praised at the time, they soon lost their original forms. Buildings occupied land originally set aside for recreation in Philadelphia, cows grazed on the Boston Common, and real-estate interests thwarted the Washington proposals. In the 1830s and 1840s four factors stimulated renewed interest in parks. First, Baron Von Haussman's beautification of Paris through boulevards

55

and park squares captured world attention. Second, cemeteries outside northeastern metropolises—Philadelphia's Laurel Hill, New York's Greenward, and Boston's Mount Auburn—featured landscape gardening, mowed lawns, and winding roads. These "cities of the dead" became tourist attractions and stimulated interest in similar projects for the living. Third, in an era before the acceptance of the germ theory of disease, anticontagionist medical authorities argued that parks purified the air by acting as "lungs" in congested sections. Fourth, popular writers, capitalizing on a nostalgia for the country shared by many city residents, argued that parks recaptured rural values in an urban setting.

In the 1850s the "City Beautiful" aspects of the park movement in the United States began with a prize competition to design Central Park in New York. The co-winner, Frederick Law Olmsted, directed construction and afterwards became the recognized national expert on park design. Projects that he directed in the 1870s, including Back Bay Park in Boston and Fairmont Park in Philadelphia, added to his reputation and generated interest in a number of other cities. By 1880 Baltimore and Washington had fine park systems; Detroit and Milwaukee had extensive plans. While most people recognized the need for parks, obtaining them was another matter: costs for land, plans, and beautification ran high, usually requiring the expenditure of tax dollars or the issuance of city bonds. Many medium-sized communities had no parks. Among these were Gloucester, Woonsocket, and Scranton in the Northeast; Alexandria, Norfolk, and Chattanooga in the South; and Fort Wayne, Youngstown, and Oshkosh in the Midwest. Numerous other places had inadequate facilities: Reading had a 5-acre unimproved tract, Covington a small grass plot, and Dubuque two squares covered with shade trees. In the West the frontier cities did little better or worse than their older counterparts.[14]

There were no parks in Atchison, Leadville, and Houston; several other places had hardly any worthy of the name Austin's system consisted of four 1.7-acre plots and 23-acre Pease Park. They remained in a natural state; the city council balked at appropriating money for maintenance. Dallas had some small public picnic grounds. Galveston boasted 15 acres of squares regulated by the three aldermen of the Committee on Public Squares and Esplanades. Officials at Lincoln expended between

$50 and $100 per year on a 10-acre tract. Seventy-four acres designated as park land in Lawrence remained unimproved. The fencing of 6 acres donated at St. Joseph had cost about $200. Denver residents generally avoided two small untended spaces. Each of the seven designated parks in Stockton were 300 feet square. Los Angeles, with 6 acres of municipal pleasure grounds valued at $800, and Oakland, which had six squares "visited very little," claimed that numerous attractive lawns and gardens made any further action unnecessary. The mayor of Los Angeles said, "Our city is 6 miles square, contains 10,000 acres of orchards and vineyards, which answer for public parks." An Oakland official commented, "There are no large parks in Oakland, and, as most of the houses are surrounded by gardens, their want is not felt to any appreciable extent." While the arrangements may have dissatisfied many plain people—few probably found much recreational enjoyment looking at vineyards owned by farmers or the lawns of the wealthy—they were better than those in Kansas City. There, what had been done was as good as nothing at all. A bureaucrat admitted, "The city has one small park or block of ground, containing 2.11 acres, used originally for a cemetery, of which it retains possession from the fact of its still containing the remains of persons buried therein. There is no attempt at maintenance except mowing the grass." Families picnicked and little children played games among the gravestones.

A number of frontier communities had better than average parks. Salt Lake City had four squares in different parts of town. Brigham Young reserved three squares in the original plat; officials later purchased another for $5,000. Fences, trees, and walks cost $10,000. Fifty-acre San Pedro Park was the largest of three in San Antonio. At Portland, a 40-acre $32,000 park, half a mile away from town on high rolling hills covered by fir and dogwood trees, annually attracted more than 35,000 patrons. Professional engineers planned Omaha's Hanscom Park. Sacramento and Leavenworth used grounds belonging to and maintained by other public agencies. The state of California owned Capitol Park in Sacramento, which contained 30 acres of terraced lawns, shrubbery, patent-stone walks, and shade trees. At Leavenworth the United States Army allowed access to the military reservation. "It is provided with graded and public ways, with romantic drives, with smooth grass plots, and shady and cleanly kept ground,"

Leavenworth's mayor stated. "It is a much finer, better, and far more extensive park and pleasure-ground than the municipality could afford to maintain, and being within 15 minutes' walk of the center of the city, it completely supplies the demand for public pleasure-grounds, and obviates the necessity of such a place maintained by the city."

The most magnificent parks in the West were in San Francisco. Among them was the nationally known Golden Gate Park of 1,050 acres, which was three miles long and half a mile wide. It had many roads and foot paths, plus thick foliage and thousands of trees not indigenous to the San Francisco Peninsula. The attendance figures for 1879 attested to the park's wide use; 748,000 persons entered in carriages, 826,000 on foot, and 35,000 on horseback. On an average, every San Francisco resident visited the grounds at least six times annually—a tribute to a lovely facility that remained in the ensuing decades a magnificent example of the better aspects of park planning.[15]

In keeping with national norms, many cities had undertaken concerted efforts to beautify their thoroughfares. Dallas fostered tree planting by paying a two dollar bounty for any that reached two years of age. Authorities in Houston advocated planting, leaving the matter to "individual taste." Galveston did better— the municipality set saplings along most streets. The city of Lincoln planted trees, requiring that lot holders pay all the expenses. Omaha requested citizens to place box elders, soft maples, or other rapidly growing species in front of houses. St. Joseph provided shade trees for the "better" districts; Kansas City placed maples and elms on "improved" property. Measures enacted in the late 1860s in Topeka promoted the planting of shade trees, with the aim of creating "a city in a forest." City ordinances in Salt Lake City required the placing of houses twenty feet back from the front line of lots, the intervening space designed for trees and shrubbery. In Denver abutters had almost universally put trees in front of their premises. Oakland authorities planted trees along most major avenues. Most homes in Stockton had some foliage. Portland encouraged trees; San Francisco discouraged them. An official in the California city reported, "The climate here is such that sunshine is preferable to shade, and, owing to the strong and continuous winds from the ocean, it is difficult to keep growing trees in an upright position." Trees failed to take

root in Leadville and Virginia City. Where practical, city governments nurtured the planting of trees for shade and beauty, usually asking householders to accomplish the task at their own volition.[16]

The streets beneath the mulberries, elms, maples, and oaks were uninviting. In 1880 few western cities had more than a small percentage of paved streets; officials made no attempt to improve upon eastern practices. In Austin a stretch of a main artery, Congress Avenue, had a broken stone finish. The other 72 miles of streets remained untreated on the grounds that the "mostly gravel" soil negated the necessity for improvements. "The streets become muddy under heavy rains," an observer contended, "but a few days of sun and wind restore them to good condition." Lincoln and Houston had no pavement at all. A Houston editor said that black mud was "a proverb in the mouths of people who stop in or pass through the city's precincts." Omaha attempted to improve only 0.4 of a mile out of 118 miles of roadways. During rainy periods the streets became virtually impassable. "Generally the water wanders around at its own sweet will," a functionary admitted, adding that the municipality planned to concentrate efforts on the construction of elevated wooden sidewalks. The 58 miles of Lawrence's streets were unpaved except for 1 mile surfaced with a combination of wood and broken stone. None of Denver's 200 miles of streets had any pavement. Kansas City, which had 89 miles of roadways, had 16.4 miles coated with broken stone and 1,500 linear feet surfaced with stone blocks. Work gangs in Leadville threw slag on muddy thoroughfares and hammered sidewalks out of worn-out pit timbers. None of the uniformly 137-foot wide streets in Salt Lake City received any treatment. Stockton's municipal force regularly shoveled fresh gravel on 1 out of 99 miles of roads. Los Angeles used broken stone on approximately 10 percent of 200 miles of streets, leaving the rest in a natural state. San Francisco spent an estimated $15,000,000 between 1856 and 1880 constructing 500 miles of streets. Cobblestones covered 20 miles, stone brick 20, asphalt 5, wood 31, and broken stones 57.[17]

No one knew what substances worked the best; all existing types had drawbacks relating to cost, durability, traction, and cleanliness. Only a small percentage of American streets had any veneer other than gravel or broken stones. Many places experimented with entirely paved surfaces, including the city of Portland. There, over $100,000 expended in 1879 on macadam, con-

sisting of broken stones cemented by bituminous material, went for naught. It melted on hot days and wore out in less than a year. Technology was not advanced enough to solve such problems, and the streets of Portland and other western towns continued to become quagmires when it rained and dusty traps when it did not.[18]

The urban frontier West failed to lead the nation in creating architectural masterpieces, designing cities, laying out parks, or building streets. Of course, not every town had as poorly tended thoroughfares as Omaha, as tedious a plat as Stockton, as undistinguished buildings as Los Angeles, and as inadequate parks as Kansas City. Outstanding mansions graced Atchison. A beautiful natural setting overcame design vagaries at San Jose. The parks of San Francisco were of a distinguished character. Portland made commendable attempts to improve streets. Yet there was no new society. The western towns borrowed basic concepts from the East, whether or not they suited the environment.

CHAPTER 4

Sanitation Practices

Nineteenth-century American cities were unpleasant places. Excrement collected on thoroughfares. Dead animals moldered at intersections. Garbage piled up in yards. Household wastes ran onto the ground or into open gutters. Privy vaults and cesspools overflowed and leaked. Sewers polluted streams and afforded poor drainage. Human wastes and industrial by-products contaminated drinking water. Inadequate cleaning practices ensured dirty towns in the eighties. A city force at Burlington, Vermont, swept the streets four times a year; Davenport spent $500 annually to have the chore performed. Steubenville had no system of garbage disposal. Scavengers in Fitchburg turned offal into swill. In Baltimore people dumped household wastes into the streets. Laundry slops seeped into wells at Kalamazoo. Keokuk had no regulations regarding privies. No city worried about industrial waste: chemicals from the paper mills at Holyoke killed fish in the Connecticut River; Madison, Wisconsin, brewers discharged slops into Lake Monona. Neither Rockford, Illinois, nor Council Bluffs, Iowa, had systems of sewerage. Open ditches carried away sewage in Pensacola. Newark's forty-eight miles of sewers drained through exposed outfalls into the Passaic River or the tidal streams in the salt marshes. The waterworks at Erie pumped water directly from Lake Erie into mains; the Louisville Water Company drew five million gallons of Ohio River water daily into two distributing reservoirs and a standpipe. Poughkeepsie had one of the few waterworks, out of 598 in the nation, that filtered water.[1]

The frontier cities faced similar sanitation problems, and the results in the West were much the same as in the East. Street cleaning received modest attention. At the bottom of the spectrum were Stockton, Salt Lake City, and Kansas City. The Stockton city clerk said that "properly speaking," no municipal cleaning existed. "The city employs a man with his horse and cart every Saturday, at $2.50 per day, to go around the principal streets and pick up the dirt and sweepings from stores and cart them away," he declared, "and that's all there is to it." In Salt Lake City, cleaning occurred intermittently. A clerk admitted, "The system is defective, and as the city becomes more densely populated a more effective one must be adopted." An unusual plan in Kansas City guaranteed inefficiency. For $2,500 yearly, workers swept the more heavily traveled streets after three inches or more of "mud" had accumulated.

Most cities had procedures that were little better. St. Joseph spent $10,000 annually to have the business district swept every other week. An official observed, "As a whole the system is very defective, but the class benefited by it, together with the force of habit, are powerful enough to continue it." Portland, using a method abandoned as impractical in New York in the 1830s, left chores to abutters. Sacramento and Lawrence combined public and private means. Property owners swept the leavings into piles in the middle of streets and municipal employees carted away the accumulations. Houston cleaned roadways sometimes as often as once a day, especially in what officials called the "sickly season." A public gang at Galveston scoured important routes three times weekly. Austin hired an "efficient" crew on a regular basis. Leadville daily employed "four mules and twelve men." Hogs supplemented the efforts of city workers in Los Angeles. Until the mid-nineteenth century many persons considered pigs, by virtue of their eating habits, an effective means of cleaning streets. In 1880 San Francisco had the only mechanical sweeping machines in the West—they followed a schedule that allowed busy streets to be swept once a week and lightly used ones every other month. However, even though special problems resulted from grades and drifting sand, the service had a low priority. This situation prevailed elsewhere: authorities believed adequate performance levels impossible.

Rapid urban population growth and conditions created by

the rise of heavy industry helped to emphasize the need for systematic corporate and technological responses to street cleaning. Against a backdrop of public concern over recurring epidemics, pioneers in the public health movement argued that municipalities must spend more for a variety of protective services, including street cleaning. These problems began to receive attention in technical journals, in monographic works, and in government compilations. The growing interest did not lead automatically to clean streets. The main thrusts of science and technology were in other directions, and other endeavors attracted the best available engineers. Firms selling cleaning equipment did little research and development. Early models of street sweepers, consisting of a primitive revolving-brush apparatus drawn by a horse, functioned so unreliably and cost so much that only a few cities bothered to purchase them. Unpaved streets continued to defy cleaning methods. Paving did not seem to help; many experts contended that it only created new problems. They noted that manure, which constant wagon travel supposedly worked into the surface of unpaved streets, turned paved ones into virtual cesspools. During an eight-hour working day a thousand horses left behind ten tons of manure and five hundred gallons of urine. A town the size of Leavenworth had over five thousand work animals. Whether a community did little cleaning or a lot, the "horse city" defied adequate cleaning.[2]

"Street dirt" collected in the western cities was disposed of in various ways. Austin and Dallas deposited the matter in the country, while San Antonio burned it inside the city limits. Sweepings at Houston covered "low places in the suburbs." Omaha relied upon "rain and overflows" to wash away loads tossed indiscriminately on the river bank. Crews in Lawrence shoveled leavings on "low places in back streets." Topeka sold manure to farmers; Denver "prisoners" carted it a mile away from town. Leadville dumped a "considerable" distance from habitations. Salt Lake City filled holes in vacant lots, and Stockton did nothing. A Los Angeles official claimed that the disposal of sweepings on the river bank had "no deleterious effects," because "trade-winds" carried the "smell" away. Kansas City and St. Joseph floated residue down the Missouri River; Oakland and San Francisco threw scrapings directly into San Francisco Bay. The ultimate disregard of human needs occurred at Galveston, where under cover of night

the municipal force buried "street dirt" on the public bathing beach.[3]

Dead animals were of special concern. Persons frequently left deceased beasts lying in the streets. Horses had a way of dying at inopportune moments. If no one was around, citizens of all classes were tempted to leave the scene rather than bear the burden of removal costs. Out of necessity, almost all governmental units had carrion regulations. Some cities left the disposal process to owners. In Austin they were required to take bodies to designated grounds a thousand yards beyond the city limits. Ordinances required individuals in San Antonio to bury remains at a depth of at least four feet in a local quarry. Such approaches worked haphazardly—only 50 large animals and 600 dogs were carried out of Austin in a typical year—so a few cities divided responsibility. At Lawrence, where measures called for removal of dead brutes within twenty-four hours, city crews buried those of unknown ownership on a Kansas River sandbar. The St. Joseph street commissioner sold abandoned animals to a glue factory. Other cities contracted for the service. A scavenger in Kansas City received about $400 yearly; he sold the best carcasses to meat packers and threw the worst into the Missouri River. Omaha's contractor marketed bodies at a phosphate plant, located outside the town. Leadville's trash man charged $4 to remove a large animal and $1 for small creatures. He took about 240 bodies annually to a remote spot, burning them when they accumulated and when the wind seemed right. In some places the task was performed entirely by public authorities. Los Angeles included animal removal in the street-cleaning budget; Portland left matters to the police. These agencies considered the duty secondary to their primary responsibilities; neither approached the state of bureaucratic efficiency demonstrated by Oakland's "city pound-master." In 1879 he reported the dispatch into the bay at a cost of $1,187 of 59 horses, 11 cows, 41 sheep, 14 goats, 95 hogs, and 69 calves.[4] Although rules and plans existed, dead animals continued to cause concern; in most towns newspaper editors frequently wrote about decaying horses lying by a curb for many days.

Garbage and ashes needed systematic attention. The time was past when householders could throw refuse into the streets; the health requirements of an age that accepted the germ theory necessitated more systematic responses. Licensed owners of butcher

carts removed garbage in Galveston. A poorly run city crew collected trash on an irregular basis in Leavenworth. Householders and the municipality shared responsibility in Lincoln, San Francisco, Los Angeles, San Antonio, Austin, and Dallas. A combination of the "chain-gang" and "swill-gatherers" carted away garbage and ashes at Sacramento. Contractors in Denver paid the city $2,000 a year for the right to haul garbage, more than making up the amount by charging individuals $2 annually. Under a poorly enforced garbage law in St. Joseph, dwellers buried some on their property, city workers threw some in the river, and scavengers fed some to hogs. In Leadville a contractor monopolized the garbage business. Kansas City and Omaha ordinances ordered residents to dump rubbish into the Missouri River. Portland stipulated that householders transport garbage out of the city during early morning hours; Oakland designated San Antonio Creek and San Francisco Bay as dumping points. Private garbage and ash collectors operated in both communities. Lawrence made householders take care of "offensive matter," with the same results that most other localities experienced. A frustrated and defensive city employee explained, "The system is good, but fails somewhat in execution by reason of laxity of individuals in entering complaint."[5]

Human waste generated severe problems. The refusal of late nineteenth-century sewage authorities to accept the germ theory of disease, despite conclusive evidence to the contrary, complicated things. Most were self-taught. No American university offered courses in sanitary engineering; persons established their credentials on the job or by taking guided tours of the sewers in London, Paris, and the Low Countries. In the seventies the leading expert was George E. Waring, Jr., a flamboyant reformer who entered the sanitation field after working as a scientific farmer, United States Army recruiter, and writer of horse stories for little girls. An ardent noncontagionist, he believed that "sewer gas" caused disease. Arguing that epidemics stemmed from foul-smelling house drains and drainage ditches, he attributed poisoned atmosphere to "the exhalations of decomposing matters in dungheaps, pigsties, privy vaults, cellars, cesspools, drains, and sewers . . . to the development of the poison deep in the ground, and its escape in an active condition in ground exhalations."[6] In the aftermath of the Memphis yellow-fever epidemic of 1878 that killed five thousand people, the federal government hired Waring to con-

struct a new system for the stricken community. There, he advocated the concept of "separate systems" designed to prevent fever outbreaks by avoiding the mixing of waste products that caused noxious odors. He proposed different mains for water runoff, household waste, and human excrement. The project had important results; it precipitated a nationwide boom in sewer construction. Previously, only a few larger cities, Chicago, Philadelphia, New York, and Boston, had extensive sewerages. The urban frontier ended before the full impact of the increased construction activities reached many towns, so most of them did not benefit from the new developments.

The largest sewerage system in the West was in San Francisco. The city had 126 miles of lines in 1880, of which 75 had been built in the previous four years under a plan prepared by William P. Humphreys, who agreed with Waring's approach. In advocating the design, Humphreys had sharply criticized the old system, which featured large three-by-five-foot mains with wooden outfalls that he called "elongated cesspools" badly choked with offensive matter. "This evil must go on increasing from year to year until some change is effected and some remedy applied," he had declared. "Each sewer appears to have been built independent of all others and without regard to the duty it has to perform." A noncontagionist, Humphreys believed that large mains made "sewer gas" a certainty. Furthermore, he asserted the existing outfalls at some points assured serious accumulations: "Along the busy water-front of the city some of the sewers do not extend out into the bay, but stop short, terminating inside of the rubble-stone bulkhead, where the offensive matter is deposited, and the liquid matter allowed to escape as best it can, rendering the slips between the wharves at times offensive to the last degree of endurance. All of these sewers should be carried out to the ends of the wharves. . . . Discharging at such points, the tide will speedily remove the sewage matter away from the city, and there will be no offensive smell about the wharves."[7] Humphreys converted the sewerage into a "combined system," with storm water and foul sewage carried by the same mains. Building an entirely new "separate system" would have cost too much money. Even so, San Francisco spent a great deal on sewers. During 1879–80 alone the city expended $78,000 on 22,000 feet of lines.

Only five other cities in the West had anything resembling

sewerage systems. At Portland, where nearly every sewer had an outlet connection to a main, the sewers ran down hills to the swift-flowing Willamette River. The system featured clay pipes eight to twelve inches in diameter, conveniently located manholes, and outfalls extending to the river bottom. Oakland had forty-eight miles of cement and vitrified clay sewers, all laid in the 1880s. Most emptied into San Francisco Bay. Four miles of mains and six miles of laterals served Los Angeles. Because the terrain impeded disposal, workers collected deposits to use in fertilizing gardens, vineyards, and orchards. Ten and a half miles of sewers at Sacramento drained five hundred acres in the business district. Mains ran down alternate streets; laterals entered from alleys at right angles. Two employees regularly flushed the lines and removed sediment. Kansas City had some stone conduits in natural watercourses, with a few laterals hooked into the arrangement. The channels, of various sizes and shapes, did a poor job of handling human excreta. A creek in the downtown district supposedly carried waste to the Kansas River. At St. Joseph brick lines followed ravines and other drainage channels. Authorities realized that the system worked imperfectly; large laterals discharged into smaller mains, and no maps existed. It was little consolation that things were much worse in many other places.

The rest of the cities ignored sewage problems. At Leavenworth an eighteen-inch pipe ran the length of the main street to a discharge point in the Missouri River. A twelve-inch line in Lincoln serviced three downtown buildings. There were a few small sewers in Dallas. A number of places allowed human waste to run directly into open ditches. Typical was Salt Lake City, which had no plans to construct sewers. The Mormon center depended on surface drainage helped by the irrigation channels that followed the street plan. Supposedly, irrigation water flowed swiftly enough to prevent the accumulation of filth. While this seemed to work in suburban areas, the heavy discharges in the business district overloaded the ditches, causing very bad odors. In Stockton sewage thrown into gutters or onto backyards had contaminated the ground. Despite charges that the situation threatened to "produce a fatal result on the health of the city," the council had done nothing more than discuss the matter.[8]

In lieu of sewers most western cities disposed of liquid household wastes and human excreta in privy vaults and cesspools.

Privy vaults held sewage until persons pumped it out and carried it away; cesspool contents filtered into the subsoil. Authorities disagreed over which method worked the best. Advocates of the cesspool, while admitting that some sewage drained into the soil, argued that a natural purification process occurred. Privy vault supporters said that excreta poisoned underground springs. They defended their system on the basis of its alleged watertightness. Unfortunately, most vaults leaked and contaminated the soil as much as cesspools; it made little difference which approach a town followed. Few adopted totally one or the other, although the accepted method was to use privy vaults for excreta and cesspools for household wastes. In any event, both arrangements were widely used. In 1877 Washington had fifty-two thousand vaults and pools; Chicago had thirty thousand.[9] In using them, the West kept pace with the rest of the nation.

Household wastes gave rise to serious problems. In Austin kitchen slops ran into privy vaults and street gutters; in Dallas porous cesspools necessitated the abandonment of numerous wells in the center of town; and in Galveston laundry fluids flowed into alleys and leaky cesspools. Lincoln's kitchen slops ended up on the ground, Omaha's went into cesspools, Topeka's ran half into gutters and half into cesspools, and Denver's passed into cesspools or privy vaults. At Oakland health authorities attributed several cases of impure well water to pollution from the escape of the contents of pools and vaults. The mayor of Sacramento admitted that the subsoil was "to a very great extent highly charged with sewage." In St. Joseph overflowing cesspools had hurt the quality of the drinking water in the older parts of the city. The best disposal practices were in Portland. The sewers received nearly all household wastes; none entered street gutters, and very little flowed into cesspools. The placement of the water supply intakes a considerable distance from town on the Willamette River precluded the possibility of contamination.[10] Such practices were the exception elsewhere rather than the rule.

Human excreta that seeped into the ground represented a worse menace. A number of cities in 1880 still depended on cesspools: Topeka and Kansas City (50 percent of households), Leadville (99 percent), and Denver (20 percent). "Zymotic diseases" from wells located near cesspools plagued Salt Lake City. In Dallas at least a third of the privies leaked. To combat this, an

ordinance ordered privy vault owners to convert to the "dry-earth system" within a specified time interval. Measures in Galveston that required brick or stone privies had no effect; most fell into disrepair. Lawrence claimed to have watertight privies because ordinances rigorously regulated construction. In what may have represented more realistic assessments, officials in Omaha, Los Angeles, Sacramento, and St. Joseph—which had detailed laws—said that almost all privies leaked.[11]

Towns handled satiated privy vaults and cesspools in a variety of ways. San Antonio enforced a rough-and-ready rule: persons dug a hole, used it until nearly full, shoveled dirt into it, and dug another hole. Galveston dumped night soil into the harbor. Licensed scavengers in Houston sold box contents for fertilizer. In Topeka sealed wagons transported the product to farmers in the surrounding area. Vineyard and orchard owners near Los Angeles hauled away excreta. Farmers bought the contents of the many vaults in Salt Lake City and the few in Portland. Denver and St. Joseph both forbade selling night soil for fertilizer. Atchison and Kansas City dumped raw sewage into the Missouri River. Regulations stipulated that persons in Lawrence empty privies in the dead of night and bury the contents away from the city "near running water."[12] Given the casual attitude of westerners toward excreta, it made little difference one way or the other that no city had ordinances covering industrial pollution.

A problem closely related to the removal of wastes was the availability of water for households. In the beginning, wells were the major source of water in a town, unless a stream was near at hand. As a community grew, the need for a water system became imperative. Until the 1840s water service was furnished by private enterprise, except in Philadelphia and New York, which had public works. Promoters became increasingly reluctant or unable to undertake construction. This, coupled with a belief that something as basic as water should not be a source of profit, led to an increasing number of municipally owned waterworks. They cost a great deal of money, almost always requiring the issuance of bonds. La Crosse expended $70,000 on a system erected in the 1860s, accounting for over 90 percent of the total amount of money spent by the city since its founding three decades earlier. At the conclusion of the Civil War, there were sixty-eight public and eighty private waterworks in the United States.[13] The trend con-

tinued, and by 1880 municipalities owned over half the works. The movement toward public proprietorship had not extended to the West, where urban dwellers seemed unwilling to pay the costs. Of the fifteen systems in operation, all except Sacramento and St. Joseph had private managers. Both Lincoln and Omaha intended to build municipal systems; Leavenworth had contracted for a private works. Several localities—Austin, Galveston, Lawrence, Topeka, and Salt Lake City—had no plans.

The frontier waterworks were about the same in quality as those elsewhere. Even in cities with waterworks, many inhabitants continued to draw drinking water from wells. "There was for some time but poor patronage for the water works," a San Antonio writer recalled. "People had to be educated to the importance of their new acquisition. Prejudice had to be overcome." Although surface water was often polluted, there was no assurance that water pumped through pipes was of a purer quality. Most works allowed only a brief period of "settling" to remove solid particles, and there was no treatment to eliminate bacterial or industrial pollution. Atchison, St. Joseph, and Kansas City drew water from a seriously contaminated source, the Missouri River. Atchison's private works did not bother to let water settle in the winter months, and during the summer waited only from eight to twelve hours before distributing water through eight miles of pipes. St. Joseph's public facility delayed delivery only a few more hours.

There were several different types of works in the West. The $100,000 Dallas Water Supply Company pumped an average of 1.5 million gallons of spring water into a standpipe, from which it was distributed. At San Antonio two Worthington pumps driven by two large double-turbine waterwheels raised San Antonio River water to a distributing reservoir near the main plaza. Water from the Los Angeles River at Los Angeles was distributed through a gravity system that had twenty-three miles of pipe. The $500,000 concern supplied an average of 125 gallons daily to each customer. Oakland's waterworks had a gigantic artificial lake, with a capacity of 20 million gallons, formed by an earthen dam three hundred feet long and seventy-five feet high. The $3,000,000 mechanism brought 5 million gallons of water to the city through a larger conduit. Cotton cloth stretched on frames acted as a filter, which was cleaned every twenty-four hours. San Francisco's waterworks compared favorably with those in other metropolises. The works,

70

built at a cost rumored to be between $8,000,000 and $15,000,000, brought 2 million gallons daily to the city from three storage reservoirs with a combined capacity of 24 million gallons. There were five thousand water meters—the only ones in the West—in San Francisco. Powerful hydraulic pumps at Stockton raised water from deep wells to a water tower. Every western town strove to provide piped water, but the emphasis was on delivery rather than upon quality. No one in Houston objected when the waterworks drew water from the same placid bayou in which the municipality dumped sewage.[14]

In western towns, as in other American cities, the streets were clogged with filth, the garbage rotted, sewers functioned inadequately, privy vaults and cesspools leaked, and the water tasted bad. Urban dwellers on the frontier were not pioneers as far as innovative solutions to sanitation problems were concerned.

Health, Fire, and Police Protection

From ancient Alexandria, Tyre, and Babylon to frontier San Francisco, San Jose, and San Antonio, urbanites held certain basic fears in common. The psychological stresses and strains of people living in close proximity to one another in an environment that promoted an individualistic response on one hand and a collective one on the other, coupled with a nagging feeling that the city might represent some sort of evil and cancerous anomaly in society, led some city dwellers to think of the dangers of urban life. Urban dwellers realized that cities had risen and fallen before and that this might happen again. War no longer posed an immediate menace: the battlefields of Europe were far away, the Civil War was over, and the Indians had retreated into remote regions or had moved to reservations. Few individuals worried about earthquakes, tidal waves, tornadoes, or floods, for natural calamities were unpredictable. Technological solutions to some disasters seemed at hand, perhaps in the form of higher dikes or more substantially constructed buildings. Rather, the average city resident worried about three basic threats to safety. One of these was ravaging disease—the possibility of great epidemics of cholera, typhoid, smallpox, diphtheria, yellow fever, and even bubonic plague. Another was fire—a conflagration sweeping across the community, burning all in its path and leaving thousands homeless. The third was crime—lawless elements preying on the innocent and helpless. Because of these fears, all the western cities attempted to establish agencies to guard the health of the com-

munity, to organize fire fighting systems, and to provide a measure of police protection.

Every 1880 community except Lawrence and Salt Lake City had a board of health charged with the responsibility of preventing epidemics and combating them if they happened. The city clerk at Lawrence stated that the council had discontinued a board in 1870 and saw no reason to establish a new one. A Salt Lake City bureaucrat justified inaction by citing what he considered special circumstances: "The city for its population probably covers a larger area of ground than any other in the Union. Outside of the business center the houses are detached. The streets are mostly 137 feet wide, and the sanitary regulations of compactly built cities have not, to the present time, been found necessary here." Other places had profited from experience gained from past calamities, such as the 1850 Sacramento smallpox epidemic that killed several hundred people, including most of the physicians.[1]

The composition of the various boards differed considerably: Austin's consisted exclusively of medical doctors appointed by the mayor; in Dallas it was selected by the council and included a health officer, three physicians, and four laymen; and in San Antonio its members were the mayor and aldermen. Omaha's health organization included the mayor, the president of the council, and the city marshal. The city physician directed an independent body of four medical men in Leavenworth. Kansas City's board embraced the mayor, fire chief, police chief, city physician, and two appointees; Leadville's, the mayor, two aldermen, and one citizen. The most novel arrangements were in two California cities. The legislature stipulated that the board in Sacramento have five practicing physicians, all holding degrees from medical colleges of "recognized respectability." In San Francisco, where the mayor acted as *ex officio* president of the board, power rested with four physicians in "good standing" appointed by the governor for five-year terms. The body elected a health officer, who had to hold a medical degree and to live in San Francisco. In keeping with national trends, no single organizational pattern had developed in the West. Still, despite inconsistencies, the goals were similar.

Boards of health had the traditional duties associated with their functions since colonial times. Most had far-reaching inspection powers. Sacramento's could search any building for irregularities; Galveston's examined all vessels that entered port.

The burial of the dead and the regulation of cemeteries came under the jurisdiction of most boards. Several had authority over various public agencies—San Francisco's board supervised the almshouse and the industrial school; Stockton's observed conditions in the city jail. Boards exercised wide control over the regulation of contagious diseases. This involved the quarantine of victims, the display of flags on infected dwellings, the removal from school of pupils exposed to contagion, and the implementation of vaccination programs. During epidemics, health officials exercised sweeping prerogatives. In Austin the single restriction in emergencies was that the council continued to exercise authority over the appropriate funds. The board in Lincoln could apply "all lawful measures" to stop an epidemic; Leavenworth's could do "what becomes necessary." Topeka claimed to have "competent and efficient officers" who were "fully alive to the sanitary requirements of the age." Oakland's had the option of proceeding regardless of cost. An ordinance in Leadville allowed the board to take "such measures . . . deemed necessary to prevent the spread of contagion or infection." All this looked impressive on paper, but the boards of health had very little real power.

Limited annual budgets in 1880 made it impossible for boards of health to carry out their duties with efficiency and dispatch. The Austin board had no budget; the president received a yearly salary of $600 in his capacity as a city official. Galveston had a deceptively large appropriation of $6,500, but it included the costs of street sanitation. Annual expenses in Omaha totaled $240, in Los Angeles $1,500, and in St. Joseph between $3,000 and $4,000. Atchison spent a "nominal" amount of money; Leavenworth, none at all. The largest health expenditure in the West was the $30,000 in San Francisco, where most of the funds went for the management of facilities unrelated to health care. Small amounts of money meant there were inadequate staffs. The Dallas board had one employee; its counterpart in Houston, a health officer and inspector. Los Angeles had two salaried employees, the chief health officer and an assistant called a "stewart." Oakland hired one full-time physician at $100 monthly and three part-time at $25 a month. These small organizations had hardly any chance of effectively guarding the populace. Of course, just as little money was available in other towns across the country: $600 in Youngstown, $100 in Concord, and $300 in Lynchburg.

Monetary restraints severely restricted services. Inspectors made only one thorough survey of health conditions in Dallas once a year. Neither Omaha nor Atchison had full-time investigators. Houston, Portland, and Kansas City claimed to do better, although the uniformly low levels of inquiry had almost no effect on community health. Occasionally, a recurring problem required constant scrutiny. In San Francisco the annual death rate per thousand was 18.50 for Caucasians and 21.22 for Chinese. One-third of the deaths among whites were children under five years of age. Most of the Chinese population consisted of adults, so almost all the Chinese who died were over twenty-one. A disturbed official attributed the high adult death rate in Chinatown to underground quarters and improper ventilation that resulted in an unhealthful atmosphere. "I have over and over again urged the enforcement of the cubic-air law as the only means of correcting the sanitary evils of the Chinese quarters," he lamented. "By constant vigilance many nuisances are abated, and a great deal of money expended to make this portion of the city even tolerable; but so long as these people are permitted to live as at present in overcrowded dens, socially, morally, and in a sanitary point of view they are a curse to San Francisco." Boards of health had no real way of avoiding epidemics. After one started, the aim was to isolate the sick in a "pest house," which was normally a dilapidated building in an out-of-the-way place. Galveston maintained a quarantine station at the extreme eastern end of Galveston Island, San Antonio supported a small hospital conspicuously marked by a "small-pox flag," and Kansas City transported victims to a snake-infested island in the Missouri River.[2]

Statistics in the nonepidemic reporting period of 1879–80 for thirty-one selected American cities showed an average death rate per thousand of 22.28. The male rate was 23.99 and the female 20.72. For the entire nation, deaths totaled 18.0 per thousand. Table 5-1 shows the proportions of death in one thousand of the living population in four western communities.[3]

All the cities had lower death rates than the national average: Oakland's were among the best in the country. These statistics compared with those per thousand of 25.4 for New York, 22.2 for Indianapolis, and 18.2 for Nashville. Because of younger populations in general, western cities had lower death rates than those in the Midwest, Northeast, and South.

TABLE 5-1
DEATHS PER THOUSAND FOR 1879–80

City	Number of Deaths			Deaths per Thousand of Living Population	
	Total	Male	Female	Male	Female
Denver	469	288	181	13.4	12.8
Kansas City	627	354	273	11.1	11.5
Oakland	336	178	158	9.8	9.6
San Francisco	4,798	3,073	1,725	23.2	17.0

Except in San Francisco, the mortality rate for children under one was generally lower than the national average in 1879–80, as illustrated by Table 5-2.[4] The deaths per thousand among babies born within 1879–80 in cities in other sections were as follows: 161.1 for males and 126.6 for females in Brooklyn, 116.7 for males and 122.4 for females in Chicago, and 167.9 for males and 157.5 for females in Washington. However, there was no solid evidence that western urbanites were significantly healthier than their contemporaries in other sections.

Frontier cities spent more money defending themselves against fires than disease. Blazes posed an ever-present danger for closely packed communities housed for the most part in wooden buildings. Sometimes, several small fires took their toll; at others, one conflagration could shatter a fine fire protection record. Between 1874 and 1880, Houston incurred $2,000,000 in losses without suffering a large conflagration. The only two fires of importance in Lincoln during the seventies brought heavy losses. The state

TABLE 5-2
MORTALITY RATE FOR CHILDREN IN 1879–80

City	Deaths per Thousand Among Those Born Within the Year		Deaths per Thousand of Living Population	
	Male	Female	Male	Female
Denver	83.1	65.0	132.1	133.3
Kansas City	91.9	65.6	143.1	88.7
Oakland	64.9	46.3	86.1	68.0
San Francisco	179.2	151.0	74.8	62.7

insane asylum went up in flames, and an opera house burned shortly after its opening. In September of 1878 Omaha experienced its first serious fire when the $200,000 "commodious and elegant" Grand Central Hotel burned to the foundations. Even though Los Angeles, Salt Lake City, and Oakland claimed in 1880 never to have had an important fire, the ringing of the fire bell caused as much apprehension in those places as in others with bad records.

Great conflagrations swept through the hastily built West Coast cities of gold-rush days. In San Francisco a $2,000,000 fire that leveled a block in the heart of town on 4 December 1849 served as a portent of things to come. On 4 May 1850 flames caused $4,000,000 damage, ravaging three blocks in the same vicinity as the first disaster. While new structures covered the area within ten days, the builders might as well have saved the trouble. Another great fire in the district on 14 June resulted in losses estimated at $5,000,000. Hastily erected replacements lasted only a short time. Those that survived a $300,000 blaze on 14 September turned to ashes in a $1,000,000 catastrophe on 14 December. Incredibly, an even worse fire followed. On 4 May 1851 flames consumed 1,500 buildings valued at more than $10,000,000 in the business district, and on 10 June a $3,000,000 fire attacked ten blocks in another part of town. After that the construction of more substantial structures and the organization of a more efficient fire department sharply cut the number of conflagrations, although an 1876 fire consumed 142 buildings, and 62 more burned in a blaze the following year. Sacramento, built originally of muslin, calico, canvas, sails, logs, boards, tin, and boxes, did not experience a disastrous fire until 2 November 1859, when seven-eighths of the city burned, with damage estimated at between $5,000,000 and $6,000,000. Stockton had worse luck. The place burned to the ground in 1848 and 1851, while still a tent city. Then, after it acquired more permanent structures, fire destroyed the town twice in 1855 and once again ten years later. A Stockton leader rationalized the calamities by stating, "In fact these fires increased rather than depressed business, as in many cases the material used for the buildings was being prepared before the fire was dead."[5] This was obviously small consolation, given the scope of the destruction.

As the frontier drew to a close, many western communities

continued to rely on volunteer fire departments. Normally, a town progressed from an all-volunteer force, to part-volunteer and part-professional, and finally to an all-professional department. Atchison reached the first stage of upgrading on 1 January 1880, when it added a paid staff that included a chief, an assistant chief engineer, a fireman, a driver, a pipeman, and a night engineer. At a single stroke the city increased its annual payroll by $3,000. The chief, who contended that "harmony" accompanied the change-over, admitted certain difficulties in his first annual report: "On assuming this . . . position . . . I was much embarrassed on account of the deficiency in apparatus to work with, a lack of a sufficient water-supply (for the first year at least), and the bad and un-serviceable condition we found the hose in, and with an incon-venient way to transport them to fires. During this time no provi-sions were made for fire alarms; consequently too much time was often consumed in finding out the locality of the fire. Some of these embarrassments have in part been overcome, such as a sufficient supply of water, the purchase of a new hose, horse-carri-age, etc., but yet enough remain to prevent the organization of a good and efficient department, such as a city of the proportions and pretentions of Atchison demand." The apparatus owned by the department consisted of a "second-class" steam fire engine, a two-horse hose carriage, a two-wheel hand hose cart, a two-horse hook-and-ladder truck, six fire extinguishers, and fifteen hundred feet of usable hose. Conditions were so similar elsewhere that the chief's summary applied to many other western towns. Yet the volunteer method persisted, as it did in one other section, the Northeast, where many cities—including Norristown, Wilming-ton, and Reading—continued to count upon amateur firemen.

Two frontier cities that had professional departments were Galveston and Omaha. Both had forces representative of those in other medium-sized American cities. The former employed an eighteen-man contingent for around $18,000 annually; the latter's fourteen fire fighters earned a yearly aggregate of about $21,000. For the twelve months ending 30 April 1880, Omaha's itemized expenses included $1,200 for the chief's salary, $13,252.56 for maintaining three engine companies, $1,585.52 for the hook-and-ladder, $108.22 for fire alarms, $456.40 for general expenditures, $4,400 for a new engine, and $676 for a piece of land. In terms of equipment, Galveston had six steamers, two hook-and-ladders, and

six hose-carriages. Omaha boasted four engines, including a hook-and-ladder. Galveston used nineteen horses to Omaha's twelve. Both cities needed good fire protection because of their large number of commercial and manufacturing establishments. Docks and packing houses contained many combustible materials. In an average year, in which the Omaha Fire Department responded to forty-three alarms, a single blaze in a meat-packing plant accounted for $137,000 out of $175,000 in losses.

Kansas City emphasized fire prevention more than either Galveston or Omaha. Ordinances divided the most heavily settled sections of the Missouri community into two fire districts. Within their limits regulations specified the thickness of outside walls, the use of incombustible materials for roofs and chimneys, and the necessity for the doors of theaters to swing outward. In an effort to improve efficiency, the twenty-man department used a telephone system to receive fire alarms. In 1880, 98 out of 118 alarms came over the telephone. Still, Kansas City suffered an unfortunate fire year, with $342,310 worth of property destroyed.

Cities normally concentrated on increasing the size and efficiency of their protective forces. San Francisco had a fine fire department: 303 men operated a large number of engines, tenders, hose-carriages, and hook-and-ladders. The annual budget came to $285,000, more than twice as much as in Pittsburgh, a city of similar size. San Francisco had 1,300 hydrants and 55 cisterns. Even more impressive were the 120 miles of wire and 150 signal boxes in the telegraphic alarm system. The San Francisco Fire Department held a high rank nationally, and so did the one in nearby Stockton. To counter the bad fires that had engulfed the community with depressing regularity, Stockton organized one of the world's largest, on a per capita basis, combination professional and volunteer departments. Some 240 men stood ready on a moment's notice to man 18 engines and a massive accumulation of other equipment. This "overkill" arrangement worked effectively; in 1880 the town incurred $10,438.94 in fire damage—an average of less than a dollar per capita.[6] No force, however, could deal with a complete disaster, as the San Francisco department learned during the 1906 earthquake.

Police protection in western towns has become the subject of many stories of frontier days. In novels, movies, and television, stories are seldom constructed around a brave public-health

officer fighting an epidemic. If, indeed, the plot deals with a widespread outbreak of cholera or typhoid, the individual responsible for saving the town is a young physician in private practice. Then, too, no "western" ever features the fire chief as the hero. If a dance hall catches on fire, it is saved by a bucket brigade of volunteers. But law enforcement officers play heroic roles. Their lot usually is to appear as brave defenders of conventional morality, who face and gun down a wide variety of vicious criminals and paid killers who terrorize western towns.

In the morality plays about the American West the lawmen play a role analogous to the knights of old—they are brave, bold, resourceful, and honest in the extreme. While there may have been such men on the frontier, particularly in the cattle towns of Kansas and Texas, there were none in the cities of the urban frontier of the 1870s. The reason was obvious—almost all had regular and formally constituted police forces, copied in concept and organization directly from the East. Nationwide advancements in law enforcement had come with dramatic suddenness. As late as 1840, when most western European nations already had centralized and competent police forces, American cities relied upon inefficient constables by day and ineffective night watchmen. While some large places, including New York, Boston, and Philadelphia, created systematically structured forces in the 1840s and 1850s, low levels of municipal spending, the belief that strong police departments were incompatible with democratic institutions, and nefarious political practices precluded the establishment of organized police forces in most cities. New York police, originally appointed directly by the mayor, did not have uniforms until 1857, when the state legislature reformed the system and established a metropolitan police board. Although several other states followed suit by temporarily taking jurisdiction over departments in large cities, the building of police forces remained essentially a local endeavor.

Major improvements in the police came after the Civil War, when the full impact of urbanization and the attendant problems of labor unrest, family instability, overcrowding, transiency, ethnic tensions, and economic disparities raised serious questions about public safety. Widespread draft riots in both the Union and the Confederacy served as portents of things to come. In 1877 great civil disturbances swept through the East during a crippling rail-

81

road strike. On another level, organized criminal bands of former soldiers, who had acquired special wartime skills in logistics and explosives, posed another threat to urban stability. There was a general belief that crime and disobedience were on the increase, and the response was a simple and direct one that involved spending more money to upgrade police departments to what most people perceived as professional levels. This occurred so quickly that by the end of the seventies there were few qualitative differences between police forces around the country. Without much fanfare and without any federal assistance, cities had accepted the "police idea."[7]

An official called either the chief of police or the city marshal, or in the case of Oakland, captain of police, commanded western urban police departments. They obtained their posts in a number of ways. The board of police selected the Dallas city marshal; the mayor, the Lincoln chief of police; the police commissioners, the Los Angeles chief of police; the mayor and council, the Lawrence city marshal; the city council, the Leadville city marshal; and the mayor and two elected commissioners, the Kansas City chief of police. In Stockton the chief of police was chosen in an annual election. The head law enforcement officers were well paid. In 1880 average annual per capita income in the United States was $175. It was $392 in California, $234 in Oregon, and $134 in Utah.[8] Compared with these figures, chiefs or marshals received $1,200 in Dallas, $720 plus "certain fees" in Lincoln, $1,200 in Omaha and Topeka, $700 in Lawrence, $2,160 in Leadville, $4,000 in San Francisco, $1,200 in Stockton, and $2,000 in Kansas City. Police officials performed a variety of functions, ranging from supervising the issuance of building permits in Lincoln to the serving of special warrants issued by the police courts in Stockton. They seldom made arrests, contrary to the view conveyed in western stories. Their main job was to supervise the department. This important and responsible task left little time for the kind of life depicted in books or on film. The chief law enforcement officials of the frontier cities were essentially desk men and administrators. Others handled the more glamorous and perilous tasks.

The designations, duties, and pay scales of peace officers below the command level were much the same from place to place. Most men worked standard twelve-hour shifts and earned good wages.

As a rule of thumb, the ratio of officers on patrol to the general population was about one to one thousand. In all instances, the men were called "patrolmen," "police officers," or "policemen," never "deputies." The force in Austin consisted of nine men, with one on duty at the station, one on mounted patrol at night, one on guard at the jail, and six on night foot patrol. Daytime enforcement depended almost exclusively upon alarms. Many citizens carried whistles. Several other communities had safety precautions similar to those in Austin. Two sergeants and eighteen patrolmen in Leadville covered only the six-block area of town with the most taverns, dance halls, and houses of prostitution. Paid $100 a month, they worked eight hours a day in the winter and twelve in the summer. Dallas had a deputy marshal who received $75 per month, two mounted police compensated at $65 monthly, and ten patrolmen on a monthly salary of $55. Everyone worked twelve hours daily, making rounds throughout the entire town. San Antonio had two assistant marshals, one of whom received $125 and the other $100 per month, plus eighteen patrolmen paid $70 monthly. Both San Antonio and Dallas had provisions for special police. Omaha's force of a deputy marshal and eight patrolmen, all of whom received $840 per annum, walked beats exclusively in the downtown. Ten men in Atchison, making $600 annually, each patrolled three miles of streets on twelve-hour shifts. Six men in Lawrence, compensated at a rate of $700, worked twelve hours a day with no regular patrol routes. In Los Angeles ten men had annual salaries of $800. Working an arduous schedule of eight hours on and eight off, two guarded the center of the city on horseback and eight covered the residential areas on foot.

Generally, the larger the city the bigger and better the department. Kansas City had a captain, one clerk, two sergeants, two roundsmen, two detectives, one special duty officer, two jailers, two mounted men, and twenty-four patrolmen. For salaries ranging from $750 to $1,140 yearly, the men worked twelve-hour duty tours. They were under strict regulations. Police faced dismissal if they consistently missed the 6:00 A.M. roll call, used unnecessary force in making arrests, beat prisoners, drank intoxicating liquor, or slept on duty. The rules warned officers not to enter "public houses, bawdy places, saloons, houses of assignation, or any other houses of public nature, unless called in officially."

83

In San Francisco, in addition to numerous high-ranking officers, 337 patrolmen helped uphold the law. Each man received $1,200 a year and averaged nine hours a day. Forces in San Francisco, Kansas City, and elsewhere found themselves seriously limited in terms of coverage and response time. Almost all officers walked—the few mounted police were the exception—and carried a whistle. The portion of town invariably given the most attention was the business district, with residential property owners usually left to their own devices.

The police in all the western frontier towns but Lawrence and Stockton wore uniforms. Even in such "six-gun towns" as Dallas, Leadville, and San Antonio, officers made rounds attired in formal navy-blue clothing, usually with brass buttons, often double breasted, and sometimes with a vest. Additionally, men generally carried a billy club, a whistle, a single handgun—never two as in fictional accounts—and handcuffs. Most forces required patrolmen to purchase their own uniforms and appurtenances. It was not unusual for a recruit to spend between $50 and $100 before starting to maintain the peace. In Omaha the uniforms consisted of double-breasted frock coats and trousers of blue cloth and blue caps. The men carried a billy, a revolver, and "Philip's patent police nippers." Hardly outdone, the Oakland police dressed in dark-blue beaver cloth uniforms, complete with brass buttons, dress coats, and straight vests. They carried a variety of equipment, including a club and pistol. The Kansas City police walked their beats in stylish blue suits with shiny brass buttons. Besides paying $75 for clothing, the officers furnished their own side arms and other equipment—a Colt revolver, a fourteen-inch club, and a pair of nippers. The most elaborate dress was in Portland, where the chief of police ran the clothing concession. He sold uniforms of blue beaver cloth, stiff round-top felt hats with gold cords, and matching overcoats, all for the "wholesale" price of $110. The city furnished brass buttons, stars, and belts, requiring each man to procure his own short club and pistol.[9] Few motion pictures or television shows ever feature frontier lawmen in gaudy uniforms. No blue-coated "deputy" subdues a criminal by hitting him with a billy and adroitly applying handcuffs. Even so, more often than not that was what happened.

Over the years, one sensational account after another emphasized the lawless nature of frontier society. Indeed, a Topeka

promoter related crime to civic progress. "Criminals and dis-reputable characters are always, to a greater or lesser degree, at-tracted to the larger and more flourishing centers," he wrote. "Topeka, being the capital of the state, and a thriving, busy city, it is not wholly exempt from this rule."[10] In the West of myth, criminals came close to overpowering the righteous. Bad men robbed banks and killed the innocent until stopped by vigilantes or brave sheriffs. While the dime novels read so avidly in the East dwelled on the activities of paid gun hands and sensuous dance-hall girls, some of the stories had an urban dimension. The Barbary Coast on the San Francisco waterfront received attention as a "grand theater" of crime inhabited by a "stagnant pool of human immorality"—a sort of West Coast version of the Lower East Side in New York, the First Ward in Chicago, or the French Quarter in New Orleans. The "sins of the city" literature moved West.[11] The narratives differed from the traditional cowboy story because the settings could have been anywhere in the country, not just in a single region.

B. E. Lloyd's 1876 exposé, *Lights and Shades in San Francisco*, depicted the Barbary Coast as a cauldron of sin and corruption. "The material is ready at all times, and should the favorable cir-cumstances transpire to kindle it into destructive activity, scenes as startling as those that won for the locality its christening, would be re-enacted," he wrote. "Even in the presence of a strong police force, and in the face of frowning cells and dungeons, it is unsafe to ramble through many of the streets and lanes in this quarter. Almost nightly there are drunken carousals and broils, frequently terminating in dangerous violence; men are often garroted and robbed, and it is not by any means a rare occurrence for foul murder to be committed. 'Murderers' Corner' and 'Deadman's Alley' have been rebaptized with blood over and over again, and yet call for other sacrifices. Barbary Coast is the haunt of the low and vile of every time. The petty thief, the house burglar, the tramp, the whoremonger, lewd women, cut-throats and murderers, all are found there. Dance-houses and concert saloons, where blear-eyed men and faded women drink vile liquor, smoke offen-sive tobacco, engage in vulgar conduct, sing obscene songs, and say and do everything to heap upon themselves more degradation, unrest and misery, are numerous. Low gambling houses thronged with riot-loving rowdies in all stages of intoxication are there.

Opium dens, where heathen Chinese and God-forsaken women and men are sprawled in miscellaneous confusion, disgustingly drowsy, or completely overcome by inhaling the vapors of the nauseous narcotic, are there. Licentiousness, debauchery, pollution, loathsome disease, insanity from dissipation, misery, poverty, wealth, profanity, blasphemy and death, are there. And hell, yawning to receive the putrid mass, is there also."[12]

Statistics in 1880 for San Francisco and other places did seem to indicate a high number of two of the elements associated at the time with a high crime rate: houses of prostitution and liquor saloons. The number of establishments admitted officially by local authorities were as shown in Table 5-3.[13] San Francisco had more saloons (8,694) than any other city in the United States except New York (9,067), which was five times larger. A city of comparable size to the Golden Gate metropolis, New Orleans, had 429. Galveston with 489 saloons had more than any other city in the country under 50,000 in population, and Leadville's 150 easily surpassed all places below 15,000. But other localities had numbers that did not seem out of line: 170 in Kansas City (55,789) against 178 in Cambridge (52,669), and 7 in Lincoln (13,003) as opposed to 65 in Macon (12,749). Authorities needed accurate statistics for these establishments for revenue taxing purposes. Houses of prostitution were another matter; they operated outside the law, so the totals were of questionable authenticity. Even so, there was no question that many western towns lived up to the section's "wide open" reputation. Only twelve cities in the United States claimed more or as many "resorts" as Leadville's 100. Galveston's 55 houses, Stockton's 40, and Portland's 30 ranked inordinately high. When it flourished, Virginia City certainly had more than the 20 listed. Of course, "vice" thrived in other places: houses numbered a national high of 517 in Philadelphia (847,170), the City of Brotherly Love. There were 365 in New Orleans (216,096), 166 in Toledo (50,137), 34 in Dayton (38,678), and 25 in Greenville, South Carolina (6,100). The number of people taken into custody for prostitution, soliciting, or entering houses of ill fame was as unimpressive in the West as elsewhere. Vice drives—such as the one on 5 houses in Lincoln that netted 95 "ladies of the night"—were exceptional occurrences. More typical was San Francisco, where no prostitutes appeared on the police blotters in 1880, although the police hauled

TABLE 5-3
HOUSES OF PROSTITUTION AND LIQUOR SALOONS IN 1880

City	House of Prostitution	Liquor Saloons
California		
Los Angeles	12	70
Oakland	10	215
Sacramento	....	....
San Francisco	....	8,694
San Jose	....	....
Stockton	40	57
Colorado		
Denver	7	200
Leadville	100	150
Kansas		
Atchison	5	48
Lawrence	0	18
Leavenworth	6	120
Topeka	....	32
Missouri		
Kansas City	....	170
St. Joseph	10	200
Nebraska		
Lincoln	5	7
Omaha	17	147
Nevada		
Virginia City	20	....
Oregon		
Portland	30	110
Texas		
Austin	....	....
Dallas	5	52
Galveston	55	489
Houston	....	....
San Antonio	6	70
Utah Territory		
Salt Lake City	5	34

in 547 persons for pimping. Many other cities, including Omaha and Atchison, while noting apprehensions for prostitution, failed to cite specific numbers, evidently in an attempt to either look as moral as possible, to hide the laxity of enforcement, or to avoid indicating collusion between the authorities and vice elements.[14]

Recorded statistics suggest that the western cities—just as the smaller cattle towns of Kansas—were no more violent than those in the East. As in other parts of the country, an overwhelming number of arrests on the urban frontier involved drunkenness. The Sacramento chief of police tersely listed his biggest problem as "whiskey." In 1880 Lincoln had 264 arrests, of which 121 were for being drunk and disorderly. San Francisco police apprehended 21,063, of which 9,127 were in the column for drunks; Portland had 2,578 arrests, including 1,466 for overindulgence. In the older sections, drinking accounted for 18,678 of 24,884 arrests in Boston 2,973 of 7,432 in Cleveland, and 4,391 of 13,558 in Washington.[15] Differences in arrest statistics related to a number of factors, including crime rates, police manpower, departmental enforcement policies, periods of civil unrest, and ethnic harassment. In Oakland 37 percent of all those arrested were Irish, who numbered 10 percent of the population, while native Americans, accounting for 68 percent of the population, had an arrest rate of 34 percent. In 1880 Oakland's arrest rate was 62 per thousand population, Los Angeles' 83, San Francisco's 90, Sacramento's 121, and Stockton's 145. Overall, southern and western cities generally had higher rates than cities in the Midwest and Northeast.[16]

A special kind of crime existed in communities with significant numbers of Chinese. This was the use of opium. The police chief in Portland carried on a crusade against the drug: in 1879 he charged twenty-seven persons with keeping opium houses and sixty-four with visiting them. He explained in his annual report that the problem went far deeper than the Oriental population: "Another evil, and a rapidly growing one, is the habit of opium-smoking, which is ruining the health and destroying the minds of many of our young men and girls. There are a large number of these dens, kept principally by Chinese, where men and women, young men and girls—some not over 13 years of age—congregate and indulge in this vile and filthy habit, and sleep off the stupor, subject to the insults and indignities that may be committed upon

them by those not under the influence and by the Chinese themselves. Some of the females who frequent these places are married and have families, and young girls of the most respectable class of society. Could their names be published society would stand amazed. It is almost impossible for the police to find out these places, as they are generally in rooms to reach which it is necessary to pass through dark, winding passages and doors fastened and guarded, sometimes requiring a guide; and when the den is reached all is dark, the inmates having escaped over roofs and by underground passages. Some more stringent and severe measures should be taken to break up these dens of infamy. No wonder that so many of our young girls fall from virtue. From the best evidence I have, there are about 500 to 600 white males and females who visit these dens in this city."[17] Portland faced a crisis of major proportions, because the chief had brought to a head a situation ignored in other cities.

The proportions of murders in western towns were about the same as elsewhere. In 1880 New York led the nation with thirty-seven homicides and New Orleans was second with twenty. The number reported nationwide in 492 cities of five thousand or more in population was 294. In the West, Atchison recorded five killings; San Jose and Galveston both two. The mayor of Omaha set the tone in noting, "It is a remarkable fact that during the past year [1880] no commission of a capital crime has occurred in the city, nor has there been scarcely a case of street robbery or garroting." Police work did not appear particularly dangerous, even though the Stockton force was the single one that carried neither guns nor clubs. Only a few municipalities in 1880 reported police casualties. In Atchison a man described as a "drunken Negro" shot and killed a patrolman, and in Leavenworth an officer died when he fell off a wagon. But fatalities were the exception rather than the rule.[18] There were no classic "OK Corral" or "High Noon" shootouts. More representative was the situation in Sacramento, where the sole injury to a peace officer the entire year was a broken wrist.

While their basic job was to uphold the law, the police in several cities claimed commendable crime-solving records, doing exceptionally fine jobs in recovering stolen items. During 1880 in Austin police returned $3,307 in property to owners out of $5,472 stolen, in Lincoln $250 out of $1,000, in Oakland $8,432

89

out of $15,687, and in Portland $7,339 out of $8,874. In San Francisco, in spite of the possibilities for easy fencing, the police recovered $43,708 out of $104,303 in pilfered goods. Although western urban lawmen did not always "get their man," they did well enough to draw the envy of many places outside the section that had larger numbers of detectives.

Many persons arrested served some time in jail. Almost always, the correctional facilities were despicable places on the order of the one in Omaha. Describing the quarters, the mayor wrote, "They are unfit to be the recipient of the vilest prisoners. . . . To keep prisoners confined in their present rooms during the summer would be an act of inhumanity." In 1880, 100 of the 867 individuals arrested in Omaha served time behind bars. In Oakland 1,177 of 2,141 persons arrested went to jail. The Oakland mayor stated in an annual report that most members of the chain gang were Chinese. "They cannot earn a dollar a day easier," he said, "as prison does not disgrace them with their own class." He argued that most would pay their fines if the city instituted a new policy of cutting off prisoners' pigtails. At Portland the number incarcerated was 889 out of 2,578. The total jailed in San Francisco came to a low 2,030 out of 21,063 arrested— a statistic explained by the fact that large numbers of men and women were apprehended for such nonjailable offenses as using obscene language (1,037), committing misdemeanors (1,745), and obstructing traffic (576). Of course, the courts did not convict everyone arrested. In Portland the judicial authorities fined 1,917 persons, sent 889 to jail, dismissed 194, and held 104 for later appearances. St. Joseph judges fined 1,013 and jailed 686 out of 1,712 arrests, discharging only 13. All in all, for annual public expenditures ranging from $9,000 in Lawrence to over $500,000 in San Francisco, the western towns received a high level of police protection.[19]

The exigencies of urbanization necessitated better protection for people crowded together in packed quarters. At times the growth of cities threatened to outstrip progress in protection. The public health movement in Europe in the 1830s and 1840s did not flourish in America until after the Civil War. Fire protection methods throughout the nineteenth century remained much the same as in the previous one. Disciplined police appeared

in New York over a decade after their introduction in London. In the new cities of Kansas, Texas, and California the local leaders showed an interest in determining on the basis of past and existing knowledge the means of protecting their communities. The extent to which they succeeded or failed depended on existing norms and not upon new methods that originated in the West.

CHAPTER 6

The Application of Technology

The nineteenth century witnessed a number of technological achievements that affected the quality of urban life. Many changes followed logically after breakthroughs occurred. The perfection of gas service systems made possible much better lighting than that furnished by kerosene lamps. Gas brightened streets, illuminated homes, offices, and factories, lengthened the winter day by making close work practicable in the evening hours, and changed the sleeping habits of millions of people. The incandescent electric lamp and the electric carbon arc lamp, both introduced in 1879, increased the efficiency and inevitability of a process already under way. A somewhat similar evolution affected the transmittal of information. The telegraph, which spanned the nation by the Civil War's end, speeded the flow of personal and business news, and wrought the almost instantaneous dispatch of data from city to city. The telephone in 1876 held promise of improving the transmission of messages, although problems remained with transmitters, switchboards, and wire noises. Still, even limited advances in fields like communication and lighting had profound impacts.

Just as important was the transportation revolution in the nineteenth century. The introduction of steamboats following the War of 1812 greatly improved river and lake travel. The perfection of the railroad in the 1850s allowed for a rapidity of traffic previously unknown, making feasible in the 1870s the creation of national markets. On another level, the development of improved

urban transportation represented a great technological triumph. The 1820s saw the introduction of the omnibus, the 1850s the general use of the horsecar, the 1860s the construction of the steam-powered elevated, the 1870s the operation of the cable car, the 1880s the application of electric power, and the 1890s the development of subways.

As western communities grew, the problem of moving people from one part of town to another became more critical. One type of conveyance used to carry commuters was the ungainly horse-drawn omnibus, which crowded from twelve to twenty persons into a small space. Dallas was one of the few frontier cities that had a sizable line. It consisted of six vehicles, thirty horses, and ten employees. The fare of 25¢ a mile was one of the highest in the United States. By contrast, in Denver an omnibus company that owned seven carts charged 50¢ a ride to take riders anywhere inside the city limits. Lincoln had a herdic line; small two-wheel horse-drawn omnibuses with side seats and an entrance in the back carried passengers for 5¢ a trip. While many towns had a couple of omnibuses that wandered the streets looking for fares, other communities either had none or preferred lines running on regular schedules. Lawrence and Leavenworth had no public transportation. While Austin and Houston had horsecar railroads, neither community had omnibuses. The heavy omnibus, which badly damaged streets during rainy weather, was sometimes a total solution and at others only a supplement to other forms of transportation.

By 1880 almost every American city of more than five thousand population had a horsecar railroad. In that year there were about three thousand miles of track and nineteen thousand cars in operation. Despite detractors who derided horsecar railroads as slow, dirty, and unsuitable for long distances, animal power was more practical for most communities than steam, the only other source of locomotion available prior to electricity. Steam engines caused unpleasant vibrations and scattered oil and hot ashes on pedestrians, particularly when used on elevated tracks or in subways. Steam generators for cable-car lines were so expensive that the systems were worth the cost only on steep grades. Horsecar railroads delivered passengers to their destinations in relative safety and had numerous advantages. The heavy cars moved on surface rails without danger of sinking into the mud, the braking

systems stopped the vehicles within relatively short distances, the average speed of three to five miles an hour was more than adequate for all except the largest mertopolises, the regularity of routes increased the efficiency of commuting, and the drivers needed little training.

A horsecar railroad proclaimed a city's pretensions of urban greatness. Leadville, at the bottom of the pretension list, had less than a mile of track on the main street. The route operated only three months of the year, charging 10¢ a ride. Los Angeles and Oakland had somewhat more elaborate systems. The former, with 11 miles of track, employed 10 cars, 40 horses, and 15 men. The latter operated with 13 miles of track, 29 cars, 115 horses, and 46 men. Los Angeles charged 5¢ a ride. Oakland sold four tokens for 25¢, making its single rate 6¼¢. The railroad in Portland had 1.5 miles of track, in Stockton 2 miles, in Austin 1.5 miles, and in Houston 3 miles. Portland's line used 9 employees, 5 carriages, and 25 horses. The 5 men, 13 horses, and 4 carts of the Stockton Street Railroad Company annually carried 100,000 passengers. Austin's 6 cars, 14 horses, and 9 workers hauled 20,000 riders in 1879. The firm in Houston owned 16 cars, 2 horses, and from 50 to 55 mules. Employees numbered 37. The most impressive animal-powered operation was in Kansas City. Over 17 miles of track carried some 60 cars—several of diminutive size to conform with the city's precipitous grades—pulled by 360 Missouri mules.[1] The hilly terrain had already stimulated discussions that ultimately led to a combination elevated and cable system.

San Francisco had already turned to cable cars as a solution to its serious grade difficulties. Andrew Smith Hallidie, a Scottish immigrant, designed the first cable systems. A grappling device attached to a moving cable towed cars along at speeds up to ten miles an hour. Original plans called for running over fairly flat surfaces. Traction companies in Chicago and Philadelphia built extensive lines, but heavy upkeep costs and frequent cable breaks prevented successful competition with horsecar railroads. The hills of San Francisco gave the cable car a new lease on life. Horses could not pull loads up the abrupt elevations, some of which rose as much as eighty feet in a four-hundred-foot block. In 1873 Leland Stanford's California Street Cable Railroad Company built the first line in the city. It ran up Nob Hill to Stanford's palatial mansion. By 1880 there were ten miles of track, in which local

residents took great pride. The cars efficiently solved the question of rapid and cheap transportation of passengers over precipitous grades.[2]

A city official described the cable-car operation in detail: "On these lines a trench 3 feet deep is dug between each line of rails from one end of the road to the other, and a permanent channel, either of wood or iron, constructed therein. This channel is connected with the street above by a slot from 7/8 of an inch to 1 inch wide. In the channel is stretched a wire rope running on sheaves, and driven by an engine placed at some convenient point. The passenger cars are attached to a 'dummy,' which also has seats for passengers, with which is connected the 'grip,' that drops down through the slot in the roadway and grasps the moving cable. The cars are thus easily hauled up the steep grades. When it is desired to stop a car the grip in the cable is unloosed and the cable is allowed to run through it, while the dummy is at rest. Of the roads now in operation one passes over a hill 325 feet high, another over one hill 300 feet high, and another 280 feet high, while the highest point reached by the other two roads is 200 feet. When the roads were first constructed it was thought that they must all be laid on straight streets without any curves; but a road is now in course of construction which will have a curve of about 60°, and around this the cars will be allowed to run by force of gravity, the grip on the cable to be relaxed just before the curve is reached. When one cable road crosses the other at right angles the cars pass over the point of intersection by force of gravity. In this case the grip, having been loosened and raised, passes above the intersecting cable and grasps it again on the other side."[3] The bumping and lurching cars, complete with their characteristically surly grip men, had become a regional curiosity, and some people visited the city just to ride the cars. Of course, even as the cable car emerged as an important community symbol, the horsecar railroad continued as the major source of public transportation; there were thirty-five miles of line, much double-tracked. Still, although the San Francisco horsecar routes were the most extensive in the West, nothing caught the public fancy as much as the cable cars.

Many other communities hoped that gaslights would identify them as being successful and prosperous. All towns of consequence tried to light their streets. Inevitably, a private concern gained a franchise to do the work. The cost per individual lighting unit

96

varied greatly, from $60 a year for the lamps of Galveston to $22 for Kansas City. The number installed differed from place to place. Leadville's citizens strolled in the glow of 100 lamps; Leavenworth's population made do with 60. There were sharp variations in quantity and quality. St. Joseph had 430 street lights, Kansas City 605, Omaha 160, Galveston 179, and San Francisco 3,500. Besides contracting with municipalities, gas companies when possible made the service available for other purposes. Major buildings usually had gas jets, as did a number of dwellings. The price varied; a Los Angeles producer charged customers $4.50 a thousand cubic feet, while Kansas City and St. Joseph users obtained the same amount for $2.50. Other cities fell between the two extremes; the cost was $3.50 in Oakland and $3.00 in Denver. There was no relationship between volume of production and price. Kansas City and St. Joseph paid the same, although the works in the larger city manufactured seven times as much gas, which theoretically should have resulted in a lower charge. In 1880 Salt Lake City had already installed Bush System electric lights on East Temple Street. Denver issued a contract in the spring of 1880 for a limited number of electric lights.[4] Thus, western cities continued to show a willingness to introduce the latest eastern improvements.

Another tremendously important invention, the telephone, quickly reached frontier communities. Even though the systems that existed in 1880 were either losing money or turning small profits, few believed this situation would prevail for very long. The telephone companies for western cities enumerated in Table 6-1 loomed as "blue chip" investments. The 148 American telephone companies that the census gathered statistics on had 32,734 miles of wire and a net income of $770,516. A Colorado observer boasted, "It is said that Denver is far ahead of any city of twice her size in the matter of telephone connections, and one of the local papers wittily remarks that the city is almost darkened by its network of telephone wires in every direction."[5] Technological innovations played important roles in western cities and in creating a spirit of community. Even so, gas lines, telephones, and horse-cars were not enough to sustain progress; continual development and expansion of the hinterlands were needed. In the nineteenth century this meant building a regional transportation network with strong national connections. While highways and rivers

TABLE 6-1

STATISTICS ON TELEPHONE COMPANIES IN 1880

City	Name of Company	Miles of Wire	Net Income
California			
San Francisco	Pacific Bell Telephone Co.	565	$7,158
San Jose	American District Telegraph and Telephone Co.	15	$2,100
Colorado			
Denver	Bell Telephone Co.	....	....
Denver	Colorado Telephone Co.	700	$18,178
Denver	Western Union Telegraph Co.	....	....
Leadville	Leadville Telephone Co.	220	$ 555
Kansas			
Atchison	Atchison Telephone Exchange Co.	45	$ 547
Leavenworth	Leavenworth Telephone Exchange Co.	175	$1,303
Topeka	Topeka Telephone Co.	80	$ 590
Missouri			
St. Joseph	St. Joseph Telephone Exchange Co.	225	$1,596
Nebraska			
Omaha	Omaha Electric Co.	179	$4,145
Oregon			
Portland	Portland Telephone, Telegraph, and Electric Co.	100	$1,362

formed important parts of plans, the railroad was the key. The iron "T" rails, the standardized gauge, the production of more substantial trains and engines, the perfection of reliable air brakes, the construction of bridges that stood up under continual heavy loads, the use of better signals, the development of steel tracks, and numerous other advances made feasible the lengthy systems needed in the West. A high degree of corruption, vision, and enterprise marked the building of the first transcontinental line and other components of the Pacific railroad strategy. By the 1870s rails spanned the continent and ribbons of steel spread like octopuses' tentacles over the wastes of New Mexico and Arizona, the plains of Kansas and Texas, the mountains of Colorado and Nevada, and the valleys of California and Oregon.

All communities anticipated the day they would see the first smudge of black smoke on the horizon and hear the rumbling sounds associated with the arrival of the first train, and believed it would usher in a veritable new age of commerce and industry. "The work is done," trumpeted a Kansas City editor after a key railroad decision. "The anxiety and toil of ten years is ended! . . . Let the heathen [rival Missouri River cities] rage . . . sunk in the turbid waters of the river, are many of the cities of this valley. Oblivion has sealed the fate of many a place deemed immortal!"[6] When the iron horse was slow in coming, optimists prepared in advance for the great day. Atchison interests constructed a railroad bridge in 1874–75 over the Missouri River. Leaders boasted about the details of the project: its wrought-iron structural parts rested upon a stone foundation, its length was 1,182 feet, its drawspan swung on a large circular pier, its approaches were 2,000 feet long, and its flooring was capable of handling any kind of traffic. Eulogizing the local builders of the bridge, the Atchison Board of Trade stated, "The mere fact that a company of capitalists are willing to undertake an enterprise involving so large an outlay of money during a period of such general depression, proves conclusively that Atchison has commercial advantages possessed by no other city in the Missouri Valley. For these gentlemen are building the bridge as a legitimate business enterprise, firmly convinced that it will pay for the investment. They have carefully calculated both the cost and the business it will do, and found that a bridge is needed to accommodate the trade already centered here. . . . The investment is a good one, upon which a handsome profit can be realized."[7] The failure to immediately gain railroads from the East and the loss of key trunk lines in Kansas dampened enthusiasm and severely curtailed aspirations. The iron horse failed Atchison at a crucial juncture, just as it did Leavenworth, Portland, and Leadville. But it favored Kansas City, Los Angeles, and other places, helping fundamentally to shape the western urban mosaic.

The steel bands of imperial destiny bridged the gaps of distance and helped end the frontier. The thrust of rails changed geographical identities. By the conclusion of the railroad-building period, as the area entered the new century, the cities on the eastern fringe—Omaha, Lincoln, Leavenworth, Atchison, Topeka, Lawrence, St. Joseph, and Kansas City—were no longer considered western towns. The railroads that they sought explained the

reason: the great technological strides were so fundamental and successful that places like Kansas City and Omaha, which continued to look westward for their prosperity, were no longer part of the region. They were in the western approaches of the Midwest. Such was the legacy of railroad building.

By 1880 several western towns had already impressive railroad connections. Kansas City had the best. Ten railroads radiated from the city. The Kansas City, St. Joseph and Council Bluffs Railroad connected at Council Bluffs with the transcontinental system. The Hannibal and St. Joseph Railroad, the Chicago and Alton Railroad, and the Missouri Pacific Railroad linked Kansas City with Chicago. Another line, the Chicago, Rock Island and Pacific Railroad, entered Kansas City over Hannibal and St. Joseph tracks. The Wabash, St. Louis and Pacific Railway ran to Indianapolis. The Kansas City and Eastern Railway operated over forty miles of narrow-gauge tracks to Lexington, Missouri. To the west of Kansas City, the Union Pacific Railroad ran to Denver. This line, first called the Union Pacific–Eastern Division Railroad and later the Kansas Pacific Railroad, afforded the original outlet for cows driven to the Kansas cattle towns. A relatively new route, the Atchison, Topeka and Santa Fe Railroad, led the thrust of Kansas City rails into the Southwest.[8] The important Kansas City, Fort Scott and Gulf Railroad tied in with routes running into Texas at either Fort Scott or Joplin. Kansas City was a great national railroad center. It handled most of the country's livestock trade. Its growth had been a hard one, involving everything from sheer luck to weighty decisions made in eastern board rooms.

The rise of Kansas City was illustrative of the struggle of western cities to obtain railroads.[9] The Kansas City railroad boom started in the 1850s, when local promoters planned state and regional lines. It was one thing, however, to plan roads in every direction and quite another to construct them. The Kansas Citians never had enough money to invest heavily in railroads, so they concentrated on persuading outside interests to build them. The community had certain assets that promised to help in achieving the ultimate objectives. Its able propagandists presented reasonable arguments that emphasized a strategic location at the juncture of major rivers. There were no well-established special interests to oppose railroads as the barge and steamboat owners

obstructed projects in numerous eastern cities. A small group of men in the Kansas City Chamber of Commerce worked together harmoniously. More fundamental was the view that partisan politics was a divisive luxury that interfered with orderly progress.

From 1855 to 1861 Kansas City's leadership generated an almost continual railroad boom. Speeches, mass meetings, rallies, parades, and barbecues aroused enthusiasm for numerous projects. The hallmark of the city was the iron horse, and it taxed the imagination of orators and editors to devise new versions of the metaphor: the iron horse slaking his enormous thirst at the Kawsmouth, the iron horse echoing along the Blue River, and the iron horse serenely surveying the majestic Kansas plains. Most promotional efforts prior to the Civil War centered on persuading the Pacific Railroad, a St. Louis line later called the Missouri Pacific, to build into Kansas City. The road broke many promises, and at the start of hostilities there was a railhead seventy miles to the east at Sedalia. Its tracks finally reached Kansas City on 21 September 1865. By then the Kansas City leaders had sought another and more desirable eastern route. The hidebound owners of the Pacific Railroad seemed primarily concerned with protecting St. Louis interests in Missouri. Moreover, even though the first Texas cattle-drives had gone to Sedalia, the directors failed to see the importance of the Union Pacific–Eastern Division, which started west from Wyandotte, across the Kansas River from Kansas City, in 1864. In fact, the Pacific management would make a horrendous blunder in refusing to give favorable rates to livestock shipper and promoter Joseph McCoy.

Kansas City leaders correctly perceived that the key to reaching Chicago markets was a railroad bridge over the Missouri River. This would allow a direct route that would not have to dip south through St. Louis, the Illinois city's rival for economic supremacy in the Midwest. There was a possibility at the Civil War's end that the first bridge to span the Missouri River would be at either St. Joseph or Leavenworth. If that happened, Kansas City might find itself off the mainstream of transportation. The line that proposed to erect the first structure over the Missouri, the Hannibal and St. Joseph, controlled the best access to Chicago. All the contending cities realized the importance of the bridge, concluding that the winner would become the regional metropolis. Kansas City emerged victorious in 1866 when the railroad decided

to shift its main line from St. Joseph; to turn it south some fifty miles to the east at Cameron, Missouri; and to cross the Missouri River at Kansas City. There were several reasons behind the decision. Kansas City business leaders convinced Boston and Chicago capitalists holding large blocks of Hannibal and St. Joseph stock that most of the fifty-mile roadbed between Cameron and Kansas City had been graded before the Civil War as part of the never-finished Cameron Road. While this stretched the truth considerably—a surveyor had walked the projected route—it was a telling argument. The railroad owners did not want to check too closely, because they had already decided to bridge the river at some place other than St. Joseph or Leavenworth. They erroneously believed the grades west of St. Joseph excessive, and wanted the shortest possible way to Texas markets. Leavenworth had a notoriously bad record of passing railroad bonds, and its leadership appeared badly divided. In addition, James F. Joy, the president of the Chicago, Burlington and Quincy Railroad, which controlled the Hannibal and St. Joseph, played a crucial role in the negotiations, strongly favoring Kansas City, where he owned extensive properties. Some persons claimed he obtained the holdings after a visit by a delegation of Kansas City businessmen, although there was no proof one way or the other.

Following the transactions, Kansas City gained the support of powerful interests. Unfortunately, an impasse remained. The contract with the railroad stipulated that the Cameron Company of Kansas City complete the roadbed. The Kansas Citians, always better promoters than builders, found it impossible to raise the money. At this juncture, Joy arranged for the Hannibal and St. Joseph to purchase the Cameron Company. After that, construction proceeded rapidly. The bridge opened on Saturday, 3 July 1869.[10] This assured Kansas City's future. About $740,000 of local money went into railroad projects in the twenty years prior to the building of the bridge; hardly an excessive amount in terms of the return on railroad investments when compared with other towns. Baltimore spent $18,000,000 in the 1830s and 1840s; Louisville granted over $2,500,000 in aid during Reconstruction.

Omaha, Denver, Oakland, and San Francisco were other important western railroad centers.[11] The main tracks of the Union Pacific extended west from Omaha to Ogden, Utah, where they joined the Central Pacific Railroad. Across the river from Omaha

at Council Bluffs, the Union Pacific met four Chicago roads, providing the "best of connections with all points to the East." In Nebraska, Omaha was the center of a network of state railroads. The Burlington and Missouri River Railroad had several divisions. It served such Nebraska towns as Lincoln, Columbus, Kearney Junction, and Nebraska City. Finally, Omaha was the terminus of the Chicago, St. Paul, Minneapolis and Omaha Railroad, which ran through Sioux City and on to Minneapolis. Denver's roads, while not as extensive in numbers as those in Omaha, helped make the city. The Union Pacific; the Denver and Rio Grande Railroad; the Denver, South Park and Pacific Railroad; and the Colorado Central Railroad helped build the Rocky Mountain Empire. Oakland, in addition to the Central Pacific Railroad, was a division point for the Southern Pacific Railroad and the South Pacific Coast Railroad. Large ferries transported freight cars and passengers from Oakland to San Francisco, which an observer described as the "practical terminus" of western rails. San Francisco had numerous regional lines. The Central Pacific's Northern Division went to Calistoga and Willows, the Oregon Division to Redding, and the Southern Division to Tulare. The Southern Pacific Coast Railroad had tracks to Santa Cruz; the North Pacific Coast Railroad terminated in Duncan Mills; the San Francisco and North Pacific Railroad stopped in Cloverdale. The Southern Pacific Railroad had built south through Los Angeles and on into Arizona, pressing toward an 1881 juncture at El Paso with the Texas and Pacific Railroad. A San Francisco official said: "In fact, all the country touched by the many railroads centering here may be said to be tributary to the city, and a large portion of the wheat crops of the state come to San Francisco to be shipped."

Railroads obviously helped some towns more than others. The building of extensive lines came as crucial times for Denver and Omaha. If the eastern leg of the transcontinental line had started in one of the other cities listed in the Pacific Railroad Act, Omaha might have remained a small town, another Rulo or Peru, two promotional failures in Nebraska. Denver might have remained unimportant if the local entrepreneurs who acquired the moribund Union Pacific–Eastern Division had failed to obtain the necessary federal legislation to build from Mile Post 405 in western Kansas through Denver to Cheyenne. The railroad

brought prosperity for Oakland that temporarily led to great expectations of breaking San Francisco's domination of the area—expectations dashed when the Pacific Coast railroad projects were centered at the Golden Gate, tightening the chains of regional domination.

For several western cities in 1880 the railroad seemed to hold promise of future greatness. Texas already possessed a regional network. At Galveston the Galveston, Houston and Henderson Railroad connected with other routes at Houston. Another line, the Gulf, Colorado and Santa Fe Railway, which passed west of Houston at Rosenberg's Junction, thrust north via Temple and Fort Worth to Denison. Houston remained the railroad center of Texas. To the north the Houston and Texas Central Railroad ran to Denison; the International and Great Northern Railroad, to Longview. The Galveston, Harrisburg and San Antonio Railway had a western terminus in San Antonio; the Texas and New Orleans, an eastern one at Orange on the Sabine River. Other short roads, in addition to the Galveston, Houston and Henderson, were the narrow gauge Houston, East and West Texas Railway that stopped at Patterson, plus the Texas Transportation Company that terminated at Clinton. At San Antonio the International and Great Northern passed through town on tracks owned by the Galveston, Harrisburg and San Antonio. The International and Great Northern ran through Austin, crossing the tracks of the Houston and Texas Central. The latter route's main line pushed through Dallas, which had two other railroads: the east-west Texas and Pacific Railroad, and a short line to Dallas called the Dallas and Wichita Railroad. Almost all observers recognized that the Kansas City connections made at Denison were the key to the success of regional railroad plans, because of needed speedy and direct access to the Midwest and Northeast. Unconsolidated lines in the South, most of which operated on other than standard gauge rails and which suffered from the effects of Reconstruction, offered unattractive alternatives.

Railroads failed to enhance the chances of a number of towns. In 1880 St. Joseph, according to a leader, was "well supplied with railroad connections." The St. Joseph and Western Division of the Union Pacific joined the main line at Grand Island, furnishing a link to the Far West. The Kansas City, St. Joseph and Council Bluffs was an imposing north-south artery. The St. Joseph and

104

Des Moines ended at an unimportant railhead in southern Iowa. The basic problem, however, was a direct western connection. The decision of the Hannibal and St. Joseph to divert its main line and the construction out of Omaha of the Union Pacific crippled St. Joseph's hopes at crucial junctures. Atchison had trouble obtaining an eastern line; the Chicago, Rock Island and Pacific Railroad and a short branch of the Kansas City, St. Joseph and Council Bluffs arrived too late to influence the course of events. Two other roads had only regional significance. The Burlington and Missouri River Railroad went straight west to Lenora in Central Kansas. The Missouri Pacific's north-south route swung through Atchison. The main line of the Atchison, Topeka and Santa Fe, upon which promoters had based great hopes, no longer started in Atchison. Sacramento's situation was more dismal. Unable to take advantage of its status as the starting point of the "Pacific Railroad," the city soon became just another division point on the Central Pacific. Several branch lines provided service to the northern California communities of Placerville, Shingle Springs, and Napa Junction. Portland would soon experience the same railroad expectations followed by bitter disappointments. In 1880 two roads, the Oregon and California Railroad to Roseburg and the Western Oregon Railroad to Corvallis, seemed to place Portland in a position to continue dominating the Northwest after the arrival of eastern rails. Of course, this failed to happen, although it did happen in another town that eagerly waited for cross-country connections—Los Angeles.

For other localities the railroad had limited effect or led to domination by more powerful centers. Lincoln, unimportant until the 1870s, was fortunate to have as good connections as it did. The Union Pacific built a branch into the city from its main line, north of the Platte River, at Valley. The Burlington and Missouri River, with offices in Lincoln, had constructed lines throughout southern Nebraska and on into Colorado and Kansas. Blunders by Leavenworth interests in dealing with railroads doomed the town to secondary status prior to the coming of any major connections. By the end of the seventies, Leavenworth had a branch of the Union Pacific and a trunk of the Missouri Pacific. Two fast express trains daily made eastern connections at St. Louis. A local route, the Kansas Central Railroad, had tracks from Leavenworth to Minneapolis in central Kansas. Topeka and

Lawrence failed to benefit in a larger sense from the main lines of the Union Pacific and the Atchison, Topeka and Santa Fe. They were too far east to turn the cattle drives to their advantage and too close to Kansas City to do much more than augment already existing marketing arrangements. Leadville's location mitigated against serious railroad plans. The community was fortunate to have two Denver roads, the South Park and the Denver and Rio Grande. The Southern Pacific, the South Pacific Coast, and the Central Pacific ran through San Jose, increasing the city's subservience to San Francisco. Stockton, on the Central Pacific, had no chance of prospering as a rail center, despite the construction by local promoters of two insignificant roads: the Stockton and Copperopolis Railroad that terminated thirty miles away at Milton, and the Stockton and Visalia Railroad that had thirty-four miles of track running to Oakdale.

Salt Lake City had the worst railroad links of any major frontier town. There were only three short routes. The Utah Western Railroad terminated thirty-seven miles to the west at an uninviting spot in the salt flats. The Utah Southern Railroad ended at Frisco, Utah; the Utah Northern Railroad connected with the Central Pacific at Ogden. Salt Lake City lay south of the transcontinental, which passed around the northern rim of Great Salt Lake. While direct east-west rail communications were not crucial to the continued growth and development of the city, construction activities helped Ogden and Logan. In fact, they might have gained supremacy in Utah if they had succeeded in overcoming the strong commitment of the Mormon hierarchy to Salt Lake City. While rails alone sometimes failed to bring victory, as many places learned to their sorrow, no one denied that they increased the chances of success. An inability to obtain railroads had the seeds of disaster, as Virginia City, without any lines, learned.

Wherever the railroads went they established superiority over other land transportation. By the time of the building of important railroads, roads and trails extended to all western cities. The Oregon Trail, the Central Overland Road, the Leavenworth and Pikes Peak Express Route, the Santa Fe Trail, the Southern Overland Mail Route, the California Trail, the Smoky Hill Road, and other wagon trails snaked across the vast expanse of the West. These famous routes of the Indians, the explorers, the mountain

men, and the pioneers tended to follow the easiest grades and to lead to water. Crudely built and inadequately maintained local and private roads complemented the main stems, surveyed and laid out by the United States Army and the Department of Interior. Over the vast network rumbled the broad-wheeled wagons of the emigrant trains, the heavy wagons of the commercial freighters, and the stages carrying mail and passengers.

By the 1860s large numbers of people and tremendous amounts of freight moved over the roads. The towns along the Missouri served as outfitting points for migrants, and as supply points for mining operations, army bases, and Indian agencies. Denver and Salt Lake City sold supplies for the trail. Thousands of tons of provisions moved with regularity. In 1865, according to one observer, 1,256 men, 4,197 wagons, 27,685 oxen, and 6,164 mules moved 42 million pounds of freight out of Atchison alone. Equally impressive were the entrepreneurial dimensions of the California Stage Company, a Sacramento concern. The line operated stages every twenty-four hours on a regular seven-day schedule over a 700-mile route between Sacramento and Portland, as well as numerous feeder routes in California. This system, which employed close to 200 men, used 1,000 horses and 134 coaches for twenty-eight daily runs over 2,000 miles of road.

Just how significant roads were in determining the final patterns of urban development was a moot consideration, because of the railroad. Moreover, it would have taken advances in vehicle design and far better road construction to serve an increasingly large population. As it was, roads enabled San Francisco and Salt Lake City to capture important hinterlands and Atchison to establish itself as a medium-sized city before the arrival of railroads. The connections aided places like Lawrence, San Jose, and Dallas in hewing out local marketing areas. Draft animals and wagons remained in wide use following the completion of railroads. Some main routes, though, lost most long-haul freight almost immediately: overland stage and wagon lines went out of business on the Santa Fe Trail after 1878 when the Atchison, Topeka and Santa Fe Railroad reached New Mexico. Even so, long wagon trains remained a common sight until railroads started running special "immigrant trains" in the 1880s.[12]

Traffic on inland and coastal waters formed another part of frontier transportation. Canals were never extensively used, be-

cause of a combination of topography and the passing of an era. The canal boom east of the Mississippi ended with the Panic of 1837. In 1880 there were only two short canals of significance in the West, one aiding Galveston and the other Portland. The Brazos Canal between Galveston and the Brazos River, dug in 1850–51, was 38 miles long. Eight miles were canal; the rest, lake and coastal waters. The canal, open to vessels with a draft of up to four feet, allowed passage over 150 miles of previously unreached rivers. Of equal importance was the Willamette Canal at Oregon City. Two-thirds of a mile long, it by-passed a falls. Completed in 1873, it annually handled over 30,000 tons of freight and carried around 30,000 passengers.[13]

Steamboats were of greater consequence, in spite of the limited navigability of Western streams. As a general rule, steamboating grew in direct correlation to settlement and declined in relationship to railroad construction. Still, some steamboating held on tenaciously, often in combination with railroads. While the "Arizona fleet" of the Colorado Steam Navigation Company running between San Francisco and Yuma, via the Gulf of California and the Lower Colorado River, came to an abrupt end when the Southern Pacific reached Yuma, paddle- and side-wheelers continued to churn along the Gulf Coast and on the Texas rivers, the Missouri and its tributaries, and in Pacific coastal regions. Texas shipping interests moved large numbers of passengers and substantial quantities of freight on the serpentine Brazos and its tributaries, some of which were open to traffic only a couple of weeks a year. On the Missouri River railroad extensions interrupted the long hauls by steamboats, but the boats continued to operate profitably for years between the railroads. Forty-four steamers operated on the Missouri, Platte, and Kansas rivers, along with the Red River of the North. Twelve thousand tons of boats represented a capital investment of $500,000. They carried over 100,000 passengers and 200,000 tons of freight. More impressive were the statistics for the Pacific trade, with 319 inspected craft. Of these, 178 were in California, 89 in Oregon, and 52 in Washington. The steamboats averaged slightly over 300 tons and cost around $20,000. During 1880 they hauled two million tons of freight and transported seven million passengers. The service had been even more important before railroad competition forced several lines out of business.

Pacific Coast steamboats carried a substantial share of traffic. They chugged in California along the Sacramento, San Joaquin, and American rivers, and conducted ferrying operations on San Francisco Bay. In Oregon and Washington the Columbia River had 300 miles of navigable waters from its mouth, except for railroad portages of 6 miles at the Cascades and 15 miles at the Dalles. Steamboats traveled 155 miles of the Willamette, and worked such streams as the John Day's, Umatilla, Walla Walla, Snake, Rogue, Coos, and Coquille. By the seventies the Oregon Railway and Navigation Company, owned indirectly by the Northern Pacific Railroad, dominated the larger share of the business.[14] Still, impressive statistics aside, steamers played an inconclusive role in furthering urbanization. They helped Portland, Kansas City, Galveston, and San Francisco to develop extensive hinterlands. They allowed Stockton, Atchison, and Sacramento to expand their economic bases. But they failed to generate the rapid expansion needed to make impressive cities out of the "steamboat towns" of Fort Benton, Yuma, and Yankton. Yuma's markets fell before the onslaught of the Southern Pacific. The Missouri River had enabled Yankton, South Dakota, and Fort Benton, Montana, to build vast hinterlands, but both lost their trade after being by-passed by railroads. Shippers routed most of the old Yankton traffic through Minneapolis–St. Paul and Bismarck, and railroads boomed Great Falls, Montana, at Fort Benton's expense.

Ocean trade was more crucial in the building of an urban West. The towns helped the most had excellent natural harbors and good connections into the interior. San Francisco was a major American port. "From his windows on Russian Hill one saw always something strange creeping through the mists of the bay," a long-time resident recalled. "It would be a South Sea Island brig, bringing in copra, to take out cotton and idols; a Chinese junk after sharks' livers; an old whaler, which seemed to drip oil, home from a year of cruising in the Arctic. Even the tramp windjammers were deep-chested craft, capable of rounding the Horn or of circumnavigating the globe; and they came in streaked and picturesque from their long voyaging."[15] In 1880 the customs district reported the entering and clearing of 1,291 ships engaged in the foreign trade and 531 in the coastal trade and fisheries. Imports totaled $41,265,317 and exports $37,213,443. By way of comparison, Boston in the same year ranked second nationally in imports,

with $68,609,658 worth, and third in exports, with an amount of $58,023,587. San Francisco dominated the Pacific Coast trade as far north as Alaska and south as Panama. The only other Pacific ports of consequence were Oakland and Portland. On the Gulf of Mexico, Galveston had wharfage for approximately 100 vessels and numerous small craft. In 1880 some 368 ships in the foreign trade entered or cleared, with imports of $1,107,241 and exports of $16,712,861.[16] Over the next several decades new ports—Houston and Corpus Cristi on the Gulf, and San Diego, Long Beach, Seattle, and Tacoma on the Pacific—would rise. But San Francisco and the others garnered enough trade to remain important in the face of new competitors.

The frontier communities profited from the technological advances of the nineteenth century. Gaslights brightened the night, telephones speeded the transmission of messages, and inter-urbans eased travel. The railroads, the steamboats, and the horse-drawn wagons bound the West together, while at the same time changing sectional boundaries. Equally significant was the readi-ness of westerners to draw on technological achievements perfected in other places. Gaslights and telephones had appeared swiftly on the frontier. Once in a while a western city led in using specialized new means, as San Francisco with the cable car and Denver with electric lighting. The application of inventive genius helped urban life as understood by easterners to move to the West very quickly. By 1880 the cities of the "Great West"—despite the mythology fostered by pulp magazines and dime novels—were no longer frontier outposts.

CHAPTER 7

The West of Magnificent Cities

Town promoter William Gilpin was born into a wealthy Pennsylvania family in 1813 and died in 1894. In the course of a colorful life he participated in numerous western promotional projects. Some of his designs failed, most notably his schemes for making vast sums of money at "Linn City," an early name for Portland, or at "Centropolis," his designation for the Kansas City area. On another occasion his grandiose San Luis Valley project in Colorado met with less than success. He never made much money on the 600,000-acre tract. Investors did not respond positively to his claims that the "immense elliptical bowl" was a "colossal staircase" and "elevated bench" of "constant brilliancy" abounding in "crevices charged and infused with the richest ores."[1] While no great cities sprang from the wilderness of the San Luis "gold belt," temporary setbacks seldom discouraged Gilpin for very long. He cut his losses and moved on to another venture.

After the Civil War, Gilpin concentrated on promoting Denver, which he called "Cosmopolis." In an 1870 address he linked the growth of Denver to broader aspirations. "It is to the infallible judgements and the intrepid valour of the pioneers that the American people owe the selection of Colorado and the auspicious site of Denver," he said. "With the pioneer army rests the glory which has vindicated the mission of America, which preserves, enlarges, and perpetuates the Continental union of the states . . . enervated by nepotism to the foolish fashions of Europe. . . . Advancing to meet and embrace this fresh and splendid arena

111

. . . the pioneer army selects *Denver*." Viewing the Rocky Mountain city as the center of the world, he declared: "Here the geography and drainage of the Atlantic comes to an end; that of the Pacific is reached. Infallible instinct adheres to the Isothermal Axis! Here is the propitious point to receive the column from Asia, debouching from the ocean and the mountains to radiate and expand itself *eastward* over the unobstructed area of the Mississippi Basin! We consent to face about! The rear becomes the front! Asia in the front; Europe in the rear! . . . *Denver* is . . . a focal point for the great radiating rivers, six in number, whose channels form a multitude of unbroken grades descending to the Atlantic."[2] Gilpin made a large amount of money in Denver real estate. He indicated without undue modesty that he "found no great difficulty in making a million or two of dollars."

In the twilight of his life Gilpin continued to write and lecture widely on the importance of the American West. He took a measure of satisfaction from his financial success and the coming to pass of many of his early assertions. Observers who had once considered him a buffoon or lunatic finally began to take him seriously. As early as 1853 he had believed that a transcontinental railroad was essential to human progress. He stated that the road would reverse "a standing inconvenience in the pathway of mankind" by bridging a gap in the "universal comity of all nations of all continents." Removal of the "distracting barrier" would "fill out and complete the cricle in which three continents and a hundred nations bind the hemisphere of the north in one endless and graceful zodiac." By 1890 his "harmonizing railroad" assumed international proportions. A "Cosmopolitan Railroad" would cover all the continents, crossing oceans on bridges and car ferries. It would create a vast marketing community designed to further trade and understanding between races, assuring generations of peace. "The cosmopolitan railway will make the world one community," he asserted. "It will reduce separate nations to families of one great nation."

He saw the urban West as the unifying element in the "Cosmopolitan Railroad." Shortly before his death he commented, "The future is not fulfilled. It is still in its infancy. I was laughed at nearly half a century ago and can afford to be laughed at now. I probably shall not live to see it, but the future generations will build a railroad up through Alaska and cross the Behring Strait to

Siberia, and on through to China, India and the Russian empire. There are 100,000 live, wide-awake engineers in this country, who could build a railroad to the moon if you would give them money enough. . . . My old Centropolis, Cosmopolis, and Linn City, will be as I predicted. My prediction of the building of this great railway does not seem half so wild as my old theory did to the Missouri farmers when I wanted to lay off a townsite and call it Centropolis, where now nearly a quarter of a million people live, but this greatness is only in its infancy!"[3]

Gilpin died peacefully in his sleep during the early hours of 20 January 1894, half a year after Frederick Jackson Turner read a paper, "The Significance of the Frontier in American History," before a summer meeting in Chicago of the American Historical Association. Discussing the importance of the 1890 census announcement of the closing of the frontier, Turner stated, "The peculiarity of American institutions is, the fact that they have been compelled to adapt themselves to the changes of an expanding people—to the changes involved in crossing a continent, in winning a wilderness, and in developing at each area of this progress out of the primitive economic and political conditions of the frontier into the complexity of city life. . . . From the conditions of frontier life came intellectual traits of profound importance. . . . The result is that to the frontier the American intellect owes its striking characteristics. That coarseness and strength combined with acuteness and inquisitiveness; that practical, inventive turn of mind, quick to find expedients; that masterful grasp of material things, lacking in the artistic but powerful to effect great ends; that restless, nervous energy; that dominant individualism, working for good and for evil, and withal that buoyancy and exuberance which comes with freedom—these are traits of the frontier, or traits called out elsewhere because of the existence of the frontier. . . . And now, four centuries from the discovery of America, at the end of a hundred years of life under the Constitution, the frontier has gone, and with its going has closed the first period in American history."[4] In general terms Gilpin would have agreed with Turner, particularly on the greatness and uniqueness of the West. However, Gilpin considered urbanization a continuing phenomenon that would carry forward long after there was no more free land. The rise of cities would not stop with Kansas City, Denver, and San Francisco. Although

Gilpin died before Phoenix, Las Vegas, and Oklahoma City became major components of the American urban network, he would hardly have expressed surprise.

By 1890 the frontier had ended for towns that ten years earlier were citadels of civilization in the barren expanses of the West. They emerged from their formative years as mature communities that could not afford to rest upon their laurels. The cruel process of town building continued unabated. To remain a contender for great urban honors, a city needed to constantly generate increased economic growth to sustain rapid population growth. Certain developments had already seemingly set various cities on unalterable courses. Regional dominance followed Kansas City's obtaining the first bridge over the Missouri River, and Denver became important by manipulating the route of the Union Pacific–Eastern Division. Stockton, Lawrence, and Lincoln appeared doomed to the second rank. Natural disasters lay ahead for Galveston (the tidal wave of 1900) and San Francisco (the earthquake of 1906). Dallas and San Jose appeared to have limited prospects. And, while hope abounded in Los Angeles, in 1880 it ranked nineteenth in size on the urban frontier and two hundred and third nationally. Cities established by aggressive promoters and sustained by decades of optimistic propaganda seldom accepted defeat. They persevered, whatever the odds, as long as there was a chance of success.

Nine of the old frontier cities had growth rates in excess of 100 percent in the 1880s, as Table 7-1 shows.[5] The spectacular growth rates for Omaha and Lincoln showed the impact of increased settlement in Nebraska. Most of Los Angeles' 350.64 percent enlargement came after the Atchison, Topeka and Santa Fe reached the community. New Texas trade areas brought upward movement in Dallas. Portland lost ground in terms of economic importance in the Northwest, even with a 163.90 percent augmentation. Because of a forty thousand jump in suburban residents, Kansas City actually did better than its recorded 137.91 percent. Salt Lake City's growth disappointed local leaders and reflected the relatively sluggish economy of Utah Territory. Topeka's 100.67 percent left it far in arrears of Kansas City.

Nine other of the twenty-four communities grew faster than the national average of 26 percent, as Table 7-2 illustrates. Economic progress in Texas allowed San Antonio's population to rise

TABLE 7-1

NINE FRONTIER CITIES WITH GROWTH RATES OVER 100 PERCENT IN THE 1880s

City	Population		Increase	
	1890	1880	Number	Percent
Dallas	38,067	10,358	27,709	267.51
Denver	106,713	35,629	71,084	199.51
Kansas City	132,716	55,785	76,931	137.91
Lincoln	55,154	13,003	42,151	324.16
Los Angeles	50,395	11,183	39,212	350.64
Omaha	140,452	30,518	109,934	360.23
Portland	46,385	17,577	28,808	163.90
Salt Lake City	44,843	20,768	24,075	115.92
Topeka	31,007	15,452	15,555	100.67

by 83.32 percent, Houston's by 66.88 percent, Austin's by 32.34 percent, and Galveston's by 30.73 percent. St. Joseph had a growth rate of 61.34, although it fell behind Omaha and Kansas City. San Francisco's 27.80 percent seemed small, but it represented a population aggrandizement of 65,038. San Jose, Oakland, and Stockton added people too slowly to attain economic independence.

Three towns had rates below the national average, and three others actually decreased markedly, as shown by Table 7-3. Sacramento's growth rate was unimpressive, compared with other Cali-

TABLE 7-2

NINE FRONTIER CITIES THAT GREW FASTER THAN THE NATIONAL AVERAGE IN THE 1880s

City	Population		Increase	
	1890	1880	Number	Percent
Austin	14,575	11,013	3,562	32.34
Galveston	29,084	22,248	6,836	30.73
Houston	27,557	16,513	11,044	66.88
Oakland	48,682	34,555	14,127	40.88
St. Joseph	52,324	32,431	19,893	61.34
San Antonio	37,673	20,550	17,123	83.32
San Francisco	298,997	233,959	65,038	27.80
San Jose	18,060	12,567	5,493	43.71
Stockton	14,424	10,282	4,142	40.28

115

TABLE 7-3

SIX FRONTIER CITIES THAT GREW MORE SLOWLY THAN THE NATIONAL AVERAGE
IN THE 1880s OR LOST IN POPULATION

| City | Population | | Increase | |
	1890	1880	Number	Percent
Atchison	13,963	15,105	—1,142	— 7.56
Lawrence	9,997	8,510	1,487	17.47
Leadville	10,384	14,820	—4,436	—29.93
Leavenworth	19,768	16,546	3,222	19.47
Sacramento	26,386	21,420	4,966	23.18
Virginia City	8,511	10,917	—2,406	—22.04

fornia medium-sized towns. Leavenworth, Lawrence, and Atchison suffered from Kansas City's increasing dominance of Kansas trade. The discontinuance of mining activities brought sharp drops of 22.04 percent in Virginia City and 29.93 percent in Leadville. The day was at hand for these communities to reassess and scale down the aims that had sustained them at the height of their eminence.

During the 1880s a number of places underwent the initial stages of urbanization. Eight localities achieved populations of 15,000 or more: Fort Worth, Texas; Kansas City and Wichita, Kansas; Pueblo, Colorado; Tacoma, Seattle, and Spokane, Washington; and San Diego, California. The cattle town of Fort Worth became a serious rival of Dallas, going from a population of 6,663 to 23,076, a gain of 246.33 percent. Another cattle town, Wichita, crushed such local rivals as El Dorado, Caldwell, and Wellington in a spirited battle for domination of a flourishing regional market in south-central Kansas and Oklahoma Indian Territory. At the start of the eighties, Wichita had 4,911 inhabitants; in the next ten years it grew by 385.71 percent to 23,853. Kansas City, Kansas, by incorporating several adjoining localities, rose from 3,200 to 38,316 people, an increase of 1,097.38 percent. Pueblo gained 663.38 percent, going from 3,217 to 24,558 residents, in the course of hewing out a trading area in southern Colorado. Tacoma and Seattle were small villages of 1,098 and 3,533, respectively, in 1880. During the decade they advanced with incredible speed; Tacoma by 3,179.23 percent and Seattle by 1,112.48 percent. The former had 36,006 persons and the latter 42,837. More fantastic was the rate of 5,592.00 percent for Spokane,

where railroads and lumber combined to start a great boom. The number of citizens rose from 350 to 19,922 in ten years. San Diego's 512.78 percent enlargement, which translated into a population increase of from 2,637 to 16,159, seemed almost small by comparison.

The future held various degrees of hope and brightness for these towns. Kansas City, Kansas, had no real prospects of achieving an independent identity. Wichita had vast possibilities if it could corner the Oklahoma trade. Pueblo had a chance to establish a promising subregion, if it succeeded in countering vigorous competition from Trinidad and Colorado Springs. Fort Worth posed a major threat to Dallas, with both cities already engaged in a bitter struggle. San Diego's fine harbor engendered a high measure of optimism among the business leadership. The progress and prosperity that followed the arrival of the railroad in Tacoma and Seattle convinced promoters that both cities might advance within a short time to the status of a major metropolis. Spokane looked confidently ahead to solidifying authority over eastern Washington, northern Idaho, and western Montana.

The rapid ascent of new centers signified that urbanization in the West had entered another era. Numerous cities that moved from small beginnings in 1880 to between 8,000 and 15,000 by 1890 reflected the changed conditions. The building of trunk and feeder railroads opened vast territories to settlement and speculation. The movement of farmers into Kansas, Nebraska, and the Dakotas; the spreading of the cattle industry into eastern Colorado, Wyoming, and Montana; the mining of mineral wealth in the mountains of Montana, Arizona, and New Mexico; and the cutting of timber in Idaho, Washington, and northern California had a tremendous impact. These developments created a need for a network of marketing communities within the hinterlands of already established or emerging regional metropolises.

The 1890 census reported that "all over the west smaller cities have sprung up as if by magic." In Texas, Denison increased from 3,975 to 10,958, Laredo from 3,521 to 11,319, Waco from 7,295 to 14,445, El Paso from 736 to 10,338, and Paris from 3,980 to 8,254. These places all enjoyed growth rates of more than 100 percent; El Paso led with 1,304.62 percent. Kansas towns that crossed the 8,000 mark were Arkansas City (1,012 to 8,347), Fort Scott (5,372 to 11,946), and Hutchinson (1,540 to 8,682). Six

117

Nebraska towns surged beyond 8,000: Beatrice from 2,447 to 13,836, Hastings from 2,817 to 13,584, Kearney from 1,782 to 8,074, Nebraska City from 4,183 to 11,494, Plattsmouth from 4,175 to 8,392, and, within a few years after its founding, suburban South Omaha to 8,062. On the upper Great Plains, Sioux Falls, South Dakota, climbed from 2,164 to 10,177, for a 370.29 percent advance. In the Wyoming High Country the trading and railroad town of Cheyenne, after many false starts, added 8,234 people in the eighties, reaching a total of 11,690. At the base of the Rockies, Colorado Springs jumped from 4,226 to 11,140. Ogden, Utah Territory, grew from 6,069 to 14,889, and Butte, Montana, from 3,363 to 10,723. Alameda, the port for Oakland, moved from 5,708 to 11,165. Another California town, Fresno, expanded from 1,112 to 10,818.

In 1880 only twelve western towns had populations between 5,000 and 8,000. Five—Alameda, Fort Scott, Fort Worth, Ogden, and Waco—surpassed the 8,000 figure ten years later. Three experienced disappointing increases. In Texas, Marshall moved from 5,624 to 7,207; Sherman from 6,093 to 7,335. Vallejo, California, edged ahead from 5,987 to 6,343. Three others suffered losses: Tucson, Arizona Territory, dropped from 7,007 to 5,150 for a 26.50 percent decline; Santa Fe, New Mexico Territory, retrogressed 6.78 percent, going downward from 6,635 to 6,185; the mining town of Silver Cliff, Colorado, plummeted from 5,040 to under 2,500. The remaining place, Wyandotte, Kansas, no longer existed as a separate incorporation.

Twenty-six new communities had entered the 5,000 to 8,000 category by 1890, for a grand total of thirty-one in that range. Texas contained six: Corsicana (6,285), Gainesville (6,594), Palestine (5,838), Brenham (5,209), Brownsville (6,134), and Tyler (6,908). Despite a growth rate of 185.10 percent in Tyler, no place added as many as 4,500 inhabitants. There were seven towns in Kansas: Emporia stood at 7,551, Newton at 5,605, Ottawa at 6,248, Parsons at 6,736, Pittsburg at 6,697, Salina at 6,149, and Winfield at 5,184. There were 6,380 people in Independence, Missouri. Two Nebraska cities crossed the mark: Grand Island (7,536) and Fremont (6,747). Fargo, North Dakota, had 5,664 residents, and Laramie, Wyoming, 6,388. In Colorado there were 5,523 persons in Trinidad, 5,161 in Highlands, and 5,108 in Aspen. Four other places were in California: Santa Barbara

(5,864), Santa Cruz (5,596), Santa Rosa (5,220), and Berkeley (5,101). The Oregon coastal city of Astoria showed an enumeration of 6,184. The undramatic nature of the addition over ten years of 2,601 people in Newton and 3,297 in Trinidad obscured important changes. Even though few of the localities had chances of sustaining a rapid rise, they added flesh to the bones of western urbanization.

The West added population at a greater rate than the rest of the nation from 1880 to 1890. One state, Nevada, lost 16,505 residents, suffering a drastic drop of 26.51 percent; a "stand-still" in mining disarranged the economy. New Mexico, Arizona, and Utah territories experienced small dilations, and only a quickening of agricultural settlement in Colorado prevented a reduction. However, the accelerated pace elsewhere more than made up for losses or slowdowns. The Dakotas increased by 278.41 percent, Nebraska by 134.06 percent, Kansas by 43.27 percent, and Texas by 40.44 percent. Many pioneers moved into the newly opened portions of Oklahoma Territory. Wyoming grew rapidly. Montana and Idaho soared, the former by 237.49 percent and the latter by 158.77 percent. Washington vaulted ahead fivefold, experiencing a 365.13 percent rise. Oregon gained 79.53 percent; California's ratio was 39.72 percent. "Mining, commerce, and manufactures in the western states and territories are in a much more advanced stage, as shown by the greater proportion of the urban element," wrote the compilers of the 1890 census. "Considered as a whole, the urban element in the Western division in 1890 constituted 29.99 per cent of the whole population, while in 1880 it constituted 23.97 per cent. It has therefore gained somewhat more rapidly than the total population."[6]

Fifty-four of the 448 cities of over 8,000 in the United States in 1890 were in the West. Four of these were among the twenty-eight metropolises of more than 100,000. San Francisco ranked eighth, Omaha twenty-first, Kansas City twenty-fourth, and Denver twenty-sixth. During the eighties the nation's urban population enlarged from 11,318,547 to 18,284,385, so that at the decade's end 29.10 percent of 62,622,250 Americans resided in places of 8,000 or more. In the same period the number of western urban dwellers almost tripled, going from 603,493 to 1,753,543. The 1890 census concluded that only Idaho, Arizona Territory, New Mexico Territory, North Dakota, and Oklahoma Territory

had no "urban populations." Five states were over 20 percent urban. California at 40.98 percent and Colorado at 37.07 percent were far above the national average. Washington was 28.27 percent urban, with all the growth having occurred in a ten-year period. In the same span, Utah Territory went from 14.43 percent to 28.73 percent; Nebraska from 9.62 percent to 24.46. Five other states had urban components of over 10 percent: Oregon (18.14 percent), Nevada (18.60 percent), Wyoming (19.26 percent), Montana (18.58 percent), and Kansas (11.62 percent). South Dakota was only 3.10 percent urban; over 30 percent of Missouri's urban residents lived in Kansas City and St. Joseph. Though the statistics may have disappointed some boosters, they afforded further proof that the urban frontier had ended.

In building cities western pioneers followed what they understood best. They rigidly copied older concepts of urban planning. Architecturally, they ignored Indian and Spanish forms. The governmental structures followed earlier norms. Police, fire, sewerage, street, and health departments displayed no changed features. Schools and churches moved westward almost *in toto*. The telephones and telegraphs, the railroads and steamboats, and the horsecars and cable cars were hardly unique. The ethnic composition of western communities resembled those in the land's other parts. Entertainment furnished no novelties, and the same applied to the general pursuit of culture. Neither promotional frenzy nor the pursuit of economic power was confined to the West.

The frontier cities were similar to those throughout the rest of the nation. Omaha's grid was much like that of Milwaukee. The buildings in St. Joseph resembled those in Terre Haute. Packing houses in Kansas City produced the same products as those in Chicago. The structure of government in San Jose and Atchison differed little from that in Shreveport and Akron. Police in Denver operated the same as those in Pittsburgh. Sacramento's fire department adhered to the same standards as its counterpart in Evansville. The sewerage of Los Angeles was the same quality as that of Newport, Rhode Island. San Antonio's street department functioned along the same lines as the one in Troy. The public health department in Dallas paralleled that in Winona. Schools in Lawrence and Leavenworth hardly varied from pedagogical establishments in Bangor and Petersburg. About the same

percentage of parishioners attended church in Topeka as in Lansing. San Francisco and Chicago had telephones, railroads, steamboats, horsecar lines, and cable cars. The ethnic composition of Lincoln compared with that of Council Bluffs. Opera houses in Leadville and Virginia City catered to the identical needs as the ones in New Orleans and East Saginaw. Portland, Oregon, and Portland, Maine, wanted exemplary cultural institutions. The promoters of Stockton, Austin, and Salt Lake City worked as hard as those in Chicopee, Macon, and Rockford. All cities—in the West as well as in the East—hoped to achieve greatness and used comparable means as they strove for success.

The cities of the West represented an extension of a process older than the Republic—exploration, settlement, and growth, a process that resulted in a nation of cities. This trend was already under way in 1880, when the West no longer meant fur-trading operations in Idaho, gold rushes in California, or cattle drives in Texas; instead, it meant street-cleaning machines clattering up the hills of San Francisco and steam engines moving freight in Houston. The urban frontier saw cities stretching from Kansas City to Los Angeles. This was the vision that Gilpin held, and this was what happened.

Notes

CHAPTER 1: THE URBAN WEST

1. Much has been written about William Gilpin and his role in the development of the West. The most recent biography is Thomas Karnes, *William Gilpin: Western Nationalist* (Austin, 1970). Still, his life and ideas must be pieced together from a variety of sources. Gilpin, never averse to promoting his own activities, paid $1,000 for a short biography by Hubert H. Bancroft, *History of the Life of William Gilpin* (San Francisco, 1889). Gilpin gave an interview to a Colorado friend, Will C. Ferrill, which the *Rocky Mountain Herald* in Denver reprinted on 4 January 1913. In addition to numerous articles, Gilpin authored three books: *The Central Gold Region* (Philadelphia, 1860), *Mission of the North American People* (Philadelphia, 1873), *The Cosmopolitan Railway* (San Francisco, 1890). Bernard De Voto revived interest in Gilpin in "Geopolitics with the Dew on It," *Harper's Magazine* 188:313–323 (March 1944). See also Charles Vevier, "American Continentalism: An Idea of Expansion, 1845–1910," *American Historical Review* 65:325–326 (January 1960); Kenneth Porter, "William Gilpin: Sinophile and Eccentric," *The Colorado Magazine* 37:245–267 (October 1960); Charles N. Glaab, "Visions of Metropolis: William Gilpin and Theories of City Growth in the American West," *Wisconsin Magazine of History* 45:21–31 (Autumn 1961). There is a perceptive essay on Gilpin's influence in James Malin, *The Grasslands of North America: Prolegomena to Its History* (Lawrence, 1947). Of less importance is James Willard, "William Gilpin," *Dictionary of American Biog-*

raphy 7:316 (New York, 1931). Crucial to understanding Gilpin is J. Christopher Schnell, "Urban Promotion: The Contribution of William Gilpin in the Rise of the American West" (Master's thesis, University of Missouri–Kansas City, 1968). For a short summary see my article, "The Isothermal Zodiac + Concentric Circles + William Gilpin = Kansas City, Center of the Universe!" in *KC: The Kansas City Magazine* 64:28–29 (May 1974). The quotation is from Schnell, "Urban Promotion: The Contribution of William Gilpin in the Rise of the American West," 74–75.

2. Quoted by Christopher Schnell, "William Gilpin: Advocate of Expansion," *Montana: The Magazine of Western History* 19, pt. 3:30–37 (July 1969).

3. There is an excellent description of town building in Chapter 5, "Town-Building and Development of Resources," in Glenn Quiett, *They Built the West: An Epic of Rails and Cities* (New York, 1934), 82–112. See also Patrick McLear and J. Christopher Schnell, "Why the Cities Grew: A Historiographical Essay on Western Urban Growth, 1850–1880," *Bulletin of the Missouri Historical Society* 27:162–177 (April 1972); Gilbert Stelter, "The City and Westerward Expansion: A Western Case Study," *The Western Historical Quarterly* 4:187–202 (April 1973). See also my article, "Chicago's Midwest Rivals: Cincinnati, St. Louis, and Milwaukee," *Chicago History: The Magazine of the Chicago Historical Society* 5:141–151 (Fall 1976).

4. The Tacoma quote is from Charles N. Glaab and A. Theodore Brown (rev. by Charles N. Glaab), *A History of Urban America*, 2nd ed. (New York, 1976), 112; the Austin quote is from George E. Waring, Jr., comp., "The Southern and Western States," *Report of the Social Statistics of Cities (Tenth Census of the United States, 1880,* vol. 19, pt. 2, Washington, 1886), 303. The latter massive compilation is a basic source on the characteristics of the American city in 1880. It contains detailed information on such things as location, topography, railroad communications, waterworks, places of amusement, drainage, municipal sanitation, police, fire protection, public schools, and cemeteries and historical background for almost all American cities of ten thousand or more in 1880, plus certain smaller ones of regional importance. The 222 cities covered constitute the backbone of the United States' urban society in the late nineteenth century. Part I of this indispensable study is entitled "The New England and Middle States." Hereinafter cited in this and ensuing chapters as *Social Statistics of Cities,* either 1 or 2.

5. Typical was New Babylon, Kansas Territory. On paper a flourish-

ing city, it had only one permanent structure, a small saloon. John W. Reps, *The Making of Urban America: A History of City Planning in the United States* (Princeton, 1965), figures 218–219. See also J. Christopher Schnell and Katherine B. Clinton, "The New West: Themes in Nineteenth Century Urban Promotion," *Bulletin of the Missouri Historical Society* 30:75–88 (January 1974).

6. Gilpin, *Mission of the North American People,* 76.

7. Christopher Schnell, "William Gilpin and the Destruction of the Desert Myth," *Colorado Magazine* 46:131–144 (Summer 1969); Charles N. Glaab, "Jesup W. Scott and a West of Cities," *Ohio History* 73:3–12 (Winter 1964).

8. Short and concise summaries on the rise of the urban frontier can be found in Glaab and Brown, *A History of Urban America,* 105–116; Bayrd Still, *Urban America: A History with Documents* (Boston, 1974), 217–224. The best survey of a single region of the West is Chapter 6, "The Power of the Metropolis," in Earl Pomeroy, *The Pacific Slope: A History of California, Oregon, Washington, Idaho, Utah, and Nevada* (New York, 1965), 120–164. See also Earl Pomeroy, "The Urban Frontier of the Far West," John Clark, ed., *The Frontier Challenge: Responses to the Trans-Mississippi West* (Lawrence, 1971), 7–30, and Gunther Barth, *Instant Cities: Urbanization and the Rise of San Francisco and Denver* (New York, 1975), 61–91.

9. *Social Statistics of Cities,* pt. 2:554–555. See also A. Theodore Brown, *Frontier Community: Kansas City to 1870* (Columbia, Mo., 1963). The latter is the only "urban biography" done on the early stages of Kansas City's history by a professional historian, but there are numerous other compilations that deal with the history of the community. These include Theodore S. Case, *History of Kansas City, Missouri* (Syracuse, 1888); Roy Ellis, *A Civic History of Kansas City* (Springfield, Mo., 1910); Darrell Darwood, *Crossroads of America* (New York, 1948); Henry C. Haskell, Jr., and Richard B. Fowler, *City of the Future* (Kansas City, 1950); Charles Spalding, *Annals of the City of Kansas City* (Kansas City, 1858); Carrie Whitney, *Kansas City, Missouri: Its History and People, 1808-1890,* 3 vols. (Kansas City,1890). Similar kinds of local history studies exist for the other cities.

10. The first quotation is from *Social Statistics of Cities,* pt. 2:544–545. Valuable information on the early history of Omaha can be found scattered through Alfred Sorenson, *Early History of Omaha, or, Walks and Talks Among the Old Settlers: A Series of Sketches in the Shape of a Connected Narrative of the Events and Incidents*

of Early Times in Omaha, Together with a Brief Mention of the Important Events of Later Years (Omaha, 1876). Sorenson was editor of the *Omaha Bee*. He updated his earlier work in Alfred Sorenson, *History of Omaha from the Pioneer Days to the Present Time* (Omaha, 1889). See also William Bradfield, *Stories of Omaha: Historical Sketches of the Midland City* (Omaha, 1898): Train is quoted in George Leighton, *Five Cities: The Story of Their Youth and Old Age* (New York, 1939), 140.

11. The quotation is from *Social Statistics of Cities*, pt. 2:561–562. See *History of Buchanan County and St. Joseph, Mo.: From the Time of the Platte Purchase to the End of the Year 1915* (St. Joseph, 1915). The *St. Joseph Daily News* published an earlier edition of this work in 1898. Information on community origins can be found in W. A. Wood, "Beginning of the City of St. Joseph," *Magazine of American History* 26:107–114 (August 1891).

12. *Social Statistics of Cities*, pt. 2:762. Valuable data on the growth and economic character of Leavenworth can be found in W. S. Burke and J. L. Rock, *The History of Leavenworth, the Metropolis of Kansas and the Chief Commercial Center West of the Missouri River* (Leavenworth, 1880). The local board of trade claimed to have issued fifty thousand copies. Of far more limited value are two "local histories," H. Miles Moore, *Early History of Leavenworth City and County* (Leavenworth, 1906), Jesse A. Hall and Leroy T. Hand, *History of Leavenworth County Kansas* (Topeka, 1921). A recent book, J. H. Johnston III, *Leavenworth: Beginning to Bicentennial* (Leavenworth, 1976), contains much valuable material.

13. *Social Statistics of Cities*, pt. 2:751–752; the quotation is from *Atchison, The Railroad Center of Kansas: Its Advantages for Commerce and Manufactures* (Atchison, 1874), 13. Of limited value are Sheffield Ingalls, *History of Atchison County Kansas* (Lawrence, 1916), 64–83; *Atchison Centennial: 1854–1954* (Atchison, 1954). See also Joseph Snell and Don Wilson, "The Birth of the Atchison, Topeka and Santa Fe Railroad," *The Kansas Historical Quarterly* 34:113–142, 325–364 (Summer and Autumn 1968).

14. *Social Statistics of Cities*, pt. 2:739–740. See also *Lincoln: The Capital City and Lancaster County, Nebraska*, 2 vols. (Chicago, 1916).

15. Samuel Radges, comp., *Radges' Biennial Directory to the Inhabitants, Institutions, Manufacturing Establishments, Business Firms, Etc., of the City of Topeka, for 1876–1877* (Topeka, 1875), 30. See also *Topeka Illustrated, Its Progress and Importance: A*

NOTES TO PAGES 12-13

Descriptive and Statistical Review of Her Resources, Advantages and Facilities in Trade, Commerce and Manufactures, Together with a Delineation of Her Representative Establishments (Topeka, 1887). Less useful are *Historical Sketch of Shawnee County, Kansas: Prepared for the Occasion of the Centennial Celebration* (Topeka, 1876) and Mary Jackson, *Topeka Pen and Camera Sketches* (Topeka, 1890). The statehouse battle is covered in F. W. Giles, *Thirty Years in Topeka: A Historical Sketch* (Topeka, 1886), 246-255. There is no historical sketch of Topeka in *Social Statistics of Cities*, pt. 2.

16. *Social Statistics of Cities*, pt. 2: 757-758. Most of what has been written about Lawrence has dealt with its early history and the subsequent disasters. With little exaggeration, one author has written, "More, perhaps, was spoken and written about Lawrence, Kansas Territory, in the 1850's than about any other town in the nation" (Allen Crafton, *Free State Fortress: The First Ten Years of the History of Lawrence, Kansas* (Lawrence, 1954), preface). Richard Cordley, *A History of Lawrence, Kansas from the First Settlement to the Close of the Rebellion* (Lawrence, 1895), provides a detailed narrative account of the town's trials and tribulations. There are a number of accounts of Quantrill's Raid: Joseph Boughton, *The Lawrence Massacre by Quantrill August 21, 1863, as Given by Eye Witnesses of the Barbarous Scene Unparalleled in the History of Civilized Warfare* (Lawrence, 1884); John C. Shea, *Reminiscences of Quantrill's Raid Upon the City of Lawrence, Kas.: Thrilling Narratives by Living Eye Witnesses* (Kansas City, 1879); S. W. Brewster, *Incidents of Quantrill's Raid on Lawrence, August 21, 1863: The Remarkable and Heretofore Unpublished Personal Experiences of Hon. Henry S. Clarke* (Lawrence, 1898); C. R. Green, ed., *Quantrill's Raid on Lawrence* (Lyndon, Kans., 1899); *Quantrill's Raid, Aug. 21-1863; From the Autobiography of Peter D. Ridenour, Who Survived the Raid, Historical Society* (Lawrence, 1963). It would almost seem as if nothing else of importance happened in Lawrence. A refreshing change from blood and gore is an unpretentious little memoir of a woman who grew up in Lawrence in the 1860s and 1870s, Agnes Emery, *Reminiscences of Early Lawrence* (Lawrence, 1954).

17. The mayor is quoted in *Social Statistics of Cities*, pt. 2:800-803. The best condensed account of the rise of San Francisco is Quiett, *They Built the West*, 182-255. He noted in his bibliography that material on San Francisco was "practically limitless." The spirit of the town prior to the earthquake is caught in a forty-seven page account, Will Irwin, *The City That Was* (New York, 1906). See

also such varied works as Samuel Huhell, *A History of the City of San Francisco and Incidentally of the State of California* (San Francisco, 1878); *The Bay of San Francisco: The Metropolis of the Pacific Coast, and its Suburban Cities: A History* (Chicago, 1892); John Young, *San Francisco: A History of the Pacific Coast Metropolis* (San Francisco, 1912); Bailey Millard, *History of the San Francisco Bay Region* (San Francisco, 1924); Charles Dobie, *San Francisco: A Pageant* (New York, 1933); Bernard Taper, ed., *Mark Twain's San Francisco* (New York, 1963); Robert Mayer, *San Francisco: A Chronological and Documentary History, 1542–1970* (Dobbs Ferry, N.Y., 1974); Robert W. Lotchin, *San Francisco, 1846–1856: From Hamlet to City* (New York, 1974); Barth, *Instant Cities.*

18. *Social Statistics of Cities,* pt. 2:783–784. See also Joseph E. Baker, *Past and Present of Alameda County,* 2 vols. (Chicago, 1914); Edgar Hinhil, Jr., and W. E. McCann, *Oakland, 1852–1932,* 2 vols. (Oakland, 1939); Peter Conmy, *Beginnings of Oakland* (Oakland, 1961). Material on Oakland can be found in many of the books on San Francisco.

19. The quotation is from *Social Statistics of Cities,* pt. 2:789–793. See the appropriate selections on Sacramento's early history in Rodman Paul, *The California Gold Discovery: Sources, Documents, Accounts and Memoirs Relating to the Discovery of Gold at Sutter's Mill* (Georgetown, Calif., 1969), and also in Julian Dana, *The Sacramento: River of Gold* (New York, 1939).

20. *Social Statistics of Cities,* pt. 2:817–818.

21. *Ibid.,* pt. 2:816. The sketch on San Jose is short and incomplete. See also Amaury Mars, *Reminiscences of Santa Clara Valley and San Jose* (San Francisco, 1901).

22. Lucius Beebe, "Virginia City," *The Encyclopedia Americana: International Edition,* 28:165 (New York, 1970); Quiett, *They Built the West,* 222–230. See also George Lyman, *The Saga of the Comstock Lode: Boom Days in Virginia City* (New York, 1934), which covers the period to 1865. There is no material on Virginia City in *Social Statistics of Cities.*

23. *Social Statistics of Cities,* pt. 2:823–824; the quotation on city building is from Glaab, *History of Urban America,* 114; the quotation on the New England flavor is from Pomeroy, *The Pacific Slope,* 135–139. See Quiett, *They Built the West,* 339–399; Dean Collins, "Portland: A Pilgrim's Progress," Duncan Aikman, ed., *The Taming of the Frontier* (New York, 1925), 157–200; Joseph Gaston, *Portland, Ore.: Its History and Builders* (Chicago, 1911).

24. *Social Statistics of Cities,* pt. 2:779–780. The best urban biog-

raphies of Los Angeles are Remi Nadeau, *Los Angeles from Mission to Modern City* (New York, 1960), and Robert Fogelson, *The Fragmented Metropolis: Los Angeles, 1850–1930* (Cambridge, 1967). Actually, nothing much happened in an urban way in the Los Angeles basin prior to the boom that started in 1887 when the Atchison, Topeka and Santa Fe Railroad reached the area. The boom is covered in Glenn Dunke, *The Boom of the Eighties in Southern California* (Los Angeles, 1944). See also Charles Willard, *The Herald's History of Los Angeles City* (Los Angeles, 1901); James Guinn, *A History of California and an Extended History of Los Angeles*, 3 vols. (Los Angeles, 1915); Boyle Workman, *The City that Grew* (Los Angeles, 1935); William Robinson, *Los Angeles from the Days of the Pueblo* (San Francisco, 1959); Lynn Bowman, *Los Angeles: Epic of a City* (Berkeley, 1974). There are some excellent old photographs of Los Angeles in Laurance Hill, *La Reina: Los Angeles in Three Centuries* (Los Angeles, 1929). An article of importance is Oscar Winther, "The Rise of Metropolitan Los Angeles, 1870–1910," *Huntington Library Quarterly* 10:391–405 (August 1947).

25. *Social Statistics of Cities*, pt. 2:315–318; Howard Barnstone, *The Galveston That Was* (New York, 1966), 55. See also Joseph Dyer, *The Early History of Galveston* (Galveston, 1916); S. C. Griffin, *History of Galveston, Texas: Narrative and Biographical* (Galveston, 1931); Samuel Graham, ed., *Galveston Community Book: A Historical and Biographical Record of Galveston and Galveston County* (Galveston, 1945). The first decades of Galveston—as well as Houston, Austin, and San Antonio—are covered in fine fashion in Kenneth Wheeler, *To Wear a City's Crown: The Beginnings of Urban Growth in Texas, 1836–1865* (Cambridge, 1968).

26. *Social Statistics of Cities*, pt. 2:323–324; David McComb, *Houston: The Bayou City* (Austin, 1969), 41. The latter is a well-done urban biography. See also Marilyn Sibley, *The Port of Houston: A History* (Austin, 1968); Benjamin Carroll, ed., *Standard History of Houston, Texas, from a Study of the Original Sources* (Knoxville, 1912).

27. *Social Statistics of Cities*, pt. 2:327–329. There is considerable interesting material in William Corner, *San Antonio de Bexar* (San Antonio, 1890). Of less worth are Boyce House, *City of Flaming Adventure* (San Antonio, 1949); Sam and Bess Woolford, *The San Antonio Story* (San Antonio, 1950); Edward Heusinger, *A Chronology of Events in San Antonio: Being a Concise History of the City Year by Year* (San Antonio, 1951). See also Ray

Broussard, *San Antonio During the Texas Republic: A City in Transition* (El Paso, 1967).

28. *Social Statistics of Cities,* pt. 2:301–303.

29. *Ibid.,* pt. 2:311–312. See John William Rogers, *The Lusty Texans of Dallas* (New York, 1951); Stanley Walker, *The Dallas Story* (Dallas, 1954). Given the great importance of the place, there is a need for an analytical urban biography of Dallas.

30. The quotation is from W. B. Vickers, *History of the City of Denver, Arapahoe County, and Colorado* (Chicago, 1880), 241. This is a massive compilation of 652 pages, containing a great deal of undigested research material. Denver's struggle for transportation is recounted in Quiett, *They Built the West,* 143–181. See also Jerome Smiley, ed., *History of Denver: With Outlines of the Early History of the Rocky Mountain Country* (Denver, 1901); Nolie Mumey, *History of the Early Settlements of Denver (1599–1860)* (Glendale, Calif., 1942); Nolie Mumey, *Prof. Oscar J. Goldrick and His Denver: Together with His Address on the Early History of Denver, July 4, 1876* (Denver, 1959); Agnes Spring, *The First National Bank of Denver: The Formative Years, 1860–1865* (Denver, 1960); Caroline Bancroft, *Denver's Lively Past* (Boulder, 1964); Bo Griffin, *Spirit of Denver* (Denver, 1964); Sandra Dallas, *Yesterday's Denver,* Seeman's Historic Cities No. 10 (Miami, 1974); Barth, *Instant Cities;* Lyle Dorsett, *The Queen City: A History of Denver* (Boulder, 1977). There is no historic sketch of Denver in the *Social Statistics of Cities.*

31. *Social Statistics of Cities,* pt. 2:773. See Duane Smith, *Rocky Mountain Mining Camps: The Urban Frontier* (Bloomington, 1967), and Rodman Paul, *Mining Frontiers of the Far West, 1848–1880* (New York, 1963). There is colorful material on social conditions in Forbes Parkhill, *The Wildest of the West* (New York, 1951).

32. The public official is quoted in *Social Statistics of Cities,* pt. 2:829–831. Much has been written about the Mormons, but relatively little about Salt Lake City. The best local history is an old book, Edward Tullidge, *The History of Salt Lake City and Its Founders* (Salt Lake City, 1885). However, it contains much information that does not relate directly to Salt Lake City. The quote about the glories of the Mormon experiment is on page 631. There is information on Salt Lake City's economy in Leonard J. Arrington, *Great Basin Kingdom: An Economic History of the Latter-day Saints, 1870–1900* (Cambridge, 1958). Social and intellectual conditions are covered in Barth, *Instant Cities,* 39–60.

See also Richard Burton, *The City of the Saints and Across the Rocky Mountain to California* (New York, 1862).

33. This conclusion was first stated in an article by myself and Robert L. Branyan, "The Development of an Urban Civilization on the Frontier of the American West," *Societas—A Review of Social History* 1:35–50 (Winter 1971). It is discussed in Bradford Luckingham, "The City in the Westward Movement—A Bibliographical Note," *The Western Historical Quarterly* 5:299 (July 1974). Luckingham states, "By 1880 the development of an urban civilization in Western America was plainly visible. City life familiar to easterners had moved west with the people. Adopting a host of urban characteristics, newer cities drew on the history of the older urban centers. Lawrence H. Larsen and Robert L. Branyan . . . point out that a western city would occasionally lead the way in innovation, but more common was the fact that 'as the United States became a nation of cities, the physical characteristics of western urban centers differed little from their eastern counterparts.' The urban frontier was not an area demanding experiment, but it did provide an opportunity for the extension and proliferation of existing trends, and 'for better or worse, western settlers, drawing on their previous experience, carried the accepted eastern norms throughout the American West.'"

CHAPTER 2: DEMOGRAPHY, SOCIETY, AND ECONOMICS

1. The quotation is in *Social Statistics of Cities*, pt. 2:762. The best available social mobility study of a western city is Howard Chudacoff, *Mobile Americans: Residential and Social Mobility in Omaha, 1880–1920* (New York, 1972).

2. Table XV, "Native Population of Fifty Principal Cities," *Statistics of the Population of the United States (Tenth Census of the United States, 1880*, vol. 1, Washington, 1883), 536–537.

3. Table IX, "Population, as Native and Foreign-born, of Cities and Towns of 4,000 Inhabitants and Upward: 1880 and 1870," *Ibid.*, 447 (California and Colorado), 449 (Kansas), 452 (Missouri, Nebraska, and Nevada), 454 (Oregon), 455 (Texas), 456 (Utah Territory); Table VI, "Population, by Race, of Cities and Towns of 4,000 Inhabitants and Upward: 1880 and 1870," *Ibid.*, 416 (California and Colorado), 418 (Kansas), 421 (Mississippi, Missouri, and Nebraska), 324 (Oregon), 424 (Texas), 425 (Utah Territory). The material on black housing patterns in San Fran-

cisco and Denver is from Gunther Barth, *Instant Cities: Urbanization and the Rise of San Francisco and Denver* (New York, 1975), 287; for Kansas City, from a seminar paper by Dwayne Martin, "The Hidden Community," presented 14 December 1976, in my "Urban Factors in American History" graduate seminar at the University of Missouri–Kansas City.

4. Table IX, *Ibid.*, 448 (South Bend), 447 (Montgomery), 451 (Lawrence); Table VI, *Ibid.*, 418 (South Bend), 416 (Montgomery), 419 (Lawrence, Massachusetts).
5. William Corner, ed., *San Antonio de Bexar: A Guide and History* (San Antonio, 1890), 2; Table IX, *Ibid.*, 453 (New York), 451 (St. Paul), 455 (Scranton), 454 (Cleveland).
6. Table XVI, "Foreign-born Population of Fifty Principal Cities, Distributed, According to Place of Birth, Among the Various Foreign Countries: 1880," *Ibid.*, 538–539.
7. Table VI, *Ibid.*, 416 (California cities and Denver), 423 (Portland), 421 (Virginia City), 421 (Omaha and St. Joseph), 424 (Texas). The table lumps Chinese and Japanese together. However, they are broken down in *Social Statistics of Cities*, pt. 2:800 (San Francisco), 783 (Oakland). Only 149 Japanese immigrated to the United States between 1871 and 1880. Masako Herman, ed., *The Japanese in America, 1843–1973: A Chronology and Fact Book* (Dobbs Ferry, N.Y., 1973), 3. The Japanese government did not legalize labor emigration until 1884. Yamato Ichihashi, *Japanese in the United States: A Cultural Study of the Problems of Japanese Immigrants and Their Children* (Stanford, 1932), 93. For the Chinese see Betty Lee Sung, *Mountain of Gold: The Story of the Chinese in America* (New York, 1967); Stuart Creighton Miller, *The Universal Impact: The American Image of the Chinese, 1785–1882* (Berkeley, 1969).
8. The quotation is from Will Irwin, *The City That Was* (New York, 1906), 43–45; *Social Statistics of Cities*, pt. 2:824.
9. *Social Statistics of Cities*, pt. 2:779 (Los Angeles), 800 (San Francisco), 743 (Omaha), 829 (Salt Lake City), 739 (Lincoln), 766 (Topeka), 301 (Austin). An 1879 city directory for San Antonio contained the names of 3,470 people of Mexican descent. Boyce House, *City of Flaming Adventure* (San Antonio, 1949), 164. An authority on Texas urbanization estimated that a decade earlier the population was between a third and a half Mexican. Kenneth Wheeler, *To Wear a City's Crown: The Beginnings of Urban Growth in Texas, 1836–1865* (Cambridge, 1968), 147. Using the 1880 manuscript census, I counted persons with Hispanic surnames for Los Angeles, San Jose, San Antonio, and Topeka.

I then added 10 percent to the total, applying a formula developed at Mexican universities and suggested by Philip A. Hernandez of the University of Colorado at Denver. Mexicans born in the United States are not identified by race in the printed schedules for 1880. See *1880 Census Population Schedules, California, Texas, Kansas,* Los Angeles County, Microfilm T-9, Rolls 66–67; Santa Clara County, Microfilm T-9, Rolls 81–82; Bexar County, Microfilm T-9, Roll 1291; and Shawnee County, Microfilm T-9, Rolls 396–397, in the Kansas City Federal Archives and Records Center, Kansas City, Mo. There is a need for books on the Mexican-American elements. See Livie Duran and H. Russell Bernard, ed., *Introduction to Chicano Studies: A Reader* (New York, 1973), and Wayne Moquin with Charles Van Doren, *A Documentary History of the Mexican Americans* (New York, 1973). The statistics for Indians in Virginia City are from the *1880 Census Population Schedules, Nevada,* Storey County, Microfilm T-9, Roll 759, in the Kansas City Federal Archives and Records Center, Kansas City, Mo.

10. *Social Statistics of Cities,* pt. 2:739 (Lincoln), 743 (Omaha), 554 (Kansas City), 561 (St. Joseph), 751 (Atchison), 759 (Lawrence), 761 (Leavenworth), 766 (Topeka), 301 (Austin), 311 (Dallas), 315 (Galveston), 323 (Houston), 327 (San Antonio), 779 (Los Angeles), 783 (Oakland), 789 (Sacramento), 800 (San Francisco), 816 (San Jose), 817 (Stockton), 832 (Portland), 769 (Denver), 773 (Leadville), 829 (Salt Lake City). While the population of each city is broken down by sex in the *Social Statistics of Cities,* it is not in other parts of the 1880 census. So, there are no statistics for Virginia City in the printed schedules. The figures used are from the *1880 Census Population Schedules, Nevada,* Storey County.

11. Table 1, "Summary of Denominations for 124 Cities, by Cities," *Report on Statistics of Churches in the United States (Eleventh Census of the United States, 1890,* vol. 50, Washington, 1894), 91.

12. Table 7, "Communicants or Members in Cities Having a Population of 100,000 to 500,000," *Ibid.,* 98–99; Table 11, "Communicants or Members in Cities Having a Population of 25,000 to 100,000," *Ibid.,* 112–115. These tables are hard to use. A recent study of Jews on the frontier concludes that by 1876 they "were primarily an urban group who held occupations and reflected the opinions of urban America and not necessarily of western America" (Robert E. Levinson, "American Jews in the West," *The Western Historical Quarterly* 5:289 [July 1974]).

13. W. S. Burke and J. L. Rock, *The History of Leavenworth, The*

Metropolis of Kansas and the Chief Commercial Center West of the Missouri River (Leavenworth, 1880), 30; Agnes Emery, *Reminiscences of Early Lawrence* (Lawrence, 1954), 38–39.

14. *Social Statistics of Cities,* pt. 2:748–749 (Omaha), 565–566 (St. Joseph), 756 (Atchison); *Report of the Commissioner of Education: 1880 (Report of the Secretary of the Interior,* vol. 3, Washington, 1882), 22 (San Francisco), 311–312 (Houston and San Antonio), 188 (Kansas City), 202–203 (Virginia City), 102 (Leavenworth and Topeka), 32 (Denver).

15. *Social Statistics of Cities,* pt. 2:565–566, 748–749, 756; Table IX, "Statistics of Universities and Colleges for 1880," *Report of the Commissioner,* 640–675; Emery, *Reminiscences,* 93.

16. The official is quoted in *Social Statistics of Cities,* pt. 2:824.

17. Western literary trends are lucidly discussed in Earl Pomeroy, *The Pacific Slope: A History of California, Oregon, Washington, Idaho, Utah, and Nevada* (New York, 1965), 158–160. See Franklin Walker, *San Francisco's Literary Frontier* (New York, 1939).

18. Edward Tullidge, *The History of Salt Lake City and its Founders* (Salt Lake City, 1885), 589. The *Tribune* in Salt Lake City started as a pro-Mormon paper called the *Mormon Tribune.* After a "gentile" acquired it in the early 1870s, he changed both the name and the editorial policy. Pomeroy feels that western journalism had a distinctive flavor. "Although the press moved along with the theater into national orbits, drawing increasingly on the standardized offerings of the syndicates and deferring to styles set primarily in the East, it had a more distinctively regional flavor, even in the early years when the written word moved across the continent far more easily than performers and stage scenery," he says. "Westerners seemed to seek diversion, escape, and familiar entertainment on the stage; controversy in their newspapers" (*The Pacific Slope,* 154–157). Of course, the same thing could be said about other parts of the nation. The Denver material is from W. B. Vickers, *History of the City of Denver, Arapahoe County, and Colorado* (Chicago, 1880), 30–31. Robert T. Van Horn was an important Kansas City promoter in his own right. He is a leading figure in Charles N. Glaab, *Kansas City and the Railroads: Community Policy in the Growth of a Regional Metropolis* (Madison, 1962). Histories of newspapers tend to be self-serving. One of the best is William Rice, *The Los Angeles Star: 1851–1864* (Berkeley, 1947). The standard source on newspapers remains Frank Luther Mott, *American Journalism: A History, 1690–1960,* 3rd ed. (New York, 1962).

19. The quotation is from *Social Statistics of Cities,* pt. 2:302. Most

local histories contain lists of voluntary organizations. They were not unique in Austin. See also Bradford Luckingham, "Associational Life on the Urban Frontier: San Francisco, 1848–1856" (Ph.D. thesis, University of California, Davis, 1968).

20. Chapter 11, "The Rise of Sport," in Foster Rhea Dulles, *A History of Recreation: America Learns to Play*, 2nd ed. (New York, 1965), 182–199, summarizes post–Civil War trends in sports. The Houston team and its fortunes are discussed in David McComb, *Houston: The Bayou City*, 60. For information on the Kansas City franchise see *The Baseball Encyclopedia: The Complete and Official Record of Major League Baseball* (New York, 1969), 117. In 1884 a Kansas City team in the Union League won 16 and lost 63 and folded with the league.

21. *Social Statistics of Cities,* pt. 2:556 (Kansas City), 770 (Denver), 781 (Los Angeles), 325 (Houston), 331 (San Antonio), 832 (Salt Lake City), 776 (Leadville), 826 (Portland), pt. 1:454 (Boston), 111 (Albany); Vickers, *History of the City of Denver*, 291. There is a detailed theatrical history of Salt Lake City in Tullidge, *The History of Salt Lake City*, 735–767.

22. *Statistics of the Population*, 855–859.

23. Table XXXVI, "Persons in Selected Occupations in Fifty Principal Cities, etc.: 1880," *Ibid.*, 875 (Denver), 881 (Kansas City), 902 (San Francisco).

24. *Ibid.*, 707.

25. *Social Statistics of Cities*, pt. 2:312; Burke and Rock, *History of Leavenworth*, 23.

26. Table VI, "Manufactures of 100 Principal Cities by Totals: 1880," *Report of the Manufactures of the United States (Tenth Census of the United States, 1880,* vol. 2, Washington, 1883), 379–380. The manufacturing census is discussed in terms of structure and reliability in Meyer Fishbein, *The Census of Manufactures: 1810–1890 (National Archives and Records Service Information Paper No. 50,* Washington, 1973). Unfortunately the manuscript nonpopulation schedules for all places of eight thousand or more in 1880 have been lost.

27. Table VI, *Report of the Manufactures*, 436–437; *Social Statistics of Cities*, pt. 2:803.

28. Table VI, *Report of the Manufactures,* 398 (Denver), 403 (Galveston), 435 (San Antonio and Salt Lake City), 419 (Oakland), 431 (Sacramento), 432 (St. Joseph), 420 (Omaha), 407 (Kansas City). The same statistical information appears in *Social Statistics of Cities.*

29. *Social Statistics of Cities*, pt. 2:722 (Denver), 322 (Galveston),

559–560 (Kansas City), 788 (Oakland), 749 (Omaha), 799 (Sacramento), 566 (St. Joseph), 835 (Salt Lake City), 332 (San Antonio), 813–815 (San Francisco).

30. The Workingmen's Party of California, which was violently anti-Chinese, elected mayors of San Francisco and Sacramento but lasted only three years, from 1877 to 1880. It was a portent of things to come. In the following decades antagonism between labor and capital became almost the norm in western labor relations, as both sides moved into positions of power. See Pomeroy, *The Pacific Slope*, 179–184; Gunther Barth, *Instant Cities*, 150–151.

31. Numerous accounts deal with this well-known aspect of the western experience. See such works as Gilbert Fite, *The Farmers' Frontier: 1865–1900* (New York, 1966); Hiram Drache, *The Days of the Bonanza: A History of Bonanza Farming in the Red River Valley of the North* (Fargo, 1964); Louis Atherton, *The Cattle Kings* (Bloomington, 1962); Thomas Cox, *Mills and Markets: A History of the Pacific Coast Lumber Industry* (Seattle, 1974); C. B. Glasscock, *The War of the Copper Kings: Builders of Butte and Wolves of Wall Street* (New York, 1935); Duane Smith, *Horace Taber: His Life and the Legend* (Boulder, 1973); Glenn Quiett, *They Built the West: An Epic of Rails and Cities* (New York, 1934); Vernon Carstensen, "The Fishermen's Frontier on the Pacific Coast: The Rise of the Salmon Canning Industry," John Clark, ed., *The Frontier Challenge: Responses to the Trans-Mississippi West* (Lawrence, 1971), 57–60; Gene Gressley, *Bankers and Cattlemen* (New York, 1966); William Turrentine Jackson, *The Enterprising Scot: Investors in the American West after 1873* (Edinburg, 1968).

32. The San Francisco leadership is discussed in Samuel Bowles, *Our New West* (Hartford, 1869), 340–341; Stevenson is quoted in Pomeroy, *The Pacific Slope*, 127.

33. The author of a study of the early Kansas City business community states, "The example of Kansas City suggests that a major source for business profits in the development of the West lay in a nearly complete identification with the fortunes of the town site from the first stages of its growth" (Charles N. Glaab, "Business Patterns in the Growth of a Midwestern City," *The Business History Review* 33:156–174 [Summer 1959]).

34. There is a need for analytical leadership studies of western cities. The founding of the dominant business organizations in Houston is discussed in David McComb, *Houston: The Bayou City* (Austin, 1969), 51. Information on the early leadership of Galveston,

Austin, and San Antonio can be found in Wheeler, *To Wear a City's Crown*. See also John Williams Rogers, *The Lusty Texans of Dallas* (New York ,1951). Quiett, *They Built the West*, has some material on the leaders of Omaha, Los Angeles, Denver, and Portland. Business interests in Los Angeles, Portland, Virginia City, and Salt Lake City are analyzed in Pomeroy, *The Pacific Slope*. Robert Fogelson, *The Fragmented Metropolis: Los Angeles, 1850–1930* (Cambridge, 1967), contains valuable material, as does Glenn Dunke, *The Boom of the Eighties in Southern California* (Los Angeles, 1944). There are no decent leadership studies for Stockton, San Jose, Sacramento, and Oakland. For Leadville see Duane Smith, *Rocky Mountain Mining Camps: The Urban Frontier* (Bloomington, 1967). Some material on Leavenworth can be found in Burke and Rock, *The History of Leavenworth*. For Atchison see *Atchison, The Railroad Center of Kansas: Its Advantages for Commerce and Manufactures* (Atchison, 1894). The dominant groups in Lincoln, Lawrence, and Topeka have to be pieced together from local histories. The evolution of economic power in St. Joseph is detailed in John D. McCaskey, "The First Family of Banks: St. Joseph, Missouri" (Master's thesis, University of Missouri–Kansas City, 1971).

35. Expenditures in Austin for the year ending 20 October 1879 ranged from $563.57 for the city cemetery to $12,505.59 for streets and bridges (*Social Statistics of Cities* pt. 2:309–310). Most local histories contain lists and sketches of leading public officials. In some instances they even detail major political controversies. Few books about the frontier deal adequately with the connection between business interests and politicians in framing community policy. One of the few that does is Glaab, *Kansas City and the Railroads*. See also the early sections of Walter Bean, *Boss Reuf's San Francisco* (Berkeley, 1952). Machinations in smaller western communities are covered in Robert Dykstra, *The Cattle Towns* (New York, 1968).

CHAPTER 3: IMPROVING THE ENVIRONMENT

1. William Corner, *San Antonio de Bexar* (San Antonio, 1890), 2; the Los Angeles quotation is from Earl Pomeroy, *The Pacific Slope: A History of California, Oregon, Washington, Idaho, Utah, and Nevada* (New York, 1965), 141. A picture on page X of the illustrations in Pomeroy's book shows Spring Street in 1885. Most local histories contain drawings or photographs of varying quality.

2. The quotation is from *Social Statistics of Cities*, pt. 2:791.
3. Will Irwin, *The City That Was* (New York, 1906), 15, comments on the low buildings in San Francisco prior to the earthquake and fire of 1906. Howard Barnstone, *The Galveston That Was* (New York, 1966), 19–88, has fine material on Galveston's architecture. A basic study of architectural trends is James Marston Fitch, *American Building: The Forces That Shape It* (New York, 1948). See also Thomas E. Tallmadge, *The Story of Architecture in America* (New York, 1936); Christopher Tunnard and Henry Hope Reed, *American Skyline: The Growth and Form of Our Cities and Towns* (New York, 1955); Vincent Scully, *American Architecture and Urbanism* (New York, 1969). Charles N. Glaab and A. Theodore Brown (rev. by Charles N. Glaab), *A History of Urban America*, 2nd ed. (New York, 1976), 137–138, related Bogardus' contribution to urbanization.
4. Quoted in Pomeroy, *The Pacific Slope*, 137–138; Sandra Dallas, *Yesterday's Denver*, Seeman's Historic Cities Series No. 10 (Miami, 1974), 35; Gunther Barth, *Instant Cities: Urbanization and the Rise of San Francisco and Denver* (New York, 1975), 185–187; Lawrence Hill, *La Reina: Los Angeles in Three Centuries* (Los Angeles, 1929), 18; *Atchison Centennial: 1854–1954* (Atchison, 1954); W. S. Burke and J. L. Rock, *The History of Leavenworth, The Metropolis of Kansas and the Chief Commercial Center West of the Missouri River* (Leavenworth, 1880), 39; Giles Mitchell, *There Is No Limit: Architecture and Sculpture in Kansas City* (Kansas City, 1934), 12–17. There is a fine clipping file on early Kansas City buildings in the Missouri Valley Room of the Kansas City Public Library. See also *Hughes Annual Kansas City Views, 1896* (Kansas City, 1896). In a special category is a beautiful book about the city, Creative Staff of Hallmark Editions, *Kansas City: An Intimate Portrait of the Surprising City on the Missouri* (Kansas City, 1973).
5. The Chinatown quote is from Irwin, *The City That Was*, 43; the other quotation is from Pomeroy, *The Pacific Slope*, 125–127; Barth, *Instant Cities*, 187–189.
6. John W. Reps, *The Making of Urban America* (Princeton, 1965), figure 233. This magnificent book is the standard work on the history of urban planning in the United States.
7. There are small topographical maps for many of the towns in *Social Statistics of Cities*, pt. 2:301 (Austin), 311 (Dallas), 327 (San Antonio), 739 (Lincoln), 743 (Omaha), 773 (Leadville), 800 (San Francisco), 817 (Stockton), 823 (Portland), 829 (Salt Lake City), 554 (Kansas City), 561 (St. Joseph), opposite 752 (Atchison),

opposite 762 (Leavenworth), opposite 784 (Oakland), opposite 796 (Sacramento). The street design of the other cities have to be pieced together in other ways—from photographs, atlases, and observations.

8. Statements on topography for many cities appear in *Social Statistics of Cities*, pt. 2:304–305 (Austin), 312 (Dallas), 318 (Galveston), 325 (Houston), 330 (San Antonio), 740 (Lincoln), 746 (Omaha), 753 (Atchison), 758 (Lawrence), 763 (Leavenworth), 767 (Topeka), 770 (Denver), 774 (Leadville), 780 (Los Angeles), 784 (Oakland), 794–795 (Sacramento), 804 (San Francisco), 816 (San Jose), 818 (Stockton), 825 (Portland), 831–832 (Salt Lake City), 555 (Kansas City), 562 (St. Joseph). The topography of Virginia City is mentioned in Lucius Beebe, "Virginia City," *The Encyclopedia Americana: International Edition* 28:165 (New York, 1970). There is a picture of Virginia City in 1861 as the frontispiece of George Lyman, *The Saga of the Comstock Lode: Boom Days in Virginia City* (New York, 1934).

9. Corner, *San Antonio de Bexar*, 2.

10. *Social Statistics of Cities*, pt. 2:767 (Topeka), 770 (Denver).

11. *Ibid.*, 831.

12. The New England tourist was Samuel Bowles, *Our New West* (Hartford, 1869), 335; the San Francisco resident was Irwin, *The City That Was*, 17. See also *Social Statistics of Cities*, pt. 2:804.

13. The quotation is in Pomeroy, *The Pacific Slope*, 147–149. Reps, *The Making of Urban America*, 410–412, discussed Olmsted's plan.

14. There is a short and clear discussion of Olmsted's career in Tunnard and Reed, *American Skyline*, 109–111. Chapter 12, "Cemeteries, Parks and Suburbs: Picturesque Planning in the Romantic Style," Reps, *The Making of Urban America*, 325–348, traces the origins of the "City Beautiful" movement. There is good material in William Wilson, *The City Beautiful Movement in Kansas City* (Columbia, 1964), xiii–xvii. *Social Statistics of Cities*, pt. 1:210 (Gloucester), 385 (Woonsocket), 883 (Scranton), 878 (Reading), pt. 2:67 (Norfolk), 137 (Chattanooga), 446 (Fort Wayne), 429 (Youngstown), 680 (Oshkosh), 58 (Alexandria), 113 (Covington), 732 (Dubuque).

15. *Social Statistics of Cities*, pt. 2:754 (Atchison), 776 (Leadville), 325 (Houston), 305 (Austin), 313 (Dallas), 319 (Galveston), 759 (Lawrence), 770 (Denver), 819 (Stockton), 781 (Los Angeles), 785 (Oakland), 556 (Kansas City), 832 (Salt Lake City), 330 (San Antonio), 826 (Portland), 745–746 (Omaha), 795–796 (Sacramento), 764 (Leavenworth), 805 (San Francisco). See also Barth, *Instant Cities*, 200.

16. *Social Statistics of Cities,* pt. 2:312 (Dallas), 318 (Galveston), 740 (Lincoln), 746 (Omaha), 563 (St. Joseph), 556 (Kansas City), 770 (Denver), 785 (Oakland), 819 (Stockton), 826 (Portland), 805 (San Francisco), 775 (Leadville); F. W. Giles, *Thirty Years in Topeka: A Historical Sketch* (Topeka, 1886), 402–404; Edward Tullidge, *The History of Salt Lake City and its Founders* (Salt Lake City, 1885), 55.
17. *Social Statistics of Cities,* pt. 2:305 (Austin), 740 (Lincoln), 325 (Houston), 746 (Omaha), 759 (Lawrence), 770 (Denver), 556 (Kansas City), 775 (Leadville), 832 (Salt Lake City), 818–819 (Stockton), 780 (Los Angeles), 805 (San Francisco); David Mc-Comb, *Houston: The Bayou City* (Austin, 1969), 100.
18. *Social Statistics of Cities,* pt. 2:825–826. See also George A. Soper, *Modern Methods of Street Cleaning* (New York, 1909), 7, 9, 11–12, 21–22; Winston A. Walden, "Nineteenth Century Street Pavements" (Master's thesis, University of Missouri–Kansas City, 1967), 6–7, 16, 20, 23, 29, 38, 40, 45, 49, 53; Blake McKelvey, *The Urbanization of America: 1860–1915* (New Brunswick, 1963), 88–89; Otto L. Bettmann, *The Good Old Days—They Were Terrible!* (New York, 1974), 3.

CHAPTER 4: SANITATION PRACTICES

1. *Social Statistics of Cities,* pt. 1:83 (Burlington), 206 (Fitchburg), 22 (Baltimore), 634 (Rome), 225 (Holyoke), 709 (Newark), 611 (Poughkeepsie), 758 (Erie); pt. 2:723 (Davenport), 417 (Steuben-ville), 636 (Kalamazoo), 737 (Keokuk), 659 (Madison), 539 (Rockford), 705 (Winona), 719 (Council Bluffs), 124–125 (Louis-ville).
2. *Ibid.,* pt. 2:820 (Stockton), 833 (Salt Lake City), 558 (Kansas City), 565 (St. Joseph), 827 (Portland), 798 (Sacramento), 760 (Lawrence), 326 (Houston), 320 (Galveston), 308 (Austin), 777 (Leadville), 782 (Los Angeles), 811 (San Francisco). See my article, "Nineteenth-Century Street Sanitation: A Study of Filth and Frustration," *Wisconsin Magazine of History,* 52:237–239 (Spring 1969).
3. *Social Statistics of Cities,* pt. 2:308 (Austin), 314 (Dallas), 331–332 (San Antonio), 326 (Houston), 748 (Omaha), 767 (Topeka), 771 (Denver), 777 (Leadville), 833 (Salt Lake City), 565 (St. Joseph), 787 (Oakland), 811 (San Francisco), 320–321 (Galveston).
4. *Ibid.,* pt. 2:308 (Austin), 332 (San Antonio), 760 (Lawrence), 565 (St. Joseph), 558 (Kansas City), 565 (Omaha), 777 (Leadville), 782 (Los Angeles), 827 (Portland), 787 (Oakland).

5. *Ibid.,* pt. 2:321 (Galveston), 765 (Leavenworth), 742 (Lincoln), 811 (San Francisco), 782 (Los Angeles), 331 (San Antonio), 308 (Austin), 314 (Dallas), 798 (Sacramento), 771 (Denver), 555 (St. Joseph), 777 (Leadville), 558 (Kansas City), 748 (Omaha), 827 (Portland), 787 (Oakland), 760 (Lawrence).

6. George E. Waring, Jr., *The Sanitary Drainage of Houses and Towns* (Boston, 1898), 10. See also James W. Cassedy, "The Flamboyant Colonel Waring," *Bulletin of the History of Medicine* 36:163–176 (March-April, 1962); George A. Soper, "General Edwin Waring," Dumas Malone, ed., *Dictionary of American Biography* 19: 456–457 (New York, 1946); Charles Zueblin, *American Municipal Progress* (New York, 1916), 78–80.

7. *Social Statistics of Cities,* pt. 2:807–808.

8. *Ibid.,* pt. 2:826 (Portland), 785–786 (Oakland), 781 (Los Angeles), 796 (Sacramento), 556–557 (Kansas City), 764 (Leavenworth), 313 (Dallas), 832 (Salt Lake City), 819 (Stockton).

9. Charles N. Glaab and A. Theodore Brown (rev. by Charles N. Glaab), *A History of Urban America,* 2nd ed. (New York, 1976), 155.

10. *Social Statistics of Cities,* pt. 2:308 (Austin), 314 (Dallas), 320 (Galveston), 748 (Omaha), 767 (Topeka), 771 (Denver), 787 (Oakland), 565 (St. Joseph), 796 (Sacramento), 727–728 (Portland).

11. *Ibid.,* pt. 2:767 (Topeka), 558 (Kansas City), 777 (Leadville), 771 (Denver), 834 (Salt Lake City), 314 (Dallas), 321 (Galveston), 760 (Lawrence), 748 (Omaha), 782 (Los Angeles), 798 (Sacramento), 565 (St. Joseph).

12. *Ibid.,* pt. 2:332 (San Antonio), 321 (Galveston), 326 (Houston), 767 (Topeka), 782 (Los Angeles), 834 (Salt Lake City), 728 (Portland), 771 (Denver), 565 (St. Joseph), 755 (Atchison), 558 (Kansas City), 760 (Lawrence).

13. Nelson Blake, *Water for the Cities: A History of the Urban Water Supply Problem in the United States* (Syracuse, 1956), 266–269. This book is the basic historical work on the subject. See also Walter G. Elliott, "Report on the Water-Supply of Certain Cities in the United States," *Reports on the Water-Power of the United States (Tenth Census of the United States,* vol. 17, pt. 2, Washington, 1887), 1–3. The material on La Crosse is in *Social Statistics of Cities,* pt. 2:653.

14. *Social Statistics of Cities,* pt. 2:754 (Atchison), 563 (St. Joseph), 556 (Kansas City), 312–313 (Dallas), 330 (San Antonio), 780 (Los Angeles), 785 (Oakland), 806 (San Francisco), 819 (Stockton).

The San Antonio quotation in the previous paragraph is from William Corner, *San Antonio de Bexar* (San Antonio, 1890), 55.

CHAPTER 5: HEALTH, FIRE, AND POLICE PROTECTION

1. *Social Statistics of Cities*, pt. 2:760 (Lawrence), 792 (Sacramento); the quotation is from pt. 2:833 (Salt Lake City). The historical evolution of boards of health is discussed in an old, but still basic study for various aspects of public administration, John Fairlie, *Municipal Administration* (New York, 1901), 157–175. The "Public Health Movement" is covered in Charles N. Glaab and A. Theodore Brown (rev. by Charles N. Glaab), *A History of Urban America*, 2nd ed. (New York, 1976), 155–157.

2. *Social Statistics of Cities*, pt. 2:307 (Austin), 313 (Dallas), 331 (San Antonio), 747 (Omaha), 765 (Leavenworth), 558 (Kansas City), 776–777 (Leadville), 797 (Sacramento), 809–810 (San Francisco), 320 (Galveston), 820 (Stockton), 741–742 (Lincoln), 786–787 (Oakland), 781 (Los Angeles), 564 (St. Joseph), 754–755 (Atchison), 325–326 (Houston), 827 (Portland), 430 (Youngstown), 63 (Lynchburg); pt. 1:46 (Concord). *Topeka Illustrated, Its Progress and Importance: A Descriptive and Statistical Review of Her Resources, Advantages and Facilities in Trade, Commerce and Manufacturers, Together with a Delineation of Her Representative Establishments* (Topeka, 1887), 34.

3. Table XIII, "Population, Births, and Deaths, with statement of Ratios, and Deaths from certain specific causes," *Report on the Mortality and Vital Statistics of the United States* (*Tenth Census of the United States*, vol. 12, Washington, 1886), 180–183. The census began to report mortality statistics in 1860.

4. Table XII, "Population, Births, and Deaths, with Statement of Ratios, and Deaths from Certain Specified Causes," *Ibid.*, 180–183.

5. *Social Statistics of Cities*, pt. 2:324 (Houston), 780 (Los Angeles), 831 (Salt Lake City), 784 (Oakland), 801–802 (San Francisco), 818 (Stockton). The census asked cities to report their major fires.

6. *Ibid.*, pt. 2:756 (Atchison), 321 (Galveston), 748 (Omaha), 559 (Kansas City), 812 (San Francisco), 820–821 (Stockton); pt. 1:908 (Wilmington), 772 (Norristown), 880 (Reading). See Fairlie, *Municipal Government*, 150–157.

7. Fairlie, *Municipal Government*, 150–157, covers the transfer of efficiently organized police forces from London to New York, and then through the rest of the United States. Another basic work is Raymond Fosdick, *American Police Systems* (New York, 1920).

Of more recent vintage is James F. Richardson, *Urban Police in the United States* (Port Washington, N.Y., 1974). Robert Dykstra, *The Cattle Towns* (New York, 1968), shows that places on the Kansas frontier such as Dodge City and Abilene were rather tame, with little lawlessness. See also James Richardson, "The Police in the City: A History," Raymond Mohl and James Richardson, *The Urban Experience: Themes in American History* (Belmont, Calif., 1973), 164–181. Most of what historians have written about police has tended to be bureaucratic, speculative, and general.

8. Earl Pomeroy, *The Pacific Slope: A History of California, Oregon, Washington, Idaho, Utah, and Nevada* (New York, 1965), 373; *Social Statistics of Cities*, pt. 2:314 (Dallas), 742 (Lincoln), 782 (Los Angeles), 777 (Leadville), 820 (Stockton), 767 (Topeka), 760 (Lawrence), 811 (San Francisco), 559 (Kansas City). I presented some of the material on western police in a paper, "Urban Police Forces after the First Hundred Years of the Republic," at "A Conference on Historical Perspectives on American Criminal Justice," held 22–23 April 1976, at the University of Nebraska at Omaha.

9. *Social Statistics of Cities*, pt. 2:309 (Austin), 777–778 (Leadville), 314 (Dallas), 332 (San Antonio), 748 (Omaha), 755 (Atchison), 760 (Lawrence), 782 (Los Angeles), 559 (Kansas City), 811–812 (San Francisco), 820 (Stockton), 788 (Oakland), 828 (Portland); *1879 Kansas City Police Regulations* (Kansas City, 1879). Many local histories contain information on police—usually lists of names and organizational characteristics. There are also some histories of individual departments that are relatively uncluttered with worthwhile information.

10. *Topeka Illustrated*, 33.

11. See Eugene Arden, "The Evil City in American Fiction," *New York History* 35: 259–279 (July 1954).

12. B. E. Lloyd, *Lights and Shades of San Francisco* (San Francisco, 1876), 79.

13. Table CXXXVI, "Police Statistics for 1880 of Cities in the United States Having 5,000 or More Inhabitants," *Report on the Defective, Dependent, and Delinquent Classes of the Population of the United States* (*Tenth Census of the United States*, vol. 21, Washington, 1888), 566–574. See also Philip Jordan, *Frontier Law and Order: Ten Essays* (Lincoln, 1970), 138–139.

14. *Social Statistics of Cities*, pt. 2:742 (Lincoln), 812 (San Francisco), 748 (Omaha), 755 (Atchison).

15. *Ibid.*, pt. 2:798 (Sacramento), 742 (Lincoln), 812 (San Francisco),

827 (Portland), 385 (Cleveland), 48 (Washington); pt. 1:119–120 (Boston).

16. Paper presented by Robert V. Percival, "Municipal Justice in the Melting Pot: Arrest and Prosecution in Oakland 1872–1910," at "A Conference on Historical Perspectives on American Criminal Justice." This excellent paper contains a wealth of valuable comparative data. Percival notes that in Oakland, "the percentage of arrests that are made for serious crimes today is substantially higher than a century ago and dramatically higher than at the turn of the century."

17. *Ibid.*, pt. 2:827.

18. Table CXXXVI in *Report on the Defective, Dependent, and Delinquent Classes of the Population of the United States,* 566–574; *Social Statistics of Cities,* pt. 2:755 (Atchison), 765 (Leavenworth), 798 (Sacramento).

19. *Social Statistics of Cities,* pt. 2:309 (Austin), 742 (Lincoln), 788 (Oakland), 827 (Portland), 812 (San Francisco), 748 (Omaha), 765 (Leavenworth), 565 (St. Joseph), 760 (Lawrence). The quote by the Oakland mayor is in Percival, "Municipal Justice in the Melting Pot."

CHAPTER 6: THE APPLICATION OF TECHNOLOGY

1. *Social Statistics of Cities,* pt. 2:312 (Dallas), 770 (Denver), 741 (Lincoln), 759 (Lawrence), 764 (Leavenworth), 305 (Austin), 325 (Houston), 780 (Los Angeles), 785 (Oakland), 826 (Portland), 819 (Stockton), 556 (Kansas City). For general information on street transportation systems see Blake McKelvey, *The Urbanization of America 1860–1915* (New Brunswick, 1963), 75–85; Bayrd Still, *Urban America: A History with Documents* (Boston, 1974), 84–88; Frank Rowsome, Jr., *Trolley Car Treasury: A Century of American Streetcars—Horsecars, Cable Cars, Interurbans, and Trolleys* (New York, 1956), 17–34. See also Gunther Barth, *Instant Cities: Urbanization and the Rise of San Francisco and Denver* (New York, 1975), 221–225.

2. George W. Hilton, *The Cable Car in America: A New Treatise upon Cable or Rope Traction as Applied to the Working of Street and Other Railways* (Berkeley, 1971), 185–233. This work, complete with fine photographs, is the basic book on cable cars.

3. *Social Statistics of Cities,* pt. 2:805–806. See also W. W. Hanscom, *The Archaeology of the Cable Car,* compiled and edited by Walt Wheelock (Pasadena, 1970).

4. *Social Statistics of Cities,* pt. 2:319 (Galveston), 556 (Kansas City), 776 (Leadville), 764 (Leavenworth), 563 (St. Joseph), 746 (Omaha), 806 (San Francisco), 780 (Los Angeles), 770 (Denver); John Fairlie, *Municipal Administration* (New York, 1901), 281–285.
5. Quoted in W. B. Vickers, *History of the City of Denver, Arapahoe County, and Colorado* (Chicago, 1880), 239. The statistics are from Table I, "General Financial Exhibit: 1880," *Report on the Agencies of Transportation in the United States, Including the Statistics of Railroads, Steam Navigation, Canals, and Telephones* (*Tenth Census of the United States,* vol. 4, Washington, 1883), 788–792. There are census statistics for only one Denver system, the Colorado Telephone Co.
6. *Kansas City Daily Journal of Commerce,* 1 December 1866.
7. *Atchison, the Railroad Center of Kansas: Its Advantages for Commerce and Manufactures* (Atchison, 1874), 19; *Social Statistics of Cities,* pt. 2:752.
8. *Social Statistics of Cities,* pt. 2:555; *Map of the Kansas City, Fort Scott and Gulf Railroad Lines and Connections,* 1883, in the Kansas State Historical Society. A detailed railroad map proved very difficult to obtain. Robert W. Richmond, the Kansas State Archivist, found the map used in this study in Atchison, Topeka and Santa Fe Railroad papers. The map proved invaluable in piecing together the western railroad net.
9. Charles N. Glaab, *Kansas City and the Railroads: Community Policy in the Growth of a Regional Metropolis* (Kansas City, 1962), tells the story of Kansas City's railroad development from the 1850s through the 1880s.
10. The Missouri River proved difficult to bridge. Octave Chanute, the director of the project, told about it in Octave Chanute and George Morison, *The Kansas City Bridge* (New York, 1870). Over a hundred years later, the bridge still stood, continuing as it had since 1869 to serve as a major railroad artery into Kansas City. The French-born and largely self-trained Chanute built well. He later played a major role in constructing the New York elevated system.
11. The best account of railroad building remains Glenn Quiett, *They Built the West: An Epic of Rails and Cities* (New York, 1934). See also Oscar Winther, *The Transportation Frontier: Trans-Mississippi West 1865–1890* (New York, 1964), 105–119; Ray Billington, *Westward Expansion: A History of the American Frontier,* 4th ed. (New York, 1974), 546–562. The 1880 census requested towns of importance to list their railroad connections. They did, but with imperfect results—many times using the names

of roads previously consolidated. In addition to Kansas City, the connections for the cities included in this study are listed in *Social Statistics of Cities*, pt. 2:304 (Austin), 312 (Dallas), 318 (Galveston), 324 (Houston), 329 (San Antonio), 740 (Lincoln), 745 (Omaha), 753 (Atchison), 758 (Lawrence), 763 (Leavenworth), 767 (Topeka), 770 (Denver), 774 (Leadville), 780 (Los Angeles), 784 (Oakland), 794 (Sacramento), 804 (San Francisco), 818 (Stockton), 825 (Portland), 831 (Salt Lake City), 562 (St. Joseph). The census received no information on railroads from San Jose and did not solicit any from Virginia City. There is a complete list of the names of railroads in the United States in Table II, "Index to Physical Characteristics of Railroads," *Report on the Agencies of Transportation in the United States, Including the Statistics of Railroads, Steam Navigation, Canals, and Telephones*, 639–647. A basic descriptive survey is Robert Riegel, *The Story of Western Railroads* (New York, 1926). For specific lines see Robert G. Athearn, *Union Pacific Country* (Chicago, 1971); Charles Edgar Ames, *Pioneering the Union Pacific: A Reappraisal of the Builders of the Railroad* (New York, 1969); Stuart Daggett, *Chapters on the History of the Southern Pacific* (New York, 1922); Neill Wilson and Frank Taylor, *Southern Pacific: The Roaring Story of A Fighting Railroad* (New York, 1952); Keith Bryant, Jr., *History of the Atchison, Topeka and Santa Fe Railway* (New York, 1974); V. V. Masterson, *The Katy Railroad and the Last Frontier* (Norman, 1974); George L. Anderson, *Kansas West* (San Marino, Calif., 1963); William Edward Hayes, *Iron Road to Empire: The History of 100 Years of the Progress and Achievements of the Rock Island Lines* (n.p., 1953); Richard Overton, *Burlington Route: A History of the Burlington Lines* (New York, 1965); Richard Overton, *Gulf to Rockies: The Heritage of the Fort Worth and Denver-Colorado and Southern Railways, 1861–1898* (Austin, 1953). The Texas routes are surveyed in S. G. Reed, *A History of Texas Railroads* (Houston, 1941). For information on individual towns—usually the names of the early railroad leaders and key dates on the arrival of the first trains—consult the appropriate local histories.

12. Winther, *The Transportation Frontier*, 25–43. See also W. Turrentine Jackson, *Wagon Roads West* (New Haven, 1965); Raymond W. Settle and Mary L. Settle, *Empire on Wheels* (Stanford, 1949); William E. Lass, *From the Missouri to the Great Salt Lake: An Account of Overland Freighting* (Lincoln, 1972).

13. "History of Operating Canals in the United States," *Report on*

the Agencies of Transportation in the United States, Including the Statistics of Railroads, Steam Navigation, Canals, and Telephones, 21.

14. "History of Steam Navigation in the United States," *Report on the Agencies of Transportation in the United States, Including the Statistics of Railroads, Steam Navigation, Canals, and Telephones,* 21–31; Winther, *The Transportation Frontier,* 74–91. See also William E. Lass, *A History of Steamboating on the Upper Missouri River* (Lincoln, 1962); Pamela Ashworth Puryear and Nath Winfield, Jr., *Sandbars and Sternwheelers: Steam Navigation on the Brazos* (College Station, 1976).
15. Will Irwin, *The City That Was* (New York, 1906), 18–19.
16. *Social Statistics of Cities,* pt. 2:812 (San Francisco), 784 (Oakland), 825 (Portland), 321 (Galveston); pt. 1:149–151 (Boston).

CHAPTER 7: THE WEST OF MAGNIFICENT CITIES

1. J. Christopher Schnell, "William Gilpin and the Destruction of the Desert Myth," *The Colorado Magazine* 46:141–143 (Spring 1969).
2. The Denver quotation is from William Gilpin, *Notes on Colorado; and Its Inscription in the Physical Geography of the North American Continent* (London, 1870), 32–33.
3. Quoted in J. Christopher Schnell, "William Gilpin: Advocate of Expansion," *Montana: The Magazine of Western History* 19, pt. 3:30–37 (July 1969).
4. See Chapter 1, "The Significance of the Frontier in American History," Frederick Jackson Turner, *The Frontier in American History* (New York, 1920), 2, 37–38. Turner's thesis has been reprinted in many places. Turner is the subject of a very fine biography, done fittingly enough by a historian of the West, Ray Allen Billington, *Frederick Jackson Turner: Historian, Scholar, Teacher* (New York, 1973).
5. Table 5, "Aggregate Population of Cities, Towns, Villages, and Boroughs Having 2,000 Inhabitants or More in 1890, with Population for 1880 and Increase during the Decade," *Compendium of the Eleventh Census: 1890 (Eleventh Census of the United States,* vol. 1, pt. 1, Washington, 1892), 442–452.
6. "Progress of the Nation," *Ibid.,* lxxiii.

Essay On Sources

The material used in this study was gathered over a period of several years. The bulk of it is from published federal census records, local histories, and scholarly monographs. These range all the way from Table XV, "Native Population of Fifty Pincipal Cities," *Statistics of the Population of the United States* (*Tenth Census of the United States,* 1880, vol. 1, Washington, 1883), to Samuel Radges, comp., *Radges' Biennial Directory to the Inhabitants, Institutions, Manufacturing Establishments, Business Firms, Etc., of the City of Topeka, for 1876–1877* (Topeka, 1975). All the pertinent sources have been cited in full in the notes to the text. The following essay is selective and is designed to give an indication of the items found most helpful.

Of special importance is George Waring, Jr., comp., *Report on the Social Statistics of Cities* (*Tenth Census of the United States, 1880,* vol. 18, 19, pt. 1, 2., Washington, 1886). This massive compilation constitutes the basic source on the 1880 American city. It contains detailed monographic and statistical information for almost all cities with a population of ten thousand or more in 1880, plus certain smaller ones of regional importance. The tabulated index indicates the vast range of subjects that the census considered important enough to collect data about: "Cemeteries," "Climate," "Commerce and navigation," "Distance chart," "Drainage," "Financial condition," "Fire department," "Garbage," "Gas," "History," "Infectious diseases," "Inspection," "Interments," "Location," "Manufactures," "Monuments," "Municipal cleansing," "Parks," "Penal, reformatory, charitable, and healing institutions," "Places of amusement," "Police," "Population by decades, and by present division," "Public buildings," "Railroads," "Sanitary authority," "Schools and libraries (public),"

148

"Streets," "Topography," "Tributary country," "Water-courses, harbors, etc.," "Waterworks." The 222 cities included constituted the backbone of American urban society at the time. Waring solicited information from officials in twenty-three of the twenty-four cities west of the ninety-fifth meridian with populations in 1880 in excess of eight thousand. All responded, except for those in San Jose. Virginia City authorities were not contacted, despite the fact that the Nevada community had a population of 10,917. The *Social Statistics of Cities* proved indispensable in the writing of this book. Unfortunately, Waring retained custody of the manuscript schedules, and they apparently have been lost.

There is a wealth of information in other federal records. Several volumes of the *Tenth Census of the United States, 1880* (24 vols.) augment the *Social Statistics of Cities*. Vital statistics on the number of blacks, natives, foreign-born, females, males, and workers can be found throughout the *Statistics of the Population of the United States*. Industrial statistics for one hundred principal cities are in *Report of the Manufactures of the United States* (vol. 2, Washington, 1883). Waterworks in selected localities are discussed in *Report on the Water Power of the United States* (vol. 17, pt. 2, Washington, 1887). *The Report on the Mortality and Vital Statistics of the United States* (vol. 12, Washington, 1886) has information on population, birth, and death ratios. Police statistics are tabulated in the *Report on the Defective, Dependent, and Delinquent Classes of the Population of the United States* (vol. 21, Washington, 1888). There are lists of railroad and telephone companies in the *Report on the Agencies of Transportation in the United States, Including the Statistics of Railroads, Steam Navigation, Canals, and Telephones* (vol. 4, Washington, 1883). The most comprehensive source for educational trends is the very detailed and extensive *Report of the Commissioner of Education: 1880 (Report of the Secretary of the Interior*, vol. 3, Washington, 1882). Two volumes of the *Eleventh Census of the United States, 1890*, have itemized religious and population statistics: *Compendium of the Eleventh Census: 1890* (vol. 1, pt. 1, Washington, 1892), and *Report on Statutes of Churches in the United States* (vol. 50, Washington, 1894). Old-fashioned type faces, difficult-to-use indexes, and sometimes confusing tabulations, all complicate the task of the researcher. Working with late-nineteenth-century federal documents requires a high degree of patience.

Manuscript census population schedules for enumeration districts of all twenty-four towns are available through National Archives and Records Service T publications. For persons enumerated the 1880 census shows address; name; relationship to head of family; sex; race;

age; marital status; born within the year; married within the year; profession; occupation or trade; number of months unemployed during census year; whether person was sick or temporarily disabled so as to be unable to attend to ordinary business or duties; if so, what was the sickness or disability; whether blind, deaf, dumb, idiotic, insane, maimed, crippled, or bedridden; attended school within the year; ability to read and write; place of birth or person, father, and mother. While some research was done in most of the western city schedules, the greatest use was made of those for Virginia City to determine the percentage of women, and of those for Los Angeles, San Jose, San Antonio, and Topeka to tabulate individuals with Spanish last names. The census-takers wrote in longhand, some less legibly than others, and the quality of the ink used varied. Thus, one Los Angeles enumeration district is almost unreadable, while others are easily read.

Numerous county and local histories exist for the towns of the urban frontier. These works vary in content and quality. Characteristically, they are poorly organized; but most contain information not found elsewhere on town promotions, dominant groups, population trends, industrial developments, and social life. The accompanying biographical volumes, sometimes called "Mug Books," have sketches of community leaders. Some of the local histories are old enough to be considered primary sources in their own right. These include Alfred Sorenson, *Early History of Omaha, or, Walks and Talks Among the Old Settlers: A Series of Sketches in the Shape of a Connected Narrative with a Brief Mention of the Important Events of Later Years* (Omaha, 1876); *Atchison, The Railroad Center of Kansas: Its Advantages for Commerce and Manufactures* (Atchison, 1874); and Samue Huhel, *A History of the City of San Francisco and Incidentally of the State of California* (San Francisco, 1878). Books found especially valuable are Theodore S. Case, *History of Kansas City, Missouri* (Syracuse, 1888); W. S. Burke and J. L. Rock, *The History of Leavenworth, The Metropolis of Kansas and the Chief Commercial Center West of the Missouri River* (Leavenworth, 1880); *Topeka Illustrated, Its Progress and Importance: A Descriptive and Statistical Review of Her Resources, Advantages and Facilities in Trade, Commerce and Manufactures, Together with a Delineation of Her Representative Establishments* (Topeka, 1887); Laurance Hill, *La Reina: Los Angeles in Three Centuries* (Los Angeles, 1929); William Corner, *San Antonio de Bexar* (San Antonio, 1916); W. B. Vickers, *History of the City of Denver, Arapahoe County, and Colorado* (Chicago, 1880); and Edward Tullidge, *A History of Salt Lake City and Its Founders* (Salt Lake City, 1885). In a special class are two short and worthwhile reminiscences, Will Irwin, *The City That Was* (New York, 1906), about San

Francisco, and Agnes Emery, *Reminiscences of Early Lawrence* (Lawrence, 1954). Some other representative local histories are Carrie Whitney, *Kansas City, Missouri: Its History and People, 1808–1890* (Kansas City, 1890); *History of Buchanan County and St. Joseph, Mo.: From the Time of the Platte Purchase to the End of the Year 1915* (St. Joseph, 1915); *Lincoln: The Capital City and Lancaster County, Nebraska* (2 vols., Chicago, 1916); Joseph E. Baker, *Past and Present of Alameda County* (2 vols., Chicago, 1914), about Oakland; Joseph Gaston, *Portland, Ore.: Its History and Builders* (Chicago, 1911); Joseph Dyer, *The Early History of Galveston* (Galveston, 1916); Boyce House, *City of Flaming Adventure* (San Antonio, 1949), about San Antonio; and Jerome Smiley, ed., *History of Denver: With Outlines of the Early History of the Rocky Mountain Country* (Denver, 1901). Most of these, plus many others cited in the notes, can be found in the Snyder Collection on Western Americana in the University of Missouri–Kansas City General Library.

Until recently, professional historians tended to ignore frontier urbanization and to concentrate on other aspects of the western experience. The current state of the art is discussed in Bradford Luckingham's article, "The City in the Westward Movement—A Bibliographical Note," in the July 1974 issue of *The Western Historical Quarterly*. Any discussion of the urban West starts with Earl Pomeroy, *The Pacific Slope: A History of California, Oregon, Washington, Idaho, Utah, and Nevada* (New York, 1965). His chapter "The Power of the Metropolis," which has excellent social and economic information, helped to shape this book. Anyone writing about the urban West is frustrated by the lack of analytical urban biographies. Fortunately, the few in print are of high quality. The emergence of a "regional metropolis" is traced in A. Theodore Brown, *Frontier Community: Kansas City to 1870* (Columbia, Mo., 1963). Brown directed the well-financed Kansas City Project, which produced a series of case studies. Los Angeles emerges in Remi Nadeau, *Los Angeles from Mission to Modern City* (New York, 1960), and has its economic development explained in Robert Fogelson, *The Fragmented Metropolis: Los Angeles, 1850–1930* (Cambridge, 1967). Robert W. Lotchin, *San Francisco, 1846–1856: From Hamlet to City* (New York, 1974), covers the early days of the city by the Golden Gate. David McComb has written a basic study, *Houston: The Bayou City* (Austin, 1969). Lyle Dorsett's *The Queen City: A History of Denver* (Boulder, 1977) supplants all previous histories of the Rocky Mountain metropolis. Gunther Barth's *Instant Cities: Urbanization and the Rise of San Francisco and Denver* (New York, 1965) deals with broader themes. His monograph compares European and American urbaniza-

tion, provides insights about the social history of western cities, and has a good bibliography. Another valuable contribution is Kenneth Wheeler, *To Wear a City's Crown: The Beginnings of Urban Growth in Texas, 1836–1865* (Cambridge, 1968).

A number of books, articles, and theses deal directly with various western urban themes. The analyses of William Gilpin's views found most helpful are Charles N. Glaab, "Visions of Metropolis: William Gilpin and Theories of City Growth in the American West," *Wisconsin Magazine of History* 45:21–31 (Autumn 1961), and J. Christopher Schnell, "Urban Promotion: The Contribution of William Gilpin in the Rise of the American West" (Master's thesis, University of Missouri–Kansas City, 1968). John W. Reps, *The Making of Urban America: A History of City Planning in the United States* (Princeton, 1965), has maps of several communities in the West. Community economic policy is examined in Glenn Dunke, *The Boom of the Eighties in Southern California* (Los Angeles, 1944); Leonard J. Arrington, *Great Basin Kingdom: An Economic History of the Latter-day Saints, 1870–1900* (Cambridge, 1958); and Charles N. Glaab, *Kansas City and the Railroads: Community Policy in the Growth of a Regional Metropolis* (Madison, 1962). A stimulating essay on the reasons cities prospered is Patrick McLear and J. Christopher Schnell, "Why the Cities Grew: A Historiographical Essay on Western Urban Growth, 1850–1880," *Bulletin of the Missouri Historical Society* 27:162–177 (April 1972). The development of one of the major ports in the West is covered in Marilyn Sibley, *The Port of Houston: A History* (Austin, 1968). Duane Smith writes about mining camps in *Rocky Mountain Mining Camps: The Urban Frontier* (Bloomington, 1967). Robert L. Branyan and I give an overview of urban services in "The Development of an Urban Civilization on the Frontier of the American West," *Societas—A Review of Social History* 1:35–50 (Winter 1971). Population patterns in a western city are traced in Howard Chudacoff, *Mobile Americans: Residential and Social Mobility in Omaha, 1880–1920* (New York, 1972). One of the few studies of the creation of a business community is Charles N. Glaab, "Business Patterns in the Growth of a Midwestern City," *The Business History Review* 33:156–174 (Summer 1959). Robert Dykstra, *The Cattle Towns* (New York, 1968), develops several western urban themes. A significant trend is explored in Bradford Luckingham, "Associational Life on the Urban Frontier: San Francisco, 1848–1856," (Ph.D. thesis, University of California, Davis, 1968). While some materials were more valuable than others, they all contributed to the final synthesis.

The study required the use of a wide variety of general and specialized works. There is much urban material in Glenn Quiett,

They Built the West: An Epic of Rails and Cities (New York, 1934). Some of the information on Oriental settlement came from Masako Herman, ed., *The Japanese in America, 1834–1973: A Chronology and Fact Book* (Dobbs Ferry, N. Y., 1973), and Betty Lee Sung, *Mountain of Gold: The Story of the Chinese in America* (New York, 1967). Jews are viewed in an urban context in Robert E. Levinson, "American Jews in the West," *The Western Historical Quarterly* 5:289 (July 1974). Franklin Walker, *San Francisco's Literary Frontier* (New York, 1939), cover literary matters, and Frank Luther Mott, *American Journalism: A History, 1690–1960* (3rd ed., New York, 1962), journalistic ones. Representative of the accounts of economic exploitation are Louis Atherton, *The Cattle Kings* (Bloomington, 1962); C. B. Glasscock, *The War of the Copper Kings: Builders of Butte and Wolves of Wall Street* (New York, 1935); and Vernon Carstensen, "The Fishermen's Frontier on the Pacific Coast: The Rise of the Salmon Canning Industry," John Clark, ed., *The Frontier Challenge: Responses to the Trans-Mississippi West* (Lawrence, 1971). There is some good Los Angeles material in Glenn Dunke, *The Boom of the Eighties in Southern California* (Los Angeles, 1944). Architectural trends are discussed in James Marston Fitch, *American Building: The Forces That Shape It* (New York, 1948); Christopher Tunnard and Henry Hope Reed, *American Skyline: The Growth and Form of Our Cities and Towns* (New York, 1955); and Vincent Scully, *American Architecture and Urbanism* (New York, 1969). Information on street surfaces can be found in Winston A. Walden, "Nineteenth Century Street Pavements" (Master's thesis, University of Missouri–Kansas City, 1967). The key book on waterworks is Nelson Blake, *Water for the Cities: A History of the Urban Water Supply Problem in the United States* (Syracuse, 1956). There is valuable data in a paper by Robert V. Percival, "Municipal Justice in the Melting Pot: Arrest and Prosecution in Oakland 1872–1910," presented at "A Conference on Historical Perspectives on American Criminal Justice," held 22–23 April 1976, at the University of Nebraska at Omaha. Urban transportation is covered in Frank Rowsome, Jr., *Trolley Car Treasury: A Century of American Streetcars—Horsecars, Cable Cars, Interurbans, and Trolleys* (New York, 1956), and George W. Hilton, *The Cable Car in America: A New Treatise upon Cable or Rope Traction as Applied to the Working of Street and Other Railways* (Berkeley, 1971). The best treatise on railroad building remains Robert Riegel, *The Story of Western Railroads* (New York, 1926). There are a number of books on specific lines, including Keith Bryant, Jr., *History of the Atchison, Topeka and Santa Fe Railway* (New York, 1974), and Richard Overton, *Burlington Route: A History of the Burlington Lines* (New York,

1965). Other transportation trends are delineated in Oscar Winther, *The Transportation Frontier: Trans-Mississippi West 1865–1890* (New York, 1964), and William E. Lass, *From the Missouri to the Great Salt Lake: An Account of Overland Freighting* (Lincoln, 1972). The finest of many works on Turner is Ray Allen Billington, *Frederick Jackson Turner: Historian, Scholar, Teacher* (New York, 1973).

Certain obscure older items have useful material. William Gilpin expounds his theories in three books, *The Central Gold Region* (Philadelphia, 1860); *Mission of the North American People* (Philadelphia, 1873); and *The Cosmopolitan Railway* (San Francisco, 1890). Samuel Bowles discusses San Francisco's leadership in *Our New West* (Hartford, 1869). *Hughes Annual Kansas City Views, 1896* (Kansas City, 1896) has some good photographs of commercial buildings. The best work on street cleaning is George A. Soper, *Modern Methods of Street Cleaning* (New York, 1909). Plumbing matters are explained in George Waring, Jr., *The Sanitary Drainage of Houses and Towns* (rev. ed., Boston, 1898). The two most worthwhile studies of municipal systems are still Charles Zueblin, *American Municipal Progress* (rev. ed., New York, 1916), and John Fairlie, *Municipal Administration* (New York, 1901). For police see Raymond Fosdick, *American Police Systems* (New York, 1920). There is sensational and colorful material on San Francisco in B. E. Lloyd, *Lights and Shades of San Francisco* (San Francisco, 1876). The story of the construction of the first bridge over the Missouri River is told by the builder in Octave Chanute and George Morison, *The Kansas City Bridge* (New York, 1870). Last but not least, an old map made it possible to piece together the western railroad net: *Map of the Kansas City, Fort Scott and Gulf Railroad Lines and Connections, 1883,* in the Kansas State Historical Society.

Index

Academy of Music: Leadville dance hall, 35

Akron, Ohio, 120

Alameda, California: Oakland's port, 118; 1880s growth, 118

Alameda County, California: Oakland seat of, 13

Albany, New York: places of amusement, 36

Alexandria, Virginia: compared with Kansas City, 6; had no parks, 56; mentioned, 73

Alton, Illinois: greatness predicted, 7

American River, 13, 109

Anaheim, California, 14

Appleton, Wisconsin, 48

Architecture: general, 47; in Western cities, 47–50

Arizona: contributed to San Francisco's population, 22; no urban population, 119–120; mentioned, 2, 103, 117

Arkansas: contributed to Kansas City's population, 23

Arkansas City, Kansas: 1880s growth, 117

Ashes: disposal of, 64–65

Aspen, Colorado: 1880s growth, 118

Astoria, Oregon: 1880s growth, 119

Atchison, Kansas: history, 11, 22; urban planning, 11, 53, 54, 56; Roman Catholic academy in, 32; railroads, 44, 99, 105; architecture, 48, 49, 60; human waste disposal, 69; water supply, 70; public health, 75, 76; fire protection, 79; police, 83, 89;

prostitution, 88; 1880s growth rate, 116; mentioned, 7, 107, 109, 120

Atchison, Topeka and Santa Fe Railroad: established operation in Topeka, 11, 12; helped Los Angeles, 44; Kansas City route to the Southwest, 100; no longer started in Atchison, 105; mentioned, 106, 107

Atchison Board of Trade, 99

Atchison Town Company: platted Atchison, 11

Atlanta, Georgia: founded as railroad town, 4

Athens, Greece, 3

Austin, Texas: extolled by booster, 5; history, 16–17; population data, 25, 26, 27, 115; voluntary associations, 34; places of amusement, 35; railroads, 44, 104; local government, 45, 137; urban planning, 52; park system, 56; streets, 59, 62; waste disposal, 63, 64, 65, 68; lack of waterworks, 70; public health, 74–75; police, 83, 89; horsecar railroads, 94; mentioned, 7, 42, 121

Axis of Intensity: explained, 3

Babylon, 3, 5, 73

Back Bay Park: in Boston, 56

Baltimore, Maryland: importance in South, 4; row houses, 49; park system, 56; garbage, 61; railroads, 102; mentioned, 3

155

Madison, Wisconsin: industrial wastes, 61; mentioned, 48

Maine: contribution to 1880 San Francisco population, 22

Malt liquor industry: in Denver, 39; in St. Joseph, 39; in Salt Lake City, 39; in Omaha, 40

Manufacturing: discussed, 37–40; in Kansas City, 40; in Omaha, 40

Market Street: San Francisco business street, 42, 50

Marshall, Texas: 1880s growth, 118

Massachusetts: contribution to 1880 San Francisco population, 22

McKim, Mead and White: architectural firm, 49

Memphis, Tennessee: yellow fever epidemic, 65; new sewers, 66

Men's clothing businesses in San Francisco, 39

Merced Theater: in Los Angeles, 49

Methodists: in San Francisco, 31

Mexicans: as Los Angeles ethnic group, 14; population of in Western cities in 1880, 26; occupations of, 27

Mexican War: Houston grew slowly prior to, 16; mentioned, 13

Midwest: dominated by Chicago, 4; contributed to Kansas City population, 22; percentage of foreign-born in cities, 25; urban female population, 27

Mile High City. See Denver

Milwaukee, Wisconsin: large numbers of Germans, 25; mentioned, 6, 48, 56, 120

Mining: consolidated by big corporations, 41

Minneapolis: railroads, 103

Minnesota: contributed to 1880 Denver population, 23

Mississippi, University of: characteristics of, 33

Mississippi River, 10

Missouri: role of citizens in Kansas settlement, 22; contributed to 1880 Kansas City population, 22–23; contributed to 1880 Denver population, 23; contributed to 1880 San Francisco population, 23; 1890 urban components, 120

Missouri Pacific Railroad: Kansas City

connection to Chicago, 100; information about, 101; Kansas service, 105

Missouri River: importance of, 6; first railroad bridge over, 9, 99, 101, 114; bridge at St. Joseph, 10; Great Curve, 11; pollution of, 64, 65, 67, 69; as source of drinking water, 70; bridge at Atchison, 99; outfitting points, 107; steamboats on, 108; trade helped some towns, 109; mentioned, 9, 10, 11, 49, 53, 76

Mobile, Alabama, 32, 48

Monarch of the West. See San Francisco

Monona, Lake: waste discharged into, 61

Montana: as Spokane trading area, 117; cattle frontier, 41; economic development, 117; population growth, 119–120; mentioned, 4

Montgomery, Alabama: ethnic composition, 25

Mormons: founded Salt Lake City, 18; number in Salt Lake City, 31; Salt Lake Tribune against, 34; control of Salt Lake City business community, 43

Mormon Tabernacle: in Salt Lake City, 35

Musicians: number in San Francisco, 36

Napa Junction, California, 105

Nashville, Tennessee: death rate, 76

"Natural Advantages": in West, 51; of Leadville, 52; of Portland, 52

Nebraska: paper towns in, 5; population growth, 10; contributed to 1880 San Francisco population, 23; political control, 41, 44; railroad network, 103; agricultural development, 117; 1880s urban population growth percentage, 120; mentioned, 1, 4, 9

Nebraska, University of: characteristics, 32

Nebraska City, Nebraska: opposed Omaha, 9; railroads, 103; 1880s growth, 118

Newark, New Jersey: sewers, 61

New Boston, Kansas: early name of Lawrence, 12

New England: role in Houston, 16, 43;

Portland, Oregon: predated regional
growth, 4; location, 7; distance to
Los Angeles, 7; history of, 14;
William Gilpin claimed founder, 14;
importance of to Willamette Valley,
14; New England attributes, 14;
population characteristics, 22, 25, 26,
27, 31; religious data, 29; education, 33; literary societies in, 33;
West Shore published in, 33; dance
halls, 36; role of New England
merchants in, 43; cast-iron façades,
49; looked like New England town,
50; favored over Vancouver, Washington, 51; natural advantages of,
51, 52; plat resembled Des Moines',
52; streets, 52, 59–60; park system,
57; tree planting in, 58; street cleaning, 62; dead animals, 64; waste disposal, 65, 69; sewers, 67; health
services, 76; police uniforms, 84;
arrests, 88; stolen property, 90; number of persons jailed, 90; horsecar
railroads, 95; houses of prostitution,
86; opium problem, 88–89; railroads,
99, 105; served by California State
Company, 107; canals, 108; steamboats helped, 109; Pacific port, 110;
once called "Linn City," 111; cultural institutions, 121; Portland's
dominant paper, 34
Poughkeepsie, New York: waterworks,
61
Power structure: analyzed in Western
cities, 41–45
Presbyterians: in San Francisco, 31
Printing and publishing: in Denver, 39;
in Galveston, 39; in St. Joseph, 39;
in Salt Lake City, 39; in San Francisco, 39; in Kansas City, 40
Privy vaults: discussion of, 67–69; dis-
posal of contents, 69
Promoters: William Gilpin, 2–3, 6; role
in Western development, 5–6; Jesup
Scott's views, 6–7; George Train, 10;
persevered despite odds, 114
Prospect Park: in Brooklyn, New
York, 47
Prostitution: in Lincoln, 86; in San
Francisco, 86; in Atchison, 88; in
Omaha, 88
Prostitution, houses of: in Leadville, 35,
86; in Dayton, Ohio, 86; in Galves-

ton, 86; in Greenville, South Caro-
lina, 86; in New Orleans, 86; in
Philadelphia, 86; in Portland, 86; in
San Francisco, 86; in Stockton, 86;
in Toledo, 86; in Virginia City, 86
Protestants: great diversity in cities, 31
Provo, Utah, 18
Public Health movement: on street
cleaning, 63; came to U.S., 90
Pueblo, Colorado: 1880s growth rate,
116; prospects of, 117; rivals of, 117

Quantrill, William C.: burned Lawrence,
12

Racine, Wisconsin, 40
Railroaders: in Kansas City, 56
Railroads: perfection of, 93; general dis-
cussion, 98–106; Atchison, 99; Lead-
ville, 99; Kansas City, 99, 100; Law-
rence, 99; Leavenworth, 99; Lincoln,
99; Los Angeles, 99; Omaha, 99, 100;
Portland, 99; St. Joseph, 99; Topeka,
99; superior transportation, 106
Railroad Street: first Houston street, 16
Reading, Pennsylvania: inadequate parks,
56; firemen, 79
Reconstruction: impact on Houston, 16
Recreation: general discussion, 34
Redding, California, 103
Red River of the North: steamboats on,
108
Religion: importance to Salt Lake City,
18; general discussion, 27–31
Restaurant workers. *See* Hotel and
restaurant workers
Richardson, Henry Hobson: famous
architect, 50
Robert Keith & Co.: building in Leaven-
worth, 49
Robidoux, Joseph: owned trading post,
10
Rockford, Illinois: no sewerage system,
61; promoters in, 121
Rocky Mountain Empire: Denver seat
of, 17
Rocky Mountains: beauty of, 2; im-
portance of, 3, 4
Rogue River: steamboats on, 109

Roman Catholic Academy: in Atchison, 32
Roman Catholic Colleges: Creighton College, 32; St. Benedict's, 32
Roman Catholics: distribution of, 29; numbers in selected cities, 29, 31
Romanesque Revival (architecture): eclectic aspects of, 49; use in West, 49–50
Romantic architecture: in Galveston, 49
Rome, Italy, 3
Rosenberg's Junction, Texas, 104
Roseburg, Oregon: railroad to Portland, 105
Row houses: in San Francisco, 49
Ruef, Abraham: San Francisco political boss, 45
Rulo, Nebraska: town failure, 103
Rutgers College: characteristics of, 32

Sabine River: Orange, Texas, on, 104
Sacramento, California: history, 13, 48; ethnic characteristics, 25, 26, 27; number of Roman Catholics, 29, 31; industry, 39; urban planning, 53; pleasure grounds, 57; waste disposal, 65, 69; sewerage, 67, 68; waterworks, 70; public health, 74; serious fires, 78; police statistics, 88; railroad connection, 105; stage line (California State Company), 107; steamboats, 109; 1880s growth rate, 115; mentioned, 4, 7, 42, 44, 120
Sacramento River: steamboats on, 109; mentioned, 13
Sailors: in San Francisco, 36
St. Barnabas School: in Omaha, 32
St. Benedict's College: in Atchison, 32
St. Joseph, Missouri: history, 10; population data, 22, 26; religious data, 31; education, 32; industry, 39, 40; leadership lacked vision, 44; early architecture, 48; beautification, 57, 58; waste disposal, 63, 64, 65, 67, 68, 69; water supply, 70; public health, 75; police statistics, 90; gas lights, 97; railroads, 99, 104–105; failure to gain bridge, 101, 102; 1880s growth rate, 115; mentioned, 7, 53, 120
St. Joseph and Des Moines Railroad, 104
St. Joseph and Western Division of the Union Pacific Railroad, 104

St. Joseph College: characteristics of, 32
St. Louis, Missouri: lost to Chicago, 4, 101; founded as fur-trading post, 4, 9; railroad to Kansas City, 9; large German population, 25; Leavenworth rail connections, 105; mentioned, 3, 6
St. Paul, Minnesota: percentage of foreign-born in 1880, 25
Sales persons: number in San Francisco, 36
Salina, Kansas: 1880s growth, 118
Salt Lake City, Utah: history, 18, 22; population data, 25, 26, 27; journals in, 33, 34; places of amusement, 35; agricultural city, 36; industry, 39; business organizations, 43; urban planning in, 54; beautifications, 57, 58; streets, 59; waste disposal, 62, 63, 68, 69; sewers, 67; no waterworks, 70; had no health board, 74; fires in, 78; gas lights, 97; railroads, 106; importance of wagon trade, 106, 107; mentioned, 7, 32, 53, 121
Salt Lake City Board of Trade: sponsored by Mormons, 43
Salt Lake City Chamber of Commerce: gentile dominated, 43
Salt Lake Theater: in Salt Lake City, 35
Salt Lake *Tribune:* gentile newspaper, 34
San Antonio, Texas: history, 16; cosmopolitan city, 25; Chinese in, 26; Mexicans in, 26, 27; religious data, 29; education, 32; places of amusement, 35; industry, 39; railroads, 44, 104; architecture, 48, 52–53; urban planning, 52–53; park system, 57; waste disposal, 63, 64, 65, 69; waterworks, 70; public health, 74, 76; police, 83, 84; 1880s growth rate, 114–115; mentioned, 4, 7, 73, 120
San Antonio Creek: Oakland dump for garbage, 65
San Antonio River, 7, 16
San Diego, California: prospects, 5; Pacific port, 110; 1880s growth rate, 116, 117
San Francisco, California: predated regional growth, 4; beat Virginia City, 5, 14; riots against Orientals, 12; vigilance committees in, 12; helped by California agricultural growth,

Silver Cliff, Colorado: 1880s population decline, 118
Sioux City, Iowa, 103
Sioux Falls, South Dakota: 1880s growth, 118
Slaughtering and packing houses: in San Francisco, 39; in Kansas City, 40; in Omaha, 40; in St. Joseph, 40
Smoky Hill Road, 106
Snake River: steamboats on, 109
Social mobility, 22
Social Statistics of Cities: material from, 124*n*
Sodom, 5
South: dominated by several cities, 4; cities more female, 27; railroads, 104
South Bend, Indiana: population data, 25
South Carolina: contributed to 1880 Kansas City population, 23
South Dakota: 1890 urban population percentage, 120
Southern California: few Spanish structures, 48
Southern California, University of, 32
Southern Overland Trail Route, 106
Southern Pacific Coast Railroad: to Santa Cruz, 103; Oakland connection, 103; to San Jose, 106
Southern Pacific Railroad: unsatisfactory to needs of Los Angeles, 15; Oakland connection, 103; San Francisco to Los Angeles, 103; to San Jose, 106; ended steamboat route, 108
South Omaha, Nebraska: 1880 growth, 118
South Park Railroad: Leadville to Denver, 106
Southwest: Hannibal and St. Joseph Railroad into, 9
Spanish architecture: few structures in West, 48
Sparta, Missouri: promotional failure, 10
Speer, Robert: Denver political boss, 45
Spokane, Washington: 1880s growth rate, 116, 117; prospects of, 117
Sports: general discussion, 34
Stanford, Leland: owned California Street Cable Railroad Company, 95
Stanfords: San Francisco family, 41

Steamboats: introduction of, 93; Missouri River statistics, 108; Pacific trade, 108, 109; use of, 108–109
Steubenville, Ohio: garbage, 61
Stevenson, Robert Louis: San Francisco quote, 42
Stockton, California: location, 7, 13; lost to San Francisco, 5; general history of, 13; settlement attempts, 13; transition before Civil War, 13; survival of, 13; steamboats, 13, 109; population data, 25, 26, 27; no challenge to San Francisco, 44; urban planning in, 53; park system, 57; tree planting, 58; character of streets, 59; street cleaning, 62; waste disposal, 63; sewage, 67; waterworks, 71; health board, 75; fires, 78; fire department, 80; police, 82, 84, 88, 89; houses of prostitution, 86; horsecar railroads, 95; railroads, 106; second rank city, 114; 1880s growth rate, 115; mentioned, 42, 60, 121
Stockton and Copperopolis Railroad: Stockton short route, 106
Stockton and Visalia Railroad: Stockton short route, 106
Street cleaning, 62–63
Streets: in Western cities, 59–60; cleaning of, 62–63; disposal of dirt, 63; paving, 63
Subways introduced, 94
Sumner, Kansas: competed with Atchison, 11
Sutter's Fort, California: Sacramento platted near, 13

Tabor Block: in Denver, 49
Tacoma, Washington: advantages of, 5; described by Rudyard Kipling, 55; planning, 55; Pacific port, 110; 1880s growth rate, 116; prospects of, 117
Tanneries: in San Francisco, 39
Telegraph: speeded transmittal of information, 93
Telegraph Hill: in San Francisco, 54
Telephone: great potential, 93
Telephone companies: discussion of, 97
Temple, Texas, 104
Tennessee: contributed to 1880 Kansas City population, 23

Terre Haute, Indiana, 120

Territorial Enterprise: published in Virginia City, 33

Texas: political control, 41; cattle frontier, 41; frontier lawmen in, 81; railroad network, 104; 1880s growth rate, 119; mentioned, 4, 7, 22, 48, 121

Texas, Republic of: Galveston, port of, 15; Austin selected as capital, 16

Texas and New Orleans Railroad, 104

Texas and Pacific Railroad: connected with Southern Pacific Railroad, 103; Dallas rails, 104

Texas Transportation Company: Houston rails, 104

Textile workers: number in San Francisco, 36

Theater Comique: in Kansas City, 35

Theaters: in West, 35

Tobacco: cigar and cigarette makers in San Francisco, 39

Toledo, Ohio: Jesup Scott's great city, 7; houses of prostitution, 86

Topeka, Kansas: history, 12; railroads, 12, 99, 105, 106; population data, 22, 23, 26; education, 32; merchants were leaders, 44; tree planting in, 58; public health, 63, 68, 69, 75; no waterworks, 70; urban planning, 53; police salaries, 82; crime related to urban progress, 84–85; mentioned, 7, 42, 121

Traders: in San Francisco, 36

Train, George Francis: as town promoter, 10; in Omaha, 43; role in West, 43

Transportation: kinds of, 93–94; water, 107–109. *See also* Railroads

Trinidad, Colorado: rival of Pueblo, 117; 1880s growth, 118; mentioned, 119

Troy, New York, 120

Tucson, Arizona: 1880s population decline, 118

Tulare, California, 103

Tulsa, Oklahoma: unimportant until 1900s, 5

Turner, Frederick J.: formulated thesis, 1–2; frontier thesis, 113–114

Turner Thesis: did not work in city, 46

Tyler, Texas: 1880s growth, 118

Tyre, 5, 6, 73

Umatilla River: steamboats on, 109

Union Pacific–Eastern Division Railroad: connections of, 17; importance to Denver, 17, 103, 114; later Union Pacific, 100; start of, 101

Union Pacific Railroad: completion date, 10; effect on Omaha, 10; town building activities of, 43; branches of, 100, 103, 105; main line, 102; connections to East, 103; construction out of Omaha, 105; did not help Lawrence and Topeka, 106

Unitas Mountain Range, 2

United States: definition of West, 2; 1880 per capita income in, 82; extent of urbanization in 1890 in, 119

United States Army: surveyed wagon trails, 107; mentioned, 35

Urban death ratios, 76–78

Urban fears, 73–74

Urban frontier: not colorful, 4; unique aspect of, 18; non-innovative, 60; inadequate sanitation practices, 71; cities followed Eastern norms, 120–121; material on, 125*n*; theories about, 131*n*

Urban governments: structure of, 45

Urban growth rates: in the West in 1880s, 114–119

Urban planning: background, 50; American practices, 51; in West, 52–55

Utah: location of Unitas, 2; importance of Salt Lake City to, 18; 1880 per capita income in, 82

Utah Northern Railroad: Salt Lake City Road, 106

Utah Southern Railroad: Salt Lake City Road, 106

Utah Territory: Salt Lake City in, 7; U.S. troops sent to subordinate, 18; contributed to 1880 Denver population, 23; 1880s urban growth rate, 120

Utah Western Railroad: Salt Lake City Rail, 106

Vallejo, California: 1880s growth, 118

Vancouver, Washington: lost to Portland, 51

Van Horn, Robert T.: Kansas City editor, 34

SURVEILLANCE IN THE STACKS

SURVEILLANCE IN THE STACKS

The FBI's Library Awareness Program

Herbert N. Foerstel

CONTRIBUTIONS IN POLITICAL SCIENCE, NUMBER 266

GREENWOOD PRESS

NEW YORK • WESTPORT, CONNECTICUT • LONDON

Library of Congress Cataloging-in-Publication Data

Foerstel, Herbert N.
    Surveillance in the stacks : the FBI's library awareness program /
Herbert N. Foerstel.
        p. cm. — (Contributions in political science, ISSN 0147–1066
; 266)
    Includes bibliographical references and index
    ISBN 0–313–26715–4 (alk. paper)
    1. Libraries and state—United States.   2. Library science—
Political aspects—United States.   3. Librarians—United States—
Professional ethics.   4. United States. Federal Bureau of
Investigation.   5. Intelligence service—United States.   6. Internal
security—United States.   I. Title.   II. Series.
Z678.2.F64   1991
025.8'2—dc20   90–38419

British Library Cataloguing in Publication Data is available.

Library of Congress Catalog Card Number: 90–38419
ISBN: 0–313–26715–4
ISSN: 0147–1066

First published in 1991

Greenwood Press, 88 Post Road West, Westport, CT 06881
An imprint of Greenwood Publishing Group, Inc.

Printed in the United States of America

The paper used in this book complies with the
Permanent Paper Standard issued by the National
Information Standards Organization (Z39.48–1984).

10 9 8 7 6 5 4 3 2

Contents

Introduction

This book was written in response to the Federal Bureau of Investigation's counterintelligence activities in libraries, the most notorious of which were conducted under the Library Awareness Program. Because I, as a librarian, make no pretense of neutrality on these ill-advised and dangerous programs, much of this book may seem unflattering to the Bureau, though such was not my intention. My library and several others around the country are presently working closely with the FBI on a case involving major thefts of patents from library collections. We see no contradiction between our cooperation on such matters and our opposition to the Library Awareness Program.

Herbert S. White, dean and professor at the Indiana University School of Library and Information Science, has written: "The confrontation between librarians, who seek to assume the maximum use of information, and security officials, for whom the ideal state may be one in which material is destroyed before anyone can read it, is as natural and instinctive as between the mongoose and the cobra. It is not only a natural conflict but perhaps a necessary one."[1] The confrontation is unavoidable because of a simple truth: Whenever the protection of rights prevents their exercise, there will be fundamental and principled conflict. In its meeting with the American Library Association's Intellectual Freedom Committee, the FBI proclaimed, "Our job is to protect the liberties. It's very near and dear to us when we are at the same time accused of violating the very things we were sworn to protect."[2] But librarians will always be suspicious of those who justify curtailing our constitutional rights in order to protect them from foreign exploitation. We lean more toward the view of James Madison: "I believe there are more instances of the abridgement of the freedom of the people by gradual and silent encroachments of those in power than by violent and sudden usurpations."[3]

Charles Levendosky, award-winning columnist for the *Casper Star-Tribune* (Wyoming), claims that the Library Awareness Program has created a new secret classification: "information for loyal Americans only." Levendosky warns: "The modus operandi of intelligence agencies is secrecy. Those who work for federal agencies like the CIA, the Intelligence Division of the FBI, and the National Security Agency should be the last people to ask to define the limitations of the rights guaranteed to American citizens by the First Amendment."[4]

In considering the library profession's unavoidable and productive struggle with the FBI over the proper balance between First Amendment rights and national security interests, some will conclude that if librarians are correct in their stand, the FBI must be faulted for its. That view may be simplistic, because this nation has always sought the resolution of complex issues through contending forces, each of which plays an essential role in revealing socially desirable solutions. We choose adversarial structures to resolve commercial, legal, or political ambiguity through the formalized struggles of management/labor, prosecution/defense, Republican/Democrat, or countless other uneasy pairs of social forces in a common search for truth. In none of these struggles can we dispense with either adversary without disastrous consequences.

Civil libertarians and law-enforcement agencies have long maintained an unofficial rivalry in defining the balance between means and ends, but recent events have virtually raised the debate between the FBI and the library profession to the status of defining First Amendment protection. Attorney William D. North has claimed: "The American library has become, in many respects, the Nation's most basic First Amendment institution. Indeed, libraries serve as a primary resource for the intellectual freedom required for the preservation of a free society and a creative culture."[5]

It is my belief that the FBI has been neither arbitrary nor capricious in pursuing its library surveillance program but has espoused and exploited unfortunate federal executive policies with respect to technology transfer and information control because they seemed to justify and support the Bureau's counterintelligence mission. My own dealings with Bureau officials like Assistant Directors James Geer and Milt Ahlerich have been cordial and mutually cooperative. But I believe that the growing federal policy to restrict information and surveil those who would use it is anti-intellectual, xenophobic, and ultimately injurious to our national security.

One of the more interesting aspects of the heavily publicized confrontation between the FBI and the library profession was the emergence of an impressive public image for librarians, previously seen as passive and politically impotent. By recounting the background and the events, the issues and the implications of the struggle between this nation's most awesome law-enforcement agency and what had been stereotyped as the nation's most "wimpish" profession, I hope to reveal a more accurate image of these two rivals and their contest for public and political support. As of this writing, the "wimps" are ahead.

In preparing this book I have received kind assistance from many sources. After my early confrontation with the Library Awareness Program, a 1988 First Amendment Award from the Playboy Foundation gave me the confidence to begin writing on the subject and the money to buy a word processor. Scott Armstrong's National Security Archive has generously provided much of the source material for this book, and Quinlan Shea, the archive's point man on the Library Awareness Program, has given me invaluable advice on the application and interpretation of these materials. Rep. Don Edwards (D-CA) has been resolute in maintaining congressional oversight of the FBI's Library Awareness Program, primarily through hearings before his Subcommittee on Civil and Constitutional Rights, exercising a restraining influence on the FBI while giving librarians like myself a public voice.

Dr. Robert Park, director of the American Physical Society's Information Office, has been the scientific community's strongest opponent of information control and has advised me on numerous aspects of this book. Hugh O'Connor, my colleague at the University of Maryland, played an essential role in forming the book's original concept and has offered important critical comment throughout the process. Similar sound advice has been provided by Charles Levendosky of the *Casper Star-Tribune*. Anne Heanue and Judith Krug of the American Library Association (ALA), like many other librarians nationwide, have provided me with important documentation on the library profession's response to the Library Awareness Program. My wife has provided the assistance and encouragement that have sustained me throughout.

NOTES

1. Herbert S. White, "Librarians and the FBI," *Library Journal*, October 15, 1988, p. 54.

2. Transcript of meeting of FBI and ALA Intellectual Freedom Committee, September 9, 1988, p. 4. Reprinted by permission of the American Library Association.

3. Saul K. Padover, ed., *The Complete Madison: His Basic Writings* (New York: Harper, 1953), p. 339.

4. Charles Levendosky, "Sign a Loyalty Oath to Get a Library Card?" *Casper Star-Tribune*, June 5, 1988, p. A12.

5. R. Kathleen Molz, *Intellectual Freedom and Privacy: Comments on a National Program on Library and Information Services* (Washington, D.C.: National Commission on Libraries and Information Science, December 1974), p. 7.

1

Library Surveillance

BACKGROUND

Dr. Vartan Gregorian, former director of the New York Public Library and current president of Brown University, has said, "Libraries are the only unifying, neutral ground for all the elements of our culture; libraries are the only tolerant institution we have in our culture."[1] Tolerance is simply a commitment to personal liberty, from which support for intellectual freedom flows naturally. Indeed, such qualities have always made librarians somewhat politically intractable, as indicated some years ago by a study showing librarians in the forefront of American support for third-party presidential candidates. This image of librarians, seldom publicly discussed, may help to explain their consistent opposition to government intrusion on intellectual freedom.

The American Library Association's Library Bill of Rights was adopted in 1939, and shortly thereafter ALA created its Intellectual Freedom Committee "to safeguard the rights of library users, libraries, and librarians, in accordance with the First Amendment to the United States Constitution and the Library Bill of Rights."[2] In 1953, when overt opposition to rampant McCarthyism was politically dangerous and therefore infrequent, a group of librarians and publishers met to consider ways to fight this virulent wave of political censorship and its threats to intellectual freedom. Out of this meeting came the Freedom to Read Statement, which encouraged librarians and publishers to make available the widest diversity of information and expression. In judging McCarthyism and the library profession's response to it, the *New York Times* commented, "To many of us, and obviously to those who drew up the Library Association's documents and those who voted to endorse them, these censors are in contempt of the most sacred traditions of American freedom."[3]

Frederick Stielow has characterized the 1960s as the most significant decade of library activism, in large part because of the growing recognition of the immense power of information and hence the potential of the library profession. When librarians and publishers sponsored a *New York Times* advertisement opposing the Vietnam War, some in the library profession questioned the propriety of taking a seemingly partisan political stand. One letter to the *Library Journal* concluded, "Let them protest, if they must, as private citizens exercising citizens' rights, but not as librarians." But the genie was out of the bottle, as librarians joined forces with the publishing industry and broadcast media, extending the profession's commitment beyond the defense of library materials to the defense of information in general. Frederick Stielow commented: "In the broadest theoretical sense, the librarians in opposition to the undeclared war in Vietnam were promoting the essence of the profession and America itself. For . . . the government had been duplicitous in its conduct of the war. In that context librarians not only hold the right—but the duty to present the issues and demand full disclosure."[4]

More recently, librarians' refusal to be good soldiers in the FBI's Library Awareness Program has caused the political right to question their patriotism. But Stielow claims that, ironically, the library profession is simply continuing a long conservative tradition: "We have an interesting role to play in society as conservatives, reinforcing American values," noted Stielow. "Our duty and responsibility as a conservative institution is to protect Americanism. Colonel North, Admiral Poindexter and the like are prime examples of people who don't realize what it means to be an American, to be part of a democracy. We should stand as the institution that guards freedom of information, and if that occasionally puts us in a position of confrontation with the government, so be it."[5]

The FBI's Library Awareness Program, the Bureau's most extended and notorious attempt at library surveillance, must be considered in the context of the many recent federal attempts to restrict information access, but the uniqueness of this program is its attempt to recruit librarians as counterintelligence "assets" to monitor suspicious library users and report their reading habits to the FBI. In the fall of 1988 Dr. Robert Park, professor of physics at the Universtiy of Maryland and public affairs director of the

American Physical Society, ridiculed the FBI's "attempts to recruit snitches at scientific and technical libraries." He stated that

behind the FBI's clumsy recruitment effort is the conviction on the part of those responsible for keeping the nation's secrets that the traditional openness of American society is a weakness—and a threat to national security and economic health. Not content to restrict access through classification, the government has attempted to keep foreigners away from information termed "sensitive but unclassified." Now it seeks to control "commercially valuable" information.[6]

At a 1989 conference on government information, the American Physical Society took the position that these government policies had shifted the front lines of the struggle over openness from conferences and publications to libraries, and that librarians were being pressured to make an unacceptable choice. "Either the librarian becomes an accomplice in withholding information, or the information is denied to everyone, citizen and alien alike."[7]

The Library Awareness Program is not an arbitrary initiative by an isolated federal agency. C. James Schmidt of the American Library Association has described the program in a larger context as "part of a systemized, coordinated inter-agency effort to prevent access to unclassified information."[8] Former CIA Deputy Director Bobby Ray Inman has explained similar domestic excesses of American intelligence agencies: "These weren't things the intelligence agencies decided, 'Gee, wouldn't that be great to do?' They all flow from decisions at senior levels of the executive branch, [telling] the intelligence community to do them."[9]

Librarians have not been unaware of these federal inclinations. In 1985, in response to the government's growing policies of information control, the Association for Research Libraries (ARL) adopted its Statement on Access to Information, which supported unrestricted access to and dissemination of information. On January 27, 1987, the ALA Council adopted its Resolution on National Policy on Protection of Sensitive but Unclassified Information, which challenged the legality of the federal policy to restrict public access to unclassified information.

The FBI's domestic intelligence activities achieved their highest visibility in the 1960s, with FBI headquarters (HQ) alone developing over 500,000 domestic intelligence files covering over 1,000,000 Americans. Few were ever charged with a criminal offense. In Chicago alone, from 1966 to 1976, the FBI employed 5,145 informants and created 7.7 million spy files on noncriminal activities of domestic groups. In the 1970s, Congress, led by the Church Committee, sought to decrease substantially the level of such activity and to establish institutional controls over future security operations. Reforms included standing intelligence committees in both houses of Congress, a proposed legislative charter for the FBI, intelligence laws, and guidelines for the conduct of intelligence investigations. But authority for domestic security intelligence programs continued to be vague and executive in nature and was not codified in a body of written law.

The FBI's surveillance of libraries, their employees, and their users is long-standing. The Bureau's recently revealed intrusions have been a part of its counterintelligence programs, but its earlier interest in libraries seemed more related to domestic security, civil disturbances, and campus unrest. During the 1960s the FBI's activities on college and university campuses became embarrassingly excessive, and by 1967, several years before the acknowledged origin of the Library Awareness Program, the visibility of the FBI's national campus activities had reached the point where the Bureau felt required to caution agents "to restrict their physical appearances on campus, to obtain authorization for on-campus interviews, . . . and to avoid contact with faculty members critical of the Bureau."[10] But this apparent policy of retrenchment represented only a decision to increase reliance upon FBI "sources" on campus. In short, the FBI opted for more campus spies.

In March 1971, in the midst of nationwide campus disturbances, over 1,000 FBI documents were removed from a Bureau resident agency in Media, Pennsylvania. These documents, which came to be known as the Media Papers, spoke of "educators and administrators who are established sources," including a switchboard operator and a file clerk at Swarthmore College, whose identities were to be protected by the FBI. Even the Swarthmore College campus police chief was identified as a source. Such FBI surveillance extended across the country, including an administrator at the University of California at Berkeley who provided file material to an FBI agent. The Media Papers revealed eighteen agents assigned to monitor Philadelphia-area colleges with a total enrollment of some 140,000 students. Files were being maintained at a variety of institutions, including community colleges and seminaries.[11] To this day the FBI has revealed little of the official history of these early campus and library surveillance programs.

Not only did FBI surveillance of libraries precede the now-notorious Library Awareness Program, but other federal agencies shared in the assault on library confidentiality. About three years before the acknowledged origin of the FBI's Library Awareness Program, the U.S. Internal

Revenue Service (IRS) had an extended confrontation with the library profession that made national headlines. In 1970 Senator John L. Mc-Clellan's Subcommittee on Investigations, formed in 1967 to probe national violence and unrest, requested that the Alcohol, Tobacco and Firearms (ATF) Division initiate a broad program to investigate suspected users of explosives. The ATF (then part of the IRS, but later established as a separate component of the Treasury Department) decided that it might be useful to examine library borrower records to see who was reading material with any relation to explosives or guerrilla warfare. Their investigations took them to urban centers across the country, cutting a swath so wide as to reveal the names of teenagers working on term papers.

Librarians everywhere resisted these encroachments by federal agents, but they were often threatened with subpoenas. In one case a librarian who refused to provide information to ATF agents was forced to comply by the city attorney's office. As in their recent response to the Library Awareness Program, the American Library Association and the National Education Association both passed resolutions denouncing the ATF investigations and called on all librarians to report any further federal requests for library records and to defend library confidentiality and intellectual freedom.

On July 29, 1970, the secretary of the treasury, David M. Kennedy, announced a change of policy: Agents would no longer be permitted to make a general search of libraries to find out who read certain books but would be allowed to investigate what books a particular suspect had checked out.[12] We will later see the disquieting similarity between this seemingly reassuring policy statement and the 1988 "conciliatory" letter from FBI Director William Sessions concerning the Library Awareness Program. In both cases the federal government was responding nervously to resolute opposition from the library profession as well as public and media criticism, and in both cases the federal government maintained its authority to encroach upon library confidentiality in the pursuit of particular investigations.

On July 16, 1970, the American Library Association issued an advisory statement warning that

the Internal Revenue Service of the Treasury Department has requested access to the circulation records of public libraries in Atlanta, Georgia, and Milwaukee, Wisconsin, for the purposes of determining the identity of persons reading matter pertaining to the construction of explosive devices. The Association is further advised that such requests were not based on any process, order, or subpoena authorized by federal, civil, criminal, or administrative discovery procedures.[13]

The ALA's statement claimed that "the efforts of the federal government to convert library circulation records into 'suspect lists' constitute
an unconscionable and unconstitutional invasion of the right of privacy
of library patrons and, if permitted to continue, will do irreparable
damage to the educational and social value of the libraries of this
country."[14] The statement concluded by recommending that each U.S.
library adopt a confidentiality policy, advise all library employees that
library records not be released except pursuant to a court order, and resist
the issuance or enforcement of such an order until a proper showing of
good cause had been made in a court of competent jurisdiction. The
ALA's Intellectual Freedom Committee subsequently used the Advisory
Statement in the introduction to its Policy on Confidentiality of Library
Records, formally endorsed by the ALA Council during its midwinter
meeting in 1971.

In July 1970 Senator Sam Ervin (D-NC), on behalf of librarians, sent a
letter to the secretary of the treasury expressing concern over these
untoward governmental inquiries. Ervin wrote, "Throughout history, official surveillance of the reading habits of citizens has been a litmus test
of tyranny." The secretary of the treasury answered Senator Ervin's letter
on July 29, 1970, claiming that the inquiries had been made "to determine
the advisability of the use of library records as an investigative technique
to assist in quelling bombings. That survey . . . has terminated and will not
be repeated." But the secretary concluded ominously that "it is our
judgment that checking such records in certain limited circumstances is
an appropriate investigative technique." On July 31, 1970, the *New York
Times* wrote: "To its watchful librarians the country owes a vote of thanks.
To itself it owes an alertness against any repetition of the IRS's deplorable
venture."[15]

On August 5, 1970, representatives of ALA and the IRS met in Washington, D.C., and issued a joint statement agreeing to develop guidelines
acceptable to both organizations. The statement concluded:

In reaching this accord, the principals recognized that due notice will have to be taken of
the individual's right to privacy as well as the agency responsibility to administer the
statutes. In the work ahead, an attempt will be made to identify areas of reconciliation
that would give the Government access to specific library records in justifiable situations
but would unequivocally proscribe "fishing expeditions" in contradistinction to the
investigation of a particular person or persons suspected of a criminal violation.[16]

The guidelines anticipated in the joint statement never appeared, and in
retrospect, ALA's attempts at "reconciliation" with a marauding govern-

ment agency seem naive. Such conciliation is unlikely in the context of the Library Awareness Program.

Still, the skirmish with the IRS had apparently raised the political consciousness of the library profession. During its annual convention in 1971, the ALA adopted a resolution supporting the right of the *New York Times* and other newspapers to print the text of the Pentagon Papers. The ALA convention also heard from Zoia Horn and Pat Rom, two librarians from Bucknell University, who described FBI surveillance within their campus community.

ZOIA HORN AND THE HARRISBURG SEVEN

In 1970 Zoia Horn was head of the Reference Department at Bucknell University in Lewisburg, Pennsylvania. The only other major institution in Lewisburg was the federal penitentiary, which at that time happened to house Father Philip Berrigan, a prominent pacifist who, with a group called the Harrisburg Seven, was awaiting trial on various charges of antiwar activism. The prison offered a work/study release program to selected inmates, and the FBI secretly exploited that program by recruiting a convict named Boyd Douglas, placing him in the neighboring cell to Father Berrigan, and arranging for him to work at Bucknell's library pasting labels on books.

While occupying the adjoining cell, FBI informant Douglas represented himself to Philip Berrigan as a fellow activist opposed to the Vietnam War, and Berrigan never questioned his motives. When Douglas would leave the prison on his work/study program, Father Berrigan would give him letters to deliver to his friend and confidant, Sister Elizabeth McAlister. Douglas would open the letters and photocopy them for the FBI.

Zoia Horn recalls that Boyd Douglas "seems to have sought me out. . . . Fr. Berrigan was by then his neighbor in the penitentiary in a part of the prison reserved for trusted inmates." Douglas would offer to take notes from Horn to Berrigan, but Horn never agreed to do this. Douglas then asked Horn to invite Sister Elizabeth and other friends of Father Berrigan to her apartment to meet with interested students and faculty. Horn says, "I was delighted. Two sisters and two priests came after a visit with Fr. Berrigan, and there was much coming and going. . . . At no time was there ever any discussion that was more than that of concerned people searching for democratic ways to effect change."[17]

Horn told me that Douglas "was always arranging meetings, and because we were a small campus in a small town, he became familiar with most of the anti-war people in the area. He told the professors and students that he was in prison for opposing the Vietnam War, but, of course, he was not there for that reason at all. Douglas was the only person I ever met in the anti-war movement who said he would use fire-arms. I said, 'Oh, come on, you must be kidding,' but he said it might be useful."[18] Horn says, "Boyd Douglas, it turned out, was an informer and *agent provocateur* for the Federal Bureau of Investigation. He smuggled and transcribed letters to Father Berrigan and attempted to instigate acts of violence."[19]

As to whether Boyd Douglas was also used by the FBI to monitor readers and reading materials in the library, Zoia Horn told me: "I don't know and probably will never know. He certainly was in a position to do so if he had wanted to. From my viewpoint, the very presence of a government informant in the library creates a chill in the atmosphere and brings up images of 'Big Brother.' "[20]

On a January morning in 1971 the FBI descended on Zoia Horn and on her library colleagues and students. She told me: "It was really like a very well-planned military mission. Two agents came to my apartment, two agents visited my reference assistant, and two others visited a pair of our students. I asked them what they wanted, and they said they could not tell me, but I would soon learn their purpose if I would answer their questions. I decided not to answer any questions, because I didn't trust the FBI at that point." Librarian Horn was given a subpoena requiring her to appear before a grand jury the next morning. She says, "I still didn't know what it was all about, nor did the other three."[21]

It was not until the evening of the grand jury's first day that Zoia Horn learned that she was involved in a conspiracy case. Father Philip Berrigan, Sister Elizabeth McAlister, several priests, and others were charged with planning to kidnap Henry Kissinger and blow up heating tunnels in Washington, D.C. (After the trial, one juror commented, "I thought the whole thing was kind of funny, the idea of a bunch of priests and nuns zipping off with Henry Kissinger.")[22]

Horn says, "We were to believe that the same priests who stood quietly in communal prayer at Catonsville waiting to be arrested for burning draft records were violent, lawless men." After Horn's lawyer negotiated immunity from prosecution (for what, she did not know), she was questioned by the grand jury. She recalls nearly two hours of questions: "What happened at this place, at that time? Who was there, what was said, who said it? What was being discussed? Who was discussing it? Whom do you recognize in this photograph? What are their names? Where did you meet them? What occasion was this?"[23]

After her interrogation before the grand jury, Zoia Horn travelled to Dallas to attend the American Library Association's annual conference, where she prepared and presented a Resolution on Government Intimidation. The resolution, approved by the ALA Council, "recognized the danger to intellectual freedom by the presence of governmental spies in libraries" and asserted "the confidentiality of the professional relationship of librarians to the people they serve."[24]

The actual trial of the Harrisburg Seven was set for January 1972, and Zoia Horn was again subpoenaed to testify. As an act of civil disobedience, she decided to answer no questions, choosing instead to hastily draft a written statement. She recalls, "At the bench the judge suggested that I think over my decision because there are dire consequences." The jury was removed, and Horn was granted permission to read her statement, which began: "Your Honor, it is because I respect the function of this court to protect the rights of the individual, that I must refuse to testify. I cannot in my conscience lend myself to this black charade." Horn's statement declared that freedom of thought, association, and speech had been threatened by "government spying in homes, in libraries, and universities [and] gatherings of friends, picnics, [and] parties." The angry judge shouted, "Take her away," and Zoia Horn was handcuffed to a chain around her waist and taken to the local county jail.[25]

Horn told me, "I was jailed for contempt of court, but it was a civil rather than criminal offense, so my incarceration could last only as long as the trial did." When I asked about her twenty days in jail, she laughed and recalled, "It was a small jail. There were twenty women, and eighteen of them were young enough to be my daughters. Some of them were prostitutes, some of them were there for drug dealing, and some of them were there for passing bad checks. I had expected to be in jail for about three months, and I was well prepared in my own mind."[26]

Aside from the simple desire to harass anyone with antiwar sentiments, why was the Bureau pursuing Zoia Horn and her library colleagues? Their involvement with Father Berrigan was superficial, and surely they could provide no useful information in his prosecution. Horn concluded, "I think what the FBI wanted to do in this crazy case was to corroborate the information that their informant, Douglas, had given them."[27]

On April 5, 1972, the jury announced that it was deadlocked, and a mistrial was declared on the original charges. However, Father Berrigan and Sister McAlister were now charged with letter smuggling in and out of the penitentiary. But since this was instigated and performed by the Bureau's own informant, even that charge was subsequently dropped.

Zoia Horn sees dangerous parallels between her ordeal and today's Library Awareness Program. "To have what is equivalent to Big Brother and the Thought Police as a presence in the library is just not permissible in this country. The library is a sacrosanct place, and the FBI has no business there. It undermines the very thing that the government is supposed to support, which is freedom of thought and speech and public debate. Librarians cannot accept the role of informants." Horn concluded: "It is so important for librarians to take a very strong stand. The government can spend an inordinate amount of time investigating people who are not criminals in any way. There is no way justice can come out of this."[28]

By 1975 the Harrisburg Seven had been freed, the Treasury Department's campaign against libraries was concluded, and librarians were virtually celebrated as media heroes. But even as these federal forces completed a strategic withdrawal, fresh troops had secretly begun a new assault on libraries through a program destined for similar controversy and popular rejection.

THE LIBRARY AWARENESS PROGRAM

In July 1986 I published an interview with then Senator Charles Mathias on the little-known but increasing phenomenon of FBI agents visiting libraries and requesting the names and reading habits of users, particularly foreign nationals. In this context I quoted to Senator Mathias the ALA Code of Ethics, which supports library confidentiality for "information sought or received and materials consulted, borrowed, or acquired." Senator Mathias responded:

That seems to be in harmony with the tenor of court opinions, which generally hold that there has to be some reasonable grounds for suspicion, rather than an indiscriminate inquiry of this kind. I think the statement you have read is in harmony with those judicial views. . . . I would be very sensitive about the effect, including diminishing use of libraries, that could result if people thought they were going to be questioned about what they had read. . . . We've been very sensitive to that sort of thing here in the Senate. In a similar area, the Defense Department has tried to restrict the authors of scholarly or scientific works from participating in conventions, seminars, or scientific meetings if they have ever received a defense grant. I believe that such restrictions would have the same stifling effect as does imposition on library privacy.[29]

At this time only a few librarians were aware of the FBI's intrusions on library confidentiality, but within a year the Bureau's Library Awareness Program was exposed nationwide. On September 18, 1987, a front-page article in the *New York Times* described an FBI visit to Columbia University in June of that year. The American Library Association had provided information on the Columbia incident to the *Times* after receiving a letter from Paula Kaufman, director of Academic Information Services at Columbia, complaining of that visit. In her letter Kaufman stated, "They explained that they were doing a general 'library awareness' program in the city and that they were asking librarians to be alert to the use of their libraries by persons from countries 'hostile to the United States, such as the Soviet Union' and to provide the FBI with information about these activities."[30]

The *New York Times* article paraphrased the FBI's description of the Columbia visit as "a Library Awareness Program that is part of a national counterintelligence effort," but this claim seemed to contradict the visiting agent's description of a "program in the city." Was there really a formal program involved here, and was Library Awareness Program its code name? Initially the FBI responded to such questions ambiguously, sometimes denying that there was any program at all and even suggesting that librarians themselves had made up the name.

On July 1, 1987, Judith Drescher, chairperson of the American Library Association's Intellectual Freedom Committee, wrote the FBI to inquire about its program. In his July 31 response, FBI Assistant Director Milt Ahlerich said, "You wrote seeking information regarding what you call the FBI's library awareness program." Apparently, at this point the FBI was unwilling to acknowledge the program name as its own, and by avoiding the use of capital letters Ahlerich was suggesting that there was no formal program at all. Ahlerich acknowledged that the Bureau's New York office (NYO) had been contacting area libraries to reduce the availability of unclassified technical information and added:

We have programs wherein we alert those in certain fields of the possibility of members of hostile countries or their agents attempting to gain access to information that could be potentially harmful to our national security. In this regard, our New York Office has contacted staff members of New York libraries to alert them to this potential danger and to request assistance. . . . The FBI relies in great measure on the willingness and cooperation of the American people to assist us in fulfilling our responsibilities, and we have found programs of these types helpful in fulfilling our goals.[31]

On August 3, 1987, the New York Library Association (NYLA) wrote the FBI expressing support for library confidentiality and opposing "the use of intimidation by government officials as a means of obtaining information about library users." The letter concluded: "In light of these

standards we are concerned about the 'library awareness' program being
conducted by the FBI in New York City."[32] NYLA formally condemned
the program in an October 1987 statement: "The Library Awareness
Program jeopardizes the rights to confidentiality of library patrons in
violation of the Library Bill of Rights and New York State Law, and . . .
the New York Library Association . . . calls on the Bureau to desist from
any further attempts to involve library staffs in reporting on library
users."[33]

Rep. Major R. Owens (D-NY), a former Brooklyn librarian, had understandably strong views on the Library Awareness Program, and his office
contacted the American Library Association on the very day that the *New
York Times* broke the story. Owens characterized the program as "a new
low for the anti-intellectualism of the Reagan administration"[34] and explained, "I have a double-barreled sense of outrage at this kind of know-
nothing intimidation by the FBI! My district faces a drug crisis of huge
proportions, about which the FBI does a very poor job, then they waste
taxpayers' money on this anti-intellectual absurdity."[35]

Shortly thereafter, Senator Paul Sarbanes told me of his strong opposition to the Library Awareness Program:

I don't think this sort of thing should occur without a court order or very strong grounds
for legal proceedings. It should never be a fishing expedition. This is a free society and
the free exploration of ideas is an essential part of a free society. . . . The library
profession's current practice of requiring a court order sounds like an appropriate response
to a situation that should not have occurred in the first instance."[36]

In October 1987 the ALA's Intellectual Freedom Committee released a
lengthy advisory statement outlining the threat posed by the FBI's program
and recommending a firm response based on existing ALA policy. The
advisory warned that libraries are not "extensions of the long arm of the
law or of the gaze of Big Brother," and it defined the role of libraries "to
make available and provide access to a diversity of information, not to
monitor what use a patron makes of publicly available information."[37]

The ALA advisory made reference to "a general library awareness
program," the FBI's descriptive term. But in subsequent media coverage
the term acquired capital letters, and even the FBI began speaking more
formally of a Library Awareness Program. Throughout this period the FBI
offered confusing and contradictory descriptions of the program. Quinlan
Shea of the National Security Archive, a Washington-based research
organization, recounts:

In September [1987], Deputy Assistant Director Fox of the New York Office called this a national counter-espionage program. In January, Deputy Assistant Director DuHadway of the Intelligence Division at Bureau Headquarters said it was limited to three cities: New York, Washington, and San Francisco. That same statement was made by Director Sessions in April, before the Senate Appropriations Committee. In May, however, before the Senate Judiciary Committee, he changed his position and said it was only in New York.[38]

During the 1988 congressional hearings on the Library Awareness Program, Rep. Don Edwards (D-CA) expressed similar confusion: "We had testimony from both the director and somebody else in the FBI that the program was also taking place in San Francisco and Washington, D.C. . . . He [the Director] said it is actually restricted to New York City although there have been other activities in connection with San Francisco and Washington. Now what do you suppose the Director meant by that?"[39]

Librarians like myself found the FBI's explanations unsatisfactory, especially the suggestion that the Bureau had been targeting only New York libraries. Two of my own branch libraries at the University of Maryland at College Park had been visited by the FBI in May 1986, and one had been the subject of FBI surveillance years before. Did the FBI have separate program names for each state? Or were they all part of a master program whose name was not being revealed?

On July 10, 1987, the National Security Archive submitted a Freedom of Information Act (FOIA) request seeking all documents relevant to the Library Awareness Program, and on August 21 the FBI responded that there were no records relevant to the request. On September 30, 1987, the National Security Archive submitted another FOIA request, this time to the FBI's New York office, reiterating its desire for all relevant documents. On October 14 the FBI admitted that its original response had been in error, that there were indeed documents available on the FBI's program, and that such documents were being forwarded to the FBI headquarters in Washington, D.C. But by April 1988 the FBI was still claiming that "no release of records was imminent."[40] On June 2, 1988, the National Security Archive filed a lawsuit arguing that the requested FBI documents were being denied without legal justification and asked the court to order their release.

Origins in the New York Office

Finally, in July 1988, after twice denying the existence of the program, the FBI released thirty-seven heavily excised pages to the National Security Archive describing counterintelligence activities by the Bureau's New

York office in the city's libraries. At the same time, Assistant Director James Geer told Congress:

FBI investigations since the early 1960s have thoroughly documented SIS [Soviet Intelligence Services] contacts with librarians in specialized science and technology libraries, SIS instructions to develop sources to steal microfiche containing specific technical reports from those libraries, SIS targeting of libraries for clandestine meetings, and SIS efforts to recruit the librarians and students associated with these libraries. In response to this effort, the New York Office (NYO) initiated an awareness program, which has come to be known as the Library Awareness Program."[41]

No mention of Library Awareness Program appeared anywhere in the NYO documents, though there were frequent references to a "Bureau-approved code name" or "Bureau code word for our investigation." Unfortunately, each occurrence of the actual code name was blacked out, but in at least one instance the number of letters in the code name was seen to be inadequate to accommodate a term like "Library Awareness Program." More recently acquired FBI documents suggest that DECAL (Development of Counterintelligence Awareness among Librarians) may have been the Bureau's code. In any case, the incidents outlined in these documents provide conclusive evidence that what was described was indeed what is today called the Library Awareness Program.

All pages were unnumbered and stamped "SECRET" or "TOP SE-CRET," and all names and dates were expunged throughout (Figure 1.1). However, in a subsequent meeting with the ALA's Intellectual Freedom Committee, FBI spokesmen revealed that the Library Awareness Program functioned from 1973 through 1976 and 1985 to date. Though the majority of each page was blacked out, the pastiche of information in the released FBI documents revealed a program proposed by the New York office, considered skeptically by FBI headquarters, but nonetheless implemented off and on in the New York City area. One document stated: "The NYO, recognizing the potential threat to our national security, has opened a case titled [deleted] 00:NY. From this control case all records regarding the above will be set forth. It is recommended that future communications relating to Soviet interest in libraries and librarians be directed to the [deleted] case as opposed to captioned case file."[42] Another of the released memos reported: "It is noted this case is maintained as a repository for information regarding KGB interest in developing librarians as sources of information. The GRU also is involved in this area."[43]

The documents reveal the NYO's initial request for headquarters approval for its library surveillance program and the HQ response that "the

Figure 1.1
Heavily Censored Page from FBI's New York Office Documents

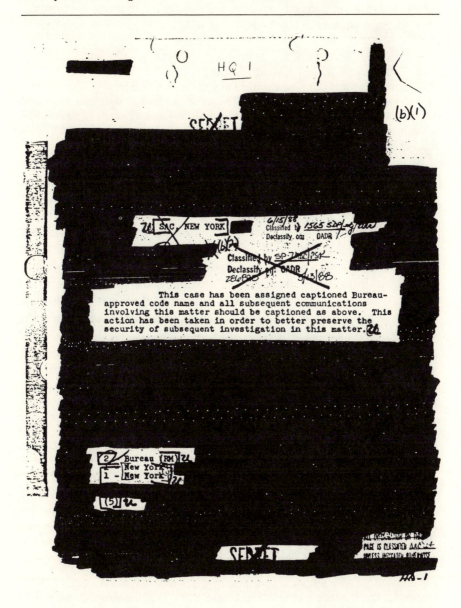

This case has been assigned captioned Bureau-approved code name and all subsequent communications involving this matter should be captioned as above. This action has been taken in order to better preserve the security of subsequent investigation in this matter.

Bureau desires that your office submit an estimate as to the approximate number of librarians who may be interviewed and the amount of manpower that might be expended."[44] The NYO then assured HQ that "it is not believed the manpower expended per case would be excessive. . . . The NYO recommends strongly the Bureau authorize implementation of this program without delay."[45] HQ responded:

The Bureau does not feel that in light of other investigative priorities the results which might be obtained warrant a substantial expenditure of manpower at this time. . . . At those libraries where there is no classified material but where there is material which is of interest to SIS, it is recognized that SIS may indeed acquire such data. In an open society, however, it is impractical to prevent all Soviet acquisition of such readily available material, and we must recognize realistic limitations in this regard.[46]

It is important to note that FBI HQ thought it impractical but not inappropriate to prevent all Soviet access to unclassified and unrestricted technical material. This pragmatic view of information control led to HQ's eventual approval of NYO's program, and to this day it remains the FBI's attitude toward denying unclassified information to Soviet citizens or, for that matter, to American citizens somehow regarded as undesirable. In any case, FBI HQ advised NYO: "Of course, where there is specific information developed concerning SIS interest in a given library, then such selective interviews of personnel of that facility would be fully warranted and will be considered on the merits of the specific case."[47]

Another of the heavily censored FBI documents described activities under the program as follows:

The librarians are apprised of this Bureau's responsibilities with regard to the protection of the U.S. They are further apprised that the technical needs of the Soviet Union can frequently be derived from any variety of publications regarding current and 'cutting edge' technologies that can be located in their facilities. If the librarian is cooperative and pursue[s] other countries of interest, the Soviet bloc countries will also be included.[48]

A subsequent "Six Month Progress Letter" affirmed:

This is a reinstituted program which attempts to Develop Counterintelligence Awareness (DECA) among those who manage special information libraries within the New York metropolitan area and have no classified contractual interest with the United States Government but have historically been the targets of recruitment and sources of information for the Scientific and Technical Branch (Line X) of the Soviet Committee for State Security (KGB).[49]

The use of the term "reinstituted" suggests that this communication may have occurred around 1985, when the Library Awareness Program resumed after a supposed hiatus.

The documents eventually summarized the program as follows:

Captioned program is maintained as a respository for information concerning SIS interest in scientific and technical libraries or librarians within the New York metropolitan area, which would not be covered by the DECA program, as well as selectively contacting specific libraries it could reasonably be assumed would be of particular interest to the SIS. Asset reportings have revealed the SIS frequently attempted to obtain information from such libraries and developed personal contacts at these libraries."[50]

Since the FBI normally uses the term "asset" to describe anyone working with or providing information to the FBI, can we conclude that some librarians in New York were cooperating with the Library Awareness Program? We will examine that question later.

The final pages of the NYO documents revealed unequivocally that the operation being described was indeed what is currently known as the Library Awareness Program: "Columbia University, Manhattan, New York, was contacted by [deleted] and advised of this program. [deleted] indicated it was Columbia University's policy not to divulge any information which would impinge on the right to privacy of any individual who might utilize their library system. [deleted] stated that neither she nor any librarian employed at Columbia would be able to assist the FBI."[51] The name excised in the first sentence is that of the FBI agent. The name excised in the final two sentences is recognizable as Paula Kaufman, the librarian at Columbia who blew the whistle on the Library Awareness Program, resulting in the September 1987 exposé in the *New York Times*. In fact, the FBI memo concluded by describing the American Library Association's complaints about the program and the resulting *New York Times* article.

Damage Control

FBI Director Sessions expressed early concern about the "negative publicity" surrounding the Library Awareness Program and claimed, "If a majority of the American public were to perceive that cooperation with the FBI is unfashionable and unnecessary, then our efforts to carry out our mandated responsibilities would be much more difficult."[52] In March 1988 Director Sessions issued a secret memo stating: "The New York Office is instructed to resume its contacts of librarians in the New York

City area to alert them to the FBI's interest in hostile intelligence services (HOIS) operations targeting libraries." Sessions told his agents to contact only those scientific and technical libraries that had typically been targeted by HOIS. To avoid further embarrassment in the media, he designated James Fox in the New York office and Milt Ahlerich, assistant director for congressional and public affairs, as the only persons authorized to discuss the program on behalf of the Bureau. Sessions emphasized, "Other FBI Special Agents should refrain from discussing [deleted] with the press," and he warned, "The New York Office should not refer to [deleted] as the Library Awareness Program."[53]

On March 22, 1988, Special Agent in Charge (SAC) William Warfield sent a secret memo to Bureau supervisors stating: "Recent media attention has been focused on the NYO's Library Awareness Program, a program designed to alert librarians of scientific and technical libraries of the interest of hostile intelligence services in their holdings." The memo repeated the "admonition" that only Assistant Director Ahlerich and James Fox were authorized to discuss the program and recommended an active role for FBI HQ in justifying the program to Congress and national library associations. The Warfield memo concluded: "Supervisors are instructed to inform all personnel that no public comment is to be made on this program, and any requests for a speaker to address library groups, classes, etc. should be forwarded to ADIC [Assistant Director in Charge] Fox without any commitment made to the requestor."[54] Indeed, with the exception of a brief series of radio and television discussions surrounding the congressional hearings in June and July 1988, the Bureau has maintained an almost complete media boycott concerning its activities in libraries.

In February 1988 the Bureau was invited to serve as a panel member at the Nassau Library System's April 11 trustee workshop. The invitation stressed, "In order to make sure that trustees receive an accurate and complete report concerning the 'Library Awareness Program,' it is extremely important that representatives from both the FBI and affected libraries have an opportunity to describe the program."[55] The Bureau declined.

The FBI's evasive action reached its most disappointing level in May 1988 when the Bureau rejected a formal request from the American Library Association for a briefing on the Library Awareness Program. Subsequently, Frederick Stielow, professor at Catholic University's School of Library and Information Science, wrote to FBI Director Sessions requesting further information on the program, claiming that there were "basic problems in communication and a lack of historical context on both sides." Stielow said that the FBI's own library staff was "well versed in the language and ethical issues of librarianship" and recommended that the Bureau form a committee of scholars, librarians, and agents to analyze the situation. Stielow concluded: "In addition to positive publicity, the latter step could prove instructive and a learning experience for both sides."[56] The Bureau declined.

At the opening of the New Jersey Library Association's December 16, 1988, workshop, the chairperson stated:

In putting together this program, "Spies in the Aisles," the most astonishing aspect was the complete absence of the adversarial position, namely the FBI. The FBI refused to participate. The Bureau was approached in New Jersey, New York, and Washington, D.C., but we could get no response. They would not admit to a definitive Library Awareness Program, provide a position paper, or cooperate in any manner. Therefore, we have taken the liberty today to include the FBI in our discussion. You will see before the podium an empty chair, and we have decided to honor the FBI by putting the name FBI on it. I hope you will keep in mind that they are here in spirit.[57]

On those few occasions where FBI agents agreed to speak in a library program, they were cautioned by headquarters to be extremely taciturn. A September 21, 1988, memo from FBI Cleveland described headquarters' authorization for a special agent to deliver a prepared speech to the Cleveland chapter of the Special Libraries Association, but the memo warned: "FBIHQ advised that the speech must not address or reference the subject of the FBI 'Library Awareness Program.' In accordance with the above advisement, SLA representative . . . was telephonically advised instant date of the above conditions, and that no question-and-answer period would follow the presentation. . . . Speaker will depart immediately following presentation."[58]

On October 31, 1988, the president of the ALA Student Chapter at Louisiana State University's library school wrote to the FBI expressing her vital concern over the Library Awareness Program, stating: "We would like to hear, first hand, your views on the need for patron disclosure. We would welcome a visit from a representative who could explain your position for us." On January 18, 1989, the FBI's Milt Ahlerich declined the invitation, saying, "We don't normally provide FBI Headquarters personnel to discuss investigative programs with university organizations."[59]

As late as December 1989, the FBI was still avoiding public discussion of the Library Awareness Program, declining to appear on the same Washington, D.C., radio show that in July 1988 had featured a debate between Assistant Director Ahlerich and myself. In that same month the editor of *Library Trends* actually asked FBI Director Sessions to submit a paper on the "ethical aspects" of the Library Awareness Program. Assistant Director Ahlerich responded for Sessions, saying that the director would be unable to furnish the requested essay.

The FBI continued to impose a low public profile on its Library Awareness Program, with the admitted hope that the entire controversy would blow over and recede from public visibility. But in July 1989 Alex Trebek, host of the popular television game show "Jeopardy," kept the issue before the public when he posed the following question to a contestant: "This Bureau's nationwide Library Awareness Program is intended to ferret out Soviet spies." The FBI must have felt that its campaign of silence had finally worked when the contestant was unable to provide the stylized answer: "What is the FBI?"

NCLIS: Secret Complicity

While attempting to isolate its critics by denying them information, the FBI rewarded its few allies in the library community through private channels. The most dramatic example of this was the Bureau's notorious "closed meeting" with the National Commission on Libraries and Information Science (NCLIS) in January 1988. NCLIS was an agency nominally representing the nation's librarians, but even before its involvement with the Library Awareness Program, NCLIS had a record of complicity with the forces of information control and a servile obligation to federal power. Formed in 1970 to inform the president and Congress on the library and informational needs of the nation, NCLIS consists of fourteen presidentially appointed members, only five of whom need be professional librarians or information specialists. Most commissioners have been businessmen, and that emphasis has been even more pronounced among those designated as NCLIS chairpersons.

On November 17, 1987, NCLIS Chairman Jerald Newman wrote Director Sessions inviting him to brief the commission on the Library Awareness Program. A recently released FBI memo admitted, "Newman also assured a representative of the FBI would be extremely well received at this meeting."[60] The Bureau's response to the invitation was enthusiastic and optimistic; one memo recommended: "It is believed that addressing the NCLIS meeting will reap favorable benefits for the FBI, and contribute to the development of counterintelligence awareness in this important area." Another memo stated: "Line X of the KGB has found the nation's libraries a safe and effective depository to complement its intelligence collection efforts. To challenge these efforts the FBI needs the complete and unwavering support of the NCLIS and of America's librarian community."[61]

On January 14, 1988, in San Antonio, Texas, NCLIS was given an official briefing on the Library Awareness Program by Thomas DuHadway, the FBI's deputy assistant director. Perhaps because the presidentially appointed commission gave DuHadway and the Bureau's controversial program an uncritical reception, it chose to keep the substance of the meeting secret from the library profession and the public at large.

None of the commissioners had been cleared to receive a classified briefing, so what could have been so sensitive in this meeting that it required such extraordinary precautions? A Freedom of Information Act request produced a partially censored transcript of the meeting, revealing the shocking details of NCLIS collaboration with the FBI's Library Awareness Program. The NCLIS proceedings proved to be a threat to good taste, not to national security.

At a particular point in the NCLIS transcript, Chairman Newman's personal attacks on the American Library Association and individual librarians were deleted under an exemption allowing agencies to withhold information that would violate personal privacy. Quinlan Shea of the National Security Archive submitted a FOIA administrative appeal of that excision, in which he stated:

It is a virtual certainty that, as a matter of law, the information on page 56 does not meet this [privacy] standard. If it did meet this standard in the context of public disclosure, the Commission would still have to release it to any persons involved. But this is not personal privacy material at all. We have a statement by the Chair of your Commission . . . at an official meeting of the Commission. If it pertains to third parties . . . it is simply not protectable under Exemption 6. This will be true no matter how derogatory Mr. Newman's comments may have been.[62]

Nonetheless, at a closed NCLIS executive meeting in October 1988, Chairman Newman convinced the commissioners to reject the appeal. Whose privacy was being protected? Not that of the librarians being attacked, but rather that of the attackers, whose indiscretions were presumably better kept private. This category of restricted information, certainly not sensitive or classified, might best be characterized as "insensitive but unclassified."

During the FBI's briefing with NCLIS, Chairman Newman gave unqualified support to the FBI but was vituperative in describing the American Library Association. Newman proclaimed: "You know the real problem, if I may say in this closed meeting, is the Intellectual Freedom Committee. . . . I will say they are the problem. They have made it look like the FBI is going after every library and they are coercing them into reporting on whoever comes in and borrows books. . . . [The FBI] is being made the scapegoat in order to give people publicity . . . for the American Library Association, and that to me is a disservice."[63]

Newman admitted, "I'm supposed to be impartial, but I am inclined on behalf of what the Bureau is doing." After telling the commission that the Soviet threat in American libraries was "rivalled only by the Red Chinese," Newman introduced a notion repeated several times at the meeting, that the traditional ethical obligations of the library profession are in conflict with patriotism and even with the Constitution. "We have the responsibility, as Commissioners, of being sure there's freedom of access [to] information, but I think we have another responsibility in upholding the Constitution of the United States, . . . which is a higher responsibility, and that includes citizens protecting our democracy and our republic." Newman said that the commission's primary concern should be to support the government's position, "since charges have been made against the FBI that could undermine their efforts to protect the security of our nation."[64]

When Commissioner Elinor Hashim, a librarian, stated, "The Constitution includes the First Amendment which librarians are really hung up [on]," Commissioner Wanda Forbes responded, "We could do with a few less librarians who are so naive in these things."[65] Commissioner Margaret Phelan chimed in: "My brother-in-law, we used to laughingly say, not laughingly but in jargon, he chased commies. He was with the FBI. He is not living, but he didn't die in the line of service, so I sort of am very partial to the FBI."[66]

Newman told the commissioners of his defense of the Library Awareness Program in an address before the Nassau County Library Association, and the angry response of the librarians. Newman concluded: "Well, when people are that rigid you can't talk to them. . . . If that indicates that I seem to favor the FBI, so be it. . . . I told you before we started . . . I don't see absolutely anything wrong with what they're doing. I mean if they're doing anything wrong, then God save this Republic."[67]

Newman continued to blame all the problems of the Library Awareness Program on the American Library Association and its Intellectual Freedom Committee in particular. When NCLIS Executive Director Vivian Arterbery suggested that the FBI might not have handled its Columbia University visit in the most professional way, Newman responded personally. "My daughter is a graduate of Barnard, which is a part of Columbia University, and . . . it just so happens that the person who blew the whistle [on the FBI] was the principal Viet Nam, anti-war person on campus. So let's understand it wasn't done in a vacuum."[68]

Newman was, of course, caricaturing Paula Kaufman, who had been a graduate student at Columbia University in 1968 and 1969. But Kaufman has stated that she never "participated or even stood around" in any of the demonstrations at Columbia. She characterized Newman's allegations as "totally irresponsible, if not defamatory," pointing out, "And even if I had been involved in the anti-war movement, what relevance does that have?" Kaufman has turned the NCLIS transcript over to the counsel's office at Columbia for possible legal action. Jerald Newman, on the other hand, has said that he will apologize if his statements about Kaufman are proved false, but he still complains that Kaufman's refusal to cooperate with the FBI is "part of a whole pattern or trend, a pattern of being anti-establishment."[69]

During the briefing one commissioner asked Deputy Director Du-Hadway why the FBI had not revealed the details of the Library Awareness Program to the public. Newman answered for DuHadway, as he did frequently throughout the meeting, saying that "the FBI does not want to talk to the general public because it reveals how much interest they do have in pursuing this program." When asked why the Bureau gave no briefing to the ALA, Newman said, "It gives them more ammunition."[70]

Commissioner Forbes then gave her prescription for patriotism: "I think we should all read a book by J. Edgar Hoover called 'Masters of Deceit.' . . . To me that opens your eyes to so much and I think that every high school student in the country should read that book." Forbes then urged the commission to oppose the American Library Association's Intellectual Freedom Committee (IFC), saying, "I would hate to think that NCLIS ever kind of pandered to the IFC."[71]

At the conclusion of the meeting, NCLIS Chairman Newman warned the commissioners:

If you are asked what went on in this meeting, all you're to say is the FBI presented its side of the story and we're analyzing it. Now I know that you will be under pressure; there are members of the ALA Intellectual Freedom Committee and the ALA themselves [who] are going to say they saw it on the agenda and they are going to say, "What went on?" We have to be big boys and girls and we have to say, "We had a closed meeting. The FBI presented their side of the story, . . . and other than that I have no comment."[72]

After the transcript of the dramatic NCLIS meeting was made public, the library profession responded with outrage and disbelief. In an editorial titled "Should Librarians Support NCLIS?" *Library Journal* expressed shock at Chairman Newman's admission of partiality toward the FBI, concluding: "It has been obvious for years that the commission will always be the captive of whatever party occupies the White House. NCLIS climbed into bed with the Information Industry Association early in the Reagan years, making a joke of its vaunted role as an 'honest broker.' Now NCLIS exhibits fundamental hostility to librarians and ALA, which has steadfastly supported it from the beginning."[73]

The *Wilson Library Bulletin* denounced the "collaborative position of the National Commission on Libraries and Information Science," and it editorialized harshly on the history of NCLIS: "Since it was organized in 1970, NCLIS does not have a distinguished record of accomplishment. . . . There are so few policy organizations concerned with information science that NCLIS was doted on mostly for what it stood for. Apparently it has not stood for much."[74]

In asking, "Where Was NCLIS?" *Library Journal* emphasized the apparent willingness of NCLIS commissioners to "pass a litmus test of party loyalty," concluding: "That mocks their much vaunted claim that NCLIS is 'an honest broker.' . . . Neither NCLIS nor its chair ever apologized for the gratuitous remarks about ALA. NCLIS has never taken a position on the FBI Library Awareness Program, even though Congress has sought advice in hearings."[75]

In a November 1988 letter to *Library Journal*, Betty Turock of the Rutgers School of Communication, Information, and Library Studies expressed grudging support for NCLIS: "Throwing out a commission because of the stupidity of some of its current members hardly gets to the heart of the matter." She instead advised: "A permanent watchdog committee should be set in place within ALA that issues periodic reviews and recommendations for improvements so that NCLIS is never again allowed to move so far from the basic values and tenets of the profession without realizing that it stands to lose the support it most needs—that of the nation's librarians."[76]

Alphonse F. Trezza, a former executive Director of NCLIS, asked: "What should we do now that we are angered and outraged by the remarks by some of the commission members on the issue of intellectual freedom (IF) and the right of privacy? The FBI policy regarding surveillance of library patrons, however vague the identification, is an affront to librarians, libraries and the association." Trezza criticized the NCLIS decision to hold a closed meeting with the FBI on so sensitive an issue as the Library Awareness Program and characterized the commission's discussion as "non focused, rambling, and, at times, incoherent. To make matters worse, some individual members of the commission made statements that were contrary not only to ALA policy but to the widely held beliefs of the professsion at large." Trezza concluded that the commissioners as individuals "have the right to be wrong, to be less than wise, and to be insensitive," but that "ALA should continue to support NCLIS, the agency."[77]

A recent commentary by Herbert S. White, dean of the School of Library and Information Science at Indiana University, captures the disappointment felt by many:

Perhaps the saddest note in all of this is sounded by NCLIS Chair Newman who weighs in on the side of the FBI with a number of sweeping generalizations about individuals who might dare to refuse to cooperate, although he acknowledges that "he is supposed to be neutral." No, he isn't supposed to be neutral. He is supposed to be on our side, on the side of the free and open use of unclassified information, and in opposition to anything that would constrain that use. That, I have long thought, is what libraries are supposed to do, and what NCLIS was established by Congress to support and defend."[78]

NCLIS Chairman Jerald Newman remains an unrepentant ideologue, despite the massive professional criticism of his conduct. He continues to defend the Library Awareness Program, which he insists "hit a raw nerve in our library community, and apparently with the Soviets also."[79]

Newman claims that NCLIS was simply "trying to be a broker between ALA and the FBI." But IFC Chairman James Schmidt concluded that ALA's relations with NCLIS had suffered because of the commission's secret involvement with the FBI and could only improve if that involvement would diminish. Schmidt described Newman's performance as "uninformed," adding that "one could express some unease at a chair of such a commission who displays so little sensitivity to the matters of great philosophical concern to the library community."[80]

After ALA President Patricia Berger mentioned at her inaugural address that NCLIS had approved of the Library Awareness Program, Newman indignantly denied the charge. While not disputing that members of the commission have agreed with the FBI's program, Newman claimed that technically the commission had not taken a position on the matter. Newman subsequently stated, "My agreement with the FBI program is not a vote of the commission. You can agree or disagree with me and I can accept that, but I don't accept it where there's distortion."[81]

Newman demanded that Berger correct in print the alleged distortion, but Berger responded with a letter reaffirming her conclusion that NCLIS had indeed endorsed the FBI's program. Berger pointed out that "most of the NCLIS commissioners who registered an opinion, including you, accepted and approved of the FBI's Library Awareness Program activities and of the Bureau's raison d'etre for that Program as well. Any other interpretation of NCLIS' posture in that meeting strikes me as transparent dissembling."[82]

Berger described as "disheartening" the NCLIS assumption that national security and First Amendment rights are mutually exclusive. She characterized the FBI's assumptions about "suspicious patrons" as seriously flawed and complained: "*It is most unfortunate* that not a single NCLIS Commissioner ever once questioned those assumptions. Instead, NCLIS appears to have embraced them whole cloth and without examination." Berger, like the rest of the library community, doubted the ability of NCLIS to function "either effectively or credibly as an 'honest broker', much less as a national leader, on library and information science matters." She concluded: "I believe if any person or entity has public explaining to do, that entity is NCLIS. More precisely, you as NCLIS Chairman owe the library profession a public explanation."[83]

The name of the commission belies its statutory remoteness from the library profession and its values. Even if one could anticipate a commission truly independent of the president, which we cannot, or an enlightened president whose appointees would represent progressive attitudes toward intellectual freedom, there would appear to be no way to avoid battle lines drawn between librarians and businessmen on the commission. Because librarians are relegated, by statute, to a minority role on the commission, their support for intellectual freedom and open access to information has often seemed incompatible with the dominant businessman's view of information as a commercial and political product to be sold, bartered, manipulated, or withheld from inappropriate eyes, foreign or domestic, depending on the economic or foreign-policy interests of the day.

In a weary gesture at its midwinter meetings in January 1989, the ALA Legislation Committee recommended that an ALA member be designated to monitor future NCLIS behavior. The proposal was accepted by the ALA Council, and the Executive Board subsequently funded a recommendation that a member of the committee monitor three or four NCLIS meetings each year. This formal expression of mistrust bordering on contempt made it hard to imagine a comfortable relationship between NCLIS and the library profession in the foreseeable future.

The ALA Board has authorized a letter to NCLIS expressing "the deep disappointment of the association at statements by individual commissioners . . . which are at best uninformed and at worst exhibit a cavalier disregard for the privacy rights of all library patrons as a fundamental ethical principle of the library profession." At ALA headquarters there was even a resolution urging Congress to zero-fund the commission, and sentiment was against a NCLIS-sponsored White House Conference on Libraries and Information Service. When the possibility of improving the commission through better appointments was considered, one ALA comment was, "We will get three more ideologues in July, and what the hell good will that do?"[84]

But recently there have been encouraging signs of change. In early 1990, Charles Reid replaced cold warrior Jerald Newman as NCLIS chairman, and there have been some strong additions to the NCLIS staff.

The most visible and significant result of these changes was the recent NCLIS statement of Principles of Public Information Policy. On April 5, 1990, the draft statement appeared in the *Federal Register*, along with an announcement of a public meeting to be held on April 30 "to elicit the views, comments, concerns, ideas and information from interested persons and organizational representatives." NCLIS Vice Chairman Lee Edwards, who had led the commission's Information Policy Committee in preparing the new statement of principles, convened the public meeting. Edwards read each of the eight specific NCLIS principles, covering everything from timely information access to the privacy of those who use it, the latter seeming to be incompatible with the FBI's Library Awareness Program. Comments were solicited from the large audience of librarians, scholars, and information specialists, and many important clarifications and enhancements were offered.

At its June 29, 1990 meeting, NCLIS unanimously adopted the final draft of its Principles of Public Information, and urged its use by all branches of Federal, state, and local government and the private sector. The Commission said the document was based on the assumption that public information is owned by the people and is held in trust by the government. There remains some doubt about whether federal agencies will heed a non-binding statement of principles. Still, such an initiative suggests the possibility of a thaw in relations between NCLIS and the library community.

The FBI Meets Congress

After the NCLIS revelations, pressure began to build to bring the FBI before Congress, a group likely to be less hospitable than NCLIS. On January 14, 1988, Brenda Brown, president of California's Marin County

Library Commission, wrote Rep. Barbara Boxer (D-CA) to express concern over the Library Awareness Program:

We vigorously protest the use of librarians as surveillance personnel to spy on library users—to identify suspicious persons from "a hostile power." The FBI would have us convert library check out counters into counterintelligence operations, snooping on library patrons who might look or sound "foreign" or have a foreign name. We believe this violates our rights protected under the First Amendment of the Constitution. We request that the House investigate this infringement of our personal freedom.[85]

In April 1988 the American Civil Liberties Union (ACLU) wrote the Senate Select Committee on Intelligence "to express our concern about the FBI's counterintelligence activities focused on the library community." The ACLU recommended: "At minimum, the Committee should request that the FBI produce guidelines and procedures on the Library Awareness Program and related activities. In addition, the existence and implementation of this FBI Program suggests that it is time for Congress to act to preserve the integrity of certain institutions, such as libraries, by imposing appropriate restrictions on intelligence gathering activities."[86]

In June 1988 the ACLU wrote to Rep. Don Edwards (D-CA) urging that he initiate an investigation of the Library Awareness Program for the purpose of requiring the FBI to (1) provide guidelines and procedures on their programs in libraries, (2) abide by state law, (3) honor the professional and ethical codes of the library community, and (4) circumscribe the scope of intelligence-gathering activities in libraries. Similarly, People for the American Way asked Edwards to request that the Bureau comply with law and ethics, adding, "In the event that the FBI refuses to comply, we would urge the Congress to take measures through the authorization and appropriations process to limit the scope of FBI intelligence gathering in our nation's libraries."[87]

Also in June, a librarian from Ouachita Baptist University wrote Edwards: "I would like to see the FBI's 'Library Awareness Program' stopped. At the very least, the program should be closely monitored by Senator Boren's Select Committee on Intelligence or Congressman Stokes' Permanent Select Committee on Intelligence. I hope that the appropriate congressional committees investigate the 'Library Awareness Program' and hold public hearings." The Georgia Library Association wrote Edwards to strongly urge his subcommittee to investigate the Library Awareness Program, concluding: "This program must be stopped, and I urge you to support the library community's efforts to curtail this insidious FBI practice."[88]

By summer 1988 Representative Edwards succeeded in organizing hearings on the Library Awareness Program before his Subcommittee on Civil and Constitutional Rights, which heard testimony from the FBI and representatives of the library community. But shortly before the first day of hearings in June, a secret FBI memo to Director Sessions stated:

For all practical purposes, Capitol Hill itself is an open area for Soviet officials, but a restricted one for FBI agents intent on continuing physical surveillance or pursuing the identity of Soviet contacts. . . . In a similar vein but less restrictive are the policy guidelines for the conduct of counterintelligence investigations upon the grounds of academic institutions. Of concern, however, is the possibility these pending hearings will result in new guidelines restricting investigative contacts in libraries and creating not a policy umbrella but a policy net. If aggressively handled, perhaps hearings and resultant publicity could serve as a platform from which to alert all librarians nationwide of the threat faced by the U.S. from hostile intelligence services.[89]

On June 20, the first day of hearings, Chairman Edwards stated that "this is a matter important enough for Judge Sessions to not only attend in a subsequent hearing, but to announce a whole program that would extirpate this noxious activity completely out of the FBI, to repudiate it in the widest audience possible." Edwards claimed that the Library Awareness Program "is simply a witch hunt for—they don't even know what." Rep. John Conyers (D-MI), a member of the subcommittee, described the Library Awareness Program in the context of other questionable FBI activities: "[W]e are being beset upon by an intelligence agency that has gone far, far afield, and in my judgment has never come back to limiting these excesses. . . . When you take it in conjunction with all of the excesses, it seems to me that we have a very, very serious situation."[90]

Witnesses testifying against the Library Awareness Program included C. James Schmidt from the American Library Association, David Bender from the Special Libraries Association, and Duane Webster from the Association of Research Libraries. In addition, Paula Kaufman and I were the witnesses representing particular libraries visited by the FBI. Schmidt told the subcommittee: "The requests of the FBI that library staff monitor and report the use of the library by any patron chills the First Amendment freedoms of all library and database users. The Library Awareness Program is a threat to the fundamental freedom of this nation. If continued, it will seriously and unnecessarily invade the intellectual life of citizens."[91]

Duane Webster characterized the Library Awareness Program as "a deliberate effort to control and intimidate library staff to cooperate in monitoring library use." He claimed, "Even the suggestion of library manipulation by such Government requests will have a frightening effect on library users. . . . Such perceptions profoundly inhibit the freedom of citizens to receive and exchange ideas." Webster said that the FBI's program would require librarians to "ascribe motives to the use of library resources and then report their judgments to the FBI. In effect the FBI is asking librarians to police the use of libraries."[92] Webster rejected this information-policing role as the antithesis of a librarian's professional code of ethics and urged Congress to take prompt action to stop the program's abuses. David Bender of the Special Libraries Association (SLA) deplored the Library Awareness Program but spent much of his testimony refuting the rumor that his organization had cooperated with the FBI and challenging the Bureau's claim that the Soviets had obtained valuable information from SLA's offices (see Chapter 3).

On July 13 the FBI had its say. Assistant Director James Geer testified in defense of the Library Awareness Program, but he also faced a lengthy question-and-answer session with the subcommittee. He attempted to rebut the earlier testimony from the library profession, complaining that "the FBI was described as looking over the shoulders of library patrons to see what they are reading. I can assure you that the FBI is not now nor has it ever been interested in the reading habits of American citizens." But Representative Conyers told Geer that his comments seemed to contradict a great deal of the previous testimony, leaving "two unreconciled positions on a subject."[93]

Chairman Edwards told Geer:

What disturbs some of us about this program is the FBI's apparent failure to recognize the special status of libraries in our society. . . . The FBI should recognize that libraries and books and reading are special. In our nation libraries are sacred institutions which should be protected and nurtured. Going into libraries and asking librarians to report on suspicious users has ominous implications for freedom of speech and privacy. Everybody in this country has a right to use libraries, and they have a right to do so with confidentiality.[94]

Edwards reminded Geer that "the words 'counter-intelligence' or 'national security' do not justify anything and everything. There have to be some limits based on the values we share as a society. One of these values is the special position we give to libraries." Edwards concluded: "I would hope that the FBI would reconsider this program, admit that it is over-broad, and get on to more productive work."[95]

When Geer was asked if he felt that there had been an "overreaction" to the Library Awareness Program by the library community, he answered: "Well, there has. I mean there clearly has. . . . I do not think if the facts at all had been understood there would have been any reaction like this. . . . I follow and agree with some of the chairman's comments about the sensitivities, but it truly did get overblown." Chairman Edwards responded: "Well, the word should certainly go from Headquarters . . . that before they get permission to move ahead with a program that has caused this much anguish . . . they had better have a very carefully, narrowly drawn charter of some sort that protects the agents, protects the office, and protects the rights of privacy and State laws." Geer answered, "Agreed."[96]

FBI Meets IFC

On March 30, 1988, C. James Schmidt, chair of the American Library Association's Intellectual Freedom Committee, wrote to FBI Director William Sessions to request that the Bureau provide a briefing for the IFC on the Library Awareness Program. Schmidt suggested that the meeting be held in July at the ALA's conference in New Orleans, saying that "such a meeting would permit both organizations to understand more fully the nature of the program, the concerns of each, and to correct such misunderstandings as may exist." Schmidt pointedly reminded Sessions of the Bureau's January briefing for NCLIS and concluded: "We thus are encouraged to expect that you will extend the same courtesy to the Intellectual Freedom Committee of the American Library Association." The anticipated courtesy was not forthcoming.[97]

On May 18, 1988, Director Sessions wrote Schmidt that "in view of our heavy commitments, it will not be possible to designate an FBI representative to meet with your Committee during July in New Orleans." On June 6 Schmidt responded to Sessions: "On behalf of the more than 45,000 members of the American Library Association, I convey our disappointment that the Bureau is unwilling to provide the briefing requested in my letter of March 30, 1988. Inasmuch as the Bureau has not previously offered to meet with the Intellectual Freedom Committee nor otherwise discussed your Library Awareness Program with us, we note with regret the passing of an opportunity to exchange information and points of view."[98]

But the pressure generated by congressional hearings on the Library Awareness Program finally forced the FBI to meet with representatives of the IFC on September 9, 1988, at the District of Columbia Public Library.

Among the librarians attending were C. James Schmidt, chair of the IFC, Judith Krug of the Office for Intellectual Freedom, the president and vice president of ALA, and ALA's legal counsel. Representing the FBI were James Geer, Thomas DuHadway, James Fox from the Bureau's New York office, and two other agents.

Both the agents and the librarians behaved with courtesy and restraint, with few confrontations and no major revelations. Geer defended the Library Awareness Program by stating: "In the 1970s, when we had this program, not one word was said about it. Nobody at this table seems to be aware that it even existed. So I've got to assume that we did it properly and we got some information that was very helpful. . . . You as a librarian may have been concerned . . . , but your patrons didn't get concerned until they started reading this in the press."[99] Geer's arguments were much the same as those he presented to Congress, but he tried to characterize the program as almost inconsequential within the overall counterintelligence obligations of the Bureau.

After the meeting, Schmidt wrote to Geer, thanking him for his participation and characterizing the meeting as "useful." Schmidt noted, "I recall that you appeared to recognize that library staff might . . . legitimately decline to respond to questions from agents which the staff determine to violate ethical, legal or policy guidelines." Finally, Schmidt commented: "I conclude by observing that while I wished for a broad agreement as a result of getting together, I did not realistically expect one, given the difference in principle which exists."[100]

In an interview with *American Libraries*, Schmidt stated: "I think it was important for both organizations to say as a matter of record that they have had a face-to-face meeting." He concluded, "We didn't learn much more from them than we already knew. . . . We heard a principled argument from them . . . and they heard a principled concern from us."[101]

The Controversy Escalates

The Federal Bureau of Investigation has tried to put the best face on it, but the Library Awareness Program has been a public-relations disaster. Despite FBI efforts at damage control, the national response to the Library Awareness Program became increasingly hostile. Judith Keogh of the Pennsylvania Library Association wrote FBI Director Sessions to protest the FBI's program, stating: "Free access to information is one of the fundamental principles of a free society. Libraries must uphold the rights of patrons to pursue information without the fear that library staff will 'spy' on them to any government agency. . . . Librarians are employed to serve the needs of their patrons, not to act as agents for the governments." Keogh quoted from an editorial in the *Philadelphia Daily News*: "Setting up a network of informants alerted to report anyone they consider 'suspicious' encourages the kind of paranoia and divisiveness which inspire just the kind of environment we deplore in countries whose 'spies' we are supposed to be protecting ourselves against—an environment in which neighbor informs against neighbor and child informs against parent." Keogh concluded succinctly: "The 'Library Awareness Program' must be ended."[102]

The Association for Research Libraries issued a statement on "Library Users' Right to Confidentiality" condemning "the efforts of any government agency to violate the privacy of library users, to subvert library patron records, and to intimidate or recruit library staff to monitor so-called 'suspicious' library patrons or report what or how any individual uses library resources. Such actions are an affront to First Amendment freedoms, individual privacy, and all citizens' right to know. These actions violate the basic tenets of a democratic society."[103]

On June 1, 1988, the Board of Trustees of New York's East Meadow Public Library wrote FBI Director Sessions expressing concern over "the reported efforts of the Federal Bureau of Investigation to recruit librarians as quasi-agents." The FBI's suggestion that librarians judge the character, motives, and national loyalties of library patrons was characterized as "ludicrous" and "anathema" to librarians. The letter, copies of which were sent to President Reagan, members of Congress, and the media, concluded:

Librarians, and library trustees, are committed to assuring that information and materials are provided to all patrons in a helpful and non-judgmental manner. Anything else is, we believe, unreasonable, intrusive, and a direct violation of a patron's constitutional rights to privacy and to freedom from governmental harassment. We urge the Bureau to develop methods of investigation and surveillance that do not involve members of this (or any) profession, and to recognize that the 'Library Awareness Program', so-called, is an ill-conceived, inappropriate, and unacceptable procedure.[104]

On July 8, 1988, ALA's Resolution in Opposition to FBI Library Awareness Program called for the immediate cessation of the program "and all other related visits by the Bureau to libraries where the intent is to gain information, without a court order, on patrons' use."[105] The resolution, committing ALA to use all resources at its command to oppose the Library Awareness Program, was sent to President Reagan, FBI

Director Sessions, NCLIS, and appropriate Senate and House subcommittees.

At the conclusion of its 1988 annual conference, the Special Library Association Board of Directors, under pressure from its membership, endorsed a statement opposing the Library Awareness Program. At its 1988 business meeting, the Society of American Archivists passed a resolution condemning the Federal Bureau of Investigation's Library Awareness Program. The Medical Library Association affirmed its commitment to the unrestricted access to information by the general public and condemned any efforts of the FBI to compromise the ability of the public to exercise its right to free access to information. Other library organizations, like the American Association of Law Libraries, passed similar resolutions.

Margaret Truman told the 1988 ALA conference in New Orleans that her father, former President Harry S. Truman, had little use for J. Edgar Hoover, but that no president dared fire him. Now, years later, Margaret Truman saw the Library Awareness Program as a "distinctly dubious surveillance operation" reminiscent of the Hoover era. She stated: "These intelligence people, whether in the CIA or FBI, never give up. They are forever trying to make informers out of us. They don't seem to understand that a country in which every citizen informs on every other citizen, and every citizen reports to the authorities, is nothing more than a police state."[106]

Margaret Chisholm, former president of the ALA, wrote, "The specter of having the FBI, or its surrogates, gazing over one's shoulder, following one through the stacks and to the photocopy machine, and making reports on database searches of items requested through interlibrary loan, must, perforce, having a chilling impact on the First Amendment rights of each and every one of us."[107] *Library Journal* presented a similarly grim indictment of the Library Awareness Program: "The FBI has hampered the free exchange of ideas by creating an unwholesome climate of fear and mistrust. The Bureau must bear the burden of having hindered intellectual advancement and slowed the enrichment and diversity of human culture."[108]

Toni Carbo Bearman, former NCLIS executive director, wrote Attorney General Richard Thornburgh to request the complete cessation of the Library Awareness Program. She called the program "ineffective, embarrassing, and controversial" and claimed that it was "eroding the privacy and freedom of library patrons in our country."[109]

The *Wilson Library Bulletin* stated:

Libraries have a much more complicated view of the world than does the bureau. We believe in building bridges, opening communications, revealing secrets. We want as much as possible known. We think it would be progress if KGB agents checked out armloads of books and kept them overdue. The KGB doesn't understand our historic role or contemporary position. We're here to divulge information, to educate, enlighten, change, and alter. We're here to scatter knowledge. Not to spy on our users but to help them surveil life.[110]

The *Los Angeles Times* said: "The idea that the FBI is asking librarians to watch and report about what people read is intolerable. . . . If the FBI has probable cause to suspect someone of spying, it can seek a court order to gain access to his library records. Otherwise, what people read is no business of the government. No fishing expeditions in libraries, please. If the Bureau won't stop this practice on its own, Congress should order it stopped."[111]

Arthur Kropp, president of People for the American Way (PAW), warned of the chilling effect of the Library Awareness Program and the Bureau's efforts to make researchers into espionage suspects. PAW concluded: "The FBI's Library Awareness Program is an affront to the intellectual freedom at the core of our open democracy, and a gross violation of citizens' constitutional privacy rights. . . . And the notion that citizens would come under suspicion based on the spelling of their names or the sound of their voice is repugnant in a free and open society."[112]

The American Association of University Professors approved the following resolution:

Freedom of inquiry is at the core of all academic endeavors. The FBI has recently admitted the existence of a Library Awareness Program under which FBI agents solicit information from librarians and others in technical and research libraries on the use of library resources by persons from certain foreign countries. . . . The Seventy-Fourth Annual Meeting condemns the FBI Library Awareness Program as an assault on the confidentiality of library records and a chill on the scholar's right to free access to libraries.[113]

At the 1988 convention of the American Federation of Teachers (AFT), the delegates resoundingly approved a resolution condemning what the convention report called "FBI efforts to turn the local library into a hospitality house for Big Brother."[114] The final resolution, introduced by the United University Professions of New York, read:

WHEREAS, the right of all individuals to full and confidential access to the unclassified materials in U.S. academic and research libraries is being undermined by an F.B.I. program innocuously labelled the Library Awareness Program, in which library staff are expected to monitor 'suspicious' library patrons and report on what or how library resources are being used; and

WHEREAS, librarians' code of ethics, as well as laws in 38 states, prohibit the disclosure of patron names in connection with requests for information; and

WHEREAS, many professional associations, such as the American Library Association, the Special Libraries Association, the Association of Research Libraries and the Research Libraries Group have spoken out in strong opposition to the Library Awareness Program; and

WHEREAS, a free and democratic society requires the uninhibited exchange of all ideas and information:

RESOLVED, that the AFT convention condemn the efforts by the F.B.I. to violate the privacy of library users and to intimidate or recruit librarians or other library staff to conspire with its Library Awareness Program, and urge the AFT to encourage public and Congressional opposition to the F.B.I.'s actions.[115]

Support for the FBI

There are librarians and scholars who would be less severe with intruding FBI agents and complicitous library employees, but they are hard to find. At a New Jersey Library Association workshop on the Library Awareness Program, Dan Figurido, executive director of the New Jersey Library Association, said, "As I see it, the FBI is not concerned with what we have in our libraries. . . . They are concerned with the person using that information. This is what they need to know. Who are the people who come to our libraries to use information that they can bring back to their countries?" Figurido claimed, "The FBI might want to know who those agents are, to identify them and stop them from obtaining that information." While admitting that librarians must serve their patrons and respect their privacy, Figurido said that the question that interested him was whether a librarian has the right to cooperate with the FBI on his own time. He concluded: "I see that the answer really comes down to a moral choice that the individual must make. Do I as a person, on my own time, willingly work with the FBI or do I not?"[116]

Bradford Westerfield, professor of international relations and political science at Yale University, took a similar position when he told a gathering of librarians, "The question, then, is, to what extent should librarians cooperate . . . to discover those Soviets that are trying to take advantage of these facilities." Westerfield proposed that "where there is no prohibiting state law, and where the job requirements are not being short-changed in order to do the spy-catching," library employees off the job should be allowed to provide information about a suspected spy. But Westerfield assured us, as did the FBI, that such counterintelligence work by librarians should be conducted only "where it is not going to create . . . massive exposés of the reading habits of ordinary Americans."[117]

This possibility of independent sleuthing by librarians fascinated Figurido and Westerfield, but it has been categorically rejected by the library profession. For example, in a 1989 article in *Library Journal*, three professionals analyzed the issue in the context of a hypothetical library employee, Michael, who claims, "I'm going to contact the agents on my own time. No one can interfere with what I do *on my own time* in my off-work hours."[118]

All three of the *Library Journal* analysts rejected the employee's claim. Martha Makosky, a public library director, said Michael was "free to talk with agents on his own time about matters that he learns about in his own private life," but she concluded, "He is *not* free to give any privileged and confidential information that he learned about as part of his library job. It makes no difference where or when he gives out the information, the differentiation is where he got the information in the first place. Information he got through his job is not his to divulge: it belongs to the library."[119]

Another of the analysts wrote, "As a professional with major management/supervisory responsibility, Michael should realize that the term 'on my own time' never applies." He concluded that if Michael chose to cooperate with the FBI in contradiction to state law and the orders of his supervisor, "his action should be treated as insubordination and handled appropriately."[120]

Within the popular press, there was virtually no editorial support for the Library Awareness Program, except in the *New York Post*. Under the heading, "Liberal Paranoia, Library Division," the *Post* stated, "America's librarians have the peculiar notion that they've struck a blow for civil liberties by frustrating FBI efforts to prevent foreign spies from plundering U.S. public and academic libraries. . . . In fact, librarians have refused even to allow the FBI to teach them how to identify possible spies . . . or monitor scientific and technical information more effectively."[121]

Aside from the editorial's easy acceptance of "monitoring" reading habits in public and academic libraries, the *New York Post* was embarrassingly uninformed in its claim: "As a result of this opposition, FBI director William Sessions has restricted the program to New York." We have seen that the Library Awareness Program had its origins in the FBI's New York office, and, by definition, all FBI operations under that program name were confined to the New York City area since the program's inception. In addition, the *Post*'s suggestion that the cavilling of intractable librarians has confined all FBI surveillance of libraries to

New York is directly contradicted by Director Sessions' official insistence that nationwide library surveillance has been and will remain a permanent part of the Bureau's ongoing counterintelligence program. Nonetheless, the *New York Post* called the library profession's response "a particularly bizarre example of library paranoia" and concluded: "It's time for the librarians to grow up. This may sound corny, but the FBI is simply asking them to do their patriotic duty. They should stop complaining and comply."[122]

A specialized government publication titled the *Employee Security Connection* was also somewhat sympathetic to the Bureau. Its editorial stated: "The FBI has been getting a bum rap from the nation's keepers of the stacks—the librarians. . . . The issue at hand is the Bureau's Library Awareness Program, in which the FBI seeks information on possible Soviet-bloc intelligence gathering by simply asking librarians to report suspicious requests by these library patrons."[123]

There were, of course, a considerable number of op-ed articles by FBI spokespersons and representatives of organizations sympathetic to the Library Awareness Program. The FBI statements tended to be almost identical to its official press releases, with little new information or personal opinion. But conservative advocates like Phyllis Schlafly, president of the Eagle Forum, were more outspoken. In an article titled, "It's Librarians' Duty to Help Catch Spies," Schlafly complained, "Unfortunately, the American Library Association is posturing with sanctimonious rhetoric about 'intellectual freedom' and 'privacy rights.'. . . To protect themselves, as well as student library users and American security, librarians should cooperate with the FBI in identifying Soviet agents."[124]

On CBS TV's "Nightwatch," Daniel Popeo, representing a group called the Washington Legal Foundation, went even further in chastising ALA spokesperson Judith Krug after she affirmed the library profession's obligation to protect the confidentiality of user records. "If I were a librarian sitting at home right now listening to you, I would be very angry. And if I were a member of your Association, I would say you do not speak for me." In defending the Library Awareness Program, Popeo claimed that "the only people who have anything to fear are the spies."[125]

It Only Hurts When We Laugh

Unlike previous assaults on library confidentiality, such as the ill-fated Treasury Department campaign described earlier, the Library Awareness

Program seemed less fearsome than ridiculous when revealed in the press. A joke made the rounds in 1988 that described an FBI agent's report to Director William S. Sessions that the Bureau had successfully apprehended six Libyans. To which Director Sessions responded, "No, no! I said librarians."

Cartoons caricaturing the Library Awareness Program have appeared throughout the national and local press, with Herblock, the dean of political cartoonists, actually lampooning the Program in two consecutive months. One cartoon showed FBI Director Sessions hiding on a library shelf among the Russian literature collection, while the other pictured a menacing FBI agent spying in the stacks as a librarian complained to the police that he was "lurking around here . . . acting kind of un-American" (see Figure 1.2).[126] Larry Wright in the *Detroit News* drew a picture of three elderly, bespectacled female librarians converging on a reader and announcing, "You're busted Mr. Foreigner! We're librarians for the FBI!"[127]

Television has taken a similarly lighthearted view of the Library Awareness Program. The CBS TV "Evening News" said, "It is the unlikeliest fight of the year—G men versus librarians, adversaries who share a penchant to work quietly in the pursuit of the truth . . . but neither side is giving an inch. . . . When it comes to quiet determination the FBI has nothing on librarians."[128]

Political satirist Mark Russell ridiculed the FBI's paranoia about library users with foreign names and accents, claiming, "So far they've arrested Henry Kissinger, Zbigniew Brzezinski, and Michael Dukakis." Russell then paid a musical tribute to the Library Awareness Program with a ditty entitled, "We're the Library Hit Squad of the FBI." The song proclaims:

> As we surround the libraries,
> J. Edgar Hoover would be pleased,
> Put back that book unless you wish to die.
> Is that an accent that I hear?
> Then we'll take your name right here,
> We're the Library Hit Squad of the FBI.
>
> Oh the Hit Squad has the power,
> It's the Bureau's finest hour,
> Since we gunned down Dillinger in '34.
> Unless the book shelves are patrolled,
> Our precious freedom is on hold.
> Let the agent search your book bag as you go out the door.

Figure 1.2
Herblock Leads the Cartoon Attack on the Library Awareness Program

© 1988 by Herblock in the *Washington Post*.

So prepare to take the blame
If you've a foreign name,
Checking books out could be treason so don't try.
I see you're checking out Ulysses,
Alright sucker, drop and freeze,
We're the Library Hit Squad of the FBI.[129]

Of course, columnists like Art Buchwald could not resist the Library Awareness Program. In a column titled, "I Was a Bookworm for the FBI," Buchwald described proper library surveillance. "Get a seat near the door. Have a copy of Richard Nixon's book in front of you and bend over and pretend you're reading it. Out of the corner of your eye, notice who comes in and what books he's reading." Buchwald reported the FBI claim that there are thousands of spooks with forged library cards manufactured in Budapest, and he said that the Bureau suggests that librarians spit on each card to see if the ink runs.[130]

The *Miami Herald* was incredulous over FBI visits to Florida's Broward County Library. "Absurd! It's just absurd for anyone to think that spies are infesting Broward's West Regional Library . . . its shelves laden with best sellers and Winnie the Pooh. . . . If it weren't so serious, the FBI's Library Awareness Program would be ridiculous." The *Herald* concluded: These FBI inquiries smack of the tactics of Joe McCarthy, that malevolent who infected the U.S. Senate 35 years ago. The FBI should sink this fishing expedition of a program—*now*. As for the libraries, thank heaven that professional librarians take seriously their duty to protect the nation's readers against such capricious invasions of privacy."[131]

Rick Horowitz wrote in the *Philadelphia Inquirer*: "The FBI has put together a cheery little something called the 'Library Awareness Program.' It's designed to step up America's effort against foreign espionage by bringing in the big guns—librarians." Horowitz advised the reader, "Chortle all you want to. Guffaw. The FBI is not amused. They may not see foreign agents lurking under your bed anymore—they're all hiding in the stacks."[132]

One writer in the *Baltimore Sun*, seeing the dubious success of the FBI's program in libraries, offered some equally absurd hunting grounds for spies, including ballet schools, barber shops, the Daughters of the American Revolution, and New York's Russian Tea Room. He admitted, "There is as yet no hard evidence of a KGB presence in the DAR, but if it could become a Russian target, why shouldn't the FBI extend its vigilance there as well?"[133]

The *Atlanta Constitution* editorialized: "The FBI's Library Awareness Program was always slightly absurd. No, the Bureau didn't dispatch agents to reading rooms to spy on patrons by peeking through holes cut in newspapers—but the project wasn't much more sophisticated."[134]

Jack Anderson wrote: "The FBI has gone too far in its search for card-carrying members of the KGB—library cards, that is. U.S. agents swagger into libraries, flash their badges and ask librarians to keep an eye peeled for patrons with foreign-sounding names and suspicious reading habits." Anderson concluded: "The mystery remains why the FBI clings to any trace of this bizarre 'counterintelligence' mission. . . . The benefits appear negligible and the program stomps all over privacy laws in 38 states, not to mention the right of people in this country to read books without being spied on."[135]

Anne Hagedorn of the *Wall Street Journal* said: "If Big Brother isn't watching you, that may be because he's spending a lot of time at the library. But Big Brother, a.k.a. your friendly FBI agent, isn't brushing up on Shakespeare. . . . He's recruiting librarians as deputies in the fight against Soviet espionage. . . . So your FBI in peace and war has leapt into action trying to enlist patriotic librarians in the War Against Illicit Research."[136]

Time magazine said that the name Library Awareness Program "sounds like a high-minded effort to get kids to check out *Huckleberry Finn*," but instead it is "spy vs spy in a battle of the bookshelves."[137] A *New York Times* editorial began, " 'I Spy for the FBI'—that's not a mystery novel but a fantastic tale of local librarians saving the nation from card-carrying enemy agents." The *Times* ridiculed the FBI's "spooks in the stacks" program but drew a serious conclusion: "Sensible librarians protest such subversion of their profession and they're right."[138]

An editorial in *USA Today* warned, "The next time you visit your library, you might find the librarian checking you out along with the books—just in case you're a Soviet spy." The editorial gave a sympathetic view of librarians' concerns, stating, "They don't want to spy on their readers, so they're asking the FBI to do its own job and leave them alone. And they're right."[139]

Even the victimized library profession was unable to overlook the comic aspects of the Library Awareness Program. Gregg Sapp, writing for the *Idaho Librarian*, said, "Ever since the FBI alerted librarians to be aware of Soviet spies in the stacks, I've been suspicious of anybody who looks just a little too Ukrainian." Sapp described his response to the Soviet threat: "In my library, I've launched an operation that I call 'Assignment Rasputin.' Our entire right-minded reference staff has agreed to deliberately give incorrect answers to anybody suspected of being, having been, or having ever known a Communist." Sapp described a suspicious phone call from someone who wanted to know the name of the U.S. secretary of state. "When I considered the potential havoc that the Soviets could wreak with such delicate strategic information, I answered without hesitation: 'Sylvester Stallone.' J. Edgar Hoover, God rest that noble man's soul, would have been proud." Sapp concluded with a warning to other librarians: "So, librarians of the free world: beware of those scheming communists who lurk in every study cubicle. . . . Hopefully the FBI will get smart and launch a counter-espionage program, and, when they do, let me volunteer to be the first librarian to infiltrate the Soviet bibliographic colossus."[140]

In December 1989 a science librarian wrote the *New York Times* in eager anticipation of hostile intelligence agents. "Of course, a spy would be noticed or even remarked on. Americans don't do science anymore. It's too hard." The letter admitted, "Meanwhile, since I am prejudiced in favor of the . . . scientifically literate, any spy who wanders into my orbit will be waited on hand and foot. There are too few customers as it is." But the librarian had no fear that FBI agents would intrude on her library. "The sight of books gives some people hives."[141]

In summing up the FBI's odd struggle with librarians, Herbert S. White claimed that "this particular battle makes the FBI look not so much nasty as silly, and that is bad for the country. We need an effective FBI, one we can rely upon." But White urged librarians and the public at large not to take the Library Awareness Program lightly, warning, "Stupidity should not be allowed to masquerade as security."[142]

The Big Chill

Shortly after the Library Awareness Program was exposed in the national press, the New York Library Association wrote to Rep. Don Edwards, warning:

Should the citizens of this nation perceive the library and its staff as a covert agency of government watching to record who is seeking which bits of information, then the library will cease to be creditable as a democratic resource for free and open inquiry. Once the people of this country begin to fear what they read, view or make inquiry about may at some future time be used against them or made the object of public knowledge, then this nation will have turned away from the very most basic principle of freedom from tyranny which inspired this union of states.[143]

Representative Edwards, himself a former FBI agent, spoke skeptically of the Bureau's purposes: "They think they can learn what the Russians are doing scientifically if they know what they are reading. But turning librarians into agents is terribly chilling. It's reminiscent of the domestic intelligence files the FBI kept for many years. I thought those bad old days were gone."[144] Edwards reflected: "One wonders what's going to happen to people who write controversial, creative works if they think they are going to be looked at by an FBI agent . . . or be reported by library employees who are working for the FBI."[145]

Indeed, as we criticize and ridicule the Library Awareness Program, we should recognize that the public's judgment of the FBI may have less ultimate impact on society than the public's altered image of libraries. What good social purpose is served if, as the result of public debate over the Library Awareness Program, the FBI is seen as a sinister intruder on library confidentiality, while simultaneously, librarians are seen as weak and possibly obliging collaborators? The traditional relationship of trust and confidence between librarians and library users is so long-standing that we tend to overlook its obvious fragility. Library patrons simply take it on faith that their reading habits will not be used to judge or embarrass them. How could it be otherwise? But that faith, nurtured by a century of unwavering library ethics, can be eroded quickly, perhaps irrevocably, by even the perception of library complicity in federal surveillance such as the Library Awareness Program. A few disturbing examples should be warning enough.

In July 1988 the *New York Times* printed a letter from a professional researcher under the heading, "Big Brother Is Reading over Your Shoulder." The researcher described how he requested back issues of a U.S. government periodical at the New York Public Library and was exasperated by a series of bureaucratic delays and intrusive questions from the librarian. The letter writer concluded that the problems he initially attributed to disgruntled civil servants were in fact evidence of the FBI's Library Awareness Program in action.[146] This episode demonstrates how a relatively trivial local library complaint became magnified and distorted into a charge of library complicity in federal surveillance.

A concerned spokesperson for the New York Public Library wrote in response, attempting to reassure the readers of the *New York Times*: "We are disturbed by the insinuation . . . that the New York Public Library or any member of its staff cooperated with the Federal Bureau of Investigation in its Library Awareness Program. . . . We do not compromise the reader's right to privacy at any cost."[147] Was the original letter writer convinced? Had a seed of doubt been planted in the minds of all New York Public Library users?

After the FBI visited the Brooklyn Public Library (BPL) in search of "suspicious activity," the chilling effect on library use in Brooklyn became apparent. On July 15, 1988, a researcher telephoned the BPL to ask for information on the proceedings of a Soviet Communist Party Congress. When the caller was told that she could come to the library and consult the *New York Times Index* for such information, she said, "If I come in and ask for that material, will you report me to the FBI?" The librarian attempted to assure the caller that she had nothing to fear, but to no avail. The caller said that she was reluctant even to send a messenger to the library for the information, because she still feared the library's complicity with the FBI. Finally, the intimidated caller declined to pursue her research, explaining, "I just don't want to get in trouble with the Government."[148]

Representative Edwards confronted the Bureau over its inability to recognize the chilling effect of its invasive library activities. "You have not measured what you are doing to freedom of speech and privacy and so forth against the panic that you are causing in this country. And it is real." In explaining the Library Awareness Program's effect on libraries, Edwards told Assistant Director Geer that "this is what happens when the word gets out, and the word is out, that you are conducting surveillance in libraries. So all kinds of imagining and fear is going to run through the libraries of this nation. . . . [O]nce something like this starts, there is no end to the panic that overtakes our precious libraries, and that is what is going on today."[149]

NOTES

1. Vartan Gregorian, President, New York Public Library, "The New York Public Library and Its Challenges," keynote speech to the American Library Association's Annual Conference, June 28, 1986.

2. Kathleen R. Molz, *Intellectual Freedom and Privacy: Comments on a National Program for Library and Information Services* (Washington, D.C.: NCLIS, 1974), p. 11.

3. Ibid., p. 13.

4. Mary Lee Bundy and Frederick J. Stielow, eds., *Activism in American Librarianship, 1962–1973* (Westport: Conn.: Greenwood Press, 1987), pp. 35, 39–40.

5. Herbert N. Foerstel, "Frederick Stielow Considers Librarians as Activists," *Crab*, May 1987, p. 9.

6. Robert L. Park, "Restricting Information: A Dangerous Game," *Issues in Science and Technology*, Fall 1988, p. 62.

7. Introductory statement by the American Physical Society, Coalition on Government Information, Washington, D.C., January 6, 1989.

46   *Surveillance in the Stacks*

8. "New Theory on FBI Program," *American Libraries*, February 1989, p. 104.

9. "Inman: Little Chance of Intentional Domestic Spying," *Christian Science Monitor*, April 17, 1984, p. 3.

10. Frank J. Donner, *The Age of Surveillance: The Aims and Methods of America's Political Intelligence System* (New York: Knopf, 1980), p. 157.

11. Ibid.

12. Ibid., p. 329.

13. "Memo to Members," *American Libraries*, July–August 1970, p. 658.

14. Ibid.

15. Molz, *Intellectual Freedom and Privacy*, pp. 25–26.

16. "Memo to Members," *American Libraries*, September–October 1970, p. 771.

17. Noel Peattie, *A Passage for Dissent: The Best of Sipapu, 1970–1988* (Jefferson, N.C.: McFarland, 1989), pp. 359–60.

18. From my interview with Zoia Horn, May 1989.

19. Peattie, *Passage for Dissent*, p. 360.

20. From my interview with Zoia Horn, May 1989.

21. Ibid.

22. Nancy Zaroulis and Gerald Sullivan, *Who Spoke Up? American Protest against the War in Vietnam, 1963–1975* (Garden City, N.Y.: Doubleday, 1984), p. 379.

23. Peattie, *Passage for Dissent*, p. 359.

24. Ibid., p. 360.

25. Ibid., pp. 357–60, 362.

26. From my interview with Zoia Horn, May 1989.

27. Ibid.

28. "FBI Asks Librarians to Help in the Search for Spies," *Philadelphia Inquirer*, February 23, 1988, p. 1A.

29. Herbert Foerstel, "Senator Charles McC Mathias—Library Friendly Legislator," *Crab*, July 1986, p. 5.

30. "Libraries Are Asked by FBI to Report on Foreign Agents," *New York Times*, September 18, 1987, p. 22.

31. Letter from Milt Ahlerich, FBI Assistant Director, Office of Congressional and Public Affairs, to Judith A. Drescher, Chairperson, ALA Intellectual Freedom Committee, July 31, 1987. October 30, 1989, FOIA release to National Security Archive.

32. Letter from Helen F. Flowers, President, New York Library Association, to John Otto, Acting Director, FBI, August 3, 1987. October 30, 1989, FOIA release to National Security Archive.

33. "The Talk of the Town," *New Yorker*, May 30, 1988, p. 24.

34. "Informer Please," *Common Cause Magazine*, November/December 1987, p. 10.

35. "A Professional and Patriotic Duty," *Library Journal*, May 1, 1988, p. 4.

36. Herbert Foerstel, "Senator Paul Sarbanes Encourages Librarians and Their 'Essential Work,' " *Crab*, January 1988, p. 4.

37. ALA Office for Intellectual Freedom, "ALA Intellectual Freedom Committee Advises Librarians on FBI 'Library Awareness' Program," October 1987, p. 3.

38. Quinlan J. Shea, speech before the American Society of Access Professionals, July 28, 1988, p. 2.

39. U.S. Congress, House Committee on the Judiciary, *FBI Counterintelligence Visits to Libraries: Hearings before the House Subcommittee on Civil and Constitutional Rights of the Committee on the Judiciary*, 100th Cong., 2d sess., June 20 and July 13,

1988 (Washington, D.C.: GPO, 1989), p. 125 (hereafter cited as *FBI Counterintelligence Visits to Libraries*).

40. Ibid., p. 339.

41. Ibid., pp. 110–11.

42. FBI memo to [deleted] from SAC, New York. Date deleted. Part of the October 30, 1989, FOIA release to the National Security Archive.

43. Handwritten FBI memo to SAC, New York from [deleted]. Date deleted. Part of the October 30, 1989, FOIA release to the National Security Archive.

44. *FBI Counterintelligence Visits to Libraries*, p. 285.

45. Ibid., p. 291.

46. Ibid., p. 292.

47. Ibid., p. 293.

48. Ibid., p. 301.

49. Ibid., p. 312.

50. Ibid., p. 322.

51. Ibid., p. 320.

52. Ibid., p. 57.

53. Memo from Director, FBI, to ADIC, New York, March 14, 1988. October 30, 1989, FOIA release to National Security Archive.

54. Memo from SAC William H. Warfield to all [deleted] Supervisors, March 22, 1988. October 30, 1989, FOIA release to National Security Archive.

55. Letter from Joseph Green, Director, Nassau Library System, to FBI Agent [deleted], February 24, 1988. October 30, 1989, FOIA release to National Security Archive.

56. Letter from Frederick J. Stielow, Co-chair, ALA/SAA Joint Committee, to William Sessions, Director, FBI, September 6, 1988. October 30, 1989, FOIA release to National Security Archive.

57. Introductory remarks by chairperson at December 16, 1988, Workshop of the New Jersey Library Association. Transcribed from video tape.

58. Memo from FBI Cleveland to Director, FBI, September 21, 1988. October 30, 1989, FOIA release to National Security Archive.

59. Letters from Theresa Campbell, L.S.U. School of Library and Information Science, to Federal Bureau of Investigation, October 31, 1988; and from Milt Ahlerich, Assistant Director, FBI, to Theresa Campbell, L.S.U. School of Library and Information Science, January 18, 1989. October 30, 1989, FOIA release to National Security Archive.

60. Memo from Director, FBI, to FBI, New York, January 7, 1988. October 30, 1989, FOIA release to National Security Archive.

61. Memos from FBI agent D. E. Stukey to Assistant Director James Geer, December 29, 1987, and January 7, 1988. September 1989 FOIA release to the National Security Archive.

62. Letter from Quinlan J. Shea, Jr., National Security Archive, to Daniel H. Carter, Commissoner and Acting Executive Director, U.S. National Commission on Libraries and Information Science, June 8, 1988, p. 3.

63. FBI presentation to U.S. National Commission on Libraries and Information Science by Thomas DuHadway, San Antonio, Texas, January 14, 1988, pp. 49, 77.

64. Ibid., pp. 1–4.

65. Ibid., pp. 35, 38.

66. Ibid., p. 42.

67. Ibid., pp. 48–50.

68. Ibid., p. 53.

69. "FBI Wanted Her to Catch Spies in Columbia Stacks," *New York Daily News*, May 1, 1988, p. 25.

70. FBI presentation to U.S. National Commission on Libraries and Information Science by Thomas DuHadway, San Antonio, Texas, January 14, 1988, p. 64.

71. Ibid., p. 76.

72. Ibid., p. 77.

73. "Should Librarians Support NCLIS?" *Library Journal*, April 1, 1988, p. 6.

74. "The Unlikeliest Fight of the Year," *Wilson Library Bulletin*, May 1988, p. 4.

75. "Where Was NCLIS?" *Library Journal*, August 1988, p. 4.

76. Betty Turock, "NCLIS: An Unbiased Assessment," letter to *Library Journal*, November 1, 1988, p. 6.

77. Alphonse F. Trezza, "In Support of NCLIS," letter to *Library Journal*, August 1988, p. 6.

78. Herbert S. White, "White Paper," *Library Journal*, October 15, 1988, pp. 54–55.

79. "NCLIS, under New Exec, Views Priorities in Atlanta," *American Libraries*, December 1988, p. 922.

80. "Transcript of Closed NCLIS Meeting Details FBI's 'Library Awareness Program,' " *American Libraries*, April 1988, p. 244.

81. "ALA President, NCLIS Chair, Tangle over FBI, Khomeini," *American Libraries*, November 1989, p. 948.

82. Letter from Patricia W. Berger, President, ALA, to Jerald C. Newman, Chairman, NCLIS, September 8, 1989.

83. Ibid. Emphasis in original.

84. "The Unlikeliest Fight of the Year," *Wilson Library Bulletin*, May 1988, p. 4.

85. Letter from Brenda Brown, President, Marin County Library Commission, to Rep. Barbara Boxer, U.S. House of Representatives, January 14, 1988. September 1989 FOIA release to National Security Archive.

86. Letter from Morton Halperin, Director, ACLU, to Senate Select Committee on Intelligence, April 21, 1988.

87. *FBI Counterintelligence Visits to Libraries*, pp. 327, 329.

88. Ibid., pp. 343, 347.

89. Memo from FBI Los Angeles to Director, FBI, May 27, 1988. October 30, 1989, FOIA release to National Security Archive.

90. *FBI Counterintelligence Visits to Libraries*, pp. 64–67.

91. Ibid., p. 13.

92. Ibid.

93. Ibid., pp. 105, 107, 124.

94. Ibid., p. 105.

95. Ibid.

96. Ibid., pp. 160–61.

97. Ibid., pp. 366–68.

98. Ibid., p. 374.

99. Transcript of meeting of FBI and ALA Intellectual Freedom Committee, September 9, 1988, p. 48. Reprinted by permission of the American Library Association.

100. *FBI Counterintelligence Visits to Libraries*, pp. 375–76.

101. "ALA Members Meet with FBI, Get Concessions on Library Visits," *American Libraries*, October 1988, pp. 743–44.

102. Letter from Judith L. Keogh, Pennsylvania Library Association, to William S. Sessions, Director, FBI, April 4, 1988. September 1989 FOIA release to National Security Archive.

103. *FBI Counterintelligence Visits to Libraries*, p. 17.

104. Letter from Margaret McCartney, President, East Meadow Public Library Board of Trustees, to William Sessions, Director, FBI, June 1, 1988. September 1989 FOIA release to National Security Archive.

105. *Memorandum*, ALA Office for Intellectual Freedom, July–August 1988, Attachment II.

106. "Margaret Truman Looks Back," *Newsletter on Intellectual Freedom*, September 1988, p. 182.

107. "People for American Way Fund Suit against FBI Library Informant Plan," *Publishers Weekly*, June 17, 1988, p. 16.

108. "Library Directions in 1988," *Library Journal*, January 1989, p. 55.

109. "More Blasts at the FBI," *American Libraries*, March 1989, p. 189.

110. "The World Is a Dangerous Place, Etc.," *Wilson Library Bulletin*, October 1988, p. 4.

111. "Librarians and Gumshoes," *Los Angeles Times*, April 25, 1988, sec. 2, p. 6.

112. *FBI Counterintelligence Visits to Libraries*, p. 339.

113. Ibid., p. 362.

114. "The FBI Library Awareness Program," *American Federation of Teachers Convention Report*, 1988, p. 51.

115. Ibid.

116. Interviews with Dan Figurido at the New Jersey Library Association workshop, "Spies in the Aisles," December 16, 1988.

117. Remarks by Bradford Westerfield at the New Jersey Library Association workshop, "Spies in the Aisles," December 16, 1988.

118. A. J. Anderson, "How Do You Manage?" *Library Journal*, June 15, 1989, p. 38.

119. Ibid., p. 39.

120. Ibid.

121. "Liberal Paranoia, Library Division," *New York Post*, November 14, 1988, p. 24A.

122. Ibid.

123. "FBI, Libraries Lock Horns," *Employee Security Connection*, Summer 1988, p. 3.

124. Phyllis Schlafly, "It's Librarians' Duty to Help Catch Spies," *USA Today*, May 24, 1988, p. 10A.

125. "Nightwatch," CBS TV News, April 29, 1988.

126. Herblock cartoons, *Washington Post*, June 7, 1988, p. A22, and July 24, 1988, p. C6.

127. Larry Wright, cartoon, *Detroit Press*, July 24, 1988.

128. Nancy Kranich, "The KGB, the FBI, and Libraries," *Our Right to Know*, Summer 1988, p. 5.

129. From Mark Russell's Public Television series, 1988 (permission by Dan Ruskin).

130. Art Buchwald, "I Was a Bookworm for the FBI," *Washington Post*, April 28, 1988, p. C1.

131. "Read It and Weep," *Miami Herald*, April 22, 1988, p. 24A. Emphasis in original.

132. Rick Horowitz, "When the FBI Decides to Go by the Books," *Philadelphia Inquirer*, March 9, 1988, p. 13A.

133. Victor T. Levine, "On the Trail for the FBI," *Baltimore Evening Sun*, July 27, 1988, p. A13.

134. "A New Chapter for FBI Library Gumshoes," *Atlanta Constitution*, November 18, 1988, p. 22A.

135. Jack Anderson, "FBI Still Checking Out Libraries," *Washington Post*, December 15, 1988, p. Md17.

136. Ann Hagedorn, "FBI Recruits Librarians to Spy on 'Commie' Readers," *Wall Street Journal*, May 19, 1988, p. 32.

137. "Spying in the Stacks," *Time*, May 30, 1988, p. 23.

138. "Librarians as Counterspies," *New York Times*, September 28, 1987, p. A24.

139. "Don't Ask Librarians to Be Spy Catchers," *USA Today*, May 24, 1988, p. 10A.

140. Gregg Sapp, "Some Editorial Thoughts . . . on Libraries and Espionage," *Idaho Librarian*, July 1988, p. 50.

141. "At Least a Spy in a Library Would Read," *New York Times*, December 5, 1989, p. 34.

142. Herbert S. White, "White Paper," pp. 54–55.

143. *FBI Counterintelligence Visits to Libraries*, pp. 348–49.

144. Hagedorn, "FBI Recruits Librarians," p. 32.

145. "Librarians Challenge FBI on Extent of Its Investigation," *Publishers Weekly*, July 8, 1988, p. 11.

146. "Big Brother Is Watching over Your Shoulder," letter from Jeff Heyman to the *New York Times*, July 22, 1988, p. A?.

147. "Public Library Preserves Intellectual Freedom," letter to *New York Times*, August 2, 1988, p. A18.

148. ALA Office for Intellectual Freedom, *Memorandum*, September–October 1988, p. 4.

149. *FBI Counterintelligence Visits to Libraries*, p. 121.

2

The FBI in Libraries: Analysis, Survey, and Prognosis

REACTIVE VERSUS PROACTIVE

Kathryn Bradford, a spokesperson in the FBI's Public Information Office, has described the Bureau's library contacts outside of New York: "Those agents are just following logical leads, which might take them into a grocery store as often as a library. It's a misconception that the FBI is swarming around libraries."[1] When James Geer defended the Library Awareness Program before Congress in July 1988, he complained of the previous testimony by librarians who "tried to equate FBI contacts of librarians outside the New York City area with an expansion of the Library Awareness Program." Geer claimed: "All FBI contacts at libraries outside the New York City area have been in response to specific investigations involving basically Soviet and Soviet bloc nationals. . . . And I would like to separate out these things because . . . we are not talking here about a nationwide FBI program."[2]

The FBI has made every effort to separate its Library Awareness Program from its general counterintelligence activities in libraries, but to the obvious irritation of the Bureau, librarians just do not seem to appreciate the difference between these two categories of library surveillance. Are librarians simply being dense, or is this a distinction without a difference? Neither. Librarians are not interested in distinguishing between the Bureau's internal program labels if the threat to libraries remains the same. Librarians judge the counterintelligence animal by its appearance and behavior. If it looks like a duck, walks like a duck, and quacks like a duck, then it is a duck, and we have no use for that bird in our libraries. But the FBI distinguishes the two programs on the basis of their purported origin, purpose, and geographical location, rather than the behavior of its agents in the field.

The FBI defines the Library Awareness Program to be a counterintelligence "awareness" program confined to New York City, all other FBI visits to libraries being "investigative" in nature and directed at particular suspects. Yet I can find little to distinguish the Library Awareness Program contacts, such as the 1987 visit to Columbia University, from the "investigative" contacts, such as the 1986 visit to the University of Maryland at College Park (UMCP). Director Sessions has told Congress:

The active approach of the Library Awareness Program, which alerts librarians generally of the Soviet intelligence service threat, should not be confused with reactive interviews of librarians in other areas of the United States which are in response to an investigative lead involving a specific Soviet national. . . . Since the FBI has no way of ascertaining the purpose of a Soviet contact . . . without interviewing those contacted, these reactive interviews are an absolute necessity in fulfilling our counterintelligence responsibilities.[3]

Sessions subsequently wrote Representative Edwards, before whose subcommitteee he had testified:

In many cases the FBI will have already identified known or suspected hostile intelligence service officers and co-optees. When the FBI needs information about the activities of such persons, it will continue to contact anyone having that information, including librarians. Such contacts will be nationwide, and such contacts will be no different from any other FBI investigation. These contacts will, however, differ from Library Awareness Program contacts in one significant respect. In the Library Awareness Program, the FBI will be asking librarians to help in the initial identification process. . . . In any other contacts with libraries, the information sought will concern specified subjects.[4]

In his written testimony before Congress, Assistant Director Geer repeated Sessions' view: "The proactive approach of this program [Library Awareness Program], which alerts librarians generally of the SIS threat, should not be confused with occasional interviews of librarians in other areas of the United States which are in response to specific investigative leads involving Soviet or other Soviet bloc nationals."[5] On the "MacNeil-Lehrer Report" Geer referred to eighteen to twenty "reactive" contacts, claiming that "each and every one of these cases outside of New York pertained to specific investigations and had nothing to do with the Library Awareness Progam."[6]

In August 1988 Rep. Louis Stokes, chairman of the House Select Committee on Intelligence, wrote to Nancy Kranich of the New York

University Libraries: "In both Library Awareness Program and other counterintelligence interviews of library officials, the Bureau often asks for information about library users in addition to whatever awareness briefings of foreign intelligence activities may be provided. Such enquiries are at the heart of the concern and confusion expressed in correspondence to the Committee." Stokes also stated that the FBI contacts with libraries outside of New York "usually relate to specific counterintelligence investigations."[7] The use of the word "usually" in Stokes' authorized statement was an admission that the FBI's fishing grounds extend across the country, further compromising the program distinctions claimed by the Bureau. Quinlan Shea, of the National Security Archive, has questioned these nationwide investigative visits: "The FBI insists that they are the result of specific 'investigative' leads. Reports from the visited librarians, however, are indistinguishable from those from librarians inside the New York area. They all look like very broad trawling expeditions to me."[8]

When James Geer and other FBI spokespersons met with the American Library Association's Intellectual Freedom Committee in September 1988, they were asked if each of these eighteen cases outside of New York involved a library staff member observed in direct contact with a Soviet. Geer explained, "In each of them it involved a specific case . . . and had nothing to do with library awareness. Now if an agent who was in there pursuing that lead chose to try to explain himself to the library by perhaps using some of the same language—I can't answer [for] that."[9] There's the rub. If FBI agents use "the same language" in pursuing both counterintelligence programs, how are librarians to distinguish between them?

Even the FBI seems unsure of the distinction. A heavily censored February 1988 FBI memo described the Bureau's visits to New York City libraries, saying, "The third case very likely had nothing to do with the Library Awareness Program, but was a routine follow-up interview as part of a contact case."[10] Very likely?

Even the number of FBI visits logged in the two FBI programs, twenty-one and eighteen respectively, are counts provided by librarians, not by the Bureau. When the IFC asked Assistant Director Geer for a specific list of FBI visits to libraries, he said that he was unable to verify particular visits or the identity of agents involved. "I could provide you with what I got from either your group, your testimony, or the media. Other than that, I don't have any kind of indices I can draw on. . . . I cannot go back without conducting a massive project."[11] I have been told that the FBI's files do not allow easy access to the names of contacted librarians, but I cannot believe that the Bureau has no log of its visits to libraries.

An IFC member told FBI representatives, "I don't understand the distinction between the Library Awareness Program and these other kinds of efforts. . . . If the only contacts under the Library Awareness Program were contacts in which the FBI had . . . specific information about Soviet interests, then how is that program any different from the general program?"[12] Perhaps exasperated by his inability to communicate the difference between the two programs, James Fox, head of the Bureau's New York office, told the IFC: "Virtually everybody, every profession across the United States, wants to help us put away the drug dealers, catch the kidnappers, eliminate these evil people, and the librarians do too. So that second program is the one that is so often confused with the Library Awareness Program. It's wrong to call the second one a program."[13] So now we have a program and a nonprogram, but the agents in both seem to act the same way.

AWARENESS VISITS: THEY LOVE NEW YORK

Columbia University

Because we are told that all Library Awareness Program visits were in the New York City area, a look at some representative FBI contacts with New York libraries should give a flavor of that program. When the *New York Times* broke the story on the program in September 1987, Columbia University was represented as the battleground on which librarian Paula Kaufman confronted the FBI. As mentioned earlier, the *Times* story quoted from Kaufman's letter, which concluded, "I explained that we were not prepared to cooperate with them in any way, described our philosophies and policies respecting privacy, confidentiality and academic freedom, and told them they were not welcome here."[14]

This dramatic confrontation had occurred on June 7, 1987, when two female agents from the FBI's New York office approached a clerk at Columbia University's Mathematics and Science Library, asking that he report on the activities of foreigners who use that library. A professional librarian overheard the conversation and told the agents that they would have to speak to Paula Kaufman, the university librarian. Kaufman has speculated that had her reference librarian not discovered the initial contact, the clerk might very well have cooperated with the agents, who were trying to make him violate or circumvent the New York State law protecting the privacy of borrower records.

A recently acquired FBI memo indicates that the agents arranged a June 8 meeting at which they explained that librarians were often targets of intelligence officers who seek "unclassified, publicly available information relating more often than not to science and technical matters." The agents told Kaufman that "singular information may be of little value, however, a compilation of these materials often assist these countries in their research programs." The memo recounts: "Kaufman informed the agents that if the FBI wanted any information from Columbia University regarding its library users, a court order would be necessary.... While Kaufman was not rude or hostile to the agents, she was emphatic that she was not willing to cooperate with the FBI on this matter.... The agents felt that continuing the interview would serve no useful purpose at that time."[15]

During the July 1988 hearings before the House Subcommittee on Civil and Constitutional Rights, Paula Kaufman described the behavior of the FBI agents during their Columbia visits:

They asked us to report on who was reading what, and I refused to cooperate with them. ... They explained that libraries such as ours were often used by the KGB and other intelligence agents for recruiting activities. Citing the Zakharov case as an example, the agents warned that students and librarians, "who are traditionally underpaid," are the primary targets of these recruiting efforts. I continued to refuse to spy on our readers.[16]

In her testimony Kaufman reflected on the ethical quandary posed by the Bureau's inquiries:

The FBI's request to me to report on foreigners using our libraries is one with which I could not practically comply, even if our institution supported such cooperation, which it does not; even if such a request did not contravene my professional ethics, which it does; even if it did not infringe upon the First Amendment and privacy rights of all library patrons, which it does; and even if it does not violate the laws of the State of New York, which it does. The academic community, indeed, American society, includes persons with a variety of backgrounds, interests, and nationalities. The FBI's definition of "foreigners" is sufficiently vague, and the environment at Columbia is sufficiently international, that it becomes patently absurd to even think about how one is to identify possible spies from among our general population. Zbigniew Brzezinski, for example, who is a member of our faculty . . . , could easily fit that definition. . . . We should be looking for ways to acquire more materials on our shelves, rather than for ways to interfere with the use of what we already own.[17]

Kaufman concluded by calling upon the FBI to "end the Library Awareness Program and to desist from recruiting librarians and library staff to monitor patrons' use of libraries."[18]

Kaufman's brief but resolute encounter with the FBI earned her unexpected notoriety in the press and the well-deserved applause of librarians and libertarians. But while serving as a heroine to her peers, she was every bit the villain in the eyes of the intelligence community and its supporters. During his briefing with the National Commission on Libraries and Information Science, Deputy Assistant Director Tom DuHadway claimed that the FBI's library visits had been received very favorably by librarians, "with one exception." That one exception was, supposedly, Paula Kaufman. DuHadway insisted that even at Columbia there had been no problems, except that "we evidently struck a chord with one librarian who thought this was atrocious and said she would not cooperate, and she said it's a violation of the First Amendment and I'm going to call the Intellectual Freedom Committee at the American Library Association and she's gotten on a letter writing campaign." DuHadway referred to Paula Kaufman as "that person who wrote these letters," and he insisted that "we're not going to back away . . . at Columbia University." DuHadway attributed the FBI's lack of success at Columbia to Paula Kaufman's bad temper and the consequent difficulty in "talking to people like that," claiming that such people are "not going to make a whole lot of sense."[19]

New York University

Though the FBI intrusion on Columbia University captured most of the New York headlines, it was only one of several Bureau confrontations with libraries in the Big Apple. Nancy Gubman, head librarian at New York University's Courant Institute of Mathematical Sciences Library, told me: "In the spring of 1986, an FBI man came in and told me they were looking at the technical libraries in New York. He said one of every three U.N. delegates from the Soviet Union are spies, and wanted to know if any Soviets have come in asking for sensitive information, unusual database searches or large photocopying requests."[20] Gubman says that she was stunned and told the agent that she would not monitor library users and therefore could not help him.

Gubman told the agent that everything in the library was unclassified and available to the general public. But the agent claimed that though the materials were unclassified, some items might be "more sensitive than general library materials," particularly when organized through data-base searches. Gubman advised him that the Courant Institute only did data-base searches for its students and faculty, and in any case, the data bases contained only publicly available information. When the agent asked about photocopying, Gubman told him it was self-service and coin-operated, adding, "Anyone who can use the library can use the photocopier, and we're not going to place a camera under it." Gubman says that the agent warned her that the Soviets might offer to pay a student or a staff member to do photocopying for him, perhaps "paying five dollars for a 50 cent job, thereby establishing a rapport with him."[21] But she assured the agent that such devices were not being employed there.

Perhaps because the NYU visit predated the notorious incident at Columbia University that brought the Library Awareness Program to national attention, the visiting agent made no mention of the Bureau's program name, but today the visit is acknowledged as part of the Library Awareness Program. Gubman told me: "About two months later I received a call from another FBI agent asking if I had anything to report on 'you know what.' That was the expression he used. I said no, there's nothing to report, and there won't be anything. That was the last I heard from them."[22]

A recently released FBI memo described the Bureau's visit to NYU as a "[deleted] Program approach for GRU officers" and claimed that Gubman "did not recall any Soviet contact." The memo concluded, "No unusual problems were encountered and no assets developed."[23]

In May 1988, shortly before the congressional hearings on the Library Awareness Program, Nancy Kranich, director of public and administrative services at NYU, wrote subcommittee chairman Don Edwards recounting the incident at NYU:

The agent asked the librarian if there were members of the Soviet mission to the United Nations who requested sensitive information available through online databases or copied large amounts of unusual types of information. . . . The librarian responded to the agent's request by explaining that the administration, faculty, and students of New York University are outraged at this incident and the prospect of future FBI visits. We simply do not wish to have our readers feel that they may be under surveillance by intelligence agents. Furthermore, we want to assure all library users of their right to read freely and to explore ideas without question of their motives. At New York University we believe this type of invasion into the privacy of the American public is an unwarranted threat to our civil liberties.[24]

Joseph Murphy, chancellor of the City University of New York, condemned the Library Awareness Program in a press release, stating: "Covert surveillance activities have no place in college libraries or any other library. I share the outrage of the city's librarians who regard it as unconscionable that they should be asked to serve as informants for the FBI as part of their professional duties."[25]

NYPL and BPL

We should not ignore New York's public libraries, because the FBI certainly did not. When the *New York Times* exposed the Library Awareness Program, the public-relations director of the New York Public Library (NYPL) said that she knew of no FBI contacts with NYPL staff. But it was subsequently learned that in the spring of 1987 an FBI agent inquired about a particular library user at NYPL's Economics and Public Affairs Division. The agents returned on November 24, this time inquiring about former NYPL employees. In meetings with top NYPL officials, FBI agents insisted that the Library Awareness Program had been misrepresented, but the Bureau was nonetheless denied confidential library information.

The FBI apparently pursued its investigation of NYPL staff beyond the confines of the library. The Bureau's investigative interest in Fernando Clark, a NYPL employee, began after Clark discussed the library's ongoing exchange program with a Cuban diplomat. Subsequently, two FBI agents appeared unannounced at Clark's Bronx apartment, inquiring about materials donated to NYPL by the Cuban Mission to the United Nations. An interview with Clark on ABC TV's "Nightline" revealed the nature of the FBI's investigation.

Clark: They say they got pictures of me.

Nightline: Pictures taken where?

Clark: In the library.

Nightline: Here in the NYPL?

Clark: Right. And they got a telephone conversation. So then I started to get very intimidated and I was angry.[26]

Apparently the FBI had photographed Clark inside the library with the Cuban diplomat and taped his office calls to the United Nations, though the Bureau has strongly denied this. Clark immediately reported the incident to the library administration, and one member of the library's senior policy group was quoted as saying, "The FBI was told not to contact anyone, and they went ahead and did it anyway. They are escalating this awareness thing." The head of the library then met with James Fox of the FBI's New York office, and a library official later said of the meeting, "Its purpose was to say we felt we were being harassed. Mr. Fox was terribly charming and said we had to understand what the F.B.I. is charged by Congress to do."[27]

Interviewed on television in 1988, then New York Public Library Director Vartan Gregorian said, "We thought it was an unwarranted intrusion into the private affairs of a member of our library . . . and that's against our rules, regulations, and expectations." On the general issue of library surveillance, Gregorian stated, "We consider reading a private act, an extension of freedom of thought. And our doors are open to all. We don't check IDs. . . . We're the Free Library of New York."[28]

Even across town in Brooklyn, public libraries were not free from the FBI, as visiting agents warned the Brooklyn Public Library that "persons acting against the security of the United States" might be using their library to gather information. Another agent told a Brooklyn librarian "to look out for suspicious looking people who wanted to overthrow the government." The confused librarian told the agent that there were no secret documents there to protect, but the agent nonetheless urged him to report such people to the Bureau.[29]

Larry Brandwein, director of the Brooklyn Public Library, told the *New Yorker* magazine:

In terms of how it affects the actual, day-to-day running of the library, such a visit isn't of much consequence, for the agent was just told that we do not give out any information of any kind regarding individual use of the library. We do not give out borrower records, and we simply informed him that we would not do that, nor would we begin to do that. But the *fact* of such a visit is clearly an attempt to invade the privacy of the public in general. Libraries, as I have understood them, are nonpartisan organizations. The people using them have always assumed, and assumed correctly, that their rights to privacy are protected.[30]

A recently released internal FBI memo gave the Bureau's view of the Brooklyn visit: "On December 1, 1987, SA [deleted] visited the Brooklyn Public Library, Science and Industry Division, and spoke with [deleted] regarding New York's Development of Counterintelligence Awareness Among Librarians (DECAL) program." The memo then expressed the Bureau's exasperation with the library profession's refusal to cooperate.

The attitude exhibited by Brandwein is much more prevalent among librarians associated with publicly accessible institutions than within private organizations, which are well aware of the need to guard against competitive industrial espionage as well as safeguarding national security interests. However, this attitude has increasingly been encountered as a direct result of the publicity surrounding the incident at Columbia University and subsequent involvement of the Intellectual Freedom Committee of the American Library Association, and it should not remain unchallenged.[31]

This FBI commentary again demonstrates the Bureau's inability to distinguish between the restrictive information policies of some "private organizations" and the free access obligations of "publicly accessible" libraries like BPL. The Bureau's claim that Larry Brandwein's uncooperative "attitude" was simply the result of bad publicity surrounding the Library Awareness Program is a self-serving delusion.

Indeed, in direct response to the Library Awareness Program, the Brooklyn Public Library recently adopted its own policy on confidentiality of library records, reinforcing the New York State statute. John L. Hopkins, BPL's public information associate, said, "After the past year's run-ins with the FBI, we felt it was time to make explicit what had always been our unwritten policy."[32]

INVESTIGATIVE VISITS: FROM SEA TO SHINING SEA

University of Maryland

One of the more mysterious of the documented FBI visits to libraries outside of New York, and therefore outside the Library Awareness Program, occurred during the 1970s at the University of Maryland at College Park, where I work. It remains shrouded in mystery because the employee approached by the FBI did not report the incident(s) until she left the university several years later. What we do know is the following.

In 1982, when the technical reports librarian at the University of Maryland's Engineering and Physical Sciences Library retired from service, I conducted an exit interview with the employee, who revealed that "a few years earlier" FBI agents had questioned her about the use of our Technical Reports Center. She told me that the FBI had asked her to monitor the use of certain technical reports and to report to the FBI the names of any persons reading or requesting such reports. When I asked why she had not reported these incidents to me earlier, she said that she had felt intimidated by the Bureau's inquiries, particularly since she was a foreign national.[33]

None of the materials in the Technical Reports Center, or in the rest of the UMCP libraries for that matter, were classified or restricted. What could possibly have been the purpose for FBI surveillance of their use? Was the librarian's account of the FBI visits accurate and complete? Because of the delay in reporting these incidents, verification was virtually impossible. Adding to the confusion, the FBI initially refused to acknowledge these alleged contacts. In a private chat before we appeared together in 1988 on television's "MacNeil-Lehrer Report," FBI Assistant Director James Geer told me that he had no knowledge of these early FBI visits to UMCP, and he repeated that claim on television, stating, "I am not familiar with the case some eight years ago. I really have no easy way to identify it."[34]

Only in January 1989 did I receive official confirmation of those early FBI visits to my library. FBI Assistant Director Milt Ahlerich, who has always been as candid with me as security allows, responded to my inquiries by acknowledging the FBI contact at UMCP's Engineering and Physical Sciences Library "several years before 1980 regarding specific individuals in whom we had investigative interest." Ahlerich told me that because of the Privacy Act and the classified nature of the Bureau's investigation, he could provide no further information.[35]

But even before Ahlerich's confirmation, my doubts about those early FBI visits to UMCP were dispelled when, in April 1986, another FBI agent returned to the same branch library, the same Technical Reports Center, and again approached the technical reports librarian, though now a different incumbent held the position. Hugh O'Connor, the technical reports librarian in 1986, described a female FBI agent who approached him, flashed a badge, and asked if he had observed anything unusual that should be reported to the FBI. When O'Connor said that he had seen nothing out of the ordinary, the agent inquired about library users with foreign names or accents, asking particularly about Polish or Soviet scholars who might have used the Technical Reports Center. O'Connor told the agent that he was unable to identify such library users, but the agent tried to discuss an unnamed Soviet scholar as if they both knew him. At this point O'Connor suggested that the agent speak to me as head of the library, but as has been the pattern in most FBI visits, the agent politely declined and departed.

But the FBI agent had more than one library on her schedule that day in College Park, Maryland. I cannot verify which library was visited first, but we know that the agent visited the White Memorial Library (WML) as well as the Engineering and Physical Sciences Library on that same day in April 1986. When she arrived at WML, she approached Sylvia Evans, a reference librarian, displayed her badge, spoke of national security, and described her presence as part of an effort "to discover if people from Soviet-bloc countries were using our libraries." According to librarian Evans, the agent also wanted to know what kinds of materials these Soviet-bloc nationals were reading or requesting. Evans recalls, "I explained to the agent that all of our libraries had open stacks and were available to anyone. It would therefore be impossible to identify our users unless they asked for a particular service, like database searching."[36] Of course, the agent immediately asked if Evans had ever done a computerized data-base search for a Soviet national. Evans said that she recalled doing a MEDLINE search a few years earlier for a person identifying himself openly as a Soviet physician. Though the MEDLINE data base contains only unclassified and nonsensitive citations in the field of medicine, the agent pursued the matter, asking what subjects had been searched. At this point Evans advised the agent that the records of data-base searches were kept at the main library and she could therefore be of no further assistance.

Later, in describing the incident, Evans said, "There was something intimidating about the agent's attitude. For example, she emphasized that I should not feel obliged to protect library users who were not American citizens." Most important, Sylvia Evans did not believe that the FBI agent was investigating the Soviet physician or anyone else in particular. "The impression I had was that it was a generalized fishing expedition."[37]

I alerted the UMCP Libraries' associate director for public services, Danuta Nitecki, to these FBI visits, and she subsequently spoke by phone with FBI agent Kathryn Kaiser, presumably the same agent who made the original inquiries. Agent Kaiser expressed concern over "services given to a member of the Russian embassy," claiming that she was conducting an investigation involving national security. The agent requested the name and subject interests of a Soviet national who had used the libraries' computerized literature search service. When Nitecki questioned the appropriateness of providing confidential user information to the FBI, agent Kaiser said that she could understand the university's concern if a Maryland student were involved, but, after all, "The person in question was not a U.S. citizen."[38]

Nitecki told agent Kaiser that she would consider the FBI's request and would notify the Bureau of the university's decision. She then spoke to a campus attorney, who advised her that there was no legal requirement in Maryland to withhold such information, and that it was up to the library to follow its internal policies. The only relevant restriction noted by the campus attorney was a Maryland statute preventing a "public library" from revealing "circulation records," but the attorney pointed out that the University of Maryland at College Park was not a public library nor was the FBI requesting circulation records. (See Chapter 4 for subsequent Maryland legislation.) Despite neutral advice from the legal office, Nitecki, after review with the library director, expressed the libraries' support for the principle of protecting the privacy and confidentiality of library use, "regardless of user status or origin." Nitecki advised agent Kaiser that the library administration would give consideration to a formal FBI request, submitted on Bureau letterhead, verifying that this was an investigation involving national security.[39] But the agent never responded. There was no formal letter from the Bureau, no written statement of national security need. Either the FBI's interest was thin, or the Bureau simply chose to move on to other and better fishing grounds.

To this day the FBI has shed little light on its visits to UMCP. At the July 13, 1988, congressional hearings, when Assistant Director Geer was questioned about FBI requests for information on persons with foreign-sounding names, he stated, "I cannot imagine that it happened, but I cannot deny that it happened because I cannot even identify [it]."[40]

Just a week later, on television's "MacNeil-Lehrer Report," Geer acknowledged that general questions about foreigners were asked at the April 1986 FBI visit to College Park, but he now claimed that there was a good purpose behind such questions: "Quite frankly, that was no more than a pretext, because we knew the person we were interested in. We knew what name we were trying to get at." But correspondent Lehrer was dubious: "So rather than ask for, say, Billy Bob Brzezinski, you wanted to look at all of [the names] just in case Billy Bob's was in there?" Geer responded, "Not all of them."[41]

The FBI gave the same explanation during its September 9 meeting with the ALA's Intellectual Freedom Committee. Geer stated:

Mr. Foerstel and [I] discussed about an agent coming in some . . . two years ago, and asking a librarian about anyone who was perhaps frequenting there with some kind of foreign-sounding name. That sounds absurd on the face of it, even to me, if I did not know the circumstances. . . . The agent knew full well who and how many times this individual had been in contact with this specific employee of the library. He used a pretext to try to avoid getting into our sources and methods and what have you. He used a pretext to get that employee to come up with the name. . . . But he didn't know at that point what had developed between this employee and this person who happened to be a known intelligence officer.[42]

Earlier, Deputy Assistant Director Thomas DuHadway said of the Maryland visit:

That was not a contact made under the Library Awareness Program. It was a specifically directed investigation to a specific individual. . . . We had very good information, which we won't go into, as to what the Soviet was trying to do. . . . The least intrusive method we could utilize was to go talk to the individual with whom we knew the Soviet to be in

contact. . . . It was a contact made in the investigation of a known intelligence officer. . . .
The agent was trying to elicit information about that contact specifically with that person.
Not the intelligence officer's use of the library, not what he was doing in other instances,
but what was his association with her.[43]

These various FBI accounts of the 1986 visit to the University of
Maryland at College Park suggest interesting conclusions as well as
contradictions. The FBI commentary refers to "a specific library employee" who had been contacted by "a specific individual, . . . a known intelligence officer." Why then did the agent interrogate librarians from two
different libraries? Which one contained the specific employee? Also, in
describing the library contact, DuHadway referred to the intelligence
officer's "association with *her*." Was this an inadvertant identification of
Sylvia Evans as the library employee? And if the FBI was pursuing a single
foreign intelligence officer at College Park, why did the agent first inquire
about a Polish national, then a Soviet national? Was the Soviet physician
the "known intelligence officer"? Or is it possible that the FBI was looking
more generally for any "Billy Bob Brzezinski" among our users, as
correspondent Lehrer put it?

SUNY Buffalo

Not even snowy upstate New York was spared a confrontation with the
Bureau, though it is important to note that because this incident was outside
the New York City area, it was supposedly not a part of the Library Awareness
Program. In the fall of 1986 an FBI agent visited the Lockwood Memorial
Library at the State University of New York at Buffalo, asking the usual
questions, but this time not about a Soviet. SUNY Buffalo spokesman Dave
Webb said that "the FBI came to the library and asked to see research reference
requests made by a specific foreign student. They wanted to see library records,
databases he's searched. The University refused."[44]

According to the SUNY Buffalo campus newspaper, the FBI agents
claimed that an Iraqi student was involved in activities that would en-
danger the national security. Stephen Roberts, associate director of libraries, said that the FBI "wanted to use the library records to corroborate
their evidence," but Roberts informed the agents that the library's user
records were confidential and could not be divulged. He later explained,
"If somebody shows up with a badge, we don't just pass information across
the counter."[45]

When the agent's request was denied, he threatened to force access to the
library's records through a court order. Indeed, the FBI subsequently ob-

tained the records in compliance with a subpoena from a local federal grand jury, naming a graduate student from Iraq as the target of the investigation. The library was forced to turn over the records of all data-base searches previously requested by the Iraqi student, despite the fact that he had already returned to Iraq. Throughout its struggle for SUNY Buffalo's library records, the FBI exercised its authority in imperious style. Stephen Roberts recalled asking an agent whether he was having trouble finding parking on the crowded campus. He answered, "I parked wherever I wanted to."[46]

As a result of FBI inquiries on their campus, SUNY Buffalo library officials have reconsidered the nature and detail of user records maintained there, attempting to sever the link between a patron and the materials or services he receives. Associate Director Roberts commented: "It's interesting that the FBI has become aware of this whole new fact of information gathering. . . . But we don't want to be gathering information that puts us at odds with the people we serve. We have to look at what we're keeping and how we're keeping it."[47]

George Mason University

On January 23, 1986, the FBI came to Virginia's George Mason University, asking Head Librarian Charlene Hurt to suspend borrowing privileges for a Soviet patron, who was said to be reading materials on missiles. Though the FBI was unable to get its way, Librarian Hurt admits that the library did not turn down the FBI very firmly. She explains: "Many of our contributors are those who would say we should have cooperated. I told the FBI about the library's confidentiality policies and Virginia's confidentiality statute, but I said I would confirm my decision with the administration. Then I told my secretary to tell the FBI I wasn't in every time they called."[48] Hurt says that after the FBI's initial visit, the agent called every day for a month. Eventually the agent personally approached the librarian's secretary, saying, "It sounds like she'll never be in." The secretary replied, "You're right."[49]

The FBI then asked to see the Soviet patron's circulation records, but the information was withheld, as is required by Virginia's library confidentiality statute. Associate Provost James J. Fletcher cautiously explained: "A casual inquiry will not be honored. But the rights of privacy do have limits. . . . If they obtain the appropriate warrants, we'll have to release the information."[50]

The FBI's terse official account of its visit to George Mason bore little resemblance to the library's description:

There was no violation of the Virginia state statute restricting disclosure of library records since no requests for records were made during the FBI's contact. Additionally, the FBI's contact at George Mason Universitiy was in response to a telephone call placed by a staff member of the library who was concerned about defense documents being checked out by an individual the librarian believed to be a Soviet. These contacts were initiated by the *library*, and not the FBI.[51]

Head Librarian Hurt told me that the staff member who called the FBI was not a librarian and was new to both the library and the country. When a Soviet national approached him at the circulation desk and identified himself, the new employee first called the FBI and then his supervisor. Hurt explained: "He just became nervous when he heard the Russian name. He probably was trying to be a good American, but he really didn't understand the library's rules or ethics. Since then we've established a training program on this issue for all employees."[52]

In describing the reported Russian, Hurt said, "He had an Alexandria address, but apparently he was attached to the Soviet embassy. He had what's called a Friends of the Library Card." In any case, two FBI agents soon appeared at the George Mason University Library to investigate this friend of the library. Hurt said that the FBI was concerned that the Soviet was using the government documents collection, yet Hurt was amazed that the agents were completely ignorant of the origin and nature of such documents. "When I told them about the government documents program, they seemed to know nothing about it. I said these are documents made public by the United States Government, and if the Government doesn't want people to see them, they won't publish them. I told them about the depository program and NTIS [National Technical Information Service], and they took notes. I thought, good heavens, what am I dealing with here?"[53]

Over a year later, when the Library Awareness Program had begun to receive national publicity, the FBI called Charlene Hurt once more, asking if it could send some agents around to question the library staff. Hurt recalls: "I said, 'You know the answer to that.' The agent said, 'No I don't,' and I said, 'Well you ought to.' " Hurt concludes, "I think overall they wasted their time, and they didn't get any information. Still, I would say we are not overwhelmingly proud of the events in our little confrontation." Charlene Hurt is aware of no subsequent FBI contacts at George Mason University, and she says, "I haven't checked for a long time to see if our 'spy' still has a library card, and without his name I guess we can't."[54] As far as she knows, the Russian may have renewed his Friends of the Library Card, perhaps continuing to function as a borrower in good standing.

The Midwest

FBI agents visited the University of Cincinnati in 1976 or 1977, where, according to one librarian, they made inquiries about a Polish student. The Bureau maintained its interest there and in 1985 requested records of library use by a Soviet citizen. An FBI agent claimed that the Soviet's proper field of interest should have been mining engineering, but he had instead borrowed a book on robotics. (The Bureau's odd insistence on intellectual narrowness in foreign nationals has been expressed repeatedly by FBI spokespersons.) FBI agents returned to the University of Cincinnati in 1986 with similar inquiries about another Soviet scholar. Dorothy Byers, head librarian at the University of Cincinnati, described a "pushy" agent who attempted to convince one of her clerks of the excitement and mystery of library surveillance. But Byers refused to cooperate, and she recalls, "I resented being pulled into this. The information community shuts down if we try to limit it."[55]

Charles Osburn, former dean of libraries at Cincinnati, recalls, "I had the FBI come into my office one day. They wanted us to report the names of people who asked for certain engineering journals. They were real stony-faced—I couldn't make them laugh—and I told them we could not comply with their request." Osburn concluded, "It's not our job to be the policemen. They're the policemen."[56]

When asked for details on its Cincinnati visits, the FBI claimed that it was unable to locate any information in the Bureau's "indices." But a recently released FBI memo admitted that "through historic memory and review of files, two substantive cases were located." Most of the seven-page memo was blacked out, but one portion stated: "Cincinnati, FBI, has made contact with university library employees under proper predication and with specific investigative targets in view, of which specific intelligence was known or suspected." After emphasizing the university's strength in aerospace engineering and its ties to General Electric and the National Aeronautics and Space Administration (NASA), the FBI's memo concluded:

Cincinnati [FBI] further has concerns that the U.S. private sector and government sector affords the capital, resources and investment for research and development in technology applicable to matters falling within the purview of national security. A considerable source of this research and development would be conducted in an unclassified mode at various universities. The HIS [Hostile Intelligence Services], by penetrating this veil of educational endeavor, are capable of obtaining the research and development without exorbitant expenditure of capital, resources or investment.[57]

In 1987 FBI agents journeyed to the University of Wisconsin's library, still seeking Soviet scholars. Alexander Rolich, the library's Soviet and East European bibliographer, told of teams of agents who would watch a Soviet national while he read *Pravda*. "They wanted to know if the newspaper he was reading looked funny, or like it had been marked up." The FBI explained that this Soviet scholar had been identified by a defector as having been present at a meeting with the KGB.[58]

At the University of Michigan, Maurita Holland, head of the Engineering Library, described how two FBI agents showed her an article in *U.S. News & World Report* titled, "Drive to Keep Secrets out of Russian Hands," which suggested the role librarians might play in protecting such information. Holland recalled that there was a heavy patriotic theme: The agents expressed concern that a visiting Russian mathematics professor who specialized in graph theory was spending a suspicious amount of time at the photocopy machines.[59] "They appealed to my feelings about being a good citizen," said Holland. "I remember they wanted to close the door to my office and have a meeting. I said the door would remain open."[60]

Way Out West

In 1988 the FBI visited the University of Utah's Marriott Library, where agents attempted to monitor library use by a Soviet citizen working in the United States. The Soviet had written a letter to the library inquiring about the National Technical Information Service (NTIS), and the FBI justified its intervention by claiming that the Soviet was attempting to "use the library to gain access to the NTIS." James Geer, the FBI's assistant director, summed up the Utah case: "The Soviet did not identify himself as such, attempting to conceal his true background. After learning of the Soviet's activity, the FBI contacted the library and received information which helped identify Soviet methodology and clandestine activity."[61] In other words, the Bureau learned that foreigners, like everyone else, use the unclassified and unrestricted National Technical Information Service.

Julie Hinz, from Utah University's documents division, told the agent that the library did not provide information on borrowers. But she admits, "This was a special set of circumstances, and we did talk to the FBI." What special circumstances? The FBI said, "We're particularly interested where there is Soviet interest." Roger Hanson, the director of libraries at the University of Utah, said that he understood the FBI's concern about Soviet nationals living in the area as the result of the INF (Intermediate Nuclear Forces) missile treaty, and he commented, "We're concerned too."[62] The Bureau's inquiries eventually prompted Hanson to write an awkwardly careful letter to the American Library Association's Judith Krug to "clarify" the FBI involvement at his library:

First, the incident. On Monday, May 2, a local FBI agent contacted a Marriott Library staff member requesting an appointment to question her regarding a certain individual's contact with the Marriott Library. The appointment was set for May 4. On May 4, several staff members met with the FBI agent. He asked for information regarding the nature of the contact of a certain individual they believed had contact with the Library. Nobody could recall contact from such a person so no information was provided. After the agent left, the staff involved discussed the visit and the name of the individual presented by the FBI agent. During this discussion, a staff member did recall receiving a letter from someone in Virginia inquiring about our NTIS service/collections. The response given to that letter was referral to the NTIS headquarters' offices in Springfield, Virginia. This response was simply penciled on the bottom of the original letter and returned to the individual. Our library did not even make a copy of the letter. Our staff member put her name on the return address of the envelope. In an effort to clear the air, our staff member who responded to the letter contacted the FBI agent and related the incident stated above.[63]

When FBI agents visited the University of Houston, they asked the library to monitor interlibrary loans by foreigners. Counsel Scott Chafin said no. Chafin claims, "If they have a problem with Soviet scientists, they should not let them in. Librarians are not going to do the work of the F.B.I." The FBI agents proceeded to ask a Houston librarian to monitor computerized literature searches performed for library patrons, justifying the request by claiming that certain Russians were acquiring "economic materials" that could benefit them. But the librarian told the agent that such precautions were preposterous, since the data bases in question could be dialed up from Moscow.[64]

In 1987 two FBI agents visited the Engineering and Mathematical Sciences Library at the University of California at Los Angeles and asked the librarians about the reading habits of a visiting Russian student. In addition, they asked the librarians to inform the Bureau of anyone else "similarly suspicious in nature." The agents said that it was the librarians' duty to cooperate and claimed that everything would remain confidential. The results of this pressure were about the same as elsewhere across the country. The librarians explained that they could not cooperate with the agents in any way, because the information they sought was confidential.[65]

When Director Sessions requested information on the UCLA visit, the Los Angeles office wrote: "Los Angeles has no 'Library Awareness Program.' Contact of librarians does occasionally occur in the carrying out of legitimate investigations of [deleted]." The memo claimed that the FBI was unable to retrieve the names of librarians interviewed in Los Angeles, stating: "Although Los Angeles cannot identify the 'contact' at UCLA's Engineering and Mathematical Sciences Library . . . it surmises that it may be similar to one that concerned an interview of a librarian during September 1987."[66] All details of that interview were deleted from the memo.

Public Libraries

Perhaps because public library collections tend to be less scientific than those in university libraries, they seem to have been the subject of fewer FBI counterintelligence visits. But two cases in New Jersey and Florida have been documented. Just prior to the summer 1988 congressional hearings on the Library Awareness Program, FBI headquarters asked various Bureau offices to secretly document their visits to libraries. In a memo to Director Sessions, FBI Newark stated:

A contact at "Princeton Municipal Library," circa 1978, did result in a less than cooperative encounter. . . . A library employee, name not recalled, became rather indignant and proved to be most uncooperative. The employee summoned his supervisor, who was equally uncooperative. Even after a thorough explanation of the FBI's role in FCI [foreign counterintelligence] investigation, both remained adamant in their non-cooperation. Due to the passage of time [deleted] an indices search cannot be completed to retrieve the names of the librarians and the date of the ill-fated contact. It should be noted however, that this interview attempt was strictly reactive in nature and not an attempt to recruit a librarian. . . . As the Bureau is aware, Newark, like all Field Offices, conducted numerous [deleted]. This would have been followed as a matter of course by interviews conducted of library personnel.[67]

In Fort Lauderdale, Florida, Selma Algaze, head of the Broward County Library, said that an FBI agent tried to appeal to her "sense of patriotic duty." She said that there was "an implied threat that I should do what he asked." The agent claimed that there were "agitators" in the area who were using the library for information. When Algaze asked the agent for specifics, she was told that it was privileged information. When the agent asked to look at the library's computer records, Algaze said, "What you're asking is privileged information to us, too."[68]

Cecil Beach, director of libraries for Broward County, could not understand the FBI's concern. He noted, "Even in our technical library there isn't anything classified, nothing you couldn't get by reading something like *Aviation Week*."[69]

FBI Assistant Director James Geer claimed that the Broward County case was the only one where the FBI asked for information on an American. Geer said that the agent was seeking the address of an individual by way of the library's records, and when told that Florida law would not permit that information to be revealed, the agent simply responded, "Oh, I'm sorry. I didn't realize that. Do you have a copy of that [law]?" When the librarian displayed a copy of the law, the agent supposedly said, "Thank you very much," immediately withdrew his request, and departed.[70]

A memo from the Bureau's Miami office to the director of the FBI described how an FBI agent contacted Algaze in December 1986, "attempting to determine a residence for a subject of his investigative matter by determining if the individual had a library card and thus review the application for same." According to the memo, "SA [deleted] stated he is unaware of any 'LIBRARY AWARENESS PROGRAM'. . . and refuted any of the comments made by Algaze." The memo stated:

According to Selma Algaze, Branch Coordinator for Broward's libraries, an unidentified FBI Agent identified himself to her with display of credentials and requested her assistance in identifying "unsavory types, subversives, to see the circulation data base, individuals looking at books on bombs, guns and armaments, appealing to her sense of patriotism." Algaze stated she denied the Agent any access, stating there was a Florida statute protecting the privacy of records . . . and alleged the Agent requested she bypass this procedure to which she replied, "You don't want me to break the law, do you?"[71]

Business and Industry: The Trip Reports

Dr. Robert Park of the American Physical Society has stated, "We are fast approaching the day when electronic data bases will largely supplant conventional libraries as the repositories of scientific and technical information and will become the preferred means by which scientists communicate their findings." Park warned, "There are no measures to impede access to such systems by our adversaries that do not involve some cost to our own vitality."[72]

With this increasing predominance of electronic information, an important relationship has emerged between the library profession and the information industry, and the distinction between data bases and library collections is becoming blurred. While the commercial information industry, including private data-base companies, may have less explicit ethical guidelines concerning information access and confidentiality than does the library profession, whose traditional position on such issues is principled and long-standing, they usually share concern over federal attempts to control their information and surveil their users. Both professions recognize the increasing significance and sensitivity of their product: information.

In 1986 a number of private data-base vendors were visited by officials from various government agencies, including the FBI, Department of Defense (DOD), CIA, and the U.S. Air Force. Jack Simpson, president of Mead Data Central, one of the vendors visited, has described government attempts to monitor and control electronic distribution systems in the private sector. Mead officials disputed the government's claim that such publicly available information, "once aggregated, . . . could be used against national interests."[73] This was, of course, another federal attempt to peddle the "mosaic theory," which claims that a collection of unclassified information can somehow be reassembled to produce classified information. But the officials at Mead did not buy it. They candidly told the FBI and other inquiring agencies that previously published information should not be of concern to the government.

In another example, the FBI went beyond its usual preoccupation with scientific and technical information, visiting the Charles E. Simon Co., a private research organization that retrieves business documents from the Securities and Exchange Commission. Just as it had done in the Library Awareness Program, the FBI warned the company about the danger of foreign agents seeking its information. A company official said that the Bureau asked about anyone from the Eastern bloc who might request its services, and one FBI agent ominously claimed that "most companies, if they are patriotic . . . would be more than helpful."[74]

Little documentation has been made available to the public on these federal surveillance attempts within the information industry, and the FBI has been particularly reticent. But a series of Air Force investigations of commercial information vendors has been described in significant detail in documents recently acquired through a FOIA request. These documents reveal the machinations of the mysterious Air Force Management Analysis Group (AFMAG), whose activities with data-base vendors shed considerable light on similar surveillance by intelligence agencies such as the FBI.

The heavily censored Air Force report, *The Exploitation of Western Data Bases*, says that AFMAG was established to determine the extent of the exploitation of commercial unclassified Western data bases and to recommend methods to stem the transfer of technology through this means. The report states: "A major goal of the AFMAG effort is to identify electronic controls which could be used to deny data base access to . . . adversaries, while keeping the data bases in the public domain. A selective denial process must be established to filter out hostile access attempts."[75] The report reveals AFMAG's methodology, and by implication, that of the FBI and other agencies known to have visited the same vendors for the same purpose.

The "Trip Reports" are, as the name suggests, the notes kept on the AFMAG trips to commercial data-base vendors, and they reveal which vendors are supporting and which are resisting the process of federal restriction of unclassified electronic information. On March 7, 1986, AFMAG met with the Executive Committee of the Information Industries Association and reported: "We discussed identifying users as they established a session with the idea of determining if it was from a potential adversary. . . . They pointed out . . . that keeping track of who the users were and how they used the data base was a sensitive issue. Users do not want anyone tracking what they are doing."[76]

In a period of just four days, March 25–28, 1986, AFMAG visited NEWSNET, BRS (Bibliographic Research Service), EIC, INSPEC, and IEEE (Institute of Electrical and Electronics Engineers). The reports describe the response of BRS's executive vice president, Larry Day: "He understood our position and intentions perfectly and conveyed that BRS has a very positive interest in what the AFMAG is doing. He offered good wishes for the accomplishment of our goal and expressed the opinion that our goals are achievable and compatible with industry concerns and goals." Day also indicated that BRS already has in place all the tools to provide controlled and audited access to data bases.[77]

On April 10, 1986, AFMAG visited TELENET and expressed interest in the ability to detect the location of callers on the network through call tracing. On April 24 AFMAG visited Mead Data Central, where it discussed "protecting information in general, and in particular, user authentication devices." As we saw earlier, Mead opposes government control of unclassified information. On May 1 AFMAG visited MCI International, where it was suggested that call screening could be improved by routing all Eastern-bloc and USSR calls on a given set of trunk lines into the U.S. gateway.[78]

The May 2, 1986, AFMAG visit to the Defense Marketing Service (DMS) revealed the best example of commercial complicity with information control. DMS President Richard Slowsky told AFMAG that his company collects unclassified information on defense subjects, providing it full-text online worldwide, "except for potential adversary entities which DMS rigorously refuses to deal with." According to the "Trip Reports," DMS works regularly with the government and "has received praise for their diligent and constant patriotism." The report claimed that DMS is increasingly being used by other firms who would rather not have to make provisions for sensitive or classified information and who recognize DMS as a "safe information source." It concluded, "The visit with DMS was very enlightening and we were encouraged that a large and successful information industry entity self-imposes greater restriction than we would anticipate recommending."[79]

On April 24 AFMAG visited Chemical Abstracts Service (CAS) and spoke with representative Jim Seals. Whereas DMS was willing to control information as restrictively as the government wished, CAS was quite the opposite. The "Trip Report" stated: "We were met with an openly hostile attack on the reason for the AFMAG's existence, the information management policies of the government, the questioning of industry's right to export information at will, and the visiting of industry entities." Seals told his government visitors that the identification, marketing, control, and dissemination of sensitive but unclassified information should be exclusively a government responsibility and that it was "unconscionable to expect industry to take up the slack." This was precisely the position taken by librarians around the country who refused to become information police for the FBI. Seals explained to AFMAG that it was his industry's right, indeed its obligation, "to promulgate the free exchange of information internationally, without concern for user nationality." He complained that the very existence of AFMAG was a threat to the economic security of his company, and that "any attempt at restricting or licensing international information exchange would result in loud and long concerted objection from the American Chemical Society."[80]

WHAT NOW FOR A TROUBLED PROGRAM?

FBI Director William Sessions has called the Library Awareness Program both necessary and useful, but First Amendment advocate Nat Hentoff has offered some advice: "Sessions can begin to show the backroom boys—and the public—that he is indeed the captain and the quarterback by simply announcing that the Library Awareness Program was stupid and has now been shelved. Such candor would do the FBI—and the librarians—a world of good."[81] Rep. Don Edwards (D-CA), a former FBI agent, made a similar suggestion in a letter to Director Sessions: "Given the limited reuslts compared with the confusion and concern that it has generated, I think the Bureau would be best served by strictly limiting the program or curtailing it altogether."[82]

On July 13, 1988, James Geer appeared on ABC TV's "Nightline" and stated that the Library Awareness Program was still in existence but that there had been no recent contacts under the program.[83] A few days later, on a Chicago radio talk show, Assistant Director Milt Ahlerich was asked for the current status of the Library Awareness Program. He answered, "The Soviet threat hasn't gone away, and we are therefore bound to carry out our duties here."[84] One FBI agent admitted, "They'll discontinue the program for a while. When the fire is up, you back off." Another Bureau spokesperson suggested the permanence of the Library Awareness Program by claiming, "There's no logical end as long as there's something out there to be aware of."[85] But a New York agent gave a clearer picture of the continuing confrontation between the FBI and the library profession: "We can't let organizations like the American Library Association affect our internal policies." He referred to the hundreds of university and public libraries in the New York City area and said, "We will try to hit all of them."[86]

David Atlee Phillips, a former CIA agent, has said that even though the Library Awareness Program has been ineffective in detecting foreign spies, most of the intelligence community believes it would be unwise to curtail it in the face of public opposition. But Phillips himself believes that "although the FBI operation was clearly legal and the counterintelligence program important, FBI management should recognize that the *prudent* course would be to postpone the operation and take another look at it a few years down the road."[87]

Phillips' prescription is probably very close to the Bureau's short-term plan for the Library Awareness Program, despite the FBI's public position of cautious persistence. For Sessions to publicly renounce a long-standing program under fire would be bad for the Bureau's morale, but it is a safe prediction to say that the Library Awareness Program will take a low profile for the next few years.

On November 15, 1988, in a story headlined, "FBI to Limit Probes of Library Users," the *Washington Post* claimed, "The FBI has agreed to sharply restrict its controversial [Library Awareness] program."[88] The story was based on a September 14, 1988, letter from Director William Sessions to Rep. Don Edwards. Had Sessions decided to follow Edwards' earlier advice to limit or curtail the program? On the contrary, when an FBI spokesperson was asked if Sessions' letter signaled a major change in the program, he claimed that it was not a cutback at all and was intended only to "dispel the myths about the program."[89] Sessions' letter began: "When deemed necessary, the FBI will continue to contact certain scientific and technical libraries (including university and public libraries) in the New York City area concerning hostile intelligence service activities in libraries." The letter reaffirmed the FBI's desire that librarians report any library users who identify themselves as Soviets or Soviet-bloc nationals and who (*a*) seek assistance in conducting library research; (*b*) request research assistance from students or faculty; (*c*) remove materials from libraries without permission; or (*d*) seek biographical information from librarians. Sessions concluded by claiming that "the FBI is completely uninterested in the library activities of anyone other than those persons who meet these specific criteria."[90]

These criteria were in fact taken almost exactly from the Bureau's report, *The KGB and the Library Target, 1962–Present.*[91] Granted, this was a rather odd set of danger signs, some of them describing nothing more than normal library reference service, but Assistant Director Geer began sending out virtual carbon copies of Sessions' letter under his own name. Librarians have not responded favorably. One such letter from Geer to a public library's Board of Trustees received the following response:

> Your letter has done very little to alleviate our concern about the "Library Awareness Program." Your . . . intention to request assistance from librarians in investigating persons of interest to your agency is particularly distressing. This will of course violate your point four, wherein you state that you will not "attempt to circumvent local library management," which management of course requires Staff *not* to provide information of any kind about any patron, whatever criteria those patrons may meet. You must also be aware that libraries do not hold sensitive or classified materials, which materials would presumably be the object of "hostile intelligence gathering activities."[92]

Sessions warned that the Bureau "will inquire further as to what these individuals are seeking from librarians." This approach would presumably halt the FBI's use of foreign-sounding names or accents to identify suspicious library users, but it would once again involve the Bureau in requests for patron records. Perhaps Sessions felt that he was reassuring librarians when he stated: "We intend to ask librarians for help along the lines set forth above. If they do not wish to help, that is up to them, but we are confident that they will help if the program is explained to them properly." Sessions also claimed that "the FBI will not attempt to circumvent local library management in contacts with librarians."[93] But the FBI has usually bypassed library supervisors in pursuing the Library Awareness Program, while simultaneously denying that this was its policy.

Sessions emphasized that the restraining guidelines propounded for the Library Awareness Program did not apply to investigations of "known or suspected hostile intelligence officers and co-optees. When the FBI needs information about the activities of such persons, it will continue to contact anyone having that information, including librarians. Such contacts will be nationwide, and . . . will be no different from any other FBI investigation."[94] But we have seen that librarians have no way to distinguish between these nationwide "investigative" contacts and the Library Awareness Program.

Representative Edwards was not completely reassured by Sessions' new guidelines. In a letter he sent to me and other interested parties, Edwards said that "it is disappointing to see that the FBI continues to defend its library visits. . . . You will see from the Director's letter that the FBI intends to continue asking without a warrant for library borrowing records of individuals who have been identified as hostile intelligence officers and their co-optees."[95]

Though Sessions' letter was characterized as conciliatory by many, C. James Schmidt, chairman of ALA's Intellectual Freedom Committee, said, "I do not regard it as so. While Director Sessions says he 'shares concerns' about public and university libraries, he states that agents will continue to visit them. While he says that the Bureau will not ask for circulation lists, he states that they will 'inquire further' about what certain Soviet or Soviet bloc nationals are reading."[96] Schmidt communicated his skepticism in a letter to Representative Edwards: "I am greatly disheartened that the FBI has reiterated its intention to make requests for confidential information on library patrons. . . . This intent demonstrates that the Bureau does not understand, or has chosen to ignore, that however important its duties may be, they are subordinate to the First Amendment rights of patrons using a library or to state confidentiality laws."[97]

On November 29, 1988, Director Sessions sent an eight-page memo to all SACs defending the Library Awareness Program and other Bureau activities in libraries. The memo began: "Since 9/87, captioned program, publicly referred to as the Library Awareness Program (LAP), has been subjected to criticism by various professional librarian organizations, the news media, and some members of Congress. FBI officials, including the

Director, have cited a need for the LAP and for substantive FBI contacts with librarians in connection with specific FBI FCI investigations." Sessions again cautioned FBI field divisions to refrain from making any public statements on the program and to adhere to his September 14 investigative guidelines, adding: "Such continuing investigation would be conducted as part of the FBI's overall FCI effort and would not be part of the LAP." Apparently, once Library Awareness Program visits have identified a Soviet national using a technical library, subsequent investigation in that library is defined to be outside the program. Sessions recommended that only experienced FBI agents should be assigned cases involving contacts with librarians, and such agents should be knowledgeable about pertinent state confidentiality laws. In a significant extension of the concept of proactive "awareness" programs, the memo stated: "Nothing in the above guidelines precludes any other Field Division from implementing a Library Awareness Program if a demonstrated need exists for the establishment of such a program."[98]

This invitation to FBI offices across the country to implement their own Library Awareness Programs, as the need exists, has undoubtedly been the Bureau's policy from the beginning. How many cities besides New York have accepted the invitation? The FBI has been evasive and ambiguous on this question and has withheld relevant information in its FOIA releases. In January 1989 the FBI's Washington Metropolitan Field Office (WMFO) claimed that it had no plans to initiate a "formal Library Awareness Program" but implied that similar activities were conducted outside of a defined program. In a March discussion of the Library Awareness Program it admitted: "WMFO has established like contacts sensitive to our FCI goals."[99] Are cities like Washington conducting their own "informal" proactive programs in libraries? The evidence available is inconclusive but disturbing.

NOTES

1. "The Talk of the Town," *New Yorker*, May 30, 1988, p. 23.

2. U.S. Congress, House Committee on the Judiciary, *FBI Counterintelligence Visits to Libraries: Hearings before the House Subcommittee on Civil and Constitutional Rights of the Committee on the Judiciary*, 100th Cong., 2d sess., June 20 and July 13, 1988 (Washington, D.C.: GPO, 1989), pp. 107, 122 (hereafter cited as *FBI Counterintelligence Visits to Libraries*).

3. Ibid., p. 56.

4. Ibid., p. 152.

5. Ibid., pp. 116–17.

6. "MacNeil-Lehrer Report," Public Television, July 13, 1988.

7. Letter from Rep. Louis Stokes, Chairman, House Permanent Select Committee on Intelligence, to Nancy Kranich, New York University, August 4, 1988, p. 1.

8. Quinlan J. Shea, "The Library Awareness Program," *American Society of Access Professionals Newsletter*, October 1988, insert.

9. Transcript of meeting of FBI and ALA Intellectual Freedom Committee, September 9, 1988, p. 9.

10. Memo to SAC William Warfield from ADIC James M. Fox, March 7, 1988. October 30, 1989, FOIA release to National Security Archive.

11. Transcript of meeting of FBI and ALA Intellectual Freedom Committee, September 9, 1988, p. 26.

12. Ibid., p. 41.

13. Ibid., p. 31.

14. "Libraries Are Asked by FBI to Report on Foreign Agents," *New York Times*, September 18, 1987, p. 1.

15. Memo from FBI New York to FBI Headquarters, September 21, 1987. September 1989 FOIA release to National Security Archive.

16. *FBI Counterintelligence Visits to Libraries*, pp. 77–78.

17. Ibid., pp. 81–82.

18. Ibid., p. 83.

19. FBI presentation to U.S. National Commission on Libraries and Information Science by Thomas DuHadway, San Antonio, Texas, January 14, 1988, pp. 32–33.

20. From my interview with Nancy Gubman, June 1989.

21. Ibid.

22. Ibid.

23. Memo from FBI New York to Director, FBI, May 31, 1988. October 30, 1989, FOIA release to National Security Archive.

24. *FBI Counterintelligence Visits to Libraries*, pp. 345–46.

25. "Academic Libraries Must Oppose Federal Surveillance of Their Users," *Chronicle of Higher Education*, March 23, 1988, p. A48.

26. "Nightline," ABC TV, July 13, 1988.

27. Natalie Robins, "The FBI's Invasion of Libraries," *Nation*, April 9, 1988, p. 501.

28. "Nightline," ABC TV, July 13, 1988.

29. People for the American Way, *The FBI's Library Awareness Program Background Report* (Washington, D.C., 1988), p. 3.

30. "The Talk of the Town," *New Yorker*, May 30, 1988, p. 23. Emphasis in original.

31. Undated memo from the FBI's New York Office to FBI HQ concerning the FBI's December 1, 1987 visit to Brooklyn Public Library. September 1989 FOIA release to National Security Archive.

32. "Action Exchange," *American Libraries*, February 1989, p. 126.

33. From my 1982 exit interview with the retiring Head of the Technical Reports Center.

34. "MacNeil-Lehrer Report," Public Television, July 13, 1988.

35. Letter from Milt Ahlerich, Assistant Director, Office of Congressional and Public Affairs, Federal Bureau of Investigation, to Herbert Foerstel, University of Maryland, January 30, 1989, p. 2.

36. From my interview with Sylvia Evans, September 1989.

37. Ibid.

38. From my interview with Danuta Nitecki, June 27, 1988.

39. Ibid.

40. *FBI Counterintelligence Visits to Libraries*, p. 37.

41. "MacNeil-Lehrer Report," Public Television, July 13, 1988.

42. Transcript of meeting of FBI and ALA Intellectual Freedom Committee, September 9, 1988, p. 22.

43. Ibid., p. 32.

44. "FBI Asks Libraries to Help It Find Spies on Campuses," *College Press Service*, January 18, 1988, p. 3.

45. "Sensitive but Unclassified: Government Threatens Access to Data Bases," *Crab*, May 1987, p. 1.

46. Robins, "FBI's Invasion of Libraries," p. 500.

47. "Sensitive but Unclassified," p. 1.

48. Interview by Herbert Foerstel with Charlene Hurt, June 1989.

49. "FBI's Invasion of Libraries," p. 500.

50. "FBI Admits Spy Attempt at Fenwick," *Broadside*, June 12, 1989, p. 1.

51. *FBI Counterintelligence Visits to Libraries*, p. 158. Emphasis in original.

52. From my interview with Charlene Hurt, June 1989.

53. Ibid.

54. Ibid.

55. Robins, "FBI's Invasion of Libraries," p. 499.

56. "FBI Asks Libraries to Help It Find Spies on Campuses," *College Press Service*, January 18, 1988, p. 3.

57. Memo from FBI, Cincinnati, to FBI, New York, and the FBI Director, May 27, 1988. September 1989 FOIA release to National Security Archive.

58. Robins, "FBI's Invasion of Libraries," p. 500.

59. Ibid., pp. 499–500.

60. Ann Hagedorn, "FBI Recruits Librarians to Spy on 'Commie' Readers," *Wall Street Journal*, May 19, 1988, p. 32.

61. *FBI Counterintelligence Visits to Libraries*, pp. 117–18.

62. Natalie Robins, "Library Follow-up," *Nation*, June 25, 1988, p. 885.

63. *FBI Counterintelligence Visits to Libraries*, p. 382.

64. Robins, "FBI's Invasion of Libraries," p. 499.

65. Ibid., p. 500.

66. Memo from FBI Los Angeles to Director, FBI, May 27, 1988. October 30, 1989, FOIA release to National Security Archive.

67. Memo from FBI Newark to Director, FBI, May 27, 1988. October 30, 1989, FOIA release to National Security Archive.

68. Robins, "FBI's Invasion of Libraries," p. 499.

69. Hagedorn, "FBI Recruits Librarians," p. 32.

70. Transcript of meeting of FBI and ALA Intellectual Freedom Committee, September 9, 1988, p. 13.

71. Memo from SAC, Miami, to Director, FBI, April 22, 1988, pp. 2–3. September 1989 FOIA release to National Security Archive.

72. "Effort to Limit Access to Unclassified Data Bases Draws Criticism," *Chronicle of Higher Education*, March 4, 1987, p. 12.

73. Hagedorn, "FBI Recruits Librarians," p. 32.

74. People for the American Way, *FBI's Library Awareness Program Background Report*, (Washington, D.C., 1988), p. 6.

75. Office of the Assistant Vice Chief of Staff, Headquarters, U.S. Air Force, *The Exploitation of Western Data Bases*, June 30, 1986, Appendix F, p. 1.

76. [U.S. Air Force], memorandum for record, April 1, 1986, meeting with the Executive Committee of the Data Base Committee of the Information Industries' Association.

77. [U.S. Air Force], memorandum for record, "Trip Report," April 4, 1986, at Bibliographic Research Services.

78. Ibid., May 6, 1986, visit to MCI International.

79. Ibid., May 8, 1986, DMS/On Line.

80. Ibid., May 7, 1986, Chemical Abstracts Service.

81. Nat Hentoff, "The FBI in the Library," *Washington Post*, July 23, 1988, p. A23.

82. ALA Office for Intellectual Freedom, *Memorandum*, October 20, 1988, p. 4.

83. "Nightline," ABC TV, July 13, 1988.

84. "Page Two," WBEZ-Public Radio, Chicago, Illinois, July 19, 1988.

85. Robins, "FBI's Invasion of Libraries," April 9, 1988, p. 502.

86. "FBI Asks Librarians to Help in the Search for Spies," *Philadelphia Inquirer*, February 23, 1988, p. 17A.

87. David Atlee Phillips, "FBI's Timing Is Questionable, Not Its Morals," *Newsday*, October 16, 1987, p. 83. Emphasis in original.

88. "FBI to Limit Probes of Library Users," *Washington Post*, November 15, 1988, p. A3.

89. Jack Anderson, "FBI Still Checking Out Libraries," *Washington Post*, December 15, 1988, p. Md17.

90. *FBI Counterintelligence Visits to Libraries*, p. 151.

91. FBI Headquarters, Intelligence Division, *The KGB and the Library Target, 1962–Present*, January 1, 1988, pp. 9–10.

92. Letter from Audrey Fixell, President, East Meadow Public Library Board of Trustees, to James H. Geer, Assistant Director, FBI, November 2, 1988. October 30, 1989, FOIA release to National Security Archive. Emphasis in original.

93. *FBI Counterintelligence Visits to Libraries*, pp. 151–52.

94. Ibid., p. 152.

95. Letter from Rep. Don Edwards, Chairman, Subcommittee on Civil and Constitutional Rights, House of Representatives, to Herbert Foerstel, University of Maryland, October 12, 1988.

96. Memo on Library Awareness Program and related matters from C. James Schmidt, Chair, Intellectual Freedom Committee, to ALA Executive Board/Council, January 8, 1989, p. 2. Reprinted by permission of the American Library Association.

97. "FBI to Limit Probes of Library Users," *Washington Post*, November 15, 1988, p. A3.

98. Memo from Director, FBI, to all SACS, November 29, 1988. October 30, 1989, FOIA release to National Security Archive.

99. Memo from Director FBI to FBI, WMFO, March 29, 1989. October 30, 1989, FOIA release to National Security Archive.

3

The Role of Librarians in Library Surveillance

THE BUREAU'S GOALS

In 1987, when the Library Awareness Program was first revealed in the press, it had to compete with three other contemporaneous FBI scandals: discrimination against blacks and Hispanics within the Bureau, harassment of political organizations like Committee in Solidarity with the People of El Salvador (CISPES), and long-standing surveillance of American authors, ranging from Carl Sandburg to Dashiell Hammett. The latter practice, a scurrilous favorite during the Hoover days, has been recently documented in the press and in books such as Herbert Mitgang's *Dangerous Dossiers*. The Bureau still maintains files on writers once considered subversive, many of them long dead, though new information is presumably no longer added to these files.

In describing the odd logic of the Library Awareness Program, author Natalie Robins has said, "In the eyes of the FBI, going from the surveillance of writers to the surveillance of books to the surveillance of the place where books live and take on a life of their own is a logical move." Perhaps out of self-consciousness over the revelations of unwarranted Bureau files on famous American authors, FBI agent Susan Schnitzer tried to assure author Robins that the Bureau's Library Awareness Program did not indulge in such excesses. "We're not looking at authors," Schnitzer said. "We're looking at people who read authors."[1] I doubt that Robins was reassured about the FBI's purposes, and I know that librarians and library users simply had their worst fears confirmed.

The FBI currently defends its library surveillance as a legitimate part of its counterintelligence program, and there is no reason to assume that it has ever felt otherwise. FOIA documents released by the FBI's New York office shed some light on the origins of the Library Awareness Program, but they made little mention of the Bureau's nationwide pattern of library surveillance and provided little insight into its purpose. As we have seen in other FBI reports and statements, the Bureau has justified the Library Awareness Program implicitly through a description of the Soviet Intelligence Services (SIS) intelligence-collection threat, rather than by stating explicitly what the FBI would do about it. It appears that we can deduce the purposes of the Library Awareness Program only from a combination of the federal government's information policy, the Bureau's rhetorical goals, and its explicit fears.

Rep. Don Edwards (D-CA), who has led the congressional fight against the Library Awareness Program, has written: "The recent controversy over FBI visits to libraries highlights the continuing debate over government information controls. The controversy also underscores the need for a new approach to information policy." Edwards claimed: "The library visits were tied to the troubling, though sometimes fitful, government effort to control unclassified information. . . . We must reexamine the basic laws that govern dissemination and access to information."[2]

C. James Schmidt, chairman of the ALA's Intellectual Freedom Committee, has recently stated: "The FBI's visits to libraries are part of a systematic, coordinated interagency effort to prevent access to unclassified information. This effort is coordinated by the interagency Technology Transfer Intelligence Committee—a group representative of 22 agencies and hosted by the CIA."[3] The Library Awareness Program is a logical accompaniment to an aggressively enunciated government policy to halt the "hemorrhage" of technology transfer, and the FBI has been performing its library counterintelligence mission under the support and cover of official federal policies of information control.

Shortly after the FBI's controversial visit to Columbia University in June 1987, Assistant Director Milt Ahlerich described hostile access to library information as the initial predicate for the Library Awareness Program. In October 1987 Ahlerich expanded the alleged threat beyond information access, claiming that foreign intelligence officers attempt to "identify and recruit American and foreign students found in American libraries," and he concluded: "The FBI's objective is to thwart this activity by endeavoring to educate, on a limited basis, knowledgeable individuals in these libraries to familiarize them with this hostile intelligence threat."[4]

In January 1988 the FBI's deputy assistant director, Thomas Du-Hadway, claimed that "90 percent of what the Soviets collect in this country is free, available, and unclassified," but he warned the National Commission on Libraries and Information Science, "There are certain sections of specialized libraries that are supposed to be restricted, and those are some of the areas that we find our Soviet friends mucking about in. They really shouldn't be there."[5] Where? From what collections within unclassified technical libraries should librarians exclude Soviet citizens? The only specific example the FBI has offered is the NTIS material, which we shall see is not off limits to Soviet citizens or anyone else.

Director Sessions has stated that "for several years now—maybe as many as ten years—we have sought the assistance of librarians in connection with specialized libraries where there are people who come to gather technical research. Believe it! That these are places where foreign, hostile intelligence persons seek both to gather information and to recruit people who will be their agents in this country! . . . We expect librarians to be aware of things that in their minds are in fact foreign, hostile intelligence gathering efforts."[6] Similarly, Assistant Director James Geer told the American Library Association that the Soviets hope "to glean all the information from libraries they can and to recruit as many librarians as they could."[7]

In January 1988 the Bureau's position paper, *The KGB and the Library Target*, claimed that "the SIS is in search of sensitive but unclassified information which provides the Soviet Union with the necessary tools to keep pace with America's scientific and technical achievements." Librarians were particularly concerned with the statement, "The FBI must logically pursue any contact between a Soviet national and an American citizen, regardless of where the contact occurs or the profession of the person contacted, and that would include libraries as the circumstances might require."[8] Quinlan Shea of the National Security Archive expressed the view of most librarians: "I don't believe that I've ever had a 'contact' with a Soviet, but if I ever do, that contact is not any of the FBI's business. . . . As far as I'm concerned, the FBI should not go into a church, or a library, or a newsroom or ask about a 'contact' between a Soviet and an American—unless they have reasonable grounds for suspecting that unlawful activity has occurred, is occurring, or is about to occur."[9]

Through its reports, testimony, and public statements, the FBI was claiming that the SIS objectives were to identify America's emerging technologies before their components became classified or restricted and to develop selected librarians, students, or professors to assist in this unclassified information gathering. But how was the Library Awareness Program to thwart such deceptively legal threats to national security? In his September 1988 letter to Rep. Don Edwards, FBI Director Sessions attempted to clarify the process: "The purpose of such contacts will be twofold: to inform these libraries that hostile intelligence services attempt to use libraries for intelligence gathering activities that may be harmful to the United States, and to enlist their support . . . in helping the FBI identify those activities."[10]

From all of this, and from the realization that the Library Awareness Program addresses only unclassified library collections, we may deduce the three goals of the program:

1. To halt Soviet access to unclassified technical information
2. To recruit librarians as FBI assets
3. To prevent Soviet recruitment of librarians as spies

But since librarians, not FBI agents, are intended to be the major players in this game, we must translate the FBI's goals into the librarians' roles.

LIBRARIANS AS INFORMATION FILTERS

A recently released FBI memo approvingly quotes from an article titled "Like Letting the KGB into the Pentagon" by former Assistant Secretary of Defense Richard Perle. The memo claims that "many of his comments are germane to the predication for the [Library Awareness] Program." Typical of Perle's quoted comments was: "We had no idea the Soviets were ripping off our technology so skillfully, so comprehensively, so effectively, right under our noses."[11]

FBI Director William Sessions says that the Library Awareness Program is designed to protect U.S. technology and military capabilities from hostile exploitation. But the ALA's C. James Schmidt says, "The Library Awareness Program is part and parcel of a whole set of activities that are products of a dangerous mindset. And that is that information is dangerous and ought not to be free."[12] In any case the FBI and ALA seem to agree that one purpose of the Library Awareness Program is to prevent the Soviets from obtaining valuable information from our scientific and technical libraries.

The FBI claims that Soviets or their agents have stolen hundreds of thousands of microfiche from libraries, but librarians say that the charge is absurd, and they would certainly know best. What laws, then, have the

Soviets violated in American libraries? Currently none. This suggests that librarians, rather than law-enforcement officers, would play the visible role in the Library Awareness Program. The FBI says that the Bureau does not have enough time or resources to keep track of every potential intelligence agent who comes into the country. The Bureau's Thomas DuHadway laments: "The U.S. government and our society don't have the manpower . . . for surveilling all of these people 24 hours a day to find out what they're doing. We just don't do that, we don't have enough money, we don't have enough manpower and it's impossible to do."[13] All the more reason why librarians are now regarded as essential cadre in the full-time effort to restrict unclassified information and surveil those requesting it.

But aside from monitoring foreign use of libraries, on what authority could librarians actually prevent foreigners or undesirables from accessing unclassified and unrestricted technical information? There have been a number of formal federal attempts to create a structure within which librarians would deny access to such information. The Unclassified Controlled Nuclear Information (UCNI) regulations were intended for just that purpose, and only after lengthy and emotional public hearings, at which librarians refused to collaborate in denying such information to "unauthorized" readers, did the Department of Energy agree to allow all UCNI information presently in libraries to remain there without access restrictions.

Similarly, the concept of "sensitive but unclassified," introduced in NSDD-145 and defined in the notorious Poindexter Memorandum, was intended precisely for the purpose of citizen complicity in information control.[14] Librarians now feel the insidious effects of export control laws, which, contrary to popular belief, control not just products, but information in library collections and even conversations. Libraries across the country are today being pressured by government agencies to remove unclassified materials from their open shelves on the basis of vaguely worded export controls.

Despite continuing pressure from the government, librarians have generally refused to act as "an additional filter" for unclassified information, as was suggested by the National Commission on Libraries and Information Science.[15] In most libraries there is nothing other than professional ethics preventing librarians from denying their collections to unauthorized readers. The export controls, like the guidelines for UCNI or sensitive but unclassified information, are already in place, and library confidentiality legislation does not address matters like sequestered collections, borrowing privileges, or even access to library facilities. With increasing federal demands to reduce technology transfer, FBI spokespersons express astonishment and disappointment at the library profession's intransigence. Why won't librarians cooperate?

Librarians are not simply being asked to accept federal authority to withhold unclassified information from their shelves. They are themselves being asked to judge, screen, and restrict both the materials and the people already inhabiting their libraries, all on the basis of vague and arbitrary national security pronouncements. Indeed, librarians are not so much expected to implement restrictive government policy as to infer their own, acting as information vigilantes with federal sanction. A few specific examples of the library profession's adamant refusal to collaborate may be instructive.

In 1987 the Department of Energy's Office of Scientific and Technical Information (OSTI) notified libraries that OSTI would "begin distributing microfiche copies of some limited access reports in September 1987." After advising libraries, "Your organization is eligible to receive reports with audience restrictions as indicated below," the OSTI notice defined these restrictions as follows: "By electing to receive this material, you are agreeing to limit access to the microfiche to only those persons and organizations authorized to receive them."[16]

The OSTI documents being offered were valuable and very tempting to technical libraries, but on principle almost all librarians refused to accept the material. For example, the Columbia University Libraries turned down the offer because it required time to deny access to anyone other than government agencies and their contractors. But the libraries that refused the OSTI reports at least wanted to know what they were missing, so the National Security Archive submitted a FOIA request to the Department of Energy. DOE refused to provide a list of the very reports that had already been offered to the libraries, claiming that the information was stored in a computer that would require a new program to be written in order to retrieve it. The Office of Hearings and Appeals subsequently overruled DOE, stating that denial of information on these grounds would allow any agency to withhold information simply by putting it in a computer.

Just what was so sensitive about these unclassified OSTI reports that required libraries to withhold them from foreigners? The FOIA request revealed that a significant percentage of these "limited-access" reports were translations of articles that appeared originally in the Soviet technical literature.

Many libraries were forced to make an even more difficult decision in July 1988 when they were informed that the heavily used NASA RECON data base was to be restricted to U.S. citizens only. Libraries such as those in the University of California system chose to cancel the invaluable NASA RECON data base rather than impose citizenship restrictions, which the university said would violate its policy against discrimination. UCLA claimed that the restrictions would be virtually unenforceable because of the large number of foreign students on campus.

Even though NASA was imposing these restrictions on unclassified information, John Wilson, NASA's data-base manager, justified them by claiming that if a data base is supported with taxpayer's money, "you can't take that wide open approach." Wilson said that the librarians would have to control access to the data base through the use of their passwords, but he tried to assure librarians that no prosecution had ever resulted from allowing foreigners to use NASA RECON. Nonetheless, university officials remained concerned over that possibility. But the fundamental concern at all University of California libraries was confidentiality and freedom of information. UC's associate vice president for academic affairs stated, "There are grounds to question the authority of a federal agency to impose such a restriction in the absence of express congressional authorization." Berkeley's head librarian said that he cancelled NASA RECON because "all of our information is at least conceptually available to anybody who comes in our doors."[17] A measure of the depth of principle involved here is the fact that libraries like UCLA and Berkeley are signing onto DIALOG, an alternative data base system that costs considerably more than NASA RECON, yet includes fewer records.

Recently NASA's John Wilson has claimed that the U.S. citizenship clause in the RECON agreement may have been misunderstood by librarians, because its true intent is to prevent the export of RECON information to foreign governments or companies. Therefore, commercial data bases like DIALOG, which contain some of the same information as RECON, would have the same constraints as RECON. Wilson says that in neither case is U.S. citizenship required for access to the information, so long as it is used in the United States for education or research. But the University of California still maintains that by signing the agreement, the university would expose itself to legal liability should a non–U.S. citizen violate the export restrictions.[18]

The FBI has not been discouraged by the library profession's rejection of the wide range of federally instigated programs restricting access to unclassified information. Early in 1987 the FBI began claiming in reports, public interviews, and congressional testimony that librarians were required to prevent Soviet citizens from "accessing" documents issued by the National Technical Information Service (NTIS). This completely spurious claim, pronounced gravely by FBI spokespersons, deserves further discussion.

The NTIS, under the U.S. Department of Commerce, collects, codifies, archives, and disseminates research publications originating in more than four hundred federal agencies. NTIS documents cover unclassified or declassified scientific, technical, and engineering research, 25 percent of which originates from foreign sources. But in February 1985 Commerce Secretary Malcolm Baldridge described a "hemorrhage" of information through NTIS to foreign governments and suggested that "new legislation, new Executive Orders, and coordinated government-wide regulations" might be required to protect NTIS. Baldridge proposed tighter screening of what goes into NTIS, requiring that unclassified but "potentially sensitive" documents be withheld.[19] During this same period the FBI had been visiting private data-base vendors, expressing its concern about open access to NTIS and other data bases.

The FBI study of technology transfer through libraries, *The KGB and the Library Target*, states:

Unclassified and nonrestricted DOD technical reports are made available to the general public through the National Technical Information Service (NTIS), Springfield, Virginia. The Soviets were embargoed from directly accessing materials through NTIS on January 8, 1980 when former President Jimmy Carter sent a letter to the U.S. Secretary of Commerce captioned "Policy on Technology Transfer to the USSR." One of the specific purposes of this executive order was to prevent the "USSR, its entities or agents," from accessing information through NTIS.[20]

A secret 1988 FBI memo referred to President Carter's alleged "embargo" letter in describing the Bureau's investigation of hostile use of NTIS in libraries. "DOC has embargoed Soviet and Communist-Bloc access to NTIS, causing these officials to seek technological information elsewhere. This investigation was predicated for determining how hostile intelligence is circumventing these restrictions." The memo then described FBI checks on any companies providing access to NTIS information, stating, "Once these checks were completed, company representatives were contacted by agents and informed of the FBI's responsibilities to thwart hostile intelligence efforts." The companies were told to contact the Bureau "in the event that hostile intelligence presents itself in the future."[21]

A subsequent FBI internal memo, written in anticipation of the 1988 congressional hearings on the FBI's library activities, complained that Soviets are able to "obtain or copy NTIS publications by openly visiting libraries that maintain NTIS stock." The memo then drew an explicit connection between NTIS access and the Library Awareness Program: "Some predicate for the FBI's Library Awareness Program (LAP) may be found in SIS officers attempting to recruit librarians to check out NTIS materials for them."[22]

In Assistant Director James Geer's written statement to the House Subcommittee on Civil and Constitutional Rights, he claimed: "The Soviets are barred by executive order from accessing materials through NTIS. Nevertheless, the SIS has made continued efforts to access NTIS to assist themselves in their technical collection efforts." Geer's statement went on to describe the University of Utah incident mentioned earlier and claimed that a Soviet national's request to access NTIS at a library was "a clear example of an SIS attempt to evade the NTIS embargo."[23]

On July 13, 1988, when Geer testified before the same House subcommittee, he went even further in response to questions from Assistant Counsel James Dempsey.

Geer: ... many, many times in some of the specific cases I have referred to, what they [the Soviets] have asked for is accessed in the National Technical Information System, [to] which they are denied access by executive order which was instituted during President Carter's Administration.

Dempsey: Denied direct access.

Geer: Denied direct access, which is an attempt to deny them access obviously.

Dempsey: And obviously, as well, they continue to have access to that material.

Geer: By going to a library in some cases, yes, and asking that it be accessed by that library and then provided to them.

Dempsey: And also they have the access through resale of that material. That material on NTIS is available abroad. ...

Geer: We cannot prevent all that. We do not have the resources to undertake to enforce the executive order.[24]

Geer has suggested that librarians might be just the human resource to enforce these alleged restrictions on NTIS. When counsel Dempsey suggested that the FBI could not prevent people from reading unclassified material, NTIS or otherwise, Geer was even more explicit: "I certainly would not hesitate to point out to the librarian that this request for information accessing through the ... National Technical Information Service was prohibited."[25]

On the very morning of Geer's congressional testimony, I had the opportunity to discuss the Library Awareness Program on ABC TV's "Good Morning America" with George Carver, former deputy director of the CIA, who warned that the Soviets "are trying to use the National Technical Information Service, which the Soviets are not supposed to do."[26] That same night, on Public Television's "MacNeil-Lehrer Report," I debated the Library Awareness Program with James Geer himself. Once more Geer described Soviet attempts "to access the National Technical Information Service, which they are prohibited by executive order from accessing."[27]

NTIS reports are openly published, unclassified, and unrestricted, like all the materials contained in the libraries visited through the Library Awareness Program. For example, my own Engineering and Physical Sciences Library at the University of Maryland has almost 1,000,000 NTIS reports that are freely available to anyone who wishes to read them. Yet once more librarians were hearing stories of the need, indeed the obligation, to restrict access.

In a July 1988 discussion on American University's Public Radio station, FBI Assistant Director Milt Ahlerich told me that NTIS was "embargoed information which intelligence officers and foreign nationals from other countries were not allowed access to. And that is exactly the type of information that the intelligence officers are obtaining."[28]

I told Ahlerich, "There has been some confusion about what the executive directive really requires of NTIS or of the materials. The National Technical Information Service is prevented from selling their documents to the Soviet Union, but the materials themselves are in no way restricted or classified. That would mean that NTIS documents in the University of Maryland Libraries or elsewhere can be read, can be 'accessed' by anyone." But some minutes later in the course of our radio discussion, Ahlerich once more stated, "We've learned that they [the Soviets] have been trying to get information through the NTIS, or access to the NTIS." Again I pointed out, "That is not illegal. There is nothing illegal about anyone reading the unclassified NTIS documents. That, once again, is a misinterpretation of the executive order. . . . The materials themselves are as unclassified and readily available as any other book or journal on our shelves." Ahlerich simply responded, "I wouldn't argue the point with you. It's certainly subject to legal interpretation."[29]

Is this really a legal ambiguity, or another attempt to bring librarians into the process of information control? Are FBI spokespersons accurately representing this mysterious executive order? The brief Carter memorandum invoked in all FBI statements was not a numbered executive order and did not even mention NTIS, so Soviet access to NTIS documents was clearly not one of its "specific purposes," as claimed in the 1988 FBI report. The January 8, 1980, Carter memo states: "Pending review, no validated export licenses for shipment of goods or technical data to the Soviet Union are to be approved. This review is to reassess what exports will make a significant contribution to the military potential of the Soviet Union and therefore prove detrimental to the security of the United States in the light of the Soviet intervention in Afghanistan."[30]

The day after his initial memo, President Carter sent another even shorter memo to the secretary of commerce directing him to immediately suspend all existing specific export licenses to the Soviet Union pending the earlier-mentioned review. Only on January 25 did the issue of NTIS enter the picture, when Francis Wolek, deputy assistant secretary for science and technology, wrote to the director of the Office of Export Administration describing the routine Soviet purchases and subscriptions to NTIS reports and asking "whether the continuation of these sales is appropriate in the light of the President's restrictions on export licenses of high technology items to the Soviet Union." Wolek suggested that it might be difficult to include NTIS in these export restrictions: "As we know, NTIS technical information is openly published material which is exported under a general export license which does not require special review by the Office of Export Administration."[31] But the Commerce Department's assistant general counsel for science and technology responded in a February 12 memo, suggesting that "in the light of President Carter's restrictions on export licenses for high technology to the USSR, NTIS . . . can be directed to suspend its sales to USSR organizations here and abroad."[32] This option to restrict "sales" was offered by the Commerce Department but not required by President Carter's memo.

Finally, on February 20, 1980, Jordan J. Baruch, assistant secretary for productivity, technology, and innovation, acting on the Commerce Department's opinion, wrote Melvin Day: "I have decided as a matter of policy to direct you to suspend all sales of NTIS materials to the Union of Soviet Socialist Republics."[33] Baruch's directive was again a DOC policy decision, not an implementation of any particular portion of President Carter's original memo. In any case no memo, response, or interpretation from the president or anyone else bore any relevance to Soviet "use of " or "access to" NTIS materials, as claimed in the various FBI statements. The only matters addressed by the Commerce Department were "export licenses" and "sales," and because NTIS material is openly published, its export did not even require review by the Office of Export Administration. In fact, Section 6 of the Export Administration Act of 1979 states that export controls applied for foreign-policy purposes require annual extension, and no such extension appears to have occurred. Dr. Robert Park, the scientific community's most influential opponent of information control, has succinctly summarized the matter: "In short, the Carter 'executive order,' which may no longer be in force, did not even indirectly apply to NTIS. An eight year old Commerce Department policy on NTIS subscription sales to the Soviets has no bearing on library use."[34]

By the fall of 1988 I assumed that the FBI's NTIS campaign had run its course, but during the FBI's September meeting with the American Library Association's Intellectual Freedom Committee, Assistant Director James Geer again presented the spectre of supposedly illegal access to NTIS reports: "[A Soviet] may just be using that library, which is true in probably four of five of the instances here, to circumvent the ban on accessing the National Technical Information Service. He can't do it directly. . . . So he goes through a library or an employee of a library, asking that library to access documents from the National Technical Information Service for him and return them to him. That's been done. We don't try to enforce an Executive Order that bans that: we can't."[35] But apparently the FBI believes that librarians can be used to implement its uninformed policy of NTIS information denial.

C. James Schmidt, chair of the ALA's Intellectual Freedom Committee, asked Geer, "Jim, is there an Executive Order that prohibits access to the NTIS reports by Russian nationals?" Geer answered, "I wish I had brought a copy with me." I wish he had too. It might have stopped this NTIS charade once and for all. But Geer continued, "I can't remember exactly how it's worded . . . but it may say 'representatives of the Soviet Union.'. . . I can't speak to the wording, but I certainly can speak to the intent. The intent is to deny them access to it."[36]

The FBI knows better, because the library community has informed it on this matter. Yet the Bureau will apparently continue to pursue this kind of disinformation in order to restrict access to openly published, unclassified reports. The fundamental intellectual contradiction remains: If library collections are unclassified and open to all, why would allowing foreign nationals to read them be harmful to the United States? Hugh O'Connor, at the University of Maryland's Engineering Library, wrote, "One gets the impression that it is not just microcomputers and better aircraft that ought to be kept out of Soviet hands, but odorless cat boxes and pop-up toasters as well."[37]

LIBRARIANS AS ASSETS

The second role for librarians in the Library Awareness Program is as an "asset" for the FBI, gathering positive intelligence for the Bureau. Though the primary purpose for the Library Awareness Program is to restrict foreign access to unclassified technical information, the FBI's detailed testimony and position papers also reveal its desire to acquire a wide variety of intelligence information from librarians and the public at large.

Director Sessions has stated that the Library Awareness Program will use librarians in the "initial identification process" of suspected foreign agents.[38] But there is considerable evidence that the Bureau's desire to use librarians as assets is directly related to the federal goal of information control, inasmuch as it allows the identification of those scientific subjects and materials that are in demand by foreign nationals. As has been acknowledged by the FBI and the federal government at large, information is flagged for future classification or designated as "sensitive" simply because it is requested by the wrong people, whether it be by Americans through the FOIA or by Soviets at an American technical library. This approach to information control bypasses any examination of the subject matter itself. Information in demand is information to be denied, and librarians could be most useful in this delicate and contradictory process of ensuring that what is most sought is least available.

The FBI speaks frequently but cautiously of its reliance on American citizens to assist it in its investigations, and though it has contacted librarians and solicited their help, the Bureau claims, "It's your decision to make, but we're not trying to make librarians into spies."[39] Late in 1989 the first hard evidence of FBI assets in libraries was acquired through a FOIA request that produced about forty reports itemizing Bureau contacts with assets in libraries from March 1986 through June 1989. On a standard form (Figure 3.1), these reports provided the name of the asset, the date of contact, the contacting agent, and the reliability of the asset. Of course, the FBI had usually excised from the released reports the names of the agent and asset and the reliability rating. But two of the reports, May 25 and May 26, 1988, contained the following reliability rating: "[Deleted] who has furnished reliable information in the past." Another of the FOIA-released asset reports stated, "On 7/29/88, asset provided the attached copies of materials."[40] But the Bureau withheld those materials, amounting to eighty-seven pages, citing FOIA exemption (b)(7)(D). That exemption is designed to protect the names of "confidential informants"

Figure 3.1
Standard Form

Memorandum   S E C R E T

To : SAC, (s) (s) (s)   (P)   Date 9/21/87   b1
                                                 b1C
From : SA   b1D

Subject (s)
        (OO: NY)

This entire communication is classified "Secret."

ASSET: (s)
DATE CONTACTED: 9/10/87, 9/18/87
CONTACTED BY: SA
RELIABILITY:

                                 (S)

                                                    (S)

                                 S)

10-13-89 156588 Plt
Declassify on: OADR

          CLASSIFIED BY G-3
          DECLASSIFY ON OADR
              S E C R E T

2-New York
  ⊕ -   )
  (2)   030672

and information provided by confidential sources. By law, this exemption can only be invoked if these sources are genuine "assets" in libraries, providing protectable information.

Who were these "assets"? Were they librarians? Library clerks? Student assistants? FBI plants like Boyd Douglas? Given the Bureau's semantic license in these matters, these assets may have had a tenuous connection with libraries, and the information they provided may not have violated library ethics or state confidentiality laws.

Recently, David Atlee Phillips, a prominent former CIA operative who had frequently recruited agents abroad during his clandestine career, met with a dozen of his retired colleagues to discuss the Library Awareness Program's use of librarians as assets. Phillips described the role of librarians in the FBI's program as "benign supporting players in a legitimate counterintelligence operation. The librarians were to be, in intelligence jargon, spotters, assessment agents or access agents." Phillips expressed his agreement with current policy in the American intelligence community not to recruit agents among the Peace Corps, Fulbright scholars, or American missionaries, but he wondered why journalists and librarians, "consenting adults" as he called them, should be off limits. "Are librarians, too, to be prevented by some sort of blanket restriction from cooperating with their own security services. . . ? Sometimes, intelligence professionals feel, they are expected to seek recruits only among pimps and whores."[41]

Having distinguished librarians from pimps and ladies of the night, Phillips described their role in the Library Awareness Program as proper but temporarily awkward. "The FBI proposal to use librarians as support agents is not, in my mind, immoral. But it is unwise. The timing is wrong." Phillips advised FBI Director Sessions to avoid outraging civil libertarians with "operations that do not promise a major counterintelligence breakthrough" and concluded, "FBI recruitment of New York City librarians is an example of what Webster was sensitive to during his tenure, and of what Sessions can now do without, given the temper of the times."[42]

Senator Patrick Leahy (D-VT), in his opening statement at the 1988 FBI Oversight Committee hearing, told FBI Director William Sessions, "The Bureau's use of librarians for counterespionage purposes seems ineffective at best. At worst, it is a direct threat to the freedoms we in this country cherish.[43] But an FBI agent from New York saw no reason for concern, and he pointed out that librarians functioning as FBI assets "would be able to see what kind of person you are. They could check out your handwriting, see whether you're a research student or whether you're crazy or whether you're a threat. There is a chance that a librarian would see some suspicious activity and call us, and we would investigate and catch someone."[44] Another FBI agent had a slightly different view of the Library Awareness Program: "It's not a program like Cointelpro or the Ghetto Informant Program of the early 1970s. It's more of a counterintelligence investigative technique—it's used for movement anlaysis."[45]

When Assistant Director James Geer testified before Don Edwards' House subcommittee investigating the Library Awareness Program, one sympathetic congressman stated: "Unlike the chairman, . . . I do think that it is worthwhile for [the] U.S. Government to find out what Soviet and bloc intelligence services are looking for in the public domain. . . . I do not think that we can ignore picking up any shred of information on what Soviet intelligence services are doing in the United States of America."[46] Here we see a greater interest in discovering Soviet information needs than in thwarting Soviet information access. This is the essence of "positive intelligence," and if any members of the subcommittee had forgotten that the Library Awareness Program focused exclusively on unclassified library collections, the congressman's emphasis on "public domain" surely reminded them.

James Geer described the broad range of intelligence that librarians could acquire: "Some of it is obviously positive intelligence. And whether it is of any use to the FBI or not, it could well be of use to other parts of the intelligence community."[47] Geer explained that the FBI is interested in anything that the Soviets are interested in and described how the Bureau would process the seemingly trivial information provided by librarians. "We analyze that material very carefully. We have professional analysts that look at everything we can determine the Soviets are interested in. That can go a long way in determining for the policy makers in this country where the gaps are in their [Soviet] technology. . . . We have to grab the scraps of information . . . that somehow are indicators to us."[48] Those scraps are to be provided by the garbage collectors, the librarians.

The FBI's report, *The KGB and the Library Target*, emphasized that a librarian or library user who has had contact with a Soviet citizen can provide the FBI with personality assessment data impacting upon the subject's recruitment or defection potential.[49] In a closed briefing Deputy Director DuHadway went even further by revealing: "We do like to know what it is they're collecting because that gives us an idea . . . as to what their intelligence needs are, where they're going, what industries they're developing, what technologies we may even need to suggest become classified." DuHadway also described how librarians can assist in "identifying intelligence officers so we can then run a double agent case or try to develop other assets, informants if you will, against them."[50] Patricia Berger, current American Library Association president, recently claimed: "Some of us believe that an unstated objective of the FBI's Library Awareness Program was and is to use the staffs of America's scientific libraries to identify persons who can later be 'turned' by the FBI to become double agents. The FBI has been less than candid regarding this matter."[51]

Despite overwhelming rejection of the Library Awareness Program by the library profession, the FBI continues to claim that librarians are "cooperating" with them. The Bureau told author Natalie Robins: "Librarians can't admit they're cooperating with us, due to the program's controversial and confidential nature. Plus there's the risk of alienating people. A librarian won't say; it would make them suspect."[52]

In discussing that matter with me on American University's Public Radio station, Assistant Director Milt Ahlerich also contradicted the popular image of librarians opposing the Library Awareness Program, claiming, "We've had lots of success. Librarians are cooperating with us despite the position that's taken by their national organizations." I expressed my doubts to Ahlerich that librarians were "cooperating," if by that he meant that they had been violating their traditional relationship of trust and confidence with library users. But Ahlerich persisted: "This is a positive intelligence program, and librarians have significantly assisted the FBI in fulfilling our counterintelligence responsibilities. . . . We've learned about the methodology, the tradecraft and tasking of intelligence officers of the Soviet Union as the result of these contacts with selected libraries."[53] He expressed the belief that it was only a small element within the library profession that was protesting the Library Awareness Program, a conclusion totally at odds with all available evidence.

The Special Libraries Association

The 1987 *New York Times* story covering the Library Awareness Program focused on the FBI visit to Columbia University, just one of twenty-one acknowledged visits to New York libraries in recent years. The story said that it was unclear whether any librarians in New York had agreed to help the FBI. The Bureau's recently released "asset reports" suggest that there was some complicity, but the matter remains unclear. The Special Libraries Association (SLA), a prestigious organization representing virtually all special libraries, has been at the center of an embarrassing controversy surrounding the Library Awareness Program. Despite SLA's official resolution opposing the FBI's program, there have been unverified charges, most of them originating within the Bureau itself, that the SLA leadership has been working with the FBI.

FBI documents have referred repeatedly to the "specialized technical libraries" targeted by the SIS, and Assistant Director James Geer has testified that librarians contacted under the Library Awareness Program have been limited to those employed in libraries listed in the Special Libraries Directory of Greater New York. People outside the library profession ask, what is so special about "special libraries"? One textbook definition states: "A special library is characteristically a unit or department of an organization primarily devoted to other than library or educational purposes. A special librarian is first an employee, a staff member of the parent organization, and second, a librarian. 'Special' really means library service specialized or geared to the interests of the organization and to the information needs of its personnel."[54] Typical of such libraries would be those within corporations, federal agencies, or the military. Given this definition, could it be assumed that because special librarians must necessarily have their first loyalty to their parent organization, often a federal agency, they would therefore be unable to follow the ethics of their profession in resolving government challenges to confidentiality? I believe that this would be an extreme and unfounded view of special librarianship. But of the New York libraries visited by the FBI, only the universities, like Columbia and NYU, and the public libraries, like NYPL and BPL, openly reported and publicly rejected the Bureau's overtures, leading some to suspect that the "special libraries" visited may have cooperated.

The controversy emerged in earnest when the transcript of a January 14, 1988, meeting between the FBI and the National Commission on Libraries and Information Science revealed FBI Deputy Director Thomas DuHadway's claim that "we went to the President of the New York chapter of the Special Libraries Association and explained to her what we intended to do. She, in turn, contacted the Executive Director of the Specialized Library Association in Washington, D.C." When DuHadway was asked how these special libraries responded to the FBI overtures, he answered, "Very favorable, fine."[55]

But the most serious charges against SLA were made by author Natalie Robins, who revealed the FBI's claim that the head of one particular library association was coordinating FBI visits to libraries. An unidentified source had told Robins that "the Bureau was working with two executives in a single library organization, one of whom was based in New York and the other in Washington." In trying to identify that association, Robins ruled out ALA, ARL, the New York Library Association, and the American Society for Information Science because of their vigorous opposition to the Library Awareness Program. When Robins asked the FBI to identify the cooperating association, she was told, "We have coordinated the program with the Specialized Library Association, but we can't say who we are dealing with there."[56] Librarians knew, of course, that there was no "Specialized Library Association," but doubts were raised because of the name's similarity to that of the Special Libraries Association.

After hearing denials from a SLA communications director, Natalie Robins returned to the FBI, where a spokesperson told her that "Specialized Library Association" was just a generic name, and the Bureau could not reveal the organization's real name. Another FBI source insisted that "the head of the association has endorsed the program. There's probably not an association that would say they are it." Still another FBI source told Robins that the mysterious association was very probably SLA, and that the collaboration with the FBI "was coordinated mostly through the New York Office." When Robins contacted an SLA chapter president in New York, he expressed outrage at being questioned but was evasive about SLA's actions.[57]

The SLA Board of Directors first discussed the Library Awareness Program in October 1987 and chose not to take a position one way or another, supposedly because of insufficient information available to them at that time. David Bender, SLA's executive director, complained, "I can't get a firm stand. I'm governed by the Board of Directors. We are remaining neutral on what the FBI is doing." Still, Bender claimed, "We're working toward the same end as the A.L.A., but just using different means."[58] In April 1988 the board once more maintained its official neutrality on the Library Awareness Program, saying that this was "due to the diversity of libraries and information centers in which the Association's membership is employed."[59]

Just what did that verbiage mean? Some of my many friends in special libraries have confided to me that it takes little courage for a university librarian to speak glibly of rebuffing inquiries from federeal agencies. But what if that agency were not an interloper but your employer? Special librarians share the principles enunciated by the library profession in their rejection of the Library Awareness Program, but many of them are in a delicate position, working for agencies like the Department of Defense or their contractors. For this reason the SLA membership deserves special applause for the pressure it brought to bear on its Board of Directors at its 1988 annual meeting, where members introduced a motion urging the board to join the other library associations in opposing the Library Awareness Program. At that time ALA President-elect and SLA Fellow Patricia Berger warned that "the profession must remain united on this issue . . . let's not let a government agency divide us." One SLA member stated, "The diversity of our collections does not negate the fundamental principles of our profession." Finally, on June 17, 1988, the SLA Board of Directors adopted a policy statement endorsing access to information and confidentiality of library records and concluding: "The Association opposes the activities of the FBI Library Awareness Program."[60]

In his June 20, 1988, testimony before Congress, David Bender, executive director of SLA, complained more of the unfounded allegations of SLA complicity with the FBI than of the Library Awareness Program itself. Bender expressed concern over the "conflicting and misleading reports" issued by the FBI that implied that SLA was cooperating with the Bureau's program. He said that these reports were, to the best of his knowledge, untrue and "serve only to unfairly implicate SLA of wrongdoing." Along with his written testimony to Congress, Bender submitted copies of three letters dealing with charges of SLA complicity. On April 21, 1988, Bender himself had written to FBI Director Sessions complaining that "the media has construed our position as one of supporting the FBI's program." Bender pressed Sessions to reveal whether SLA really was the mysterious association that had allegedly endorsed the Library Awareness Program, stating, "First, the reputation of SLA has been cast in doubt. Secondly, accurate information should be provided to the media."[61]

On May 23 SLA President Emily Mobley also wrote Sessions: "Recent reports from the FBI imply that SLA is the association cooperating with the Library Awareness Program. Although you have not replied to Dr. Bender's letter of April 21 requesting that the FBI confirm or deny SLA's endorsement of the Library Awareness Program, it seems unlikely and contradictory that SLA would cooperate."[62]

On June 7 Director Sessions finally wrote to Bender, but the letter was unfocused and unresponsive to Bender's concerns. After two pages of boilerplate generalizations about the Soviet threat and the FBI mission, Sessions said that he was deeply disturbed by public comments that would portray cooperation with the FBI in a negative light. But the closest Sessions came to answering Bender's question about SLA collaboration with the Bureau was his reiteration that "the term specialized libraries association was used by the FBI in a 'generic' sense."[63]

What can we conclude from the morass of conflicting statements and charges circulating about SLA? Unlike public and academic libraries, many special libraries will be understandably cautious in repudiating their corporate or government sponsors, and individual SLA officials may even have been co-opted by the FBI. Clearly the SLA membership had to drag its Board of Directors, kicking and screaming, into the struggle with the FBI, but even the conservative board seems an unlikely conspirator. Perhaps we can conclude nothing more from SLA's ordeal with the FBI than that it raised the association's social consciousness, making it less likely that any government agency could again divide librarians on matters of principle.

A Librarian for the FBI

One librarian, Robert Colburn, has proudly revealed his work as an FBI "asset" in an article, "I Spy: Spying on a Spy for the People Who Spy on Spies." Early in his article Colburn claimed that "80 percent of the information collected by intelligence agencies is not secret." While understating the FBI's "90 percent" claim, Colburn added the view of Charles Yost, former U.S. ambassador to the United Nations, that "most significant current 'intelligence' is published in the daily, weekly or monthly press. The principal difficulty is not too little information but too much."[64]

Colburn then described how, during early 1984, Igor N. Mishchenko, third secretary of the Ukrainian Mission to the United Nations, visited the Document Depository at Columbia University's Engineering Library, purchasing copies of several unclassified technical reports. Such purchases were a routine part of the library's service, but Colburn recognized Mishchenko's address as that of the Soviet Mission, placing Colburn in what he called "an ethical dilemma." He stated, "Here was a Soviet who obviously wanted to get his hands on U.S. technology, and librarians aren't supposed to restrict information or who gets it."[65]

Since there were no classified or restricted materials at Colburn's library, was there really an "ethical dilemma" here? Only if one regards Soviet access to openly published technical information as a threat to American security. Apparently Colburn took this view, because he quickly called the State Department to express his concerns. Three days later an FBI agent contacted Colburn and urged him to come to the Bureau the very next morning.

Colburn was met by one of the 350 or more agents assigned to cover foreign diplomats, and together they identified Mishchenko from a series of photographs. The FBI agent told Colburn that Mishchenko had done nothing illegal, because he had been working within the twenty-five–mile zone to which Soviet diplomats stationed in New York are confined, and none of the documents he had asked for was classified. But the FBI agent suggested a role for Colburn if Mishchenko continued his library relationship. "If he did, would I be willing to become what the agent called an 'asset'? Would I meet with Mishchenko, then tell all to the Bureau?" Colburn had already violated most of the explicit ethical standards of his profession by providing patron names and reading habits to the FBI, so it was not surprising when he proudly admitted, "I bought in."[66]

What followed was a succession of lunches and dinners with Mishchenko. They talked about movies, beer, Russian literature, and the Olympics. Colburn passed all of this small talk to the FBI, and the Bureau urged him to continue his contacts with Mishchenko. But first Colburn was asked to take a lie-detector test "to reassure Washington." To this point the lunchtime chats between Colburn and Mishchenko had varied from innocent to insipid, but perhaps the Bureau wished to verify whether Soviets preferred Chicken McNuggets or the Mac BLT. In any case, Colburn assured us, "I cleared the polygraph test and continued to eat my way through my own version of a second Russian grain deal."[67]

Colburn's final meeting with Mishchenko occurred in November 1984, when they again dined together. Colburn states, "During the meal, he put me through an embarrassing, simplistic and insulting lecture on 'the benefits of the Soviet way of life', where the television newscasts always ended with a positive story item and where no one 'owned anybody else.' " But aside from speaking well of his country, which apparently only spies do, Mishchenko did little else to threaten our national security. In fact, shortly thereafter, just as we were prepared for some real action, romance, violence, anything but more free lunches, Colburn's story abruptly ended as Mishchenko returned to Moscow. No laws broken, no spies trapped, just a lot of freeloading by Colburn. But in concluding his less than thrilling tale, Colburn put the best face on the affair: "I was relieved. My experience had been relatively benign. I was able to steer clear of both superpowers without jeopardizing my career or my country. Others haven't been so lucky."[68]

Perhaps if the rest of the library profession would put God and country before the stale platitudes of our profession, we could forever be free of the dreary stereotypes that plague us. But few librarians are likely to choose Colburn's anomalous path. The delightful irony of the FBI's attempt to recruit librarians as "assets" is that the same obstinacy that prevents most librarians from collaborating with the FBI will ensure their prototypical patriotism in the face of foreign intelligence officers. To whatever degree the library profession is capable of performing the FBI's surreptitious "positive counterintelligence" on its unsuspecting patrons, to that same degree must the FBI suspect the librarians' vulnerability to other unethical or illegal solicitations, foreign or domestic. I am betting that intelligence agencies at home and abroad will continue to find librarians to be infuriatingly obdurate and principled in their adherance to law and ethics and their opposition to any distortion or violation of intellectual freedom or confidentiality. In other words, as American as apple pie.

LIBRARIANS AS POTENTIAL KGB AGENTS

The ALA's C. James Schmidt told Congress that "the alleged targeting of libraries as a place of recruitment and of librarians as potential operatives by Soviet intelligence agents is unsubstantiated. There has been no evidence to support this claim."[69] But ever the cynic, the FBI adheres to its belief that not just malevolent library users, but librarians themselves are serving the SIS, and that the Library Awareness Program must protect them from KGB recruitment. FOIA documents released from the FBI's New York office mentioned the need to counter Soviet efforts to develop "sources and contacts among librarians," but such terms are applied so broadly as to include any interaction between library staff and Soviet nationals.

Such semantic confusion in the FBI's pronouncements renders its claims of frequent KGB recruitment of librarians ambiguous and unverifiable. For this reason, there is a temptation to write off the Bureau's stated desire to guard librarianship from KGB recruitment as nothing more than a counterintelligence cover, a public-relations image of a paternal Bureau protecting a naive and vulnerable profession from itself. The first source of confusion is the FBI's inclusive definition of the term "librarian." For example, in his meeting with the ALA's Intellectual Freedom Committee, FBI Assistant Director James Geer was asked, "Are you calling everybody that works in a library a librarian?" Geer answered, "Well, I can be, yes. I'm using it in a very broad context." A second FBI semantic problem concerns its definition of a KGB "source" to include anyone providing unclassified information, such as NTIS reports, to a Soviet citizen. For example, Assistant Director Geer stated, "The Soviets recruit sources that they use to collect unclassified information all over the country, simply because they don't want to be seen doing it themselves."[70] This description of a "source" would, of course, fit almost any American reference librarian, making it logical to conclude that librarians are being recruited successfully each day by the KGB.

Curiously, the Special Libraries Association has been alleged by the Bureau to be both an FBI "asset" and a KGB "source." The "asset" charge has been dealt with earlier in this chapter, and the "source" allegation seems to be equally groundless. In its report, *The KGB and the Library Target*, the FBI charged that the SIS had been acquiring valuable information from SLA's office.[71] After the SLA president wrote the Bureau to dispute the claim, Director Sessions answered:

You take strong exception to the statement that 'The SIS has utilized clandestine means to obtain large volumes of documents from the Special Libraries Association' and you assert that the statement is false and unfounded. . . . No one in the FBI has ever suggested that any librarian would knowingly provide such documents. Intelligence officers are highly trained and use covert and seemingly innocent means to accomplish their goals. They, little by little and with apparently innocuous materials, obtain significant intelligence when the information is added together.[72]

SLA tried to explain to the FBI that not only had nothing been taken from its office, but there was nothing there to take, other than the most trivial and tedious materials on library management. But the FBI remained convinced that SLA was an unwitting "source."

Regardless of semantics, the FBI clearly feels that by emphasizing the KGB recruitment issue rather than information control or positive intelligence, it is less likely to arouse First Amendment concerns within the library profession. In January 1988 FBI Deputy Director Thomas DuHadway stated: "We've had Soviets tell us that they think it's better to recruit two librarians in a science and technological library than it would be to recruit three engineers . . . , because those librarians have access to people, places and things that can front for the Soviet. . . . They think it's extremely important to have sources in libraries."[73] On the "MacNeil-Lehrer Report" James Geer advised me and the audience that the SIS "tries to develop contacts and recruit librarians."[74] Such characterizations subsequently appeared on television news, which cited "efforts by the Soviet Union to recruit librarians and develop them as spies against the United States.[75]

James Geer has warned of hostile intelligence officers utilizing America's technical libraries "to develop sources, train agents, and obtain information vital to their government's needs." Geer described the Library Awareness Program as an attempt "to inform selected librarians that they and their libraries are and have historically been significant SIS targets for intelligence activities and recruitment," and he said that the Soviets "utilize unsuspecting employees and patrons of these libraries." He claimed that payments or other inducements have been offered by the SIS to librarians "in an effort to recruit these individuals as agents, either wittingly or unwittingly."[76] Similarly, Milt Ahlerich, the Bureau's assistant director on congressional and public affairs, warned that intelligence officers "target unsuspecting librarians and citizens."[77] Again, in the context of unclass-ified libraries, the notion of "unsuspecting" librarians serving "unwittingly" as KGB agents is indistinguishable from librarians providing normal reference service to Soviet nationals.

The Bureau has been justifying the Library Awareness Program as "a very measured response to a well planned and organized effort . . . to exploit our specialized scientific and technical libraries and recruit our citizens."[78] In May 1988 FBI Assistant Director Milt Ahlerich claimed, "the Soviet Union routinely attempts to develop librarians as sources of information or recruit them as agents."[79] Ahlerich later discussed this issue with me on Public Radio, claiming that "the Soviet intelligence services are actually involved in recruiting librarians." When I asked if he could be more specific, Ahlerich answered, "Not other than to say it has occurred. We know for a fact that librarians have been recruited by the intelligence services of hostile countries. . . . We think it is incumbent on the FBI to let librarians know that they are the targets of recruiting efforts . . . and that success has occurred, with the Soviets then going to certain scientific libraries and extracting information." By saying that the recruitment of librarians results in Soviets "extracting information" from the totally unclassified libraries covered by the Library Awareness Program, Ahlerich underscores the FBI's view that any librarian providing normal service to a Soviet national is a co-optee of the SIS.[80]

On a subsequent radio show out of Chicago, Ahlerich again told me that the Soviets had frequently recruited librarians as KGB spies. "We know they have done this, and they have successfully recruited librarians in the past." Ahlerich further claimed, "We know the Soviets and their surrogates are in these libraries, recruiting the librarians and using it to their ad-vantage. And that does not seem to meet with any objections from the librarians, yet the FBI's interest in trying to counter this threat does."[81]

On August 24, 1988, I wrote to Ahlerich that I was unaware of any librarians recruited by the SIS and asking for details on such charges. Ahlerich responded by assuring me that his remarks were not intended to suggest that librarians are less loyal or less concerned about our nation's security than other Americans. He said that he wished it were possible to reveal the details of instances where librarians had been successfully recruited by the Soviet intelligence service, but such information was classified and could not be released.[82]

The Zakharov Affair

What, then, does the Bureau offer us as evidence that librarians, library employees, or even library users are targeted for recruitment by the SIS? When the *New York Times* broke the story of the Library Awareness Program in September 1987, it claimed that the program had been under way "since last spring as a result of a sensational espionage case in which a Soviet employee of the United Nations, Gennadi F. Zackharoff, recruited a Queens College student as an agent through contacts made at a library."[83] Shortly thereafter, special agent Ray McElhaney of the FBI's National Press Office read a press response describing the attempt by hostile intelligence officers to recruit students in American libraries. When asked for evidence of this activity, McElhaney could only offer the Zakharov affair.

We know that the Library Awareness Program was initiated in 1973, but curiously, the Bureau continues to maintain the centrality of the 1986 Zakharov affair in its justification for the program. Despite the fact that the Zakharov case involved no librarians or other library employees, the FBI continues to invoke this and only this case to support the charge of SIS recruitment in libraries. The FBI's earliest position paper, *The KGB and the Library Target*, devoted four pages to the Zakharov case in describing the SIS threat to libraries and librarians, and Assistant Director James Geer did much the same in his written testimony to the House Subcommittee on Civil and Constitutional Rights. FBI Director Sessions claimed, "Mr. Zakharov's use of libraries did not come as a surprise, inasmuch as FBI investigations over the years have documented a large number of cases where SIS officers have exploited contacts with specialized libraries and librarians."[84]

But C. James Schmidt, testifying for the Research Libraries Group, told the same subcommittee:

The arrest of Gennadi Zakharov in 1986 has been cited by the Bureau as an instance of the contention that libraries are sites and librarians are targets of recruitment. The public facts of that incident indicate, however, that the student who worked for Zakharov was, in fact, (a) recruited by another student, not by Zakharov; (b) asked to provide UN-CLASSIFIED materials. More damaging, yet, to the Bureau's use of this case as a cautionary example is the clear fact that this student was being "run" by the FBI from the beginning. Are we truly being asked to believe that our national security is threatened by students who, under the control of the FBI, provide copies of unclassified journal articles to Russians?![85]

Geer of course disagreed with Schmidt's view, but James Dempsey, assistant counsel for the House Subcommittee on Civil and Constitutional Rights, expressed his own doubts while questioning Geer.

Dempsey: But the one example that is most frequently cited . . . did not involve an approach to a librarian.

Geer: That is true.

Dempsey: It did not involve a Soviet diplomat going into a library.

Geer: It was within the library premises that he got the name of the student to begin with from the bulletin board.

Dempsey: But that could have been a single visit with a name off a bulletin board.

Geer: It could have been.[86]

A look at the Zakharov case suggests that it had much more to do with FBI assets than SIS agents. Leakh Bhoge, the student allegedly recruited by Zakharov in 1983 in a Queens College library, was in fact introduced to Zakharov by a fellow student, under quite different circumstances than those suggested by the FBI. Bhoge did not meet Zakharov in the library, and Zakharov may never have entered the library.

On a brief television interivew after the Zakharov affair, Bhoge said only that he was introduced to "a Russian personnel," whom he immediately suspected was a "Russian personnel." Bhoge's labored attempt to sound like an intelligence agent was ludicrous and prevented any real communication. The interviewer had to tell the audience that the "Russian personnel" was Zakharov, and after a few questions the interview was terminated. The pathetic Leakh Bhoge has not graced the media since then, and the only public source of information on the Zakharov affair remains a single 1987 article in *New York* magazine, cited repeatedly by the FBI itself. The article reveals the following:

Bhoge was a Guyanese immigrant whose early passions were geography, cricket, and spy movies. Even after he came to the United States, he sought escape at the end of each day in the movie houses on New York's Forty-second Street, where he favored spy movies. At home he read spy novels and watched James Bond movies on television. Sean Connery was his favorite actor.

At Queens College Bhoge met a student named Artie, who said that he had been earning ten dollars an hour doing research for a professor. When

Artie quit that job he introduced Bhoge to the "professor," who in fact was Zakharov. Zakharov gave Bhoge a list of magazine articles to be located in the library and photocopied. At the suggestion of a fellow student, Bhoge contacted the FBI, and an agent subsequently called him at home to arrange a meeting. At that first meeting an agent asked Bhoge if he wanted to make some extra money during the summer. He said no. The agent asked him if he had time for lunch. He said no.

But eventually Bhoge agreed to work as a paid "asset" for the Bureau. Soon FBI agents were meeting regularly with Bhoge and taking him to lunch, but Bhoge was uneasy with the way the Bureau was treating him. "I wasn't doing any smiling because, hey, this thing is getting serious now."[87]

In the meantime, Zakharov had given Bhoge his business card, identifying himself openly as a Soviet attaché with the United Nations. The FBI agent told Bhoge to take Zakharov's money, because "the motherland supplies it."[88] The agent pressed Bhoge to continue meeting Zakharov, promising that the FBI would properly reward him. But Bhoge still did not want to get involved.

The FBI had given Bhoge the code name "Plumber." Bhoge says, "I never asked why. I was scared of them." While Bhoge continued to copy magazine articles for Zakharov, often from periodicals on microfiche in the Queens College library, the FBI was paying him in the neighborhood of $300 a month, while the Bureau kept all of Zakharov's payments as "evidence." Bhoge now wanted more money from the FBI and threatened to quit, but his FBI contact pressed him to continue.[89]

Through the rest of 1983 Bhoge continued to photocopy magazine articles for Zakharov, with the FBI making its own copies of same. But Bhoge was wearying of his role as an FBI asset, and when he was assigned a new FBI contact, he told the agent, "I feel like a piece of nothing, and I don't know who I am anymore." Bhoge recalls, "I was like a dog following them." Shortly thereafter, the FBI gave Bhoge a polygraph test.[90]

When Bhoge received his degree from Queens College, the FBI placed him in a machine shop owned by an FBI agent's father. By now the FBI had outfitted Bhoge with a hidden tape recorder, to be worn during all meetings with Zakharov. In late 1986 the FBI gave Bhoge three Air Force documents to provide to Zakharov. These, having SECRET stamped on their covers, were to be the basis for Zakharov's subsequent arrest. When Bhoge met Zakharov for the final, fateful transaction, he did not reveal the true nature of the documents he carried in the envelope. "I did not want to tell him the word 'secret' is printed on the documents, because I was afraid he might leave. I said, 'Something of a classified or unclassified nature is printed on them.' " Zakharov sensed that something was wrong, but after some small talk he was smiling again. Bhoge reflects, "I now knew I had him where I wanted him."[91]

Bhoge offered the envelope containing the documents to Zakharov and said, "See man, it's secretive. See the word 'secret' marked on it? Give me my money." But while Bhoge held out his hand, Zakharov just gazed down at the envelope, and an FBI agent immediately appeared, grabbed his arm, and arrested him for purchasing classified documents. Bhoge described how it took several seconds before a surprised Zakharov looked up, but the agents told him that it was no use resisting, and they dragged him off in handcuffs.[92]

What really happened here? Nancy Kranich of the New York University Libraries has stated, "It appears that the FBI may have entrapped Zakharov, since the Bureau has failed to produce any evidence to indicate that Zakharov asked Bhoge to obtain classified information."[93] Did Zakharov ever actually take the envelope? Did he even know that it contained classified information? Ironically, the same questions were asked about Nicholas Daniloff, an American reporter arrested shortly thereafter in Moscow as a spy for having received a similar envelope. Bhoge's analysis of the Daniloff affair was interesting: "If I were him, I would have stayed away at this time from taking an envelope."[94]

Because the article from which most of this detail is taken is the exclusive public source of information on the Zakharov case, it has been elevated to the level of an official document, frequently quoted and cited in the FBI's position papers and testimony. The author, Michael Daly, concluded that though Leakh Bhoge had hoped for the sports cars and beautiful girls of the James Bond movies he enjoyed, he found instead a depressing life that revolved around fast-food restaurants. The FBI gave Bhoge his final $650 payment, bringing his earings for three years of espionage to about $20,000. Since all of Bhoge's salary from Zakharov was turned over to the FBI as "evidence," that $20,000 worth of "espionage" was for the Bureau, not the KGB. Perhaps more important and revealing was Leakh Bhoge's proud response when he subsequently became a U.S. citizen: "I hope it [is a] passport to big dollar."[95] Such is not the behavior of a patriot by whose standards librarians may be profitably judged.

Treason in the Stacks

Has the Bureau never pursued an actual library employee on suspicion of espionage? Consider the case of Harry Kenneth Clark, bookshelver at the Library of Congress. In 1975, shortly after the FBI began its Library Awareness Program, the Bureau initiated an investigation of this library employee after an informer told the FBI that Clark had attended a meeting of the Young Socialist Alliance. By 1976 the FBI had undertaken a full field investigation of Clark, despite the patently harmless nature of his job and political activities.

The FBI assigned agents from Washington, Baltimore, and Minneapolis to investigate Clark and in addition used hosts of officers from police departments around the country, as well as U.S. Park Service and Civil Service investigators. They examined Clark's high-school records, his credit files, and his family's public-housing records. Clark's fellow workers and supervisors at the Library of Congress were questioned, along with his neighbors, friends, former employers, and former teachers. Even Clark's junior-high-school librarian was quizzed about his character and reading habits.[96]

The FBI described this investigation as "minimally intrusive," but Clark found himself turned down for forty positions at the Library of Congress over a two-year period, despite an excellent work record and qualifications. Eventually, with the help of the ACLU, Clark went to court. At trial the government claimed that its investigative obligation "outweighs the entirely speculative injury to his [Clark's] First Amendment rights." Despite admitting the nonsensitive nature of Clark's position, the government claimed that "this does not mean that under no set of facts could he have been a risk to national security."[97]

But the District of Columbia Circuit Court of Appeals concluded that the FBI was required to demonstrate that its investigation served a vital governmental interest and that the full field investigation was the means least restrictive of the employee's First Amendment rights. The government requested a rehearing, but the Court of Appeals rejected that request, with only Judges Bork, Scalia, and Starr dissenting. The Justice Department remained unhappy with the results of *Clark* v. *Library of Congress*, complaining: "Application of such a stringent standard to the initial decision to undertake an investigation deprives the Government of the discretion it must have to inquire into the suitability and loyalty of its employees."[98]

Paint the Critics Red

Neither the Zakharov nor the Clark cases support the FBI charge that librarians, or even library employees, have been recruited by the SIS.

There were no library employees involved in the Zakharov affair, and there were no SIS agents involved in the Clark affair. The one case is an irrelevancy to libraries, while the other case is an absurd McCarthy-era anachronism. The library profession continues to await evidence of even a single library employee guilty of treason in the stacks.

However, recently released dcouments have revealed the depth of the FBI's paranoia and the shocking extent of its "index checks" on librarians. A February 6, 1989, memo from the FBI's New York Assistant Director in Charge (ADIC) to Director Sessions described a sixteen-month investigation of librarians: "After a review of 266 New York indices checks conducted on the names of individuals since 10/87 in an attempt to determine whether a Soviet active measures campaign had been initiated to discredit the LIBRARY AWARENESS PROGRAM (LAP), only the following eight references were noted. All other indices checks were either negative or of no significance to this study."[99]

The "active measures campaign" referred to in the FBI's memo is intelligence jargon for any effort by hostile intelligence to influence popular opinion through disinformation, propaganda, or front groups. The memo withheld the eight names allegedly involved with a Soviet campaign to discredit the Library Awareness Program, but any of the librarians who have spoken forcefully and publicly against the program could be on the list. The most disturbing aspect of the Bureau's extended investigation of librarians, begun almost immediately after the 1987 *New York Times* exposé on the Library Awareness Program, is its Hoover-era assumption that any domestic criticism of an FBI program must be Soviet-instigated. In reality, the library profession's opposition to FBI intrusions in libraries was quintessentially homegrown, the formal component of national, grass roots outrage. To suggest that foreign subversion was necessary to "discredit" a program that was instantly rejected and ridiculed by the public is to ignore the painful lessons of the Bureau's past.

The memo cited here was one of about 1,200 previously secret FBI documents released on October 30, 1989, pursuant to a FOIA request by the National Security Archive. Throughout the released material there was other evidence of continuing FBI investigations of librarians. For example, even when the FBI withheld documents, there were frequent exemption forms stating, "The withheld pages are copies of search slips on individual(s) associated with a library or library organization." In fact, this exemption was invoked to justify withholding information on approximately 450 such "search slips," with at least 266 of them made since October 1987. One search slip (Figure 3.2), dated October 17, 1985, con-

Figure 3.2
Indices Search Slip

Indices Search Slip
FD-160 (Rev. 7-21-83)

SECRET b1 b2 b7C

Date 10/17/85

TO: OFFICE SERVICES MANAGER

Subject: SPECIAL LIBRARIES ASSOCIATION

Social Security Account #

Aliases

Address: NEW YORK CHAPTER

Birth Date	Birthplace	Race	Sex
			☐ Male ☐ Female

☐ Exact Spelling
☒ All References
☐ Main Security Case Files Only
☐ Security References Only
☐ Main Criminal Case Files Only
☐ Criminal References Only
☐ Main Security (If no Main, list all Security References)
☐ Main Criminal (If no Main, list all Criminal References)
☐ Restrict Locality of

File & Serial Number	Remarks	File & Serial Number	Remarks
[redacted] (S)	I		
[redacted] (S)	NI		
[redacted] (S)	I		
[redacted] (S)	I		
[redacted] (S)	I		
[redacted] (S)	I	10-12-89 Classified by 2565 SDP/bfj Declassify on: OADR	

Requested by [redacted]
Squad [redacted] (S) Extension [redacted] File No. [redacted] (S)

☒ General Indices: [redacted]
Searched by — Date 10/17/85
☐ Confidential Indices:
Searched by — Date
☐ ELSUR Indices:
Searched by — Date
☐ ISIS:
Searched by — Date
☐ OCIS:
Searched by — Date
☐ IIS:
Searched by — Date

Consolidated by — Date
Reviewed by — Date

~~CLASSIFIED BY G-3~~
~~DECLASSIFY ON: OADR~~

[redacted]

030639

File Review Symbols
I - Identical
NI - Not Identical
? - Not Identifiable
U - Unavailable reference

*U.S. GOVERNMENT PRINTING OFFICE: 1985- [redacted]

cerned the Special Libraries Association, showing six separate FBI files located on SLA. Did the Bureau actually suspect SLA members of having KGB connections? Or was the Bureau simply trying to verify SLA members who might be sympathetic to an FBI visit? We cannot tell, because all significant information on the search slip was blacked out.

FBI Director Sessions initially said that he was unaware of the FBI's background checks on critics of the Library Awareness Program, but he said that he would have approved such checks had he been asked. "It is natural for us to check," he said. "It is routinely done."[100] A Bureau spokesperson later tried to revise and minimize Sessions' comments, and Assistant Director Ahlerich insisted that no agents were dispatched into the field to conduct such inquiries. He described them as a standard review of FBI files to determine if a person had previously written or called the Bureau or was the subject of a criminal or espionage investigation. Bureau spokesman Greg Jones claimed: "The F.B.I. at no time conducted any investigation regarding the critics or anyone in opposition to the Library Awareness Program. The F.B.I. did, however, conduct indices checks relating to individuals who had been in contact with us."[101]

Rep. Don Edwards said that his Subcommittee on Civil and Constitutional Rights had no information to support the FBI's suspicions about a Soviet influence campaign. "There is absolutely no evidence to support this theory either in any of our private briefings or public testimony by the F.B.I. on this program." Edwards added, "The F.B.I. never understood why people were upset with the Library Awareness Program. . . . It's very dismaying that the F.B.I. so failed to understand what was the source of this criticism."[102]

Joseph S. Murphy, chancellor of the City University of New York, asked Congress to look further into the Bureau's investigations of librarians, stating that the FBI had "questioned the loyalty" of librarians who wrote letters critical of the Library Awareness Program. Murphy said that it was "inappropriate and, in fact, inconceivable that librarians should be asked to serve as informants for the F.B.I. as part of their professional duties."[103]

The American Library Association's Office for Intellectual Freedom protested the FBI's actions: "It's not consistent with First Amendment principles to investigate somebody on the basis of what he reads, nor to investigate somebody because he stands up to defend a First Amendment principle."[104]

After ridiculing the Library Awareness Program as a " 'Get Smart' spy spoof," a *New York Times* editorial stated: "Now there's a new chapter. Declassified documents show that the F.B.I. conducted cursory investigations of librarians and others who publicly criticised its program. The agency says it did nothing more than a 'routine' check of in-house files to see if those who spoke out were urged to do so by the Soviets." The editorial called on Director Sessions to repudiate the Bureau's meddling in libraries, concluding: "If his agents fear spies in the stacks, let them get a court order to check it out. His main mission ought to be to end this offensive encroachment of the rights of library workers and users."[105]

John Berry, *Library Journal*'s editor-in-chief, complained: "It hurt when the FBI director impugned the patriotism of librarians who wouldn't enlist in the Bureau's Library Awareness Program. It angered us to find out that the FBI was investigating the nearly 250 librarians who refused to take part in the program." Berry then reflected on why the FBI regards librarians as such suspicious characters: "Fixated on communist subversion, the FBI tends to see all dissent as emanating from Moscow. It was predictable, alas, that agents would search for links between the suspicious librarians and the USSR. . . . The FBI nearly always sees something subversive in any opposition to its efforts to protect the 'secrets' of our government or to limit access to our libraries." Berry concluded: "We the people plant the seeds of subversion. They are there in our Bill of Rights, our elections, our free press, and, of course, in our libraries."[106]

NOTES

1. "Librarians Say No to Spying Pitch of FBI," *Virginian-Pilot*, October 29, 1988, p. B3.

2. Don Edwards, "Government Information Controls Threaten Academic Freedom, *Thought and Action: The NEA Higher Education Journal*, Spring 1989, p. 87.

3. Memo on Library Awareness Program and related matters from C. James Schmidt, Chair, Intellectual Freedom Committee, to ALA Executive Board/Council, January 8, 1989, p. 4. Reprinted by permission of the American Library Association.

4. Letter from Milt Ahlerich, FBI Acting Assistant Director, Office of Congressional and Public Affairs, to Harriet M. Turley, Eckerd College Library, October 7, 1987. October 30, 1989, FOIA release to National Security Archive.

5. FBI presentation to U.S. National Commission on Libraries and Information Science by Thomas DuHadway, San Antonio, Texas, January 14, 1988, pp. 7, 40.

6. Natalie Robins, "The FBI's Invasion of Libraries," *Nation*, April 9, 1988, p. 498.

7. Transcript of meeting of FBI and ALA Intellectual Freedom Committee, September 9, 1988, p. 7.

8. FBI Headquarters, Intelligence Division, *The KGB and the Library Target, 1962–Present*, January 1, 1988, pp. 2, 32.

9. Quinlan J. Shea, speech before the American Society of Access Professionals, July 28, 1988, p. 4.

10. U.S. Congress, House Committee on the Judiciary, *FBI Counterintelligence Visits to Libraries: Hearings before the House Subcommittee on Civil and Constitutional Rights of the Committee on the Judiciary*, 100th Cong., 2d sess., June 20 and July 13, 1988 (Washington, D.C.: GPO, 1989), p. 150.

11. Memo from FBI Los Angeles to Director, FBI, May 27, 1988. October 30, 1989, FOIA release to National Security Archive.

12. "FBI Asks Librarians to Help in the Search for Spies," *Philadelphia Inquirer*, February 23, 1988, p. 1A.

13. FBI presentation to U.S. National Commission on Libraries and Information Science by Thomas DuHadway, San Antonio, Texas, January 14, 1988, p. 18.

14. In 1984 President Reagan signed National Security Division Directive 145, designating a new category of restricted information called "sensitive but unclassified." The precise definition of "sensitive" was to be left to the unpredictable judgment of agency heads. In October 1986, National Security Advisor John Poindexter issued National Telecommunications and Information Systems Security Policy No. 2, a memo defining "sensitive but unclassified" as "information the disclosure, loss, misuse, alteration or destruction of which would adversely affect national security or other government interests. . . ." (NTISSP No. 2, October 29, 1986, Section II.)

15. National Committee on Libraries and Information Science, *Hearing on Sensitive but Not Classified Information* (Washington, D.C.: Library of Congress, May 28, 1987), p. 40.

16. Decision and Order of the Department of Energy, Motion for Clarification, Office of Scientific and Technical Information, January 26, 1988, p. 5 and attached form.

17. "UC Libraries Quit NASA Databank in Rules Dispute," *Los Angeles Times*, July 3, 1988, sec. 1, pp. 3, 31.

18. "FBI Encourages Librarians to Be on the Lookout for Spies," *Nature*, December 8, 1988, p. 507.

19. "Commerce Secretary Wants Technical Data Restricted," *Science*, March 8, 1985, p. 1182.

20. FBI Headquarters, Intelligence Division, *KGB and the Library Target*, p. 15.

21. Memo from SAC, WFO, to Director, FBI, January 15, 1988. October 30, 1989, FOIA release to National Security Archive.

22. Memo from SAC, WMFO, to Director, FBI, June 1988. October 30, 1989, FOIA release to National Security Archive.

23. *FBI Counterintelligence Visits to Libraries*, pp. 116–18.

24. Ibid., pp. 128, 138.

25. Ibid., p. 144.

26. "Good Morning America," ABC TV, July 13, 1988.

27. "MacNeil-Lehrer Report," Public Television, July 13, 1988.

28. "The Diane Rehm Show," WAMU Public Radio, Washington, D.C., July 19, 1988.

29. Ibid.

30. *FBI Counterintelligence Visits to Libraries*, p. 129.

31. Ibid., p. 407.

32. Ibid., p. 408.

33. Ibid., p. 131.

34. Ibid., p. 406.

35. Transcript of meeting of FBI and ALA Intellectual Freedom Committee, September 9, 1988, p. 43.

36. Ibid., p. 44.

37. Hugh O'Connor, "America Becomes Aware of FBI in Libraries" (Part 2), *Crab*, November 1988, p. 8.

38. *FBI Counterintelligence Visits to Libraries*, p. 152.

39. FBI presentation to U.S. National Commission on Libraries and Information Science by Thomas DuHadway, San Antonio, Texas, January 14, 1988, p. 32.

40. FBI Asset Reports dated May 25, May 26, and July 29, 1988; contained in memos to NYO from [deleted], dated May 26, May 27, and August 5, 1988. From October 30, 1989, FOIA release to National Security Archive.

41. David Atlee Phillips, "FBI's Timing Is Questionable, Not Its Morals," *Newsday*, October 16, 1987, p. 83.

42. Ibid.

43. Charles Levendosky, "FBI Noses Around for Spies in Libraries," *Casper Star-Tribune*, May 29, 1988, p. A10.

44. "FBI Asks Librarians to Help in the Search for Spies," *Philadelphia Inquirer*, February 23, 1988, p. 17A.

45. Robins, "FBI's Invasion of Libraries," p. 498.

46. *FBI Counterintelligence Visits to Libraries*, p. 106.

47. Ibid., p. 144.

48. Transcript of meeting of FBI and ALA Intellectual Freedom Committee, September 9, 1988, p. 6.

49. FBI Headquarters, Intelligence Division, *KGB and the Library Target*, p. 9.

50. FBI presentation to U.S. National Commission on Libraries and Information Science by Thomas DuHadway, San Antonio, Texas, January 14, 1988, pp. 8, 30.

51. Letter from Patricia W. Berger, President, ALA, to Jerald C. Newman, Chairman, NCLIS, September 8, 1989, p. 2.

52. Robins, "FBI's Invasion of Libraries," p. 501.

53. "The Diane Rehm Show," WAMU Public Radio, Washington, D.C., July 19, 1988.

54. Elizabeth Ferguson and Emily R. Mobley, *Special Libraries at Work* (Hamden, Conn.: Library Professional Publications, 1984), p. 4.

55. FBI presentation to U.S. National Commission on Libraries and Information Science by Thomas DuHadway, San Antonio, Texas, January 14, 1988, p. 32.

56. Robins, "FBI's Invasion of Libraries," *Nation*, p. 501.

57. Ibid., p. 502.

58. Natalie Robins, "Library Follow-up," *Nation*, June 25, 1988, p. 886.

59. "SLA Reluctantly Joins Fray in FBI 'Awareness Battle,'" *School Library Journal*, August 1988, p. 14.

60. "SLA Board Acts to Oppose FBI Library Awareness Program," *Specialist*, August 1988, p. 1.

61. *FBI Counterintelligence Visits to Libraries*, pp. 42, 51.

62. Ibid., p. 53.

63. Ibid., pp. 57.

64. Robert Colburn, "I Spy," *Washington Post Magazine*, March 2, 1986, p. 8.

65. Ibid.

66. Ibid.

67. Ibid., p. 9.

68. Ibid., p. 17.

69. *FBI Counterintelligence Visits to Libraries*, p. 29.

70. Transcript of meeting of FBI and ALA Intellectual Freedom Committee, September 9, 1988, pp. 8, 44.

71. FBI Headquarters, Intelligence Division, *KGB and the Library Target*, p. 16.

72. Letter from William S. Sessions, Director, FBI, to Emily R. Mobley, President, Special Libraries Association, July 11, 1988. October 30, 1989, FOIA release to National Security Archive.

73. FBI presentation to U.S. National Commission on Libraries and Information Science by Thomas DuHadway, San Antonio, Texas, January 14, 1988, p. 25.

74. "MacNeil-Lehrer Report," Public Television, July 13, 1988.

75. "Evening News," WJLA TV, Washington, D.C., June 2, 1988.

76. *FBI Counterintelligence Visits to Libraries*, pp. 111–13, 119–20.

77. "Why the FBI Is Interested in Talking to Librarians," *Washington Times*, February 15, 1988, p. F5.

78. "Librarians Tell Congress FBI Is Spying on Readers," *News Media and the Law*, Summer 1988, p. 38.

79. Milt Ahlerich, "Soviets Are Exploiting USA's Libraries," *USA Today*, May 28, 1988, p. 10A.

80. "The Diane Rehm Show," WAMU Public Radio, Washington, D.C., July 19, 1988.

81. "Page Two," WBEZ Public Radio, Chicago, Ill., July 19, 1988.

82. Letter from Herbert Foerstel to Milt Ahlerich, Assistant Director, FBI, August 24, 1988, and reply from Ahlerich to Foerstel, September 12, 1988.

83. "Libraries Are Asked by FBI to Report on Foreign Agents," *New York Times*, September 18, 1987, p. 1.

84. *FBI Counterintelligence Visits to Libraries*, p. 55.

85. Ibid., pp. 29–30.

86. Ibid., p. 141.

87. Michael Daly, "I Spy," *New York*, April 6, 1987, pp. 39–40.

88. Ibid., p. 40.

89. Ibid., p. 41.

90. Ibid., p. 43.

91. Ibid., p. 36.

92. Ibid., pp. 37–38.

93. Nancy Kranich, "The KGB, the FBI and Libraries," *Our Right to Know*, Summer 1988, p. 4.

94. Michael Daly, "I Spy," *New York*, April 6, 1987, p. 38.

95. Ibid., p. 47.

96. Nat Hentoff, "Treason in the Stacks," *Progressive*, May 1985, p. 28.

97. Ibid., p. 30.

98. Ibid.

99. Memo from ADIC, New York, to Director, FBI, February 6, 1989. October 30, 1989, FOIA release to National Security Archive.

100. "Documents Disclose F.B.I. Investigations of Some Librarians," *New York Times*, November 17, 1989, p. A1.

101. Ibid.

102. Ibid.

103. FBI Chief Defends Acts on Librarians," *New York Times*, November 8, 1989, p. A21.

104. "Reports That FBI Checked on Librarians Prompt Call for Congressional Hearings," *Chronicle of Higher Education*, November 15, 1989, p. A3.

105. "Card-carrying Librarians?" *New York Times*, November 17, 1989, p. A38.

106. John N. Berry III, "Editorial: Little Shops of Subversion," *Library Journal*, December 1989, p. 6.

4

The Law and Library Surveillance

FREE SPEECH AND INQUIRY

The Federal Bureau of Investigation's Library Awareness Program has come to epitomize the growing federal challenge to statutory and constitutional rights to free expression, privacy, confidentiality, and the people's right to know. The library profession has made clear its own ethical standards in these areas, but as they have been ignored or violated by the FBI and other federal agencies, the pressure to codify these standards into law has increased.

The FBI's Library Awareness Program has questioned the right of American libraries to freely communicate the unclassified information in their collections and the right of Americans and foreign nationals to freely inquire after that information. The legal challenges being offered to the Library Awareness Program on the basis of freedom of speech and inquiry have been tentative at best. In 1988 the Freedom to Read Foundation considered a direct confrontation with the Library Awareness Program through an injunction to force the Bureau to cease and desist. In its July 1988 report the foundation discussed the possibility of such an injunction and said, "We would love to be able to do this and to invite ALA to join with us in such a suit. The reality, however, is that *at this point* we do not have enough information to file such a suit." The foundation explained that where the governmental purpose is to suppress speech, the courts will almost always find that the government's activities violate the First Amendment. But if the government claims another purpose, such as enforcing the criminal laws preventing espionage, "any *incidental* suppression of speech that results from governmental efforts to achieve that other purpose will *not* violate the First Amendment, unless these government efforts are 'wholly gratuitous.' " Since the FBI denies that the purpose of the Library Awareness Program is to suppress free speech, the foundation has concluded that

in order to win a suit against the FBI, we would have to prove either that FBI contacts with libraries are so unrelated to preventing espionage that such contacts are gratuitous and unreasonable; or that the FBI's real purpose is to deter patrons from using libraries or to deter librarians from providing information to patrons. Either type of proof would be what attorneys call fact-intensive, and therefore "very expensive," and the final result of such a suit is very uncertain.[1]

Though the ALA's Intellectual Freedom Committee initially recommended that ALA join the foundation's suit, subsequent advice from counsel convinced the committee to concentrate instead on gathering further information through FOIA requests. The IFC's chair, C. James Schmidt, has concluded that "a lawsuit directly challenging the FBI Library Awareness Program would almost certainly be unsuccessful and might be strategically damaging." Schmidt believes that the court would probably conclude that librarians have not been injured directly enough by the Bureau's program to have standing to sue. Like the Freedom to Read Foundation, he also noted that courts tend to uphold official activities in support of legitimate government goals, such as counterespionage, even if they have an incidental chilling effect on speech. Schmidt claims:

To succeed in a lawsuit, we would have to sustain challenges to our standing *and* prove that the purpose of the FBI Library Awareness Program is to stifle or limit speech. The record as we now know it would make supporting this claim difficult. Second, strategically, if we were to file a lawsuit with a low prospect for success, we run the risk of establishing negative precedent on the issue of our *standing* to sue. We also risk undermining the credibility of the library profession's opposition to the FBI Library Awareness Program, because a government victory in court, even if only on standing rather than the merits, might be seen by the public as a judicial endorsement of the Program.[2]

PRIVACY AND CONFIDENTIALITY

The word "privacy" appears nowhere in the Constitution, yet it is implicit in its amendments.

The first amendment shields individual freedom of expression, religion, and association from an officious government. The third, fourth, and fifth amendments forbid unwarranted governmental intrusion into the private persons, homes, and possessions of individual citizens. The ninth amendment expressly reserves to "the People" rights, such as privacy, not enumerated in the Constitution. The fourteenth amendment's guarantee that citizens cannot be deprived of life, liberty or property without due process of law, provides an additional bulwark against governmental interference with individual privacy.[3]

The American Civil Liberties Union has stated: "Crucial to one's sense of 'self' is the right to maintain some decision-making power over what information to divulge, to whom, and for what purpose. Yet, individuals are increasingly losing control over personal information collected, maintained, used and disseminated by both the federal government and private institutions."[4]

In congressional testimony Judith Krug (ALA) and C. James Schmidt (Research Libraries Group [RLG]) went beyond the notorious intrusions of the Library Awareness Program in describing routine examples of the historical pressures on libraries to reveal confidential information:

1976: New Mexico police asked for library circulation information as part of an investigation of the "Chicano guerrilla movement."

1978: A divorced father in Illinois requested library records to find out if his daughter was using his name or that of the mother's current husband.

1978: Religious groups in Florida requested the names of persons reading certain books so they could be asked to join religious organizations.

1979: New York detectives asked for the names of people reading books on lie detectors because they suspected that somebody was trying to beat a lie-detector test.

1979: In Virginia a husband requested circulation records of his wife to prove she had been "exploring avenues of divorce" before he filed the papers.

1980: A hospital staff member asked the hospital librarian to reveal the names of other staff who had borrowed sex-therapy films.

1980: A college student in Albany, New York, found a newborn infant in an alley and brought it to the proper authorities. Investigating police asked her college library if she had previously borrowed books on infant care.

1981: The Moral Majority asked the Washington State Library to release the names "of public schools and public school employees" who borrowed the film, *Achieving Sexual Maturity.*

1985: Indiana law-enforcement officials demanded public library circulation records on books about satanism.

1988: In Baton Rouge, Louisiana, the sheriff's office ordered a library to reveal the names of people who had borrowed books on the occult, in order "to weed out the curious from the serious followers of satanism."

1988: An IRS agent in Delaware told a public library director that the "IRS is going to subpoena the library's borrower records." When the director pointed out the

library's confidentiality policies, the agent responded, "That's your problem—we
will just seize your microfilm."

1988: The police department of Whitestown, New York, asked for the records of library
patrons borrowing materials on satanism and the occult during the past four years.[5]

These incidents, like the intrusions of the Library Awareness Program,
represent a continuing threat to library privacy and the user's right to read,
inquire, and learn, free from outside judgment, control, or attribution of
motives. Librarians protect user privacy by maintaining the confidentiality
of personally identifiable information in libraries, and increasingly it is
from governmental surveillance that library users require protection. As
electronic data bases and computer systems become the repository for
most personal information, the confidentiality of library records becomes
more tenuous and the threat more disturbing.

The "open records laws" in most states are intended to serve the same
purpose as the federal Freedom of Information Act, yet they pose a legal
threat to library privacy and confidentiality. A request for library records
often pits library privacy against the legal right to inspect public documents. The American Library Association not only defends the principle
of confidentiality of library records but claims that open records laws were
never intended to provide public access to library records. The ALA
correctly states that library circulation records contain only information
on the reading habits and propensities of individual citizens, rather than
information about the affairs of government or the official acts of public
officials. The ALA's Policy on Confidentiality of Library Records (1971,
revised 1975 and 1986) recommended that libraries

1. formally adopt a policy recognizing circulation records and other records identifying
   the names of library users to be confidential in nature;

2. advise all librarians and library employees that such records shall not be made
   available to any agency of state, federal, or local government except pursuant to
   appropriate process, order, or subpoena; and

3. resist the issuance or enforcement of any such process, order, or subpoena until a
   proper showing of good cause has been made in a court of competent jurisdiction.
   (Reprinted by permission of the American Library Association.)

Bruce Kennedy of the Georgetown University Law Center has outlined
the constitutional argument for confidentiality of library records in five
steps:

1. The First Amendment protects against state action that indirectly abridges speech
   through a "chilling effect."

2. Both the right to speak and the right to receive speech are protected.
3. The right to receive speech includes using a library to receive ideas and information.
4. State action that has a chilling effect on using a library violates the First Amendment.
5. The First Amendment protects the confidentiality of library records, because their disclosure would have a chilling effect on the use of library materials.

Nonetheless, Kennedy warns that the U.S. Supreme Court has not adopted this reasoning, the stumbling block being the second premise. The right to receive speech has not been authoritatively established by the Supreme Court. Kennedy concludes: "In the final analysis, the constitutional arguments for the confidentiality of library records remain mere theories. They await acceptance or rejection in an authoritative judicial decision. This constitutional uncertainty has prompted most states to seek legislative solutions to the problem."[6]

THE BORK BILL

Before discussing state confidentiality laws, let us consider the most intriguing and revealing of all the library confidentiality bills: the federal legislation that failed. Late in 1987 Rep. Al McCandless (R-CA) introduced H.R. 3523, a bill prohibiting video rental stores from wrongfully disclosing what tapes a customer has rented. On May 10, 1988, the Senate introduced the Video Privacy Protection Act of 1988 (S. 2361), called the "Bork Bill" by some, because the issue of video privacy came to national attention when Judge Robert Bork's choice of video rentals was revealed by a newspaper during his confirmation hearings to the Supreme Court. Some referred to the bill as "Son of Bork" because the judge's son, Robert Bork, Jr., wrote an article for the *Washington Post* complaining of the trampling of his father's privacy. Curiously, the younger Bork showed only lukewarm support for the "Bork Bill" in his article, claiming instead that "the media since Watergate" were the real problem. He concluded that "as a measure to protect public persons from unreasonble intrusions into their private lives, I am afraid the new laws are irrelevant."[7] Perhaps predictably, Robert Bork, Jr., distorted the First Amendment aspect of the bill by turning the privacy issue into an attack on press freedoms, and in the process he trivialized the legislation.

But on June 29, 1988, the focus was changed when Rep. Robert W. Kastenmeier (D-WI) introduced a revised version of the Bork Bill, titled the Video and Library Privacy Protection Act (H.R. 4947). Kastenmeier explained: "After the Bork incident, my colleague Alfred McCandless introduced a bill relating to the privacy of video stores users. Since the important privacy issues addressed in that bill apply equally well to library patrons, we made the decision to expand the original bill so that it would apply to both video and library use."[8]

Suddenly, what had been regarded by many as trivial became significant and, as we shall see, disturbing to the FBI. In describing the new bill, Kastenmeier stated: "My concerns about library use are long-standing. I firmly believe that the first amendment protects the freedom to read. American citizens must know that when they enter a library, they need not worry that a government agent, or a reporter, or anyone else, will be able to find out what they are reading. People must not be deterred from reading by fears of governmental or private 'snoops.' "[9] Kastenmeier then described Rep. Don Edwards' hearings on the FBI's Library Awareness Program:

I serve on that subcommittee, and the testimony I have heard so far has confirmed my fears about invasion of library patron privacy. There are allegations that the FBI has tried to obtain circulation records from various libraries, and that it has asked librarians to report suspicious behavior by library patrons. To their credit, most, if not all, librarians have resisted these efforts, which I believe at best represent unwise policy, and at worst are a blatant violation of the first amendment. The FBI apparently denies that it is interested in obtaining circulation and other library records. If this is true, then this bill will not affect the Library Awareness Program. If it is not true, this bill will still not affect the FBI's efforts to recruit librarians to report suspicious activities. Whatever the extent of the FBI's efforts, and whatever the fate of this bill, the Congress will continue to closely scrutinize the Library Awareness Program. . . . This bill will create a uniform national standard, and will send a strong message that the Federal Government will not tolerate such invasions of privacy.[10]

Senator Patrick Leahy (D-VT) quickly introduced a Senate bill similar to Kastenmeier's, and the Video and Library Privacy Protection Act of 1988 was under way, bringing with it new allies and enemies. On July 13, 1988, the American Library Association adopted its Resolution in Support of Video and Library Privacy Protection Act, in which it affirmed the freedom of all to read and to view. The resolution stated that ALA "staunchly defends the rights of all people in the U.S. to education and entertainment without the chilling constraint of another person or entity reviewing that activity. . . . THEREFORE, BE IT RESOLVED, that the American Library Association strongly supports the Video and Library Privacy Protection Act, H.R. 4947 and S. 2361."

Like its sister statutes in forty-two states and the District of Columbia, this federal bill addressed the behavior of librarians (or video store employees), not the behavior of law-enforcement agents or other intruders. But this was not just federal duplication of state confidentiality statutes. In addition to the greater authority of federal law, the Video and Library Privacy Protection Act of 1988 would bring protection to the remaining eight states without confidentiality legislation. Also, the inconsistency and occasional inadequacy among the state statutes would be shored up by the federal law.

The federal bill defined library records to include circulation records, data-base search records, reference interview records, interlibrary loan records, and other personally identifiable records revealing an individual's use of library materials or services. In their congressional testimony in support of the Video and Library Privacy Protection Act, Judith Krug (ALA) and C. James Schmidt (RLG) assured Congress: "We do not seek to obstruct legitimate law enforcement investigations. We do seek to protect the First Amendment rights of patrons and to safeguard their privacy." They pointed out that none of the state statutes protect privacy rights of the information in multi-library, not to mention multi-state, networks, many of which share not only cataloging but also circulation information. Krug and Schmidt concluded: "Some of the state laws apply only to public libraries, not to school libraries. Some apply only to those libraries receiving state funds. This legislation would both extend the uneven coverage of privacy protection now afforded to library patrons and would extend the scope of library use that is protected."[11]

Perhaps in response to the power and comprehensiveness of the bill, the FBI reversed its earlier support for the video provisions and took aim at the library portions of the bill. A secret internal memorandum, released in response to a FOIA request, revealed the Bureau's early opposition to S. 2361. Dated May 13, 1988, just three days after the bill's introduction, the memo complained that "the bill explicitly preserves the rights of customers and patrons under state and local law." The Bureau's Counterintelligence Division (CID) stated: "CID strongly objects to the provisions set forth in the bill which would be required by a law enforcement agency to gain access to such records if necessary." CID specifically opposed

1. requiring a court order to gain disclosure,
2. affording the subject the opportunity to appear and contest that court order,
3. requiring a law-enforcement agency to offer clear and convincing evidence that the subject of the information is engaging in criminal activity and that the information sought is highly probative, and
4. requiring that any information gained unlawfully cannot be used in a court proceeding.

The memo concluded: "CID believes that . . . these restrictions for access are entirely inappropriate and therefore opposes this bill. Inasmuch as the bill has just been introduced, CID opines that the bill should carefully be reviewed by the Intelligence Division to determine what impact, if any, the restrictions pertaining to library information would have on their library awareness program and other investigations."[12]

In an August 3, 1988, statement to the joint hearing on S. 2361, Sen. Alan Simpson (R-WY) espoused the FBI's position by insisting that the bill not impinge on the "appropriate release and disclosure of personal records to law enforcement officials." Simpson concluded:

I think we need to be especially careful that we do not overly restrict the access of such information to legitimate police inquiry where it is necessary to further investigations into criminal activities which may even affect national security through espionage. It may seem absurd to state that a person's video records or library records could somehow be connected with foreign counterintelligence and espionage. But it is quite apparent that just such foreign operatives are actively engaged in the use of our vast, easily accessible library system in order to recruit intelligence sources and to uncover information which perhaps should not be so readily accessible.[13]

Rumors circulated on Capitol Hill of an imminent FBI-supported amendment to allow the Bureau to bypass virtually all provisions of the bill by producing nothing more than a written request by an FBI official claiming national security needs. No court order or other legal document or process would be required. Soon the rumors became more tangible, and behind the scenes debate was intense among the FBI, library lobbyists, and congressional staffers.

On September 22, 1988, Rep. Don Edwards, whose subcommittee was considering H.R. 4947, wrote Rep. Louis Stokes, chairman of the House Select Committee on Intelligence, expressing both support and concern for the bill:

We understand that representatives of the Federal Bureau of Investigation have spoken with certain Members [of Congress] about possible amendments to the bill. We are greatly concerned that these amendments not be permitted to impede the progress of the bill. . . . We stress that the FBI has never formally contacted us about any problems with H.R. 4947. . . . Our understanding, however, is that the Bureau has eight specific problems with H.R. 4947. Seven of the problems relate generally to the scope of materials prohibited from disclosure, and to the standards by which law enforcement agencies may seek court ordered disclosure of video and library records. The Bureau apparently believes that these standards are too onerous. . . . The eighth proposal is a request that the FBI be permitted to obtain video and library records without seeking a court order, through a national security letter.

Edwards rejected the application of such a disclosure procedure to records protected by the First Amendment, concluding:

We are more than willing to accommodate the FBI in its legitimate law enforcement needs. However, the Bureau does not need a national security letter exemption and to permit it would create such a large hole in the bill as to render our efforts futile. The insertion of a national security letter exemption would be seen by the library community as congressional authorization for the Library Awareness Program, which, as you know, has generated tremendous concern among librarians.[14]

On September 23, 1988, Judith Krug wrote to Representatives Edwards and Kastenmeier, stating: "Creating a 'national security letter' disclosure process at this time appears to ALA to grant tacit approval to the Bureau's program(s). ALA believes that taking action which appears to endorse the very activities now under congressional scrutiny naturally undermines the integrity of the investigations, and may defeat their purpose outright." Krug defended H.R. 4947's court-order standard for releasing library records, saying that it offered protection "when librarians are faced with one of the most crucial dilemmas of their profession, a choice between maintaining their professional ethics, or acceding to requests by law enforcement authorities."[15]

On September 26, David Bender of SLA and Duane Webster of ARL also wrote to Edwards and Kastenmeier, expressing concerns similar to those of ALA. Bender said:

We are chagrined to learn that the Federal Bureau of Investigation is attempting to get a 'national security letter' exemption. This would enable the FBI to get confidential library records without judicial review or notification of the subject in question. In our opinion, this circumvents the intent of the legislation and enables the FBI to obtain library records without showing cause. The Association opposes the activities of the FBI's Library Awareness Program and views this national security exemption as a way for this agency to continue, with, in essence, Congressional approval.[16]

Webster wrote:

A mandatory or permissive national security letter exemption in HR 4947 would in part authorize, or be perceived by library users as authorization, for the Library Awareness Program and other similar activities. Adoption of this exemption would also put an end to the Congressional investigation of the Library Awareness Program. Given the negative publicity and questions that remain unanswered by the FBI about the Library Awareness Program, these are not desirable consequences.[17]

The only formal communication to Congress revealing the FBI's demands was a September 27, 1988, letter to Chairman Kastenmeier from the Justice Department's Thomas M. Boyd. Speaking for the Bureau, Boyd claimed: "Of significant concern to the FBI and other law enforcement agencies is the cumulative effect that this legislation and other similar legislative initiatives have on law enforcement's ability to protect the public safety and ensure the national security." Despite the FBI's publicly expressed unhappiness with state confidentiality statutes, the Justice Department rationalized: "Federal legislation for library confidentiality is an intrusion into areas traditionally regulated by the States." The Bureau's specific "national security" proposals were prefaced with the statement: "Although these recommendations will provide for basic needs, from a public safety standpoint a general exemption would be preferred."[18] That the FBI could advocate "a general exemption" to all provisions of the bill seems preposterous, but apparently many in Congress were of a similar mind.

In addressing the specifics of the bill, Boyd's letter parroted the demands initially stated in the FBI's secret May 13 memo. It rejected the requirement that library users be informed that their records were being sought, claiming that this would be "contrary to law enforcement interests," and the requirement that there be "clear and convincing evidence" that the subject was suspected of criminal activity and that the information would be highly probative to the case. Boyd also rejected the bill's requirement that law enforcement use other less intrusive investigative processes or show that they would not succeed. Similarly, the letter complained: "H.R. 4947 also requires a showing of why the value of the information sought would outweigh competing privacy interests. These standards would effectively prohibit law enforcement agencies from obtaining video and library records for investigative purposes." Taken together, the Justice Department's arguments admit that the FBI actively seeks library records, and, more important, that its requests for disclosure would be judged unconvincing or inappropriate if weighed against less intrusive alternatives or balanced against the need for personal privacy. In conclusion, the Justice Department's letter revealed its long-rumored demand that broke the back of the Bork Bill:

A third disclosure process by 'national security letter' should be fashioned to parallel the Electronic Communications Privacy Act . . . or the Right to Financial Privacy Act . . . which permit the disclosure of telephone toll records and financial institution records when a certification is made that records sought are for foreign counterintelligence purposes. . . . Without this procedure, the FBI could not effectively monitor and counter clandestine activities of hostile espionage agents and terrorists.[19]

When the FBI subsequently introduced a real flesh-and-blood amendment to H.R. 4947, it did not formally propose the much-feared "national security letter," but it invoked all the other demands in the Justice Department's letter by deleting the entire section of the bill under "What the Agency Must Show." But the FBI still intended to remove the court-order standard for disclosure and replace it with the much less stringent national security standard proposed in the September 27 Justice Department letter. It was not the reading (or viewing) habits of potential criminals that interested the FBI, but the reading habits of foreigners and other suspicious persons.

A recently released FBI memo to Director Sessions reveals that Representative McCandless "agreed on 9/23/88 to the FBI request for a national security letter access provision amendment to H.R. 4947." But the memo complains: "Although supporting the FBI in its public safety concerns and arguments, each committee has objected to our demand that these bills contain a national security letter process."[20]

It is commonly believed that Senator Gordon Humphrey (R-NH) and Rep. Carlos Moorhead (R-CA) were prepared to introduce the FBI's "national security letter" amendment in the Senate and House, in response to an FBI memo to the chairmen of both the House and Senate subcommittees considering the Bork Bill. The FBI's demands became the basis for the ensuing political negotiation, compromise, and eventual capitulation. The possibility of a flawed or distorted federal bill, preempting hard-won state confidentiality statutes, was particularly frightening to librarians.

Dr. Robert Park of the American Physical Society rhetorically asked: "Should the FBI be exempt from library privacy laws? Should athletes with size 40 necks be exempt from steroid tests?" Park then lamented the congressional drift toward eviscerating the bill to accommodate the FBI. "The bill has strong bipartisan support, but the FBI has powerful friends, and is lobbying hard for an amendment that would have the effect of reducing library privacy."[21]

ALA's Office for Intellectual Freedom (OIF) wrote: "Hopes that the FBI may have decided to cut its losses and abandon inquiries to libraries were further dimmed when the FBI officially, though not publicly, attempted to insert into the Video and Library Privacy Protection Act a 'national security letter' disclosure process, in the form of an exemption. . . . Having failed in its efforts on the federal statute, it appears likely that the Bureau will mount a 'rearguard action' intended to seek such exemptions in state laws."[22] The OIF also learned that the FBI was planning to recommend to the president that he veto the bill if it passed without the national security letter exemption.

The day before the bill was scheduled for markup, the FBI's "legislative liaison" people went to Chairman Kastenmeier's office seeking the "national security letter" exemption. The FBI spokespersons explained that they could not accept a court-order standard for disclosure of library records because that would require them to divulge classified information to the judge when "lives might be at stake." Markup was postponed, and representatives of the ALA and the ACLU asked the House subcommittee not to support the FBI's amendment. When the House Judiciary Subcommittee began markup of H.R. 4947, Chairman Kastenmeier announced the FBI's "informal" request for a national security letter exemption. But the subcommittee refused to approve the exemption to the court-order standard in the bill, and given the stalemate, Kastenmeier said that he would not seek full committee or floor action on H.R. 4947. Action then shifted to the Senate Judiciary Committee, which met on October 5, 1988. Anticipating that an amendment proposing the FBI's exemption would be added at markup, the nervous committee completely stripped the library portion of S. 2361, leaving only the video privacy provisions. The revised bill was reported out of committee and, retitled the Video Privacy Protection Act of 1988, passed by voice vote in both the Senate and House with no attempt to add the threatened "national security letter" amendment.[23]

C. James Schmidt of ALA agreed to the deletion of the library portion of the bill, explaining: "I reached this conclusion reluctantly and only because a Senate amendment had been prepared which would have a) replaced the court order requirement with a lesser standard—a 'national security letter,' b) imposed a gag order on any library employee(s) who may have been questioned by the FBI, and c) subordinated state confidentiality laws for national security cases."[24]

Robert Park told how the FBI's friends within and without Congress eventually carried the day, forcing Congress to back down on "snooping among the stacks." Park concluded that though the FBI failed to get its amendment inserted in committee, "the danger that it would be introduced on the floor during the rush to adjourn was just too great, and the bill's sponsors reluctantly withdrew the library portion of the bill. . . . It is an interesting commentary on our times that our right to view films may be afforded greater protection than our right to read."[25]

The scientific magazine *Nature* wrote: "A congressional attempt to enact federal confidentiality laws protecting library users was made this year, but withered under a blistering attack from the FBI." The editorial questioned the Bureau's acceptance of video privacy but not library privacy: "When Congress attempted to protect library records as well—using the logic that it was perverse to protect those who wanted to watch *War and Peace*, but not those who wanted to read it—the FBI objected."[26]

On October 20, 1988, Rep. Ben Cardin (D-MD) wrote me explaining that "when the Senate Judiciary Committee considered the bill they felt there was sufficient threat from the FBI to kill the entire bill if they did not remove the provisions covering library materials." But Cardin maintained hope that a federal confidentiality law might still be attainble. He concluded: "I am very concerned that the library provisions were dropped because I am aware that the FBI has made many attempts to get information from Maryland libraries about materials that are being utilized. I am a member of the subcommittee that had jurisdiction over this matter and have requested that the subcommittee reconsider including libraries under the scope of this bill next session."[27]

Cardin's concern about intrusions on library privacy is shared by most in Congress, but his optimism about federal legislative solutions is not. One congressional source confided: "It's going to be tough getting such legislation passed. I think by pushing the issue into enactment you would again precipitate the FBI's 'national security letter' amendment. So it may be best to keep the issue on the table and before the public instead of pushing the enactment of legislation."[28]

On January 30, 1989, FBI Assistant Director Milt Ahlerich wrote me to explain and justify the passage of the act without the library confidentiality provisions: "The FBI had requested the inclusion in the original Act, encompassing both video and library privacy provisions, of a national security provision. . . . The nature of foreign counterintelligence investigations does not make the availability of a standard criminal warrant or grand jury subpoena a viable alternative."[29]

STATE CONFIDENTIALITY LAWS

By the end of 1989, forty-two of our fifty states, plus the District of Columbia, had adopted some form of confidentiality legislation restricting the examination of library records, with the motivation for these statutes varying widely. The Colorado statute was enacted in response to demands made for the library records of John Hinckley after his attempted assassination of President Reagan. Federal investigators succeeded in acquiring Hinckley's library borrower records, but the Colorado legislature sought to insulate the library system and its employees from lawsuits. Throughout the nation, state confidentiality statutes represent a recognition of the vulnerability of library records in the face of investigative interlopers, federal, state, or local, and many were in specific response to federal intrusions like the IRS raids on libraries or the Library Awareness Program.

Because the Library Awareness Program was nominally confined to New York City, the public exposure of the FBI's program brought immediate pressure on New York Governor Mario Cuomo to amend the New York Civil Practices Law and Rules to make all library records confidential, to be disclosed only by consent of the user or pursuant to subpoena or court order. As amended in 1988, the New York statute covered any library records "which contain names or other personally identifying details regarding the use of public, free association, school, college and university libraries and library systems." The new wording includes but is not limited to "records related to the circulation of library materials, computer database searches, interlibrary loan transactions, reference queries, requests for photocopies of library materials, films or records."[30]

The New York Library Association (NYLA) strongly supported the 1988 revision to the New York statute. In a press release it reiterated ALA's Policy on Confidentiality of Library Records, adding one important new recommendation: "Review internal record keeping procedures to assure that records identifying library users are limited to those essential for library operation."[31] NYLA's recommendation was a tacit recognition that no matter what the wording of a confidentiality statute, the best protection comes from limiting the amount of confidential information collected and minimizing the time it is maintained in library data bases. This approach is increasingly followed in libraries across the country, with automated systems designed to ensure such safeguards as the deletion of circulation records upon the return of borrowed materials.

Georgetown law librarian Bruce Kennedy has appropriately criticized libraries for their records-collection policies: "The Church Report condemned the federal intelligence community for collecting too much data and holding it for too long. Some libraries can be similarly condemned. . . . Libraries should become information storage centers *for* their patrons and not *about* their patrons."[32]

Some confidentiality statutes were drafted as amendments to the state's open records law, exempting library records from mandatory disclosure. But integrating a privacy provision into an existing open records law has proven troublesome. For example, in 1981 an amendment was proposed to Connecticut's open records law, adding library records to the information permitted to be withheld for reasons of privacy. But this "permissive" privacy right would have left nondisclosure to the judgment of the library, and after careful consideration the legislature opted for a privacy provision totally independent from the open records law, making nondisclosure of library records mandatory. Missouri's statute simply says that no library employee shall be required to disclose a library record. Five other states have "integrated" statutes that are permissive in the sense that a library is allowed to withhold records from scrutiny but is not required to do so. All such statutes make strong internal library policy essential for the protection of library confidentiality. Indeed, recently revealed FBI memos have shown that the Bureau is acutely aware of those states where an individual librarian's discretion is the only barrier between an FBI agent and a library user's files.

An example of the vulnerability of such "integrated" library confidentiality statutes was seen in Iowa, where library records were included under a provision in the open records law allowing their release by a court, by the lawful custodian of the records, or by another person duly authorized to release information. The question of whether this statutory privacy right could be asserted against police investigations was put before the Iowa Supreme Court, and on appeal the court held that the statute did not limit police access to library records. In the wake of this decision, the Iowa legislature amended the privacy law to provide that library records shall be released to a criminal justice agency only pursuant to an investigation of a particular person or organization suspected of committing a known crime. Even then, the records can be released only upon a judicial determination that a rational connection exists between the release of the information and a legitimate end and that the need for the information is cogent and compelling.[33] Perhaps the lesson in Iowa and elsewhere is that "integrated" privacy provisions can be carefully crafted to provide library protection, but an independent statute, free from the judicial construction of an open records law, is simpler and safer.

The scope of state confidentiality laws varies widely, covering different kinds of libraries and information. About ten of the state laws cover "libraries" without defining the term. Statutes in North Carolina, Minnesota, and North Dakota refer to libraries established, operated, or funded by state or local governmental bodies. The Alaska, New York, and Maine laws expressly mention school libraries, academic libraries, and state libraries, respectively.

Some state laws specify the types of library records covered, such as "circulation" or "registration" records, and the laws of Alabama, Florida, and Illinois have adopted almost identical definitions of these terms. Many statutes describe protected records in terms of patron activity, covering materials "requested," "obtained," or "used" by patrons. The Colorado statute prevents publicly supported libraries from disclosing information that identifies a person as having requested or obtained specific materials or service or as otherwise having used the library. The Montana legislation protects any information "retained, received, or generated" by a library that identifies a person as having "requested, used, or borrowed" library materials. South Carolina's confidentiality statute protects library records "which contain names or other personally identifying details" regarding users of libraries, and records "which by themselves or when examined with other public records would reveal the identity of the library patron."[34]

An even broader approach is found in the Minnesota and North Dakota laws, which protect the subject of a patron's research, and Minnesota's statute, which protects any records linking a library patron's name with materials requested or borrowed or with a specific subject about which the patron has requested information.

Private or special libraries are usually not included in confidentiality statutes unless they receive government funds, though the Michigan law does cover "any private library open to the public." The New Jersey law is the most comprehensive, covering any library maintained by an "industrial, commercial or other special group, association or agency, whether public or private."[35]

State confidentiality laws usually include some exceptions to privacy, most commonly pursuant to a court order or subpoena. Because, in practice, a prosecutor may be able to obtain a subpoena with little judicial scrutiny, some state laws specify particular judicial findings required before the library records may be released. For example, the Missouri law says that library records will be disclosed upon a written request of the person identified in the record or pursuant to a court order specifying that disclosure is necessary to protect the public safety or to prosecute a crime. The Montana law allows disclosure only upon a written request of the person identified in the record or a court order determining that "the merits of public disclosure clearly exceed the demand for individual privacy." The Nevada statute authorizes disclosure of library records only "to protect the public safety or to prosecute a crime."[36]

The Alabama legislation exempts from access restrictions the library that manages the records, the state education department, or the state public library service. In addition, the parent of a minor child has the right to inspect the registration and circulation records of any school or public library that pertain to his or her child. The Colorado statute allows disclosure when necessary for the operation of the library; upon written consent of the user; or pursuant to subpoena or court order. The Georgia statute specifies:

Circulation and similar records of a library which identify the user of library materials . . . shall be confidential and shall not be disclosed except:

1. To members of the library staff in the ordinary course of business;
2. Upon written consent of the user of the library materials or the user's parents or guardian if the user is a minor;
3. Upon appropriate court order or subpoena.[37]

It is assumed in all confidentiality statutes that a patron may access his own records, and as an extension of that right, fifteen states and the District of Columbia permit the release of library records when a patron consents. It is also usually assumed that library employees or officials should be able to examine library records in the conduct of official business. New Jersey, Montana, and Louisiana explicitly authorize the release of records necessary to administer the library, to enforce fines, and to collect overdue books. There are, however, dangers of interpretation here. Are university officials, including campus police, authorized to examine library records?

Maryland State Law

In a letter to Rep. Don Edwards (D-CA), FBI Director Sessions justified the Bureau's inquiries at the University of Maryland by arguing that the Maryland confidentiality statute covered "public libraries" but not university libraries. In a specific attempt to shore up that gap in the law, Maryland Delegate Samuel (Sandy) Rosenberg, with co-sponsor Nancy Kopp, introduced the more comprehensive current Maryland statute. Because I was privileged to play a major role in the passage of that bill, and because it is one of the state statutes introduced in direct response to the Library Awareness Program, it may be useful to examine the history of the bill in some detail.

Sandy Rosenberg told me how he first learned of the Library Awareness Program: "I've always been very interested in First Amendment issues. In January [1988] I saw an advertisement by the National Emergency Civil Liberties Committee in the *New York Times*, with the heading, 'The FBI Invades U.S. Libraries.' I was appalled by this blatant invasion of privacy."[38]

Rosenberg had been following the story of FBI surveillance of American authors and political organizations, but the revelations on the Library Awareness Program surprised and shocked him. He initially sent letters of concern to Maryland's state superintendent of education, the head of the State Board of Higher Education, and the president of the University of Maryland. Rosenberg admitted, "I figured all I could do at that point was throw letters of protest into the wind to express my outrage, and hope that these administrators would send the word down to the libraries under their control."[39] However, in discussing the matter with fellow delegate Nancy Kopp, who had served on the Privacy Commission that had drafted Maryland's original law, Rosenberg learned that there was an existing statute providing limited confidentiality for library records.

In his January 26, 1988, letter to President John Toll of the University of Maryland, Rosenberg began: "Our university libraries are no longer safe from the anti-communist hysteria and xenophobia of the Reagan Administration. I was appalled to read this weekend of an F.B.I. campaign to have public and university libraries help in tracking down foreign spies or other intelligence agents who may be using the libraries." Rosenberg described the library confidentiality legislation that he and Nancy Kopp planned to introduce and concluded, "We earnestly seek your support of such a bill, and in the strongest terms possible, we urge you to announce your opposition to this flouting of individual rights, whether or not you have been approached as yet by the FBI."[40] In a February 15 response to Rosenberg, Toll offered wholehearted support for the bill, emphasizing the need to extend to academic libraries throughout the state of Maryland the protection against surveillance then accorded only to public libraries.[41]

Judith Krug of the American Library Association quickly wrote Rosenberg, "I am sure it will be of interest to you to know that the Engineering and Physical Sciences Library at the University of Maryland has received a visit from the FBI."[42] As we saw in Chapter 2, a second University of Maryland Library had also been visited, and because both libraries were under my administrative responsibility, this marked the beginning of my productive working relationship with Sandy Rosenberg.

I was soon called to testify before the Maryland House of Delegates in support of the Rosenberg-Kopp Bill (H.B. 1239) and in opposition to the Library Awareness Program. Together with representatives of organizations such as the Maryland Library Association, the American Library Association, and Common Cause, we succeeded in convincing the Maryland House of Delegates to vote 133 to 0 in favor of the bill. I then testified before the Maryland Senate's Economic and Environmental Affairs Committee, and the full Senate subsequently approved the bill, again unanimously.

H.B. 1239 not only extended confidentiality protection to any "free association, school, college or university library," but it broadened the protected data to include any "item, collection or grouping of information about an individual . . . [that] identifies the use a patron makes of that library's materials, services or facilities." The latter was particularly important because it brought Maryland confidentiality law into the computer age, covering the FBI's favorite library service: data-base searches.

On May 2, 1988, I was present as Maryland Governor Schaefer signed the Rosenberg-Kopp Bill into law. On May 6 a secret FBI memo to Assistant Director James Geer expressed concern that the Rosenberg-Kopp Bill "would prohibit the FBI from reviewing, without a subpoena, the records of Maryland's academic library patrons." The memo recommended that the Maryland State Senate be provided a copy of the Bureau's report, *The KGB and the Library Target,* "accompanied by a letter clarifying misrepresentations by the press."[43]

In discussing the successful campaign for H.B. 1239, Rosenberg told me: "That no one opposed this legislation is encouraging. That I would never have been aware of the FBI's Library Awareness Program had I not read about it one evening in the *New York Times* is frightening. I just hope that other states will now see fit to follow Maryland's lead. I'm certainly willing to assist them by making available any of our information."[44]

In a letter to the *Baltimore Evening Sun,* Rosenberg stated, "Citizens using any library in Maryland will be safe from the unwarranted snooping of FBI agents under legislation enacted by this year's General Assembly. Circulation records, as well as computer data base searches, are protected from the Bureau's invasion of free expression and privacy rights under House Bill 1239, introduced by myself and Del. Nancy Kopp." Rosenberg described the FBI's visits to two University of Maryland libraries and concluded, "The fortitude of Herbert Foerstel, the libraries' administrator, in thwarting this witch hunt is now bolstered by state law."[45]

As we have seen, the FBI regards state confidentiality laws as obstacles in the path of effective counterintelligence work, and agents test the limits of these laws wherever possible. One recent ploy is the Bureau's claim that "library records," protected in most confidentiality laws, are not the same as the information contained in these records. This may seem like a specious distinction, but the FBI believes that such an interpretation would allow it to discuss the contents of library records with a librarian, so long as it did not actually inspect these records. The Bureau has, in fact, gone so far as to claim that any conversations between FBI agents and librarians are unprotected by confidentiality laws. For example, Assistant Director James Geer has testified: "Some statutes say they cannot furnish records. Some statutes say they cannot furnish information, period. If the New York statute just applies to records, then there is no prohibition . . . against individuals furnishing something of their knowledge."[46] When a librarian told Geer that not just circulation records were considered confidential, but reference interviews and data-base searches as well, Geer responded: "But not necessarily your own conversations with this person. And that can be extremely helpful. . . . I can't imagine any librarian having any reluctance to discuss with an FBI agent a conversation with a person they knew to be a representative of the Czechoslovakian mission of the United Nations."[47]

On August 22, 1989, after reading a draft of this book, Delegate Sandy Rosenberg wrote to the state attorney general, calling his attention to the FBI's claimed distinction between library records and their contents. After quoting FBI Assistant Director Geer's statements in this regard, Rosenberg asked whether Maryland's confidentiality protection could be interpreted not to apply to a conversation in which protected information was verbally disclosed.

In his September 7 response to Rosenberg, Assistant Attorney General Richard Israel said that Maryland's confidentiality statute had modified two existing laws: the Public Information Act, covering only the records of governmental units, and the Educational Article, which has no such limitation. Though Israel said that both acts "explicitly deny only a right to 'inspect' certain library records," he stated that the implementing language of the Public Information Act referred to "disclosure, access and use of personally identifiable records." Therefore, he concluded: "It is my view that current law prohibits the oral disclosure of personally identifiable library records which are records of governmental units. However, it does not forbid the oral disclosure of such information when it is found in the records of private institutions."[48]

Whereas the FBI has been devious in interpreting the scope of protected information in the state statutes, librarians have been uncertain in identifying the individuals from whom the statutes would deny library information. The intent of the confidentiality laws was obviously to protect libraries from the intrusions of federal and state investigative agencies. But who else might the laws define as an intruder? What about the user's parents? Spouse? Within a university campus, are university officials or campus police exempted from restrictions on access to library records?

After the passage of Maryland's confidentiality statute, the University of Maryland Libraries at College Park revised their administrative memo on confidentiality of library records, quoting freely from the new state law. But the sticky details of implementation are still being debated and refined. This same process is occurring at universities across the country, and matters are made more difficult by the position of neutrality taken by many university legal advisors, who are understandably more concerned with the legal and practical niceties of operating a university than with reinforcing library ethics. As a result, legal advice often suggests that library records should be freely available to virtually any member of a campus community, including campus police, in the conduct of university business.

At College Park, Maryland, the campus legal office advised that when campus police request library patron information as part of an investigation internal to the university, releasing such information should be considered part of university business and therefore not really a "disclosure." However, if the inquiry is for external prosecution, a subpoena would be required. Librarians at College Park were uncomfortable with this approach, particularly because they feared that information disclosed to campus police might be transmitted to outside investigative agencies that could not otherwise acquire it without a court order.

Many state confidentiality statutes allow disclosure of library records to the extent necessary for the proper operation of the library, leaving some latitude to library officials in deciding on internal access to records. But none of the statutes exempts the entire academic bureaucracy from library confidentiality restrictions simply because the library is a member of the campus community. The notion that confidentiality statutes do not apply within a "campus family" is disputed by the American Library Association, and there is strong indication that the sponsors of these statutes did not intend them to be bypassed so easily. The Maryland statute, in particular, makes no mention of any exemption to its restrictions. Delegate Rosenberg, fearing an interpretation that would allow campus police to access library records, wrote then Chancellor Toll of the University of Maryland to express his concern: "As the principal sponsor of the legislation extending confidentiality protections to the users of all libraries in Maryland, I am deeply disturbed by the proposed exception being carved out for investigations by Campus Police." Rosenberg explained: "Chapter 233 of the Acts of 1988 treats campus police no differently than it does any other law enforcement agency. Fishing expeditions are an unacceptable invasion of privacy, regardless of the source." Citing Toll's early support for his bill, Rosenberg concluded, "Thus, I am confident that you will prevent the implementation of this ill advised exception to library confidentiality."[49]

Chancellor Toll referred Rosenberg's letter to the state attorney general's office, and on June 9, 1989, Assistant Attorney General John K. Anderson responded:

I am told that the legal office in the Office of the President of the University of Maryland at College Park have advised that circulation records may be disclosed to Campus Police for the purpose of investigating instances of theft of library materials. This advice seems to me to be true to the letter and spirit of the Public Information Act. A stricter reading . . . would prevent the library from pursuing theft suspects because to do so would require disclosure of protected library records.[50]

Anderson claimed that the principal purpose of a circulation record is to allow the library to recover borrowed materials, a process that may involve the campus police. He concluded: "Referral to the police for this purpose is a routine use of these documents, a use for which they are kept. Thus access by Campus Police is allowed for the purpose of preserving library materials. Access for the purpose of 'fishing expeditions' is not allowed by this approach, and I know of no advice from any University legal office which would allow access for such a broad purpose." Still, Anderson perceived some ambiguity in the Public Information Act as it applied to "intra-agency requests," and he suggested a commonsense approach: "The purposes of the Act are perhaps best served when a custodian denies intra-agency requests to inspect protected records, except when the purpose of the request is one for which the record is created and kept."[51]

Delegate Rosenberg was not in disagreement with this approach and, in fact, wrote me in June 1989 to suggest, "Perhaps, the law should be amended to incorporate his [Anderson's] point that intra-agency requests for protected records should be denied, except when the purpose of the request is 'one for which the record is created and kept.' By copy of this letter, I am seeking the advice of Del. Nancy Kopp as to whether legislation should be introduced on this point."[52]

Indeed, Rosenberg and Kopp decided to address both the problem of "intra-agency requests" and the earlier discussed problem of oral disclosure of library records. On February 2, 1990, Rosenberg and Kopp introduced H.B. 986, prohibiting libraries from "orally disclosing certain records and other information," and H.B. 990, amending the Public Information Act to allow "intra-agency inspection" of public records "only if the purpose of the inspection . . . is consistent with the purpose for which the record was created."

The two amendments were eventually combined in H.B. 986, under wording that prohibited the "inspection, use, or disclosure" of a library record, except "in connection with the library's ordinary business and only for the purposes for which the record was created." The new act was adopted on February 27, signed by the governor on May 29, and took effect on July 1, 1990.[53]

Protection through Opinion

In the absence of statutory protection, Kentucky, Vermont, and Texas have relied on formal "opinions" from the state attorney general addressing the issue of library confidentiality. In 1981, when Kentucky's state librarian requested a legal opinion on whether registration and circulation records were mandatorily open to the public, the attorney general wrote, "It is our opinion that they are not." After emphasizing that the individual's privacy rights with respect to material borrowed from a public library were "overwhelming," the attorney general stated, "In fact we can see no public intent at all to put in the scales opposite the privacy rights of the individual." However, the opinion concluded that "the exceptions to mandatory disclosure of public records are permissive and no law is violated if they are not observed by the custodian."[54]

Also in 1981 Vermont's State Department of Libraries wrote the Office of the Attorney General for an opinion on the confidentiality of library records. Vermont's assistant attorney general, Merideth Wright, wrote back: "You have asked whether present Vermont law allows individual circulation records to be withheld from public scrutiny. Our opinion is that it does." Wright went on to state several exceptions to Vermont's law on access to public records, including exceptions for "personal documents relating to an individual" and "lists of names . . . when disclosure would violate a person's right to privacy." Wright affirmed that Vermont's public records law recognizes the right of all people "to privacy in their personal and economic pursuits," and he said that "that right should be protected unless the information sought is needed for public scrutiny of governmental action." The Vermont attorney general's office chose to conclude its written opinion with a quote from the Oregon attorney general that strongly advocated the right to intellectual privacy:

In our society, the private throughts of individuals comprise the most sacred bastions of privacy. The development of these thoughts is commonly nourished by reading. These private thoughts frequently develop as reflections of or reactions to the literature an individual selects. The knowledge that the disclosure of library circulation records showing the use of specific library materials by named persons may occur, may intimidate individuals in the selection of library materials, thereby chilling the obtaining of intellectual stimulation. Such disclosure also could permit inferences to be drawn as to the private thoughts of individuals. We therefore conclude that the disclosure of such circulation records would clearly constitute an unreasonable invasion of privacy.[55]

Despite the encouraging rhetoric in both the Kentucky and Vermont opinions, they say only that library records are not mandatorily open to the public. Perhaps because of the opinions' permissiveness, in March 1989 Vermont finally passed its own confidentiality law, codifying and formalizing the attorney general's opinion that had been followed since 1981.

Texas remains one of only eight states with no statutory protection for library records, relying on an attorney general's opinion as the formal basis for confidentiality of records. On July 10, 1975, the Texas attorney general wrote to the Ector County attorney general, stating:

We understand your contention to be that only the identity of library patrons is excepted from disclosure, and that you do not object to disclosure of other requested information which does not identify individual patrons. No Texas statute makes library circulation records or the identity of library patrons confidential, and no judicial decision in this state, nor in other jurisdictions, has declared it confidential. However, we believe that the courts, if squarely faced with the issue, would hold that the First Amendment of the United States Constitution, which is applicable to the states through the Fourteenth Amendment, *Gitlow* v. *New York*, 268 U.S. 652, 666 (1925), makes confidential that information in library circulation records which would disclose the identity of library patrons in connection with the material they have obtained from the library.[56]

The Texas attorney general cited extensive case law and stated, "In light of these authorities, we believe that the First Amendment guarantee of freedom of speech and press extends to the reader or viewer, and protects against state compelled public disclosure of a person's reading or viewing habits, at least in the absence of a showing of a clear and present danger which threatens an overriding and compelling state interest." After quoting a law establishing that "a state has no business telling a man, sitting alone in his own house, what books he may read or what films he may watch," the attorney general concluded, "Neither does the state have any business telling that man's neighbor what book or picture he has checked out of the public library to read or view in the privacy of his home." But while concluding that "information which would reveal the identity of a library patron in connection with the object of his or her attention is excepted from disclosure," the Texas attorney general claimed that this constitutional protection did not extend beyond the connection between the patron and the materials used. "Thus, we do not believe the fact that a person has used the library, owes or has paid a fine is confidential information."[57]

In 1988 Texas Attorney General Jim Mattox reaffirmed the 1975 opinion on the confidentiality of library records on the basis of "a long series of Supreme Court cases protecting, through privacy, various rights to receive or review information without government interference."[58] But we should not presume that all states without library confidentiality laws can rely on supportive opinions from their attorney generals. More typical are the opinions in Mississippi and Iowa, which claim that without an explicit privacy provision, library records are unprotected within an open records law.

Without Law or Other Protection

Only a few states can rely on neither law nor opinion to protect library confidentiality, and the FBI carefully monitors and exploits their vulnerabilities. In June 1988 the FBI used a "pretext telephone conversation" with the State Archives in Utah to discover that library records in Utah require a specific designation by a city council, county commission, or the library itself in order to be considered confidential. A subsequent FBI memo concluded that "a library would have to formally request the State Archivist to designate these records as private data or confidential data. [Deleted] to date none of the library systems in the state have officially requested this information be so designated. Librarians are often under the perception that their records are private; however without the formal Archivist's designation, these records are technically public information."[59]

The state of Hawaii not only lacks legal protection for library records, but Hawaii's State Librarian's Office told the FBI that "the public library system is unaware of any rules or regulations regarding confidentiality of their records."[60]

The state of Ohio has neither law nor supportive legal opinion on library confidentiality, and this has brought unending struggle to librarians and controversy to the state. Ohio Library Association (OLA) Executive Director Bonnie Beth Mitchell claims, "If people really understood what they could get about other people . . . by tapping their library records, we'd be out of the library business."[61]

The Ohio Library Association considers access to library records to be a loophole in Ohio's open records law that could be removed without changing its intent, and it has proposed legislation to exempt library records from the public scrutiny presently allowed. To circumvent the current law's conflict with First Amendment rights, many Ohio libraries have adopted internal policies that contradict the open records law. In 1983 Steven Hawk, executive librarian of the Akron–Summit County Public Library, was threatened with jail for refusing to comply with a subpoena seeking a list of books requested by a criminal suspect.

The legislation proposed by the Ohio Library Association and the Ohio Library Trustees Association would apply to any library that is open to the public, including but not limited to any public or private school, college, university, or other educational institution. The statute would protect records containing

1. information that identifies an individual as having requested or obtained specific materials or materials on a particular subject from the library; and
2. information that is provided by an individual to assist a staff member of the library to answer a specific question or provide information on a particular subject.

The proposed statute authorizes disclosure of such records by request or consent of the individual who is the subject of the record; for official library purposes; or pursuant to a subpoena or other court order, if the court "determines that there is a rational connection between the release of the requested library record and a legitimate end." While such wording sounds strong, there follows a provision that marks the proposed Ohio statute as quintessentially permissive: "A library or person may release a library record for law enforcement purposes or for use in the trial of a criminal action or proceeding, if a law enforcement officer . . . makes a request for the release of the library record and the library or person voluntarily releases the requested library record in the course of the operation of the library." A librarian who voluntarily releases such records is not legally liable "unless the release was manifestly outside the course of the operation of the library or was made with malicious purpose, in bad faith, or in a wanton or reckless manner."[62]

Despite the permissive escape clause in the proposed statute, Ohio law-enforcement representatives and advocates felt that it threatened their access to library records, which they considered to be an important investigative tool that should not be relinquished. As a result, after the confidentiality bill cleared the Ohio Senate, it was further amended and weakened in the House such that Ohio's librarians could no longer support it. Among the amendments backed by the Ohio Association of Chiefs of Police and the Ohio Prosecuting Attorneys Association was one that would completely eliminate the court-order requirement.[63]

A survey of forty Ohio libraries indicated that six of them had been asked by local and state police for information on library users and their circulation records. Eighteen of the libraries reported requests by patrons for information about other patrons. The FBI, of course, has been active in Ohio libraries, visiting the University of Cincinnati library in 1985 and 1986 to check the reading habits of Soviet citizens. But in all cases librarians rejected the inquiries, choosing to follow their internal confidentiality policies rather than comply with the open records law. The librarians were motivated not just by First Amendment considerations, but also by the fear that they would be liable if released library information resulted in harm to the patron.

Bonnie Beth Mitchell insists that Ohio's librarians are not being obstructionists: "We're not refusing to help. In fact, we want to. But we will not allow fishing expeditions, and we will not allow innocent people to be put under suspicion simply because they use a library. We're trying to protect people's rights here." The opposite position is taken by John Gilchrist, a lobbyist for the Ohio Association of Chiefs of Police: "The OLA wants the police to testify about what they're looking for at a hearing before they get a court order. That hearing, which would probably be public, defeats the whole purpose of an investigation. You don't want the person you're looking for to know you're looking for them." But the ACLU executive director, Ann Zeller, says, "Opening these records to the police or the courts would suddenly and improperly make someone a suspect merely because they like to read."[64]

Privacy and Pain in Pennsylvania

In June 1984 Governor Richard Thornburgh signed Pennsylvania State Act 1984–90, establishing that circulation records that contain borrower names or other personally identifying details shall be confidential and shall not be made available to anyone except by a court order in a criminal proceeding. On the afternoon of October 30, 1985, a woman named Sylvia Seegrist shot and killed three people and seriously wounded seven others in a Pennsylvania shopping mall near the Swarthmore Public Library. Less than two hours earlier, Seegrist had been in the library, where she had had an unpleasant encounter with a desk attendant and the library's director,

Janis Lee. Seegrist appeared agitated, angry, and upset, but she had frequently behaved this way in previous visits to the library.[65]

Immediately after the shooting, reporters, detectives, and attorneys descended on director Lee, relentlessly inquiring about Seegrist's activities in the library, her behavior, dress, questions asked, and, of course, books borrowed. A *Philadelphia Inquirer* reporter asked Lee to reveal Seegrist's circulation records, saying that a killer did not deserve the same civil rights as an ordinary citizen. Lee described her interrogation by reporters, detectives, and attorneys as a harrowing experience. "They hammered at me until I became confused. They tried to get me to say things I didn't want to say. . . . At times I was treated with disdain and even animosity."[66]

Lee distributed a memo to her library staff, emphasizing their responsibility under the law to safeguard the confidentiality of circulation records. After describing how she had been personally pressured to reveal the reading habits of Sylvia Seegrist, Lee urged her staff to be more aware of their special obligations under Act 1984–90 "to do everything in our power to uphold the law and support the civil rights of those we serve."[67]

On February 5, 1986, pursuant to a court order, both the district attorney and defense attorneys were granted access to the book cards from materials borrowed by Seegrist and the patron information corresponding to the identification number on each card. In the subsequent trial, when asked for the titles of books borrowed by Seegrist, Lee attempted to state that this information was protected by Pennsylvania law. But the district attorney interrupted brusquely, insisting that she describe the borrowed books. Though Sylvia Lee describes her testimony as "an ordeal," she thought that she could handle the questions on circulation records—the law took care of that. What she was not prepared for were questions about how Seegrist acted, what kinds of questions she asked, or what materials she photocopied—matters not protected under the law.[68]

Sylvia Lee endured the trial and interrogation, and she has expressed both doubt and pride about the legal protection available to librarians. "I have some misgivings about Pennsylvania's confidentiality law. . . . But at least we *have* a law! . . . Without the law, would I have been willing to risk my position with my staff, my board, and my public because of the civil rights of a 'cold-blooded murderer' who happened to have overdue books at the Swarthmore Public Library? . . . I doubt it." Lee concluded that policy, ethics, and ideals are all well and good, but they are easily threatened, weakened, or even ignored without the law to back them up. She warned: "I found out these things don't just happen at the workshops or in the journals. In fact they could be happening right now in your library. Are your patrons' rights being violated? . . . Are yours?"[69]

Above or around the Law

The FBI has shown undisguised distaste for state confidentiality laws, but it has been ambiguous on whether it considers those laws binding on the Bureau. On November 7, 1988, Senator Daniel Patrick Moynihan (D-NY) wrote Nancy Kranich at New York University:

The FBI claims that they have the right to investigate library files based on an Executive Order, 12333.1.14, adopted on December 4, 1981. This EO gives the Executive Branch the authority to override state law when conducting counterintelligence operations within the United States. The remaining question is whether the information found in library records is really essential to those intelligence operations—so essential that the basic right to privacy can be violated. I am doubtful that this is the case.[70]

Nancy Kranich was even doubtful that the cited executive order conferred any authority to override state statutes, and upon examination of the order she discovered that it did no such thing. Subsequently, Senator Moynihan wrote FBI Director William Sessions, stating:

As you know, the Library Awareness Program has raised many concerns about the role of the FBI and the confidentiality of library records. When first learning of the program, I was led to believe that Executive Order 12333 gave the Executive Branch the authority to override state law when conducting counter intelligence operations within the United States. I now question that understanding. . . . As you are aware, New York State law deems library records to be confidential unless the user has given consent to their release or in the event of a court order. I would hope that the FBI has recognized and operated in accordance with this law.[71]

Bruce Kennedy has noted that thus far, when federal agents have been confronted by state privacy laws, they have either abandoned their requests or complied with the law by obtaining a court order. Because this compliance has been grudging, Kennedy believes that it may reflect an agency decision that it is more expeditious to obtain a court order than to initiate litigation to test the validity of these laws. He concludes, "Nevertheless, an agency may some day contend that these laws do not limit federal investigations because the state statutes are 'preempted' by federal law."[72]

FBI Assistant Director James Geer has claimed, "There has not been one single instance that I have identified where we've received any information in violation of any state statute." Geer's claim is doubtful, and in any case he has admitted that the FBI has asked for such information, but he says that it has withdrawn its requests when told that they were in violation of state law.[73]

On December 8, 1988, FBI Director William Sessions wrote Rep. Don Edwards (D-CA), addressing the evident conflict between the Library Awareness Program and state confidentiality statutes. Sessions attached to his letter an analysis by the Bureau's Intelligence Division of fifteen FBI contacts with libraries. Six were in states that had no confidentiality statute in effect at the time, six involved no requests for library records, and one obtained records pursuant to a grand jury subpoena. The Bureau's description of its visit to Florida's Broward County Library said: "Prior to requesting any information, the FBI Agent asked the librarian if there was any legal prohibition against such disclosure. After being advised by the librarian that state law required production of a court order, the Agent left without making any further request."[74]

In a previous account of the Broward County visit, FBI Assistant Director James Geer has said that the FBI agent was trying to find the address of an individual and then "went in to the librarian and asked that very question and the librarian was quick to say that's in violation of the Florida statute." Geer described the agent's direct request for library records as "clearly something he shouldn't have done, and you can say he certainly should have been aware of the Florida statute."[75]

This ignorance of the law seems odd in the nation's premier law-enforcement agency. Recently released FBI documents indicate that all Bureau field offices were provided comprehensive information on state confidentiality laws, as well as exhaustive analysis on possible loopholes. Still, the fact that FBI requests for library records usually occur in states without confidentiality legislation implies the significance of such statutes in discouraging FBI intrusions on libraries. Indeed, Geer has expressed the Bureau's belief that state confidentiality laws unduly restrict its counterintelligence operations: "I think the statutes, when they were proposed, never considered this kind of thing. My sense of it is that the state legislatures and the legislators that put these together . . . might have built some flexibility in there."[76]

FOREIGNERS AS PERSONS

In the government report, *The Exploitation of Western Data Bases*, we are told: "In view of the authority of the government to control the admission of an alien to the United States, a logical extension is to control the interactive electronic entry of an alien in on-line transactions with a data base."[77] This quite presumptuous interpretation of the rights of foreign nationals in this country seems to be shared by the FBI. One of the Bureau's most persistent and disturbing legal claims is that foreign nationals using American libraries have no First Amendment rights, even where a state confidentiality statute exists.

We have seen that the FBI frequently inquires about foreigners in libraries—about their reading habits, data-base searches, and subject interests, as well as personal information. In fact, FBI agents continue to assure librarians that they should have no hesitation about revealing user information, so long as it does not involve American citizens. But the FBI often uses nothing more than foreign names or accents to identify these targeted "foreigners."

In his written statement to the House Subcommittee on Civil and Constitutional Rights, FBI Assistant Director James Geer said that "the FBI has not initiated any investigations of American citizens on the basis of a foreign sounding name or accent, their use of libraries and/or their reading habits." Geer insisted that "we have not sought or obtained any library records on any United States person in the Library Awareness Program or in any . . . contacts around the country over the last few years. . . . I do not want to lose sight that we are not asking for library records on Americans."[78] But after giving similar assurances to ALA's Intellectual Freedom Committee, Geer quickly added, "A Soviet or a Soviet student is another thing."[79]

On television's "Good Morning America," George Carver, former deputy director of the CIA and frequent media apologist for the Library Awareness Program, told me: "There are laws regarding confidentiality, but the confidentiality laws, I believe, do not inhibit librarians from simply reporting on what foreign officials are extensively working on in areas of high technology interest. I don't think this infringes on foreign intelligence rights or librarians any more than a neighborhood watch infringes on the rights of burglars."[80]

Librarians have been unwilling to treat foreign nationals as pariahs unprotected by the rights enjoyed by homegrown library users. In hearings before the National Commission on Libraries and Information Science, Sandra Peterson of ALA's Government Documents Roundtable told the commission that withholding information from foreigners "is a form of censorship in which librarians cannot ethically participate." One hostile commissioner asked incredulously, "Anyone in the world, no matter who they are, no matter how hostile?" Peterson answered, "If it's unclassified information, yes."[81]

Our government finds it difficult to accept the library profession's view that unclassified information should be available to anyone. In a 1982 Senate hearing on technology transfer, Senator Sam Nunn (D-GA) and Arthur Van Cook, DOD's director for information security, went to absurd extremes in lamenting the right of foreign nationals to access unclassified information through the Freedom of Information Act.

Sen. Nunn: We are saying right now if Fidel Castro wrote in to the Department of Defense and said he wanted 200 items that were unclassified that you would have to send them to him?

Van Cook: That is correct, sir.

Sen. Nunn: Quaddafi in Libya. Is that correct?

Van Cook: That is right.

Sen. Nunn: The Ayatollah of Iran?

Van Cook: Yes, sir.

Sen. Nunn: Don't you think on the face of it, that is ludicrous?

Van Cook: Yes, sir, I do.[82]

ALA's Library Bill of Rights, adopted initially in 1948, states, "A person's right to use a library should not be denied or abridged because of origin, age, background, or views." In October 1987 the ALA's Office for Intellectual Freedom stated what remains the library profession's position on the rights of foreign nationals in libraries: "It is well-established that foreign nationals residing in the United States enjoy the same First Amendment protections as do citizens of the United States. Just as aliens in this country are equally protected by the First Amendment, they are also protected, as 'persons', by the Due Process Clause of the Fifth Amendment and the Equal Protection Clause of the Fourteenth Amendment"[83] (see *Bridges* v. *Nixon* [1944], *Galvin* v. *Press* [1953]).

But the FBI defines the term "U.S. persons" narrowly to include only U.S. citizens and permanent resident aliens, a definition taken from the Foreign Intelligence Surveillance Act. The Bureau continues to pursue library records associated with foreign nationals legally in this country, because few of these persons fit the FBI's definition of "U.S. persons." But state confidentiality laws address only the behavior of librarians, not the status of library users, and these laws contain no footnotes proclaiming, "The above protection does not apply to foreigners."

During the 1988 congressional hearings on the Library Awareness Program, Rep. John Conyers (D-MI) and the FBI's James Geer had the following exchange:

Conyers: A non-citizen legally in the country should be able to peruse the library without bringing down the FBI on him. . . .

Geer: Yes, if we can separate non-citizens into separating intelligence officers from legitimate library users.

Conyers: But I am assuming that a person legally in the country is not an intelligence officer. Even, as a matter of fact, I suppose intelligence officers may get in the country legally. . . . Why should not a non-citizen enjoy the right to go to a library? You know the Constitution has been tested to apply to a lot of people who are in the country . . . even though they may not have citizenship.

Geer: You are not going to get any disagreement from me on that, Mr. Congressman.[84]

The FBI's position on foreigners in libraries remains ambiguous. FBI agent James Fox has said, "I know that Soviets here, whether they're KGB officers or not, are fully entitled to browse and use our libraries. I don't argue that point."[85] This position suggests that it is all right to let foreigners in the front door, but only after checking passports. Let them read, but only if their reading habits are shared with the Bureau.

H.R. 50: AN ATTEMPT AT LEGAL RESTRAINT

Author William Keller has analyzed the uncontrolled FBI counterintelligence programs of the past: "In general, domestic intelligence activity was not conducted pursuant to specific statutory authority, and intelligence investigations did not generate prosecutions." Keller concluded, "When an agency employs intelligence techniques that are not publicly circumscribed by institutional or legal instruments, it tends to move away from a model of a bureau of domestic intelligence toward that of a political police or beyond to an internal security state."[86]

During the Hoover era the Bureau's domestic Cointelpros were acknowledged by no legislation, regulation, executive order, or cabinet-level administrative directive. Bureau administrators recommended the establishment of these programs to the FBI director, and each was implemented solely on the authority of internal memoranda initiated by J. Edgar Hoover, with no congressional oversight, authorization, or specific appropriation. The massive use of FBI informants was solely at the discretion of the individual agent and the agency he served, and guidelines regulating informant activity were internal and unavailable outside the FBI. "First

Amendment questions regarding informants did not come before the courts because informants were rarely exposed, and the information they gathered was used for intelligence purposes, unrelated to criminal prosecutions."[87]

Despite the FBI reforms in the 1970s and subsequent internal guidelines made public by the Bureau, there remains a need for unambiguous legislative restraint on the FBI's domestic programs, such as the Library Awareness Program. Rep. John Conyers believes that the privacy rights of American citizens have been effectively nullified "by the FBI's insistence that its decision to investigate provides its own authorization." Conyers claims: "If we really believe in our professed notions of freedom of speech and association, we should provide assurance to citizens that they can exercise their rights without fear that Big Brother is watching and making entries in his ubiquitous computer. The only way to do that is to enshrine in statutory law the limits of police investigative powers in our land and to provide effective remedies for violations."[88]

Given the historical lack of legislative restraint on the FBI, there was considerable interest when, during the closing days of the One Hundredth Congress, Rep. Don Edwards and Rep. John Conyers introduced a bill entitled the Federal Bureau of Investigation First Amendment Protection Act of 1988 (H.R. 5369), intended to "regulate the conduct of the Federal Bureau of Investigation in certain matters relating to the exercise of rights protected by the first article of amendment to the Federal Constitution." On January 3, 1989, Edwards and Conyers reintroduced the bill as H.R. 50. In his initial remarks on H.R. 50, Edwards stated that he and Conyers were introducing the legislation to establish a simple principle: "The Federal Bureau of Investigation should not be monitoring first amendment activities . . . without some direct relevance to the investigation of criminal activity." Edwards said that H.R. 50

specifies that the FBI should follow a criminal standard in opening and conducting cases that may involve the collection of information on first amendment rights. . . . Our bill also addresses the question of what to do with the files after a case is closed where the FBI improperly collected information on first amendment activities. The bill would require the FBI to dispose of the records in a manner that protects the individuals whose names show up in those files. The provision ensures that the records may not be disseminated inside the Bureau and may not be disseminated outside the Bureau except to requesters under the FOIA and the Privacy Act.[89]

Edwards claimed: "The requirements in the bill are not onerous. They establish a clear reliable standard that will protect the rights of Americans and ensure that the FBI when it investigates U.S. persons, focuses on criminal activity."[90]

Among its definitions, H.R. 50 states that "the term 'United States person' has the meaning given that term in section 1801 of title 50, United States Code." Under the U.S. Code's Title 50—War and National Defense, we find the following: " 'United States person' means a citizen of the United States, [or] an alien lawfully admitted for permanent residence." But this is precisely the definition adopted by the FBI from the Foreign Intelligence Surveillance Act, by which the Bureau has justified the denial of First Amendment rights to all but a small minority of foreign nationals in this country. If there is a weakness in H.R. 50, it is the de facto endorsement of the FBI's unfettered harassment of foreign nationals in this country.

On July 20, 1989, I wrote to Representative Edwards expressing my concern that H.R. 50's use of the term "U.S. person" would leave "foreign tourists, visiting scholars, exchange students, and the overwhelming majority of foreign nationals in this country subject to the FBI's arbitrary intrusions on their privacy and First Amendment rights." I quoted from letters submitted earlier by librarians and library organizations to Edwards' subcommittee when it was conducting hearings on the Library Awareness Program. Those letters expressed the strong conviction that foreign nationals in the United States needed protection from the intrusions of the Library Awareness Program. I concluded, "Given these and other statements, already a part of the record of your previous hearings, it is clear that the library profession, and probably academia in general, feels the need to protect foreign nationals in this country, not just 'U.S. persons.' "[91]

On August 14 Edwards responded: "Your point about limiting coverage of the bill's protections to United States persons has been raised by others as well. This is certainly a matter to be addressed in hearings on H.R. 50. The intention was to allow the FBI to monitor certain foreign nationals, such as Soviet diplomats . . . , even in the absence of a criminal predicate. Perhaps it would be more appropriate to use the FBI's own 'agent of a foreign power' category, which is more limited than the category of non-U.S. persons."[92]

H.R. 50 requires that the Bureau not initiate an investigation covered by the act unless the director of the Bureau or his designee finds in writing that

1. specific and articulable facts reasonably indicate that the subject of the investigation has engaged, is engaging, or is about to engage in a federal criminal offense; and

2. the investigation is warranted, taking into consideration the magnitude of the suspected criminal offense, the likelihood it would occur, and the danger to privacy and the exercise of First Amendment rights.

With respect to the conduct of investigations covered by the act, the Bureau would be required to

1. gather only information relevant to federal criminal offenses;
2. employ the least intrusive techniques available to gather information; and
3. follow procedures to minimize the acquisition, retention, or dissemination of any information relating to the exercise of First Amendment rights or individual privacy.

The FBI First Amendment Protection Act of 1989 is broad in its focus, addressing none of the specifics of library confidentiality. It may have been aimed more at the FBI's documented campaign of harassment of American political organizations, like CISPES, than at the Library Awareness Program. But librarians consider the bill to be relevant to their concerns and useful in restraining the FBI's library surveillance programs.

On January 11, 1989, the Council of the American Library Association adopted its Resolution in Support of H.R. 50, which reads, in part:

WHEREAS, The American Library Association has demonstrated strong opposition to the Federal Bureau of Investigation's Library Awareness Program and other visits to libraries to investigate the identities and activities of library users; and

WHEREAS, Congress, in holding hearings, has also shown concern for the chilling effect that these FBI library visits have had on the exercise of First Amendment rights in libraries by citizens as well as foreign nationals; . . . now therefore be it

RESOLVED, That the American Library Association strongly supports the psasage of H.R. 50, and be it further

RESOLVED, That the American Library Association expresses its deep appreciation to Chairman Don Edwards and the House Subcommittee on Civil and Constitutional Rights for their continuing interest and concern for protecting First Amendment rights of library users.[93]

Formal hearings on H.R. 50 have not yet been held, but Representative Edwards' Subcommittee on Civil and Constitutional Rights heard testimony in June 1989 that was clearly relevant to H.R. 50, focusing on the FBI's stated policy of investigating any American who has had a contact of any kind with a Soviet or Eastern-bloc citizen. Among those testifying against the Bureau's counterintelligence excesses were witnesses from Amnesty International USA (AIUSA), dozens of whose members have been visited by the FBI in the past two years simply because they participated in AI's long-standing policy of writing letters to foreign governments to protest human-rights violations.

Chairman Edwards warned that "even though the FBI does not intend it, these visits can and do have a chilling effect on the exercise of First Amendment rights. Americans should not have to explain their lawful acts to the FBI. . . . This turns the presumption of innocence on its head." Edwards described the FBI investigations of AI as "a terrible waste of resources" and added: "We also have reports of the FBI interviewing two grade school children who had written foreign embassies seeking information for school projects. The FBI also interviewed a 73-year-old grandmother who subscribed to *Soviet Life* magazine and wrote a thank you note to the Soviet embassy for helping free the whales trapped last year in the ice in Alaska."[94]

When an FBI agent visited this grandmother/spy, Virginia Bernard, reading off her Social Security number and birth date from his notebook, Mrs. Bernard asked why she was being investigated. The agent said, "Well, you subscribe to *Soviet Life* magazine, don't you?" The agent explained, "When you subscribed to *Soviet Life*, that was Mark 1 against you. Then you wrote to the Russian Embassy. That was Mark 2." He then added, "I need to clear this up. It's in the interest of national security." At this point Mrs. Bernard's husband could not help laughing, but the agent snapped, "Don't mock me." Grandma Bernard recalls, "When I realized what the FBI man was driving at, I . . . looked him right in the eye and said, 'I'm (expletive).' I'm very angry that my tax dollars are paying for this kind of crap."[95]

The FBI's James Geer assured AI that it is not under investigation, but he said that the interviews will continue because "unfortunately, some of the foreign officials or diplomatic establishments contacted by your members are of interest to us and the fact that the contact was solely for the interests of Amnesty International does not become known to us until we conduct an interview."[96]

Two of AI's witnesses before Congress were librarians. Martha Mc-Knight, a reference librarian at the Indianapolis Public Library, told how she and another librarian were interrogated at her library by an FBI agent in December 1988. McKnight described the agent's response when her colleague mentioned the Library Awareness Program: "My interviewer professed not to know much about the issue, and asked me what I knew, to which I replied that the FBI was trying to recruit librarians as informers. He obviously did not like my choice of words, and commented that he would not have any objection to anyone knowing what he read!" McKnight told the subcommittee: "I value very highly the liberties and respon-sibilities promised to us by our Constitution, and am outraged at what I perceive to be a growing attempt to circumscribe them in the name of national security."[97]

FOIA AND THE HOPE FOR A FULL ACCOUNTING

James Madison proclaimed, "A popular government without popular information or a means of acquiring it is but a prologue to a farce or a tragedy or perhaps both."[98] Throughout this book it has been evident that virtually every significant document relevant to the Library Awareness Program, from the FBI's NCLIS briefing to its New York office documents to the "Trip Reports," had to be pried loose from the Bureau and other government agencies through the Freedom of Information Act (FOIA).

Recently, a U.S. district court denied a reporter's FOIA request for FBI documents on the grounds that "the public interest in assuring proper review of such agency's activities can be adequately addressed by the agency's congressional oversight committees." Rep. Don Edwards, whose subcommittee investigated the FBI's Library Awareness Program, re-sponded in the *Congressional Record*, saying that his subcommittee examines the activities of the FBI on a program-by-program basis and does not attempt to review every decision made by the FBI. He emphasized: "Instead, we investigate matters of concern that are brought to our attention by members of the public and in particular by the press. . . . The subcom-mittee has never sought to substitute itself for an informed public or an alert press. Nor does the subcommittee see its access to executive branch information as a substitute for the rights of access established by the Freedom of Information Act. . . . The congressional oversight process thus depends on the FOIA to an important degree."[99]

Edwards added: "The FBI's so-called Library Awareness Program offers another example of the relationship between the FOIA and our subcommittee's oversight activities." He described the considerable infor-mation on the FBI's program obtained through FOIA by reporters and librarians who then made it available to his subcommittee. "It prompted us to hold two hearings on the program and to press the Director to issue guidelines limiting it, which he did in September 1988. In conclusion, Mr. Speaker, the FOIA and the congressional oversight are sometimes com-plementary, but the principle of public accountability does not depend solely on the Congress. The public is entitled to direct access to informa-tion about its Government and the actions of the Government's agents."[100]

In 1989 the National Security Archive, the Washington-based library and research center that has played a continuing role in revealing the details of the Library Awareness Program, caught newspaper headlines with its legal victory in *National Security Archive* v. *FBI*. In a May 1, 1989, stipulation negotiated between the archive and the FBI by U.S. District Judge Louis Oberdorfer, the FBI agreed to process for public release under the FOIA more than 3,000 pages of the Bureau's internal documents related to the Library Awareness Program.

This legal struggle with the FBI had begun in 1987 when the archive submitted FOIA requests for FBI documents. When these requests were denied, the archive filed suit against the Bureau, forcing the initial release of twenty-two heavily excised documents, including the FBI's New York office communications described in Chapter 1. The FBI resisted requests for further materials and moved to dismiss the archive's suit, but Judge Oberdorfer urged both parties to accept a stipulation for processing further FBI records. The terms of the stipulation required the FBI to process

1. more than 3,000 pages of documents concerning the Library Awareness Program;
2. more than 100 internal records searches on persons affiliated with libraries; and
3. materials pertaining to speeches, media interviews, and congressional testimony by FBI officials.

All of this material was to be processed by November 1989, with interim releases in July and September, and the archive would have the right to litigate for access to any FBI records not released.

The stipulation required the FBI to "process" records, not to release them, and though much of the information presented earlier in this book was acquired through the Oberdorfer stipulation, the material the Bureau withheld may be even more significant. For example, the FBI was to process an accounting of "investigative" library visits as opposed to "awareness" visits, and it has not released that material. The Bureau also withheld all of the possible questions and recommended answers that FBI agents were trained and rehearsed to field from the media and Congress. Similarly, the material on "Libraries Contacted by the Library Awareness Program" was withheld, consistent with the Bureau's past refusal to reveal these locations. Since the FBI has stated that it chose to visit libraries whose collections were "targeted" by the SIS, the Bureau may fear that by identifying those visits it would be disclosing what the FBI knows or thinks it knows about Soviet interests. Some believe that the list of libraries visited by the FBI would divulge, by implication, the names of those librarians who have remained silent during the furor and who may therefore have cooperated with the Bureau. This would be tantamount to revealing the names of confidential informants.

Because so much information was arbitrarily withheld by the FBI, the National Security Archive will undoubtedly litigate for further FOIA releases. The archive will likely begin by preparing a "Vaughan affidavit" (in *Vaughan* v. *Rosen* the court required the Bureau to articulate, under oath and in detail, its rationale for applying each FOIA exemption to each document withheld).[101] Under the Oberdorfer stipulation the National Security Archive has the right to identify a sample of the withheld or excised material to be covered in the Vaughan affidavit, specifying the individual pages that the Bureau must justify to the court. The archive may then challenge the sufficiency of the Vaughan affidavit, and unless there is an agreed disposition between the parties, the court will decide what must be released. The district judge may rule that the Bureau can keep everything currently withheld, or he may rule that it must release some specific information. If the court is ultimately unsatisfied with the Bureau's excisions, it could strike them all down, but this would be part of a very protracted process. Either side, and possibly both sides, may appeal the court's decision.

The National Security Archive is not the only player in this legal struggle with the FBI. The American Library Association has its own pending FOIA request, which it agreed, on administrative grounds, to confine to the same documents requested by the National Security Archive. But neither ALA nor the archive are proscribed from filing another FOIA request, and because ALA did not join the archive's suit, it is not precluded from filing its own suit. After all appropriate material has been released pursuant to the Oberdorfer stipulation, ALA could file an administrative appeal to the Justice Department, asking for a reconsideration of the Bureau's excisions.

Working together, the National Security Archive and the American Library Association will surely extract further information from the FBI, shedding light on the dark excesses of library surveillance and clarifying the ethical options and legal remedies available to us all. Few of the acts and events ultimately revealed to the public are likely to inspire national pride, and fewer of the players exposed will deserve our applause, but this drama will be played out.

NOTES

1. "President's Report to Council," *Freedom to Read Foundation News* 15, no. 4 (1989): p. 1. Emphasis in original.

2. Memo on Library Awareness Program and related matters from C. James Schmidt, Chair, Intellectual Freedom Committee, to ALA Executive Board/Council, January 8, 1989, p. 3. Emphasis in original. Reprinted by permission of the American Library Association.

3. U.S. Congress, Senate, Subcommittee on Constitutional Rights of the Committee on the Judiciary, *Federal Data Banks and Constitutional Rights*, 93d Cong., 2d sess., 1974, vol. 1, p. ix.

4. American Civil Liberties Union, Washington Office, *Privacy*, (December 1988), p. 1.

5. *Video and Library Privacy Protection Act of 1988, Joint Hearing before the Subcommittee on Courts, Civil Liberties, and the Administration of Justice, House Committee on the Judiciary, and the Subcommittee on Technology and the Law, Senate Committee on the Judiciary*, 100 Cong., 2d sess., August 3, 1988, pp. 42–44 (hereafter cited as *Video and Library Privacy Protection Act of 1988*).

6. Bruce M. Kennedy, "Confidentiality of Library Records: A Survey of Problems, Policies, and Laws," *Law Library Journal*, Fall 1989, pp. 746, 754.

7. Robert H. Bork, Jr., "The Secrecy of Video Rentals," *Washington Post*, February 21, 1988, p. B8.

8. *Congressional Record–Extensions of Remarks*, June 29, 1988, p. E2227.

9. Ibid.

10. Ibid.

11. *Video and Library Privacy Protection Act of 1988*, pp. 44–46.

12. Memorandum from F. I. Clarke, Criminal Investigative Division, FBI, to Milt Ahlerich, Congressional Affairs Office, FBI, May 13, 1988.

13. *Video and Library Privacy Protection Act of 1988*, p. 134.

14. Ibid., pp. 146–47.

15. Ibid., pp. 140–41.

16. Ibid., p. 142.

17. Ibid., p. 145.

18. Ibid., pp. 148–49.

19. Ibid., p. 150.

20. Unsigned FBI memo to Director Sessions, September 29, 1988. Document 030254 in October 30, 1989, FOIA release to National Security Archive.

21. Robert Park, *What's New* (Washington, D.C.: American Physical Society, September 30, 1988), p. 1.

22. ALA Office for Intellectual Freedom, *Memorandum*, September–October 1988, p. 4. Reprinted by permission of the American Library Association.

23. "Video and Library Privacy Protection Act," *ALA Washington Newsletter*, October 24, 1988, pp. 2–3.

24. Memo on Library Awareness Program and related matters from C. James Schmidt, Chair, Intellectual Freedom Committee, to ALA Executive Board/Council, January 8, 1989, p. 2.

25. Robert Park, *What's New*, October 14, 1988, p. 1.

26. "FBI Encourages Librarians to Be on the Lookout for Spies," *Nature*, December 8, 1988, p. 507.

27. Letter from Ben Cardin, U.S. House of Representatives, to Herbert Foerstel, University of Maryland, October 20, 1988.

28. Confidential source.

29. Letter from Milt Ahlerich, Assistant Director, Office of Congressional and Public Affairs, Federal Bureau of Investigation, to Herbert Foerstel, University of Maryland, January 30, 1989.

30. N.Y. Civ. Prac. L. and R. 4509 (McKinney 1988).

31. "New Law Protects Confidentiality of Users' Library Records/NYLA Adopts Supporting Policy," *Metro*, July/August 1988, p. 6.

32. Kennedy, "Confidentiality of Library Records," p. 766. Emphasis in original.

33. Ibid., p. 758.

34. Mont. Code Ann. Section 22–1–1103(3)1987 and South Carolina Acts, Section 60–4–10, no. 108.

35. Kennedy, "Confidentiality of Library Records," p. 760.

36. Ibid., p. 762.

37. Georgia Code 1981, Section 24–9–46, enacted by the Georgia legislative in 1987.

38. From my interview with Del. Samuel Rosenberg, September 1989.

39. Ibid.

40. Letter from Samuel I. Rosenberg, Maryland House of Delegates, to Dr. John Toll, President, University of Maryland, January 26, 1988.

41. Letter from John S. Toll, President, University of Maryland, to Samuel I. Rosenberg, House of Delegates, February 15, 1988.

42. Letter from Judith F. Krug, Director, Office for Intellectual Freedom, ALA, to Del. Samuel I. Rosenberg, Maryland House of Delegates, February 4, 1988. Reprinted by permission of the American Library Association.

43. Memo from D. E. Stukey, FBI New York, to J. H. Geer, FBI Assistant Director, May 6, 1988. October 30, 1989, FOIA release to National Security Archive.

44. From my interview with Del. Samuel Rosenberg, July 1988.

45. Samuel I. Rosenberg, "Library Snoops," letter to the *Baltimore Evening Sun*, August 24, 1988, p. A15.

46. U.S. Congress, House Committee on the Judiciary, *FBI Counterintelligence Visits to Libraries: Hearings before the House Subcommittee on Civil and Constitutional Rights of the Committee on the Judiciary*, 100th Cong., 2d sess., June 20 and July 13, 1988 (Washington, D.C.: GPO, 1989), p. 128 (hereafter cited as *FBI Counterintelligence Visits to Libraries*).

47. Transcript of meeting of FBI and ALA Intellectual Freedom Committee, September 9, 1988, p. 35.

48. Letter from Richard E. Israel, Assistant Attorney General, State of Maryland, to Samuel I. Rosenberg, September 7, 1989.

49. Letter from Samuel I. Rosenberg, Maryland House of Delegates, to Dr. John S. Toll, Chancellor, University of Maryland, May 2, 1989.

50. Letter from John K. Anderson, Maryland Assistant Attorney General, to Samuel I. Rosenberg, Maryland House of Delegates, June 9, 1989.

51. Ibid.

52. Letter from Samuel I. Rosenberg, Maryland House of Delegates, to Herbert Foerstel, University of Maryland, June 13, 1989.

53. Chapter 635, Laws of Maryland 1990, codified in MD. Ann. Code State Gov't, Section 10–616(E) and Education Section 23–107.

54. Letter from Kentucky Attorney General Steven L. Beshear to James A. Nelson, State Librarian, April 21, 1981.

55. Letter from Merideth Wright, Assistant Attorney General, State of Vermont, to Patricia Klinck, State Librarian, December 1, 1981.

56. Letter from John L. Hill, Attorney General of Texas, to Bill McCoy, Ector County Attorney General, July 10, 1975.

57. Ibid.

58. Letter from Jim Mattox, Attorney General of Texas, to R. E. Stotzer, Jr., State Department of Highway and Transportation, February 29, 1988.

59. Memo from SAC, Salt Lake City, to Director, FBI, June 6, 1988. October 30, 1989, FOIA release to National Security Archive.

60. Memo from FBI Honolulu to FBI Director, May 26, 1988. September 1989 FOIA release to National Security Archive.

61. "Check It Out: Librarians Fighting for Records Confidentiality," *The News* (Frederick, Maryland), December 7, 1988, p. B3.

62. Ibid.

63. Ibid.

64. Ibid.

65. Janis Lee, "Confidentiality: From the Stacks to the Witness Stand," *American Libraries*, June 1988, p. 444.

66. Ibid., pp. 446–47.

67. Ibid., p. 444.

68. Ibid., pp. 447–48.

69. Ibid., p. 450. Emphasis in original.

70. Letter from Daniel Patrick Moynihan, United States Senate, to Nancy Kranich, New York University, November 7, 1988.

71. Letter from Daniel Patrick Moynihan, United States Senate, to William S. Sessions, Office of the Director, Federal Bureau of Investigation, December 19, 1988.

72. Kennedy, "Confidentiality of Library Records," p. 766.

73. "MacNeil-Lehrer Report," Public Television, July 19, 1988.

74. *FBI Counterintelligence Visits to Libraries*, p. 156.

75. Transcript of meeting of FBI and ALA Intellectual Freedom Committee, September 9, 1988, pp. 13–14.

76. Ibid.

77. Office of the Assistant Vice Chief of Staff, Headquarters, U.S. Air Force, *The Exploitation of Western Data Bases*, June 30, 1986, p. IV–3.

78. *FBI Counterintelligence Visits to Libraries*, pp. 118, 123, 138.

79. Transcript of meeting of FBI and ALA Intellectual Freedom Committee, September 9, 1988, p. 14.

80. "Good Morning America," ABC TV, July 13, 1988.

81. FBI presentation to U.S. National Commission on Libraries and Information Science by Thomas DuHadway, San Antonio, Texas, January 14, 1988, p. 28.

82. U.S. Congress, Senate Committee on Governmental Affairs, *Transfer of United States High Technology to the Soviet Union and Soviet Bloc Nations: Report of the Committee on Governmental Affairs, U.S. Senate, made by the Permanent Subcommittee on Investigations*, 97th Cong., 2d sess., November 15, 1982, pp. 55–56.

83. Office for Intellectual Freedom, ALA, *Extraordinary Memorandum*, October 1987, p. 3. Reprinted by permission of the American Library Association.

84. *FBI Counterintelligence Visits to Libraries*, pp. 123–24.

85. Transcript of meeting of FBI and ALA Intellectual Freedom Committee, September 9, 1988, p. 21.

86. William W. Keller, *The Liberals and J. Edgar Hoover: Rise and Fall of a Domestic Intelligence State* (Princeton, N.J.: Princeton University Press, 1989), pp. 175, 182.

87. Ibid., pp. 175, 177.

88. John Conyers, Jr., "When the FBI Is Looking through the Keyhole," *Christian Science Monitor*, March 31, 1988, p. 13.

89. *Congressional Record—Extensions of Remarks*, January 3, 1989, p. E29.

90. Ibid.

91. Letter from Herbert N. Foerstel, Head of Branch Libraries, University of Maryland, to Rep. Don Edwards, Chairman, House Subcommittee on Civil and Constitutional Rights, July 20, 1989.

92. Letter from Rep. Don Edwards, Chairman, Subcommittee on Civil and Constitutional Rights, to Herbert N. Foerstel, University of Maryland, August 14, 1989.

93. "Resolution in Support of H.R. 50," *Memorandum*, ALA's Office for Intellectual Freedom, January–February 1989, Attachment III.

94. Opening statement of Rep. Don Edwards at hearings before the House Subcommittee on Civil and Constitutional Rights, June 21, 1989, pp. 1–2.

95. E. J. Montini, "FBI Visit on Letter, Soviet Magazine Makes Grandma See Red," *Arizona Republic*, April 7, 1989, p. B1.

96. Prepared statement of Amnesty International USA before the House Subcommittee on Civil and Constitutional Rights, June 21, 1989, pp. 4–5, 7.

97. Statement of Martha McKnight before the House Subcommittee on Civil and Constitutional Rights, June 21, 1989, pp. 2–4.

98. Letter from James Madison to W. T. Barry, August 4, 1822, in *The Complete Madison* (New York: Harper, 1953), p. 337.

99. "The FOIA and Congressional Oversight," *Congressional Record–House*, January 27, 1989, p. H108.

100. Ibid.

101. *Vaughan v. Rosen*, 484 F2d 820 (1973).

Selected Bibliography

American Civil Liberties Union. Washington Office. *Privacy.* Washington, D.C.: American Civil Liberties Union, December 1988.

Bennett, James R. *Control of Information in the United States: An Annotated Bibliography.* Westport, Conn.: Meckler, 1987.

Colburn, Robert. "I Spy." *Washington Post Magazine,* March 2, 1986, pp. 8–9, 17.

Daly, Michael. "I Spy." *New York,* April 6, 1987, pp. 36–47.

Donner, Frank J. *The Age of Surveillance: The Aims and Methods of America's Political Intelligence System.* New York: Knopf, 1980.

"FBI Asks Librarians to Report on Foreign Agents." *New York Times,* September 18, 1987, pp. 1, 22.

Federal Bureau of Investigation. Headquarters. Intelligence Division. *The KGB and the Library Target, 1962–Present.* February 1988 (Effective date of study, January 1, 1988).

Hagedorn, Ann. "FBI Recruits Librarians to Spy on 'Commie' Readers." *Wall Street Journal,* May 19, 1988, p. 32.

Keller, William W. *The Liberals and J. Edgar Hoover: Rise and Fall of a Domestic Intelligence State.* Princeton, N.J.: Princeton University Press, 1989.

Kennedy, Bruce M. "Confidentiality of Library Records: A Survey of Problems, Policies, and Laws." *Law Library Journal,* Fall 1989, pp. 733–67.

Molz, R. Kathleen. *Intellectual Freedom and Privacy: Comments on a National Program for Library and Information Services.* Related Paper no. 10. Washington, D.C.: National Commission on Libraries and Information Science, December 1974.

People for the American Way. *Betraying Our Turst: A Status Report on First Amendment Rights.* Washington, D.C.: People for the American Way, 1988.

————. The FBI's Library Awareness Program Background Report. Washington, D.C.: People for the American Way, 1988.

The Right to Know. Vol. 2. Oakland, Calif.: Data Center, 1988.

Robins, Natalie. "The FBI's Invasion of Libraries." *Nation,* April 9, 1988, pp. 498–501.

———. "Library Follow-up." *Nation*, June 25, 1988, pp. 885–86.
U.S. Congress. House. Committee on the Judiciary. *FBI Counterintelligence Visits to Libraries: Hearings before the Subcommittee on Civil and Constitutional Rights of the Committee on the Judiciary.* 100th Cong., 2d sess., June 20 and July 13, 1988. Washington, D.C.: GPO, 1989.

Index

About the Author

HERBERT N. FOERSTEL is Head of Branch Libraries at the University of Maryland, College Park, and one of the leading experts on library surveillance. He has written numerous articles on the subject for the journal of the Maryland Library Association and has appeared on a variety of television programs and before congressional committees to discuss the issue.